Nov 2009

TEACHING SPEECH
Methods and Materials

KARL F. ROBINSON, Ph.D.

CHAIRMAN, DEPARTMENT OF SPEECH EDUCATION
SCHOOL OF SPEECH
NORTHWESTERN UNIVERSITY

and

E. J. KERIKAS, Ph.D.

INSTRUCTOR IN SPEECH EDUCATION
SCHOOL OF SPEECH
NORTHWESTERN UNIVERSITY

DAVID McKAY COMPANY, INC.
New York
1963

PREFACE

Many teachers will recognize that this new book owes much to a previous textbook by Karl Robinson, TEACHING SPEECH IN THE SECONDARY SCHOOL, and to the experience of many persons who have used that book since its first publication in 1951. It is hoped the new text will be useful to students preparing to teach college classes, as well as to those preparing to teach or already instructing in secondary schools.

The organization of the new book is considerably changed from that of its predecessor, the treatment of many topics has been expanded, and there are a number of completely new chapters. Material that appeared in the earlier text has been revised, sometimes radically. Part I is concerned with important considerations underlying an understanding of speech education and its practice. Part II concentrates upon methods and materials for teaching the fundamentals of speech in basic courses. Both classroom and cocurricular approaches, methods and materials for all the forms of speech, and the organization and judging of contests are discussed in Part III.

The coauthor, E. J. Kerikas, brings to the text experience in teaching junior and senior high school as well as college classes. His contributions to the book include the chapters on *Textbooks, Audio-Visual Materials,* and part of *Voice, Articulation and Related Problems,* as well as the exercises and some of the bibliographies.

ACKNOWLEDGMENTS

The authors are indebted to Paul E. Elicker, formerly Executive Secretary of the National Association of Secondary School Principals; to Robert C. Jeffrey, Executive Secretary of the Speech Association of America; to Robert Schneideman, Executive Secretary of the American Educational Theatre Association; to Bruno Jacob, Secretary of the National Forensic League; to the late Ernest Bavely, former Secretary-Treasurer, and to Leon Miller, present Secretary-

Treasurer, of the National Thespian Society; to Harold Green, Executive Secretary of Masque and Gavel; and to Woodson Fishback, State Coordinator of Curriculum, Department of Public Instruction of the State of Illinois, for permission to quote from their publications.

They are also grateful to Jessie Mercer, Senior High School, Amarillo, Texas; to Marion Stuart, High School, Champaign, Illinois; to Mary Blackburn, Community High School, Granite City, Illinois; to Elizabeth Hubbs, High School, Highland Park, Illinois; to Wallace Smith, Evanston Township High School, Evanston, Illinois; to Winifred Gahagan, New Trier Township High School, Winnetka, Illinois; to Robert Teeter, J. Sterling Morton High School, Cicero, Illinois; to Rowena Roberts, William Palmer High School, Colorado Springs, Colorado; to Evelyn Konigsberg, Principal, Washington Irving High School, New York, City; and to members of the faculty of the National High School Institute in Speech, Northwestern University.

They also wish to acknowledge the cooperation of Franklin H. Knower and Wallace Fotheringham, Ohio State University; the late Irving J. Lee, and Clarence Simon, Charlotte Lee, Robert Breen, and Kenneth Brown, colleagues at Northwestern University; Kenneth G. Hance, Michigan State University; Alan Monroe, Purdue University; A. Craig Baird, State University of Iowa; Gladys Borchers, University of Wisconsin; Walker Wilke, New York University; Paul Crawford, Northern Illinois University; Wayne Thompson, University of Illinois (Chicago); and Waldo Phelps, University of California, Los Angeles. They are also indebted to Frances Knight Robinson, Sylvia Gladish, and Margaret Hubbard for assistance and to James H. McBurney, Dean of the School of Speech, and Payson S. Wild, Dean of Faculties, Northwestern University, for their interest in the work.

Excerpts from copyrighted books and other printed materials are included by permission of the following publishers, whose courtesies are hereby gratefully acknowledged: Appleton-Century-Crofts, Inc.; William C. Brown Company; Harper and Row, Publishers; D. C. Heath and Company; Holt, Rinehart and Winston, Inc.; Houghton Mifflin Company; J. B. Lippincott Company; McGraw-Hill Book Company, Inc.; and Prentice-Hall, Inc.

K. F. R.
E. J. K.

Evanston, Illinois

CONTENTS

APPENDICES

INDEX

PART ONE

Essential Considerations
in Speech Education

CHAPTER ONE

Speech in Contemporary Education

We live in the age of the population explosion, supersonic transportation, and miracles in communication machines. By high-speed transportation we can carry a man by jet from San Francisco to New York in a few hours, or if he is space-minded, around the world in ninety minutes. By modern communication equipment we can talk to our spaceman as he flies at 17,500 miles an hour, record the sounds he makes, the things he does and sees, and in a matter of hours, replay the whole series of events for the world to hear and see. If we wish to pick up a telephone, we can dial a number and in a few seconds be in conversation with London or Moscow. If time does not allow us to travel or write letters, we can hold important conferences by long-distance telephone among persons scattered over the country and reach a decision without moving away from an office desk. Because of the scope and pace of contemporary life, our problems are complex, large, many, and often suddenly precipitated. Such a problem is our concern with the present program of education in the United States and the place of speech training in that educational scheme.

EDUCATION—THE HEART OF DEMOCRACY

Every nation has a responsibility to provide for its people an education that best fits them to live successfully and happily under its form of government, economic system and society, and as far as possible in the world family of nations. For over three hundred years the United States has dedicated itself to developing a democratic government, a system of private enterprise, and to strengthening religious and cultural institutions that guarantee the rights

3

of free men to every individual. To these ideals we are devoted as a people. We have, furthermore, championed them throughout the world and are now investing billions of dollars, the combined efforts of leaders in government, education, and religion, as well as our military might, to preserve and extend democracy in every corner of the globe.

We know that the success of democracy depends upon the intelligence, talents, and capacities of *individual citizens*, developed through *education*. To enjoy the rights of free men, they must do more than sit complacently by, congratulating themselves upon the possession of such freedoms. They must first *participate* actively and intelligently as *ordinary citizens* in all of the responsibilities of government and society. Next, many of them must develop into *leaders* needed to direct others so that democracy can succeed. Unless our people are *educated* to carry both of the responsibilities of citizenship competently and, in the case of leadership, brilliantly, tirelessly, and courageously, we may very well lose our birthright in the United States and fail in the struggle to maintain democracy in other nations of the world.

AIMS OF EDUCATION

What kind of education are we projecting to meet such needs as we rethink and reorganize our system at the present time? To those whom we would educate, education is a promise, and in a sense its aims are commitments to the young people of a nation. The United States has undertaken the greatest educational task of any nation, that of providing free, public education for all of its citizens. In attempting to achieve this end, certain aims have been worded to give specific direction to the training. The Educational Policies Commission set forth these "Ten Imperative Needs of Youth":

1. The development of salable skills;
2. The development and maintenance of good physical fitness;
3. Understanding the rights and duties of citizens in a democracy;
4. Understanding the significance of a family;
5. Knowing how to produce and use goods and services intelligently;
6. Understanding the methods of science;
7. Appreciating beauty in literature, art, music, and nature;

8. The ability to use leisure time well;
9. Respect for other persons;
10. Ability to think rationally, express thoughts clearly, and to read and listen with understanding.

These present many implications for exploring the place of speech training in helping to satisfy such needs. However, before turning to such a discussion, we should note Kramer's objectives in terms of serving the obligations of citizenship and leadership:

1. Prepare a man to earn a living.
2. Provide opportunities and the necessary resources for him to develop a "well-furnished mind."
3. Aid him in the cultivation of the power to think: to reason, to investigate, to test new ideas, to evolve new concepts, to make decisions on the basis of pertinent data, to distinguish fact and opinion, to analyze propaganda, to form sound judgments, to build worthy values, and to solve problems.
4. Foster with great care the development of articulate human beings, who are aware of their moral accountability for any ideas expressed.
5. Cultivate within the individual a social consciousness and responsibility, as well as to develop the ability to cooperate with others and to recognize the rights of others.
6. Cultivate the creative and appreciative talents.
7. Help the individual to formulate estimable moral values.
8. Provide the means for discovering those individuals endowed with special qualifications for leadership, and also provide the experiences which will enable the potential leaders to grow to the fullest of their capacity.[1]

These are challenging commitments for education in a democratic nation and in a world in which the concepts of democracy are competing with communistic doctrine.

VALUES AND PRESENT CRITICISMS

In reshaping and adjusting such goals the criticisms are not primarily those of basic aims but of (1) attitudes toward education; (2) decisions regarding the significance and relevance of disciplines and areas of study most important in carrying out our goals; (3) our standards for educational achievement and the selection of educable

[1] Magdalene Kramer, "The Role of Speech in Education: A Re-Evaluation," *Quarterly Journal of Speech*, XXXIV (April, 1948), 123–27.

individuals for leadership, especially; (4) improvement of methods and modernizing educational institutions to make them more efficient.

In general, our critics have been prompted by fear and pride as they have sought answers to the problem. A desire to keep pace and to excel in a world competition in science, speed, space travel, and the production of nuclear weapons has been linked with goals in military supremacy. Our astronauts have been watched with awesome excitement, but with great pride because they have matched or beaten Russian achievement. Fear has been equally strong in promoting criticism of education. "Who rules space rules the world" has become almost axiomatic when combined with apprehension about atomic bombs capable of mass destruction.

In trying to decide what kind of education will be best, another sensitive spot has been the question of standards of educational achievement in the United States. The charge of lack of rigor has been accompanied by a rush to get on the band wagon of hard-core subjects such as science. With this action has come a demand for higher standards for grading, performance, college admission, and for greater acceleration and concentration in learning. In some schools the humanities have been hurt by distorted, sudden decisions that mistakenly push aside art, music, drama, oral communication skills, and other studies so necessary in government, society, and human adjustment as balance wheels for the prepossession with science and mathematics.

Next has been the improvement of teaching methods and materials in order to give education to more students with greater efficiency in the use of facilities and faculty time. Wider use of audio-visual aids of all kinds has been promoted—films, closed-circuit television, overhead projectors, taped and programmed courses—all of these have been employed with team teaching, demonstration lectures with large classes, and other methods to modernize, extend, and improve instruction.

PRESENT RECOMMENDATIONS NEGLECT SPEECH TRAINING

America has been earnestly seeking answers to her educational problems. Among the principal studies of the American educational system have been those by James Conant, former president of Harvard University. Starting with the earlier work on the college and university level, *The Harvard Report on Education in a Free Society* (1945), which strongly influenced a movement to increase amounts of general education in higher education, he has written two other works, *The American High School Today* (1959) and *Recommendations for Education in the Junior High School Years* (1960).

In the high school, he lists twenty-one suggestions for improvement. Summarized, these ask a better counseling system, individualized programs, required programs for all in English (four years), mathematics (one year), social science (three or four years), and science (one year). Also included are the use of ability grouping (three levels); more work in English composition (a theme a week, with 50 per cent of English devoted to composition); diversified programs in business, industrial arts, etc.; remedial and developmental reading programs; special programs and honors courses for gifted students; more periods in the school day; scholarship prerequisites for advanced courses; academic honors lists; modification of ranking procedures in classes; summer school for bright students especially; four years of foreign language; science courses with high and "practical" levels; home rooms permitting heterogeneous grouping; social studies in the twelfth grade as an orientation to democratic problems and living.

When asked what place he recommended for speech and oral communication, Dr. Conant indicated that he classified it under English. He did not exhibit familiarity with the field of speech, however, and the text of his report makes no specific provision for study of theory or skill in the area of speech education, under English or anywhere else.

The same oversight or neglect has characterized numerous reports and surveys relating to general education at the college level since 1945, much to the distress of many persons. *The Harvard Report*, followed by *The Idea and Practice of General Education* (1950), from the University of Chicago, did not mention speech. The President's Commission on Higher Education in 1947 in *Higher Education for Democracy* mentions the need for "the ability to understand the ideas of others and to express one's own effectively . . . by tongue or pen." *Towards General Education* (1948) sets forth as a goal of general education in secondary school and colleges "the ability to speak and write clearly and with considerable effectiveness." In *General Education in School and College* (1952) a committee of faculties of Andover, Exeter, Lawrenceville, Harvard, Princeton, and Yale observes "training in speech, either public speaking or discussion, is sacrificed to training in writing. . . . the committee urges the correction of this imbalance." However, little was done. This action in part caused Francis Horn to speak as he did in the quotation following on page 9.

From this evidence, it is quite apparent that surveys and recommendations in the field of secondary education and general education at the college level have neglected the essential theory and training in skills of speech education.

SPEECH EDUCATION—AN ESSENTIAL PART OF AMERICA'S EDUCATIONAL SCHEME

In contrast to this lack of knowledge of the field of speech, the 1960 national meeting of the National School Boards Association, holding its sessions on the theme, "Education for World Leadership," devoted almost one-third of its three-day meeting to the place of speech and oral communication as vital tools for democratic leadership in our world. Eleven of these papers are printed in a volume bearing the title of the convention theme.[2]

It seems very necessary and most timely that research workers in education, administrators, deans, speech instructors, teachers in all other fields, and parents acquaint themselves with the importance of the area of speech education. The recently published Illinois guide, *Communication—Speaking and Listening*, makes this position very clear:

It is unthinkable that a national group can be committed to economic individualism, to freedom of speech, and to freedom of assembly without also providing for an educational curriculum which seeks to produce individuals who are capable of speaking and listening.

Freedom of speech and assembly are hollow terms if skills of speaking and listening are not an integral part of the education of free men.[3]

[2] *Education for World Leadership* (Evanston, Ill.: National School Boards Association, 1960), pp. 357–454.

[3] *Communication in the High School Curriculum—Speaking and Listening*, Bulletin D–1 (Springfield, Ill.: Illinois Curriculum Program, 1961), p. 3.

The second quotation further links the need for such training to citizenship and leadership:

No modern, technological, and democratic society can secure and maintain freedom for individuals in their social, economic, and political lives, without providing for deliberate and intentional speech education in those skills, attitudes, and arts which are peculiar and basic to that society's primary goals.[4]

Also supporting this position is George T. Wilkins, Superintendent of Public Instruction of the State of Illinois:

Speech is the most important of all means of communication. In the great areas of government, politics, and in the expression of our democratic rights, speech is also most important. Good speech is essential to participation in a democracy. . . . No obligation of our public schools merits greater emphasis.[5]

Speaking on a similar issue and stressing the university outlook in his address, "Oral Communication in a Technological World," is Francis Horn, President of the University of Rhode Island:

It should be evident that today's world requires that speech be a part of a student's general education. I have suggested that in our technological world and the even more fabulous world of tomorrow, effective speaking may be more important for the average individual than effective writing. Yet our schools and colleges fail to see this. . . .

Both speaking and writing are important and should be included in the general education requirements, but if there must be a greater emphasis on one than on the other I believe it should be shifted from the course in composition to the course in speech.[6]

Thinking educators realize that speech education rests upon a universal need—the need for one man to exchange his ideas and feelings, by visible and audible means, with other men so that they may live successfully with one another. This need is as old as civilization; it is not new; it is not a fad or a frill, nor something recently discovered. It has always been with us; it will always remain with us, as long as two people survive. The need exists in all occupations,

[4] *Ibid.,* p. 1.
[5] For Mr. Wilkins' complete speech, see *Speech Teacher,* IX (September, 1960), 177–79.
[6] See *Speech Teacher,* VIII (September, 1959), 197–204, for the complete address.

in all kinds of society and government, at all ages from childhood through adult years, although in somewhat varying degrees. Speech training was the core of Greek education when the democratic city states flourished; it was vital to Roman deliberation in the forum and the law court. It is today the most immediate communication need of our educational system and will be even more essential as newer, faster means of electronic transmission are developed.

Why is this statement a reasonable one?

First, speech is a *universal* form of communication. It requires only mastery of skills in any spoken language anywhere in the world for the transmission of meanings. Second, speech is the *fastest, most immediate* form of human communication. It can be transmitted and received almost immediately in a face-to-face situation or through electronic equipment. It does not require printing or distribution, but can be instantly intelligible. Third, it is the most *flexible* means of communication, allowing for adaptation to conditions that arise, and capable of rapid, specific change. Fourth, it *can be recorded easily* on tape, film, or disc; it can then be *stored,* and *transmitted* in a restricted area or broadcast widely through radio, television, or film. Fifth, it can be *programmed* or organized in "packages" as instructional materials for use by schools, information for governments and other agencies, or can be used as a sales medium or as propaganda. Sixth, because of its other qualities, and with the use of suitable transmission and receiving equipment, it is *practically limitless in its possibilities in space.* Satellites and various forms of space carriers are now being evolved and will be further developed to extend the range of human speech almost beyond belief. American Telephone and Telegraph Company is using Telstar, one of these devices, and is doing research leading to others. The fundamental point is this—the key to or base of such developments is the *spoken word!* Man's mastery and control of speech begins with skills (learned through speech education), which, when combined with amplification through science, may become the miracle of future communication and the means for education now scarcely realized.

At present our generation shows a lack of training because education has made inadequate provision for the needs of our people. If we are to resolve the problems of participation and leadership in our own democracy and hope to move more rapidly toward resolving world problems in government, in economics, and in human relations, we must give more careful, *direct attention* to speech education.

The Nature and Scope of Speech Education

Speech is a learned ability that provides man with the necessary symbol system, primarily visible and audible, that makes it possible for him to encode or verbalize his ideas and feelings so that he can use them to influence the responses of other people or things in his environment.

It can be taught successfully, and man's ability to improve his skill is proved by results reported in hundreds of researches in the field of speech and general communication, as well as by the practical examples of thousands of individuals.

Nearly 90 per cent of all education depends upon speech and oral communication, according to experts on communication media.

A program of speech education serves three broad classes of persons according to their needs: (1) those with defective speech and hearing; (2) those with "normal" speech but who need improved habits and skills; (3) those gifted persons who will become leaders in the democracy of our country and in the world.

1. *Eighteen million defectives need help.*

About 10 per cent of our population of 180,000,000 have speech difficulties so prominent that they cannot have normal, successful communication. Approximately 7,000,000 have hearing disorders, some of such magnitude that they cannot receive sounds satisfactorily. Also, related speech development may be impaired and, as a result, successful living is made difficult. Additional thousands have speech which has been retarded or destroyed by cerebral palsy, cleft palate, and similar handicaps. These persons must face a world in which more speech demands will be placed upon them than ever before in history.

Generally speaking, a speech or hearing defect makes for decreased: (a) confidence; (b) self-esteem; (c) enthusiasm; (d) happiness; (e) acceptance and understanding of others; (f) friendliness toward others; (g) cooperativeness; (h) responsiveness toward others; (i) feeling of belongingness.

A defect tends to make for increased: (a) feelings of inferiority; (b) unworthiness; (c) apathy; (d) disappointment; discouragement; (e) awe, contempt, or rejection of others; (f) antagonism toward others; (g) competitiveness; (h) withdrawing tendencies; loneliness.[7]

In a time when youth problems are on the increase, it is pertinent to note: (a) the child's whole personality would be improved by speech and hearing correction; (b) the child needs more than speech correction only.[8]

Today our elementary schools are teeming with thousands of children who will be denied the opportunity for speech and hearing rehabilitation if the services of competent therapists are not provided. The future is not encouraging. To serve these handicapped persons properly, 3,500 new special teachers are needed annually.[9] Otherwise many of these persons will go unattended, deprived of a chance to meet life on anything like even terms.

Speech correction and hearing rehabilitation are integral parts of a program of speech education.

    2. *Speech education is needed for those with "normal" speech who need to improve.*

    a. *Personal speech habits can be improved.* Ninety per cent of our population has what might be called "normal" speech. In other words, their personal speech habits are such that they do not have deviations calling attention to themselves nor do they cause the individuals with deviations to be maladjusted. Nevertheless, their speech often may be indistinct because of carelessness, their voices monotonous, too loud, or too soft from ordinary causes. They just do not produce speech which is attractive or serviceable within these "normal" limits. For these persons the important service of speech education is to *provide improvement* so that they can be more effective in their jobs and in relations with other people.

    b. *Attitudes of confidence and security in speech situations can be developed.* One of the most common remarks made by laymen

[7] From Wendell Johnson and Others, *Speech Handicapped School Children* (New York: Harper & Row, 1948), p. 60. Reprinted by permission of the publisher.

[8] *Ibid.*

[9] Max D. Steer, Chairman, Planning Committee of the American Speech and Hearing Association, January 12, 1955. (Projected to 1962, these figures could reach 4000.)

and students is "I feel uneasy or afraid when I talk to an audience." This audience may consist of one person or many. The attitude is typical. It often keeps children from "belonging." It prevents adults from sharing good ideas with a PTA or a conference group. It keeps many from taking part and assuming leadership in community affairs and government. Speech education provides training and experience which will enable persons to become better adjusted and more confident in meeting the speech situations of everyday life.

c. *Basic speech skills can be mastered.* Even with "normal" speech, children and adults find themselves confronted with problems and situations of oral communication which they cannot meet by their own devices or with the casual or fragmentary training provided by the schools.

In the elementary schools there are not only too few teachers, but most of them have not obtained in their preparation the information and methods for teaching speech improvement and the necessary basic and/or functional speech skills. Teacher's colleges have for many years stressed reading, spelling, and writing as the principal areas for direct teaching in the language arts area. There is no question of the importance of these skills. However, they have ignored or slid *indirectly* past any organized instruction in speaking, discussing, creative drama, interpretation of literature, and listening, which are very important parts of the area. This practice has caused Mardell Ogilvie to write guides to teaching speech in the elementary school.[10] These aid the teacher in helping the child to meet individual and group speech situations.

Ogilvie develops very completely and practically methods and materials for meeting informal speaking situations, giving talks, discussion, conducting a meeting, oral reading, choral speaking, puppetry, creative dramatics and play production, plus content on speech improvement. A similar emphasis and treatment is also to be found in Rasmussen.[11]

The basic skills of preparing and presenting talks, discussing

[10] Mardell Ogilvie, *Speech in the Elementary School* (New York: McGraw-Hill Book Co., Inc., 1955), Chap. 1.

[11] Carrie Rasmussen, *Speech Methods in the Elementary School* (New York: Ronald Press, 1962).

problems (with attention to analysis, critical thinking, good preparation for participation and leadership), and reading aloud need to be given a place in elementary education which permits them to be taught in a direct, organized fashion, and not "just incidentally."

Similarly, secondary education has been too easily satisfied with its efforts in providing basic speech skills. Speech education is wanted and needed by the students at this level. A survey given to recent graduates (over an extended period) of a large midwestern high school to aid administrators in curriculum revision revealed this interesting response to the question: "What have you found most necessary to success in your years since graduation that was *not* included or stressed in your secondary school education?" Over 90 per cent of the students said: "Training in speech that would enable us to speak confidently and effectively with or before people."

Such insecure attitudes and inadequacies in basic speech skills tend to create in "normal" individuals the same personality problems present in more severely handicapped persons. Schools cannot afford to neglect the important contribution of speech education in our critical times.

College students and adults usually realize their inadequacies, and at a very late date in their educational lives try to "fill in the gaps."

d. *Training in more specialized speech activities can be given.* Speech education offers significant training in more specialized activities. The word "specialized" denotes areas of performance which distinguish them from the basic or fundamental skills. However, such a distinction is purely arbitrary. Actually, the activities of debate in its various forms—drama, oral interpretation of literature, radio and television—may be just as basic or fundamental to certain individuals as are those of speaking, oral reading, and discussion. Our society demands more and more proficiency in these "specialized" skills, to the point that training in these areas is becoming essential to more and more people. Participation in government, community affairs, and social affairs necessitates the use of the techniques of advocacy (debate) when problems cannot be resolved by discussion and conference. The sharing of the best in literature through oral interpretation of various types becomes a fundamental cultural experience. Participation in drama has become so much a part of community and school recreation and a means of developing sensitivity to and appreciation of the great values to be found in dramatic literature that such experiences are not unique or "specialized," but are important areas of education and experience. Radio and television have moved from the commercial and entertainment locale into fundamental means of education and participation in which they are no longer uncommon or unusual, but are instead media which many people must know how to use, understand, and evaluate.

Speech education offers training in these activities as another part of its contribution, which is increasingly more significant.

3. *Speech Education is Vital for Training the Gifted for Positions of Leadership.*

Recent surveys among business and industrial executives and personnel directors show that 75 per cent of this group indicate speaking ability as an essential quality for success at the office-worker, junior executive, and top leadership levels.[12] Employee training programs in Pan-American Airways, International Harvester, Illinois Bell Telephone Company, General Motors Corporation, The United States Navy, American Institute of Banking, the Financial Public Relations Association, United States Steel Corporation, Republic Steel Company, the National Safety Council, and countless numbers of other concerns consider speech education so important that they employ trained instructors to provide it for their personnel. Every night throughout the school year, thousands of adults also attend night school classes in university centers to get the speech training they do not have.

In our democracy we are obligated to produce leaders in government, business, industry, education, and the other professions. Speech education, by the very statement of existing leaders, is an invaluable and essential part of leadership training. Failure to help those who have superior ability and talent to become leaders is one of the great sins of American education. All of the aspects of speech education contribute to the solution to this problem. We need articulate, creative, sensitive, resourceful, and tactful persons in posts of au-

[12] Franklin H. Knower, *Speech Education in Ohio* (Columbus, Ohio: Ohio State University, 1949).

thority. The tools of effective speaking used by leaders to impart information, to search out truth and present it convincingly, to discuss and negotiate in problem situations, to know and to share the best in our culture through interpreting literature, to appreciate drama, and to use with intelligence and integrity the mass media of radio and television are goals and services of speech education.

Desirable Conditions for the Development of Speech Education

Since speech education serves critical needs of all segments of our population, it is relevant to set forth conditions favorable to its development.

First, *the needs* (described above) *must be recognized.*

Second, *its contributions to our educational pattern should be known and appreciated* (developing adequate personal speech habits; building suitable attitudes toward speech situations; mastery of the basic speech skills; training in more specialized activities).

Third, *opportunities should be provided for teaching it in the regular curricular patterns of the elementary school, high school, and college.* It is not enough to treat this area incidentally, as an extra-class experience only, or to bury it by unfavorable integration with English instruction (in the high school) where it is lost in the eagerness of the teacher to emphasize writing skills and mechanics. Neither should it be "passed over lightly" as a stepchild in the family of writing, spelling, and reading in the elementary school.

Fourth, *work in speech education should be well-organized and broad enough to serve the needs of all levels of the school population* (handicapped, "normal," and talented).

Fifth, *continuity should be provided for speech education so that there is opportunity for repetition of experience, growth, and maturation in the habits and skills taught.*

Sixth, *flexibility should be present to allow meeting individual student needs.*

Seventh, *intelligent planning should permit the work to evolve in a manner consistent with the particular school and community conditions.*

Eighth and last, *adequate time, faculty, and budget are necessary so that the investment in speech education in our generation will pay the handsome dividends it is capable of paying to our people, to our government, to our society, and to democracy throughout the world.*

EXERCISES

1. Develop in a clear, well-organized paper the place of speech training in the total program of education, indicating the importance of its role as an academic discipline.
2. State what you believe to be the correlation between speech training and success in personal and professional life, giving statistical information, quotations, and examples to support your statement.

REFERENCES

ALY, BOWER. "Speech in the Service of Tyranny and Freedom," *Speech Teacher*, III (March, 1954), 81–88.

AUER, J. JEFFERY. "Speech and the Satellite," *Speech Teacher*, VII (November, 1958), 281–89.

BAIRD, A. CRAIG. "The Educational Philosophy of the Teacher of Speech," *Quarterly Journal of Speech*, XXIV (December, 1938), 546–53.

CONTEST COMMITTEE OF THE SPEECH ASSOCIATION OF AMERICA. "A Program of Speech Education," *Quarterly Journal of Speech*, XXXVII (October, 1951), 347–58.

HOCKMUTH, MARIE. "Speech and Society," *Bulletin of the National Association of Secondary School Principals*, XXXII, No. 151 (January, 1948), 17–34.

HORN, FRANCIS H. "Oral Communication in a Technological World," *Speech Teacher*, VIII (September, 1959), 197–204.

ILLINOIS CURRICULUM PROGRAM. *Communication in the High School Program: Speaking and Listening*. Bulletin D–1. Springfield, Ill. (October, 1961), Chap. I.

KNOWER, FRANKLIN H. "A Philosophy of Speech for the Secondary School," *Speech Teacher*, I (March, 1952), 79–85.

KRAMER, MAGDALENE. "The Role of Speech in Education: A Re-evaluation," *Quarterly Journal of Speech*, XXXIV (April, 1948), 123–27.

NILSEN, THOMAS R. "Free Speech, Persuasion, and the Democratic Process," *Quarterly Journal of Speech*, XLIV (October, 1958), 235–43.

RARIG, FRANK M. "Our Speech and Our Inter-Personal Relations," *Quarterly Journal of Speech*, XXXIV (December, 1948), 439–44.

ROBINSON, KARL F., and W. NORWOOD BRIGANCE. "The Program of Basic Skills in Speaking," *Bulletin of the National Association of Secondary School Principals*, XXIX, No. 133 (November, 1945), 19–29.

WALLACE, KARL R. "Education and Speech Education Tomorrow," *Quarterly Journal of Speech*, XXXVI (April, 1950), 177–83.

————. "The Field of Speech, 1953: An Overview," *Quarterly Journal of Speech,* XL (April, 1954), 117–29.

————. "Towards a Rationale for Teachers of Writing and Speaking," *The English Journal* (September, 1961), pp. 384–91.

WEAVER, ANDREW T.; GLADYS BORCHERS; and DONALD SMITH. *The Teaching of Speech.* New York: Prentice-Hall, Inc., 1952. Chap. I.

CHAPTER TWO

Historical Backgrounds of Speech Education

Speech education as we know it in the United States today has a long and distinguished background. It extends to the Egyptian civilization. It was richly endowed by Greek and Roman writers, teachers, and practitioners. These contributions were carried through the Middle Ages by scholars and priests who influenced particularly English writers and teachers.

In turn they affected significantly the pattern of speech training in this country. Speech training has had its greatest development in the United States, evolving over a period of three hundred years.

In this chapter we shall attempt to trace the development of speech education over a period of five thousand years. It is possible to follow two principal threads, one through theater and the other through rhetoric. Our chief emphasis will be upon beginnings; the classical influence of the Greeks and Romans; the later writers, movements, performers, and teachers, who made significant contributions; and the coming of speech education to America in the colonial period. For further information beyond this point, students are directed to the excellent volume, prepared under the auspices of the Speech Association of America, *History of Speech Education in America* by Karl R. Wallace and Others. (New York: Appleton-Century-Crofts, 1954).

Readings in this work will assist the scholar to knit other threads together—modern interpretation; public address; speech and hearing rehabilitation; radio, television, and film—with those, in theater, elocution, and rhetoric, that have provided the backgrounds for contemporary speech training.

BEGINNINGS OF SPEECH EDUCATION

Theater

The art of theater had its origin in the days of primitive man in ceremonials, dances, admonitory and fertility rites, and the animal masks of medicine men. Pictured evidence of such activities is found on cave walls in France 50,000 years old. If a definition of theater seems to demand the existence of a written play, performed by actors on a stage with scenery, costumes, and so on, the origin of theater is more recent, and its history probably covers only several thousand years. However, many thousands of years of *theater*, broadly defined, preceded *the* theater, as it is designated today.

Early plays date back to Egypt as far as 4000–5000 B.C.[1] The Pyramid Texts have been identified as dramas recording the ascent to heaven or resurrection of dead rulers; they were acted by priests and living rulers. Another dramatic form was the Coronation Festival Play, the oldest being in 3100 B.C., celebrating the coronation of the Pharaoh. Later forms commemorating this event were the Heb Sol or Coronation Jubilee Play.

In the Egyptian Passion Play (*c.* 1849 B.C.), the first stage director and actor recorded in history participated. He was I-kher-nefert, who was sent by King Usertsen III to Abydos to build a new shrine to Osiris and produce the Abydos Passion Play. This play told the story of the resurrection of the king-god (Osiris). I-kher-nefert inscribed on stone his account of the action of the play, his work as a producer, and his role as an actor who avenges his father's murder, recovers his body, and brings Osiris back to Abydos as a living god. This was the first of the passion plays, which include also the Mohammedan version and are still given today, as at Oberammergau.

Rhetoric

In his *Rhetoric*, Aristotle defines rhetoric as the "art of discovering (and using) in any particular subject the available means of persuasion." Long before his time, however, writers and teachers shared his interest in describing and teaching the oral means that men could use to influence the behavior of their fellows. They were concerned

[1] By permission from Kenneth MacGowan and William Melnitz, *The Living Stage* (New York: Prentice-Hall, Inc., 1955), Chap. 1.

with the various situations ordinary citizens and leaders had to meet, in public meetings, in courts of law, in governmental bodies, and so on. To accomplish this they determined their purposes for communicating; selected the issues to be met; found, developed, and organized their arguments and supporting materials; worded them; and delivered them to their audiences.

Over the years, the greatest growth of speech education has come in countries under democratic government with an economic system compatible with it. But people in *all times* under *all kinds of government* have recognized the importance of skill in speaking as basic to their survival and success.

Egyptian Writings

As early as 2500 B.C., an Egyptian papyrus [2] reveals records of instruction in speech training given to leaders in the government. One of these, Kegemini, was made governor of his city and vizier; the other was the son of Ptah-ho-tep. His father was vizier in the Fifth Dynasty under King Isosi, and he gave instructions to the young man to help him in his life. The matters discussed in these scrolls remain as elements in modern speech instruction, nearly five thousand years later—subject matter, the ethics of the speaker, language, the use of voice, the appearance and actions of the speaker. The suggestions were practical, based upon the experience and thinking of these early leaders.

THE GREAT ORAL CIVILIZATIONS: GREECE

The major developments in speech education in the ancient world came in the Greek civilization. Greece in the fourth and fifth centuries B.C. was not a unified country under a single authority. It was composed of various city states, each with its own government and institutions. Sparta was an aristocratic government. Athens, originally monarchical and aristocratic, had moved to a democratic government, its people dedicated to independence and the development of citizens capable of serving the state. Each citizen was expected to be active in the democracy through participating in government

---

[2] Battiscombe Gunn, *The Instruction of Ptah-ho-tep and the Instruction of Kegemini: the Oldest Books in the World—Translated from the Egyptian* (London: John Murray, 1948).

councils, pleading his own cases in the courts of law, and participating in assemblies and juries.

Actually, this democracy was incomplete because slaves did much of the menial work, thus leaving the Athenians to pursue the education of their minds, bodies, and emotions. The rich contributions of their philosophers, sculptors, architects, rhetoricians, sophists, poets, playwrights, and scientists made Athens the cultural center of the ancient world. Added to this, Athens had much military prestige at this time because of its part in the defeat of the Persian invasion in 469 B.C.

The Greeks worshipped pagan gods and paid tribute to them in such celebrations as the Dionysian festival, an event very influential in the growth of the Greek theater.

Theater

The Greek theater was different from ours today. Although details of their stage are not complete, major changes have occurred. Acting and interpretation of lines have moved away from the declaimed speeches and intense physical and emotional style. Modern plays show wide variation from the stories in verse of heroes, with accompanying chanting and dancing of a chorus. However, certain similarities in plot and climax are the same today as they were in Sophocles' *Oedipus Rex*.

The Greeks gave three types of plays: (1) tragedies, dealing with historic legends; (2) satyr plays, burlesquing such legends, with bawdy mimicry and with satyrs (half men and half goats) playing a prominent role; (3) comedies, giving a farcical treatment to the life of the time. All were given at planned ceremonies of a civic and religious nature. All employed a chorus. All were concerned with the god of fertility and wine, involving the death and rebirth of Dionysus (the Romans called him Bacchus). All were written in verse. All three used masks to allow one actor to portray several characters, or, if worn by the chorus, to suggest symbolic meaning.

Before these definite types of plays developed, choral hymns, or *dithyrambs,* were prominent in the origins of drama. In the sixth century (534 B.C.), Thespis moved the dithyramb into the emerging dramatic form by stepping out of the chorus to deliver lines. In that year he won the prize for tragedy.

The influence of Dionysus was most prominent in all of these forms. The festival was in his honor. His figure was carried in the procession preceding the plays and placed in the center of the playing area. The story of his death and rebirth dominated the plays. So involved were the three types of plays with the attributes of the god of fertility and wine that many scholars see the origin of the drama in the Dionysian festival. It attracted people from all parts of the Grecian world of which Athens was the dramatic capital. *The* theater was the Dionysian theater at the foot of the Acropolis.

In Athens this festival continued for five or six days. Usually the last three days were devoted to plays which competed for the annual prize. In the fifth century, on each of these days, a different playwright presented three tragedies and a satyr play (a *tetralogy* in which each play dealt with a single myth or group of characters; a *trilogy* if only three plays were done).

The great playwrights of the Greeks were writers of tragedy—Aeschylus, Sophocles, and Euripides—all Athenians. They were very prolific, Aeschylus writing ninety plays and winning thirteen first awards, Sophocles over a hundred plays and gaining eighteen first prizes, and Euripides ninety-seven plays with five first awards. Although most of their manuscripts were lost, there are seven of the plays of Aeschylus available today, eight by Sophocles, and eighteen by Euripides.

Aristophanes was the great Athenian writer of comedy, followed by Menander, nearly a hundred years later.

Athens remained the capital of the ancient dramatic world for nearly three centuries.

Rhetoric

Although Homer makes numerous references to the importance of oratory and the qualities of the speaker in the *Iliad* and the *Odyssey* as early as 850 B.C., the more significant writings and activities come somewhat later. Knowledge of these contributions comes through a study of (1) great speakers and teachers and (2) written sources or treatises on rhetoric.

First Teachers of Speech—the Sophists

About 467 B.C. in Sicily, the tyrants had been overthrown and a democratic state established. There were many law suits involving property which had to be settled. Since there were no professional lawyers, each citizen had to plead his own case. This practice was also followed in Athens. In response to this need, Corax, a Sophist teacher, and later his pupil Tisias, began the teaching of rhetoric, or persuasion, as a means of helping citizens to win their cases in court. This first speech teacher also wrote manuals, setting forth basic principles of speech organization. He taught men to develop persuasive methods having strong *probability* of acceptance because the available facts (not the whole truth) seemed to yield plausible conclusions. The object was to *win* the decision in the courts even though all of the facts were not available. The appeals to human motives, skill in using the fundamentals of delivery (voice and action), plus effective style or use of language were also part of this early speech instruction.

About 427 B.C. Gorgias of Leontini, a pupil of Corax and Tisias, went to Athens to visit, but remained to spend the rest of his life there as a teacher of rhetoric. Actually, he disliked the label of "Sophist" and called himself a rhetorician. Like his teachers, he emphasized rhetoric for use in the courts. He was an effective speaker and is described as "winning applause by the display of his oratorical gifts and acquiring wealth by teaching rhetoric."

Other Sophists of this period included Protagoras (481–411 B.C.) and Isocrates (436–338 B.C.). Protagoras used speech as part of the general culture in preparing men for citizenship in Athens. Because of his skill in teaching disputation, he is sometimes called the father of debate.

Isocrates, one of the greatest early teachers of rhetoric, influenced the educational scene later, but very significantly.[3] His school, founded to train young men for civic life, drew students from all of Greece. Tuition-paying students from the age of fifteen enrolled to gain the benefits of Isocrates' teaching. He contended that education should be practical, moral, patriotic, broad and interdisciplinary, and thorough. The core of his program was public speaking because it sharpened the faculty of judgment and demanded good thinking as the basis for good speech. Other subjects were classical prose and poetry, philosophy, mathematics, and history. The study of speech and debate was taught largely through the study of models and the practical application of the principles of rhetoric through

[3] See Goodwin Berquist, "Isocrates of Athens—Foremost Speech Teacher of the Ancient World," *The Speech Teacher*, VIII (September, 1959), 251–55.

exercises and contests. He stressed individual attention for each student and developed close instructor-student ties. For fifty years his school had great influence in Greek education; nearly all successful speakers of his day had training with him. Aristotle quotes him often and Cicero calls him "the master of all rhetoricians." He was truly an outstanding speech teacher of the ancient world.

The Philosophers and Philosophical Rhetoricians

All Sophists were opposed by the philosophers, such as Socrates and Plato (428–338 B.C.). The chief objections to their teachings were: (1) they were dangerous because they developed a school of skepticism; (2) they were indifferent to truth; (3) they had an aversion to patient, sincere research; (4) they had a fondness for a jingle of words; (5) they stressed persuasion rather than knowledge; (6) they sought superficial, immediate effects (approval of the crowd, winning in court, and so on).

In his *Dialogues*, the *Gorgias* and the *Phaedrus*, Plato attacked the Sophists and their rhetoric. In the first, he condemns Sophistic rhetoric as a *knack*, not an *art*, caring only for appearance, for a semblance of justice. He also condemns rhetoric because it destroys the integrity of a man's soul, for it involves conformity to the ways and means of the multitude. In the *Phaedrus*, he gives these features of an ideal rhetoric: (1) the speaker must know the truth in order to speak; (2) he must employ careful definition; (3) he must employ orderly divisions; (4) he must know the differences between human souls by reflection and experience; (5) he must adapt his discourse to the individuals to whom he is speaking; (6) he must know the nature of justice and injustice; (7) he must approach the status of the philosopher by basing his composition upon truth.

The great contribution of the time came from Aristotle (384–322 B.C.), a pupil of Plato at the Academy. In his *Rhetoric* he produced a work considered to be the most outstanding in the field. He organized an entire rhetorical system, advancing three means of persuasion: *Ethos* (through the personality of the speaker); *Pathos* (through the appeal to the emotions); *Logos* (through reasoning or logic). The work is divided into three books. Book I deals with the speaker, Book II with the audience, and Book III with the speech, concentrating upon organization, language, and delivery. Although he is a philosopher, the work is a practical one based upon his years of observation and experience. This comprehensive knowledge distinguishes his work from that of those who preceded him. He points out that the speech must be given to an audience and that the speaker must understand himself, the speech, and the audience. He insists that the speaker is most effective when his work is based upon careful study and investigation, familiarity with logical forms, and a practical knowledge of the psychology of the audience.

Great Speakers—the Attic Orators

Important for further influence in the Greek civilization were the ten Attic orators, men of unusual proficiency in the oratory of their time. Before their time Pericles had been outstanding in the delivery of ceremonial orations. This group consisted of Aeschines, Andocides, Antiphon, Deinarchos, Demosthenes, Hypereides, Isaeos, Isocrates, Lycurgus, and Lysias. Most of these men were effective practitioners and wrote speeches professionally, many of them for law courts, and some for state occasions, some for their own political advancement. They represented varying styles in the use of language in speaking. For example, Lysias was known for a plain or natural style. Antiphon for an austere style with strong word positions, usable in court procedure. Isocrates, a great teacher, was inclined to be mechanical and lacked the best voice for delivery. Isaeos, thought to be a pupil of Lysias, specialized in property cases and used a persuasive, vivid style. Reportedly, Demosthenes, the most famous name on the list, was inspired by the style of Isaeos. Demosthenes was known for his dedication to a career as a political orator and statesman, particularly in opposition to the plans of Philip of Macedonia. Many of his speeches—some sixty-one in all—are preserved, including his oration, "On the Crown." In it he answers the accusations of Aeschines, who hated him and accused him of seeking a gold crown, which the Athenians wished to present to him. The bitter contest was won by Demosthenes, who received four-fifths of the votes of the judges. Aeschines was exiled.

The Greek tradition is a rich one in the study of the development of speech education and may be explored further with profit.

Interpretation

Changing definitions of this field cause some problem in placing its beginnings. Described as reading aloud, its origins are found long before it was initiated as an art form in the Dionysian festivals in the fifth century B.C. In these ceremonies poets read their works before the multitudes and hoped to receive the prizes provided for outstanding work.

Hundreds of years earlier, bards in primitive tribes sang or recited legends and stories of the past, as well as their own creations. They were reservoirs for the poetry, story, and drama of their time. Their role as oral interpreters was clearly established.

In Greek education, interpretation was often merged with rhetoric when literature and speeches were read and declaimed in an effort to improve delivery.

Choric interpretation was used in Greek drama. The choruses in the plays provided a significant part of the lines. Thus, this form of interpretation is thousands of years old, and is not, as some persons think, a recent discovery in the field of speech education.

THE GREAT ORAL CIVILIZATIONS: ROME

Much of the Greek tradition was the basis for development of speech education in Rome. Although the Greek political structure was broken to pieces and the Roman Empire gained supremacy, Greek culture flourished in Rome. It influenced Roman living, art, education, and speech training.

Theater

Rome had dramatic festivals, also, but they were very early dominated by amusement and sports, including boxing and other displays of physical prowess. They were held often, usually whenever a convenient military success, a funeral, or a state occasion permitted For entertainment in drama, farces were brought in from the provinces, and later Greek tragedy in translation was introduced (about 240 B.C.). So frequent were these festivals that one Roman actor named Roscius (78 B.C.) is reported to have played 128 times in a single year. Because the Romans enjoyed a variety of plays, games, and violent spectacles such as gladiatorial combats, they were often staged at night by torchlight for the populace.

The Roman theater was definitely commercial. Managers organized troupes of actors, purchased the plays, costumed them, and staged them, hoping that approval by the crowd would bring financial return. The games were held in the same theaters as the plays, often on the same program. To satisfy the tastes of the audience, these performances became more and more violent and bloody. The plays degenerated into pantomimes, lewd dances, and tableaux. Many of the pantomimes retold Greek myths, with elaborate staging effects.

Playwrights included Plautus (254–184 B.C.) and Terence (185–159 B.C.). Plautus wrote comedies much like the later or new comedy of Menander in Greece. They featured political and aesthetic satire, later being replaced by humorous plots from private life. Actors wore masks, and the chorus, though present, had no connection with the plot. Terence followed his example. The theater steadily became too debased to appeal to learned audiences of good taste. In tragedy most writers adapted Greek plays. Seneca, two hundred years later (*c.* 4 B.C.–65 A.D.), was one who wrote original material, but his plays were usually read in private.

Rhetoric

Rome had two outstanding rhetoricians. Cicero (106–43 B.C.) and Quintilian (A.D. 35–100). Cicero, as counsel of Rome and a distinguished orator, was in a place of high authority. He saw the need for skills in speaking immediately usable in public life. His writings reflect this practical point of view. His *De Oratore* (55 B.C.) is a philosophical rhetoric written as a dialogue between Crassus, presenting Cicero's views, and Antonius and others, who present opposing viewpoints. In general this work upholds the orator's need for a strong basic education and broad knowledge, enabling him to speak on a variety of subjects. Further, he should have command of language, should know human emotions so that he can appeal to them, should be capable in delivery through actions of the body, gesture, and so on, possess modulation and variation of voice, and a good memory. Cicero also develops the need for much practice and, if necessary, the need for imitation of good speakers. He believes that one learns to speak by speaking.

A further contribution of Cicero comes through his development of the five classical divisions of rhetoric: *invention*—concerning the finding and development of materials for speaking; *disposition*—dealing with the arrangement and organization of content; *elocution* (style, or embellishment, as Cicero designates it)—using language effectively; *pronuntiatio* or delivery—modulating voice and using body to express ideas; and *memory*—the ability to recall materials and patterns of speech organization. He also develops a six-part organization for a speech including the exordium or introduction, the statement of the case, the establishment of the point in controversy, the support or proof, the refutation of the opponent's argument, and the conclusion.

Cicero's *De Inventione* (80 B.C.), a sophistic work, deals with the finding and using of materials. His *De Oratore* (55 B.C.) describes the characteristics of great orators and contains examples based upon his opinions of their abilities.

As a famous orator, Cicero has handed down to speech educators fifty-seven speeches in nearly complete form for study, and fifty more are known. They deal with public questions, pleas in court, and, in the case of four orations against Cataline and the fourteen *Philippics* against Antony, are invectives, many of them bitter. Because of their content, rhetorical structure, and style, Cicero's orations are outstanding in Roman history.

Quintilian, a great teacher of speech, has written probably the most famous work on the teaching of speech, entitled *Institutes of Oratory* (95 A.D.). In it he traces the education of the orator from birth to his adult success on the platform. He was greatly concerned with human values in his teaching, and, besides knowledge and skill in speaking, he places a high premium upon character and personality. An orator, he states, is "a good man trained in speaking." His pedagogical ideas, rhetorical principles, and many helpful suggestions on method are useful to the contemporary teacher.

As the Roman Empire declined and democratic practices in the courts and forum disappeared, there was much less interest in the development of original speaking as a part of education. Rhetoric was diluted and curtailed until it became essentially a study of style and delivery. Most of speech training was declamation with practice pieces utilized for material.

THE MIDDLE AGES

For nearly a thousand years during the Middle Ages relatively little development occurred in speech education. In theater, writers point out that no dramatist wrote a single great play from 400 B.C. to A.D. 1600. The church originally opposed the drama and was one of the great causes for its decline; however, it proved to be the agency by which drama and theater were ultimately restored. Church rituals and scenes from the Scriptures, such as the nativity and the punishment of man for his sins, were frequently done during the Middle Ages. Church dramas, such as *Adam* (*c.* twelfth century), done by priests and other churchmen, were presented out of doors and later moved to the market place when the trade guilds took them over. The miracle plays, morality plays, and interludes of the pre-Shakespearean day provided the bridge to an enriched, developing drama as the Renaissance gained momentum.

In rhetoric, its study, writing, and instruction were kept alive through the efforts of priests, monks, and scholars associated with religious pursuits. There is little evidence that the writings of Aristotle on rhetoric were known during this period. The *De Inventione* of Cicero was known and a few scholars were familiar with his *De Oratore*. Capella (425), Cassiodorus (543), Bede (673–735), and Alcuin (735–804) knew the *De Inventione*.

Most significant work of the period was that of St. Augustine, whose *De Doctrina Christiana* (425) indicates his familiarity with the *De Oratore* and other classical works. After a variety of teaching experiences in Africa, Carthage, and Rome, he was converted and went into Christian teaching and preaching. His treatise is a very fine one on the usefulness of rhetoric skill to the Christian teacher. Most of his suggestions on rhetoric are practical ones with certain originality in his urging the use of imitation, reading aloud *and* speaking, and particular attention to bodily action in delivery. His work did much to preserve all the good of earlier teaching for others to follow.

THE RENAISSANCE

Theater

The greatest period in the history and development of the theater came in the Renaissance. This great revival of learning blossomed out of the Middle Ages. Through the writings of Dante, Petrarch, and Boccaccio, Italy was already springing to life even before the fall of Constantinople in 1453 caused eastern scholars to flee to Italy. In addition, the invention of the printing press a little earlier amplified man's possibility to distribute his knowledge. From such stimuli, Italian theater advanced rapidly, particularly in the building of theaters, in developing production techniques, as well as in plays written and produced. Spain experienced her Golden Age with the help of her Italian neighbors. Lope de Rueda (*c*. 1558); Cervantes with his *Don Quixote;* Lope de Vega, writer of eighteen hundred comedies; and Calderón de la Barca (1600–81) were the greatest of their playwrights. The construction of theaters also played a part in their growth.

In England the great contributions of the Renaissance theater are well known. From Nicholas Udall's *Ralph Roister Doister, Gammer Gurton's Needle,* John Lyly, Christopher Marlowe, Thomas Kyd, Robert Greene, George Peele, the immortal William Shakespeare, Thomas Dekker and Thomas Heywood, Ben Jonson, John Webster, Francis Beaumont and John Fletcher came a wealth of drama unknown and unequalled previously or perhaps since that time.

In France, Pierre Corneille, Molière, and Jean Racine made great contributions in dramatic literature and built the French theater to hitherto unparalleled heights.

Rhetoric

After the very meager product of the Middle Ages, certain events occurred to revitalize rhetoric in the future, particularly in England and later in the United States. These events were the recovery of the three significant classical treatises on rhetoric. In 1416, the text of Quintilian's *Institutes of Oratory* was found. This was followed by the recovery of Cicero's *De Oratore* in 1422, and Aristotle's *Rhetoric* in 1508. It was a matter of time until translation and distribution strengthened the acceptance and use of these works in rhetorical instruction.

During this period the growth of the teaching of rhetoric was not so phenomenal as that in the theater. However, certain influences should be mentioned. About 1529 Leonard Cox's *The Arte or Crafte of Rhetoryque,* the first rhetorical schoolbook published in English, appeared in London. This is the earliest systematic attempt to acquaint English readers with the Ciceronian concept of invention.[4] Cox, an English schoolmaster, leaned upon Cicero, and upon Melanchthon's *Institutiones Rhetoricae* for his discussion. About 1553, Thomas Wilson produced *The Art of Rhetorique*, the greatest work in the Ciceronian tradition by an Englishman. He writes a systematic, learned, lively account of the five divisions of the field, devoting nearly two-thirds of his space to invention and about one-fifth to style.[5]

Between 1584 and 1642 the influence of Peter Ramus, a French writer, dominated the theory of communication in England.[6] Much of his influence was later transmitted to rhetoric in Harvard College and the American colonies, although the influence of Ramus in England seems to become obsolete after the seventeenth century. Ramus departmentalized the three liberal arts to include grammar (etymology and syntax), dialectic (invention and arrangement), and rhetoric (style and delivery). This separation had great influence upon what was taught in rhetoric in England at the time, and later significantly affected the teaching of rhetoric in America.

THE RESTORATION AND THE EIGHTEENTH CENTURY IN ENGLAND

Theater

The Restoration period was marked by the early attempts of Charles II to introduce many of the practices he knew in the French theater—the physical stage, the use of actresses, and so on. The situation was complicated further because of the lack of good plays. Puritanical opposition to the theater under the Commonwealth did not help. Under James I, the Restoration comedy began. Numerous plays "wittily depicting heartless seduction and sophisticated evil" were done by George Etherege, William Wycherley, William Congreve, and George Farquhar from 1660 to 1706. Changes in theater design followed. Next evolved not only a century of great acting, but also the entry of men of letters into playwriting. Among the actors were Thomas Betterton; Colley Cibber, a comedian; the great David

---

[4] See Wilbur Sam Howell, "English Backgrounds of Rhetoric," in Karl Wallace and Others, *A History of Speech Education in America* (New York: Appleton-Century-Crofts, Inc., 1954), p. 11.

[5] *Ibid.*, p. 13.

[6] *Ibid.*, pp. 28, 29.

Garrick, who was a director and a producer as well; Roger Kemble, and his daughter, Sarah Siddons. Many of Shakespeare's plays were done, but with scripts modified to suit players and occasions. Fine comedy came from the pens of Oliver Goldsmith (*She Stoops to Conquer*, 1773); Richard Brinsley Sheridan (*School for Scandal*, 1777); and John Gay (*The Beggar's Opera*, 1728). These and numerous other plays of this period have been produced frequently in the United States.

Rhetoric

In this period three principal contributions were made to rhetoric. In 1759, John Ward's *System of Oratory* appeared. This work departed from the Ramean influence and is definitely classical in tendency. He draws from Quintilian and uses Cicero for illustrations. Ward's work later influenced rhetoric in the American colonies by sweeping away the last vestiges of Ramean rhetoric which had dominated the early years. His treatment covers *all* of the classical divisions of rhetoric, stressing invention, disposition, and elocution most strongly.

The second writer, George Campbell, was a Presbyterian minister. His two works, *Philosophy of Rhetoric* and *Lectures on Pulpit Eloquence* together provide one of the most penetrating analyses of the bases of rhetoric in the history of the discipline. Richard Whately, a distinguished writer and a follower of Campbell, indicates that the *Philosophy* is definitely superior in depth to the work of Blair, which was a popularly received work in this period. In the *Lectures* he amplifies the explanation of the ends of oratory, adding to existing ideas in that area.

In 1783, Hugh Blair published his *Lectures on Rhetoric and Belle Lettres*, which was widely adopted by colleges. His stated purpose of the work was for those "who are studying to cultivate their taste, to form their style, or to prepare themselves for public speaking or composition." Of thirty-four lectures, Blair devotes twenty-six to language, style, and eloquence. He does, however, expand the scope of rhetoric to something more than that which is pleasing to the hearers. "A higher degree of eloquence," says Blair, "is that through which the speaker attempts not only to please, but to inform, to instruct, to convince. The highest degree of eloquence is that used to influence conduct and persuade to action."

These three sources of English rhetoric were influential in early speech education in America.

The Elocutionists [7]

A third thread in the history of speech education developed during this period after 1750. This was the attempt to improve delivery through systematic and specific methods devised by the elocutionists. Their influence was to continue for hundreds of years, into America, and into the fringes of modern speech education.

The elocutionists gained their start as a result of much criticism of the delivery of English preachers, especially by such men as Defoe, Swift, Dryden, David Garrick, and Thomas Sheridan. So aroused were some of them that they even urged the founding of an English academy to deal with the problem. The elocutionists held that the principles of effective delivery came from nature herself. Their systems were based on broad principles and upon the reader or speaker's understanding of ideas and emotions to be read or spoken. The "natural" group allowed considerable freedom in this expression. The "mechanical" group desired this natural delivery, but believed that it could come only from a study and practice of rules within nature. Their elaborate systems were attempts to organize and apply such rules. Every aspect of delivery was included in their teachings: clear-cut utterance of sounds, including a knowledge of vocal production; correct pronunciation; suitable vocal use to fit meanings; appropriate facial expression; and significant gesture, movement, and so on.

A considerable list of writers concentrated upon the new methods. In 1748, John Mason first used the word "elocution" in a book, *An Essay on Elocution*. In 1756, Thomas Sheridan began a career as a teacher of elocution after his stage aspirations had ended in failure. His *Dictionary* (1780) and *Grammar* (1780) established pronunciation as part of the field. Joshua Steele in his *Prosodia Rationalis* (1775) developed a system of correlating speech with the musical scale and ventured a method of marking that was picked up by

---

[7] See Frederick W. Haberman, "English Sources of American Elocution," in Karl Wallace and Others, *A History of Speech Education in America* (New York: Appleton-Century-Crofts, Inc., 1954), Chap. V.; also, Professor Haberman's doctoral dissertation, "The Elocutionary Movement in England, 1750–1850" (Cornell University, 1947).

other writers. John Walker was probably the most prolific writer, with six books to his credit. A former actor, he made a success of his writing and teaching of elocution. His *Elements of Elocution* (1781) was his most widely used work. The Reverend Gilbert Austin had extensive influence through his *Chironomia; or a Treatise on Rhetorical Delivery*. Published in 1806, it developed an elaborate system of rules, postures, gestures, and other techniques. An extensive array of plates and illustrations was part of the volume. This book affected the teaching of delivery as late as 1916 when some American writers were still drawing upon it.

In addition to the books described above, there were hundreds of manuals for school use and for practice at home. Most of these were written for the clergy.

THE AMERICAN COLONIAL PERIOD (1607–1800)

Speech education in America took some time to get started, despite the fact that theater, rhetoric, and elocution were quite strongly established in England by the end of this period. The colonists faced obstacles of transportation and location. Few books were printed in America at first. Most of them had to be brought from England. Gifts from personal libraries were frequent as a means of getting schools started.

The settlers, however, did not neglect education. Right away, they founded schools and colleges: Harvard in 1636, Yale in 1701. Numerous other institutions followed. Many controversial issues faced the leaders of the colonies and, later, of the new nation. Situations in the Continental Congress, the Constitutional Convention, and the meetings of the various local governing bodies often called upon men to utilize all the rhetoric they knew. Yet speech education was meager and developed under handicaps.

Theater

In the colleges there was little development in theater. Some institutions were definitely opposed to it because of religious and moral beliefs. Early activity included the presentation of a colloquy at William and Mary College in 1702; a performance of Cato is recorded in 1736. Cotton Mather voiced strong opposition to any efforts in Massachusetts. After Yale's two drama and literary clubs,

Linonia and Brothers in Unity, gave off-campus performances of such plays as *The Beaux's Stratagem* and *Love Makes a Man*, they were publicly censured by President Stiles in 1782. A rule prohibiting all public performance was passed and remained in force until 1789. Other college groups met with the same opposition, but by the end of the century certain encouraging signs appeared. Hugh Brackenridge and Philip Freneau wrote dramatic exercises on political issues for the Princeton commencement. The first American play, *The Prince of Parthia*, was written by Thomas Godfrey in 1758, and, in 1787, Royall Tyler wrote *The Contrast*.

In the commercial theater, things were not much better. Massachusetts' ban on public performances was not lifted until 1793. Before 1800, only English actors appeared in any plays presented. Walter Murray and Thomas Kean came to the colonies, and the Hallams brought a troupe from England to Virginia and New York about 1752. Until after 1783, the Revolution cramped the theater. In 1794, new theaters opened in Boston, and Philadelphia displaced New York as the center of activity with the opening of theaters there.

Rhetoric

Early rhetoric concentrated on style and delivery, following Peter Ramus' plan of assigning invention and arrangement to dialectic. There was a definite lack of classical influence; Aristotle, Cicero, and Quintilian were not known. The works of Cox and Wilson did not appear in the colonies until about 1730. The first evidences of a classical influence came in 1750 with the printing of the *Port Royal Art of Speaking*, a Ciceronian treatment. Cicero's *De Oratore* circulated at Yale and Harvard from 1743 to 1762 and later. John Ward's *System of Oratory* was popular until 1780. There was some emphasis upon rhetoric and belle lettres, and the elocutionist influence was gaining strength quite rapidly with the circulation of the works of Mason, Sheridan, Walker, and Austin. These also influenced later writings on rhetoric in America.

Lectures on Moral Philosophy and Eloquence first given at Princeton, 1768–94, by John Witherspoon, the president of the college, were published in 1810 and became the first complete American rhetoric.

There was no lack of rhetorical practice in this period. This began with speaking at college exercises, either at commencement or at special exhibitions, as early as 1768–85. Forms of activity were orations, usually given in Greek, Latin, or sometimes in English; forensic disputations, the forerunner of debates; dialogues; and syllogistic disputations, in which points of logic were contested.

Speaking in curricular studies later replaced the public exercises in a number of schools. Rhode Island made this change about 1782. There was also a revival of interest in declamation and reading contests noted at the College of New Jersey during this period. More specialized tutors were hired, each being required to teach his specialty *and* speaking and writing in order to qualify. John Quincy Adams, president of Harvard, who later held the Boylston Chair of Rhetoric, approved training in speaking as part of the curricular study. His *Lectures on Rhetoric and Oratory*, published in 1810, were a high point in the history of American rhetorical theory.

Harvard and Yale both required participation in speech activity by the end of the eighteenth century. Harvard required declamations, orations, and syllogistic disputations in the regular schedule. The president of the college lectured on rhetoric each Friday. Yale required forensic disputations weekly for juniors and seniors. In Philadelphia, Benjamin Franklin demanded training in English in writing and speaking for students at the academy he founded there, which later became the University of Pennsylvania. Debating societies in many colleges offered much training in parliamentary practice, impromptu speaking, and extemporaneous speaking.

Thus, the scene was set for important changes and developments in the years to come. In the nineteenth century, the influence of English writers continued with Whately's *Elements of Rhetoric* (1828). The American rhetorics of Genung (*Practical Elements of Rhetoric*, 1885) and Day (*The Art of Discourse*, 1867) were influential. Dr. Benjamin Rush's *The Philosophy of the Human Voice* (1827) was to affect a series of elocutionists from Porter to Trueblood, and Steele Mackaye's championship of Delsarte made another mark in this pattern.

The fields of voice science pioneered by Alexander Melville Bell and his son, the interest in the handicapped in speech and hearing, and the development of monistic psychology opened the new field of speech and hearing rehabilitation on a scientific basis.

Later the invention of the wireless paved the way for radio and television broadcasting, plus college courses in these fields.

EXERCISES

1. Using the material covered in this chapter and in the supplementary readings as a basis for your discussion, indicate what you consider to be the major problems and issues of speech education still existing today and give your approach to handling them.
2. Discuss what you consider to be the present and future trends in speech education, drawing upon historical material found in this chapter and in your supplementary readings to support your contentions.
3. Select any modern concept, body of content, or method of teaching in use today and trace its relationship to earlier sources developed in the historical backgrounds; for example, personality of the speaker, parts of the speech, style or language, use of evidence or example, use of stage make-up, theater design, choric interpretation, and so on.

REFERENCES

CICERO. *De Oratore,* ed. J. E. WATSON. Philadelphia: David McKay Co., 1899.

COOPER, LANE (ed.). *Theories of Style.* New York: The Macmillan Co., 1907.

HUNT, EVERETT LEE. "Plato and Aristotle on Rhetoric and Rhetoricians," in *Studies in Rhetoric and Public Speaking,* pp. 3–60. New York: The Century Co., 1925.

JEBB, R. C. *The Attic Orators.* Cambridge: J. E. Sandys, 1909.

MACGOWAN, KENNETH, and WILLIAM MELNITZ. *The Living Stage.* New York: Prentice-Hall, Inc., 1955.

QUINTILIAN, *Institutio Oratoria.* Translated by H. E. BUTLER. 4 vols. New York: G. P. Putnam's Sons, 1920.

ROBERTS, RHYS (ed.). *The Rhetoric of Aristotle.* Oxford: The Clarendon Press, 1924.

RYAN, J. P., "Quintilian's Message," *Quarterly Journal of Speech,* XV (April, 1929), 171–80.

WALLACE, KARL, and OTHERS. *A History of Speech Education in America.* New York: Appleton-Century-Crofts, Inc., 1954.

WHATELY, RICHARD. *The Elements of Rhetoric.* New York: Sheldon and Co., 1871.

CHAPTER THREE

Professional Careers in the Teaching of Speech

THE NEED

The great need for teachers springs from the young people of the United States themselves. Never have there been so many of them. Never have they looked so eagerly toward education for attitudes, values, knowledge, and skills to help them meet their problems in a confused world. Never has the teacher had a personal and professional role of greater importance. His influence reaches into nearly every home in the land.

The Staggering Increase of Students

In 1945–46, there were 23,300,000 pupils in the public schools. In 1954, the United States Office of Education reported a total of 33,-000,000, of which 6,400,000 were in high schools and 26,700,000 in elementary schools. College enrollments stood at 2,469,000. In 1958, figures showed 8,750,000 in high schools, 28,700,000 in elementary schools, and 3,258,000 in colleges. War babies, growing up now, are crowding high schools and knocking on the doors of colleges. An annual birth rate of 5,000,000 adds to the problem. Conservative 1965 projections indicate 48,000,000 children of school age. Of these, 10,000,000 to 12,000,000 will be in high schools and about 36,000,000 in elementary schools.

On the basis of the present rate of high school graduates attending college (over 30 per cent), there will be over 4,000,000 college students by 1970. If 40 per cent go to college, as they well may do, there will be over 5,000,000; if 50 per cent continue their education, about 6,700,000 will attend college in 1970.

If the same ratios are applied to enrollment in speech at all levels of instruction, with no allowance for new programs, there will be twice as many pupils in high school and college classes. Speech and hearing clinics for elementary school pupils will have to serve an additional 100,000 cases.

If speech training expands in the next ten years in proportion to its growth in the past ten years, by 1970 speech faculties may have to serve three times as many students. But the most important fact is that *speech programs at all levels of education, now or in the future, are no stronger than the teachers entrusted with their development and administration.* What, then, is the result if teachers are lacking to carry on this work? What happens, with speech gaining educational support, if trained faculties are not available to conduct expanding programs? The answer is obvious. The programs will be watered down, weakened, or lost. Strong teachers are needed, and needed badly.

The Supply and Demand

To serve the students, enough new teachers must be trained to keep pace. A conservative figure of 100,000 new teachers is needed each year. They must fill vacancies of those leaving the profession and also fill *new* positions. Simple arithmetic shows a need for 500,-000 new teachers in a five- to ten-year period. Needs for college teachers may run as high as 300,000 for the same period.

Turnover and Replacement

A national figure of 75,000 annual replacements is an item for serious consideration. One teacher in four leaves teaching for economic reasons, although that figure is improving because of better salaries —better, but not always enough to keep abreast of rising living costs.

Speech is in a period of growth and development. The need for teachers and replacement of teachers are critical problems. The personal and local quality of programs in this field demands capable leaders. Recently, a veteran high school teacher retired after many years in her position. She had built an unusually strong four-year curricular sequence and had an extensive reputation for excellent forensic and interpretative activities. Hundreds of former students and parents had lived successful lives because of her contribution. In her community and state she represented a stronghold for speech training. Her influence affected many colleagues. Available teachers were scarce when she left; a younger, less-dedicated person replaced her. Since that time the speech program in that school has steadily lost ground. Two elective courses have been dropped; activities in the school are sketchy. The whole cause of speech education was affected by this replacement.

The Shortage of Special Teachers

Of particular importance to the speech field is the shortage of teachers in such areas as reading, cerebral palsy, work with the deaf and hard of hearing, and speech correction. Studies of cities of over 100,000 reveal a shortage of such teachers in 40 per cent of the cities. Professor Max Steer of Purdue University, Chairman of the Planning Committee of the American Speech and Hearing Association, made this statement five years ago. Conditions have not improved since.

If we project our needs to 1965, we estimate that we shall have over 2,500,000 speech defectives needing attention. To serve the increasing numbers, we shall have to train a minimum of 3,500 speech therapists a year. This figure includes replacements for those who leave the profession and new teachers.

The Solution

The method having the greatest potentialities is the continuing, individual personal recruitment of new personnel. The speech teachers of the future are now in speech classes and activities in elementary schools, high schools, and colleges. Every one of these students should have the opportunity to consider a professional career in the teaching of speech. With suitable information and wise guidance, they can meet the need of serving future generations.

THE CHALLENGE

Service—the Corner Stone

The great challenge of a teaching career is the possibility it affords for real service. No person should enter teaching unless he places this goal at the top. Through his life a teacher influences the lives of others for good. By sharing his knowledge he kindles the spark for students to learn. He whets their minds so that they will be keen and ready to respond. Through his values and ideals, he shapes their personalities and characters. With his skills he develops behavior essential to their occupational success. By stimulating them, he develops leaders. From all of these experiences, the real teacher expects but a small reward—the hope and satisfaction of seeing his students develop into fine, outstanding adults. Material rewards are definitely secondary.

Teaching Speech—an Intensely Personal Challenge

The teacher of speech has distinctive opportunities to influence young lives. The very nature of his work places him in closer touch with his students than are other teachers. Whenever a student stands before an audience to communicate orally he places on inventory everything he is as a person. The teacher observes these qualities. He seeks to know more so that his instruction will be individual, personal, constructive. This close interpersonal tie is the core of teaching speech. Through it the teacher opens doors for the student so that his knowledge and feelings can function in all his human relationships.

The teacher also knows that the knowledge and skills he develops are *immediately practical*. Improvements made by his pupils in the morning class can be used at a luncheon discussion or in an afternoon meeting. He is sure also that the gains his students make *belong to them* as permanent parts of their education to be used throughout life.

In addition, the handiwork of the speech teacher can have a tremendous impact upon the life of our times. Today men dare not turn quickly to force. More than ever before is needed the cool, clear deliberation of persons listening, thinking, talking together at the conference table. An imperative is the enlightened exposition and persuasion of leaders with sound values to interpret these decisions. Equally essential are the sensitive understandings and appreciations revealed through interpreting and producing great literature on the platform or in the theater. Radio, television, and film need the refining influence of a cultural mind to counterbalance box office and commercial pressures.

The speech teacher has the means to wield great influence through his students.

Teaching and Other Professional Careers

With the security provided by a teaching position it is quite common for persons trained in performance areas to combine their talents with their academic lives. One speech dean moderates a national television discussion program; a high school teacher directs and acts in a community theater; an interpretation professor has a national reputation as a recitalist and platform reader; a director of forensics is an accomplished forum director.

Salaries Improving

The material rewards of teaching speech are improving. Starting salaries for beginning high school teachers without experience range between $4,000 and $5,000. Master of arts degrees move the figure up another $200 in most cases. Annual increases on salary scales run $100–$200. Merit increases and cost-of-living bonuses add to those figures substantially. Upper limits of salary scales in good systems are much higher than before: $8,000 is not uncommon; wealthier districts go as high as $10,000. Colleges are upgrading salaries at all ranks in an effort to attract and hold capable personnel. In 1958, the Research Division of the National Education Association in a national survey reported 400 professors at the $15,000 mark (many in medical schools); *top* salaries in state colleges about $11,000, teachers' college *top* at $9,500, and a small number of large and medium nonpublic colleges with a *top* exceeding $8,000; *medians* for municipal universities at $7,911; for state universities, $6,370; for teachers' colleges, $6,068; for state colleges, $5,882. Median increase, 1957–58, was 8.2 per cent. Conditions have improved somewhat since then.

Fringe Benefits Better

Group life insurance, health plans, major medical insurance, retirement funds, and in some colleges tuition exchange agreements, make the financial outlook for teachers much more pleasant and secure. These details are part of the appeal of careers in teaching.

Numerous Opportunities for Further Study

High schools and colleges are becoming very sensitive to inducements and direct help in further study for faculty members. National foundations, business and industrial sources, along with federal government agencies are financing further study and travel for teachers. The Internal Revenue Service allows deductions of educational expense for additional study required in one's teaching career. Summer vacations offer interesting opportunities for these purposes.

Enjoyable Personal Associations Offered in Teaching Speech

One of the fine benefits of a speech educator's life is the opportunity to make friends with cultured people in the profession. Such associations cannot be estimated in dollars and cents. They surround a teacher with the fun and stimulation of well-educated persons in the faculty; they put him in the center of student life that will keep him young and alive for years. As a teacher, he also has an "open door" to the finest cultural groups in the community.

THE BASIC JOB

The speech teacher must also see clearly his basic job. He must fully realize that he is dealing not only with linguistic habits but with a form of social behavior, behavior which permits individuals to make the necessary adjustments required by life in our democratic society. The adolescent, especially, is much concerned with the successful and happy outcome of these adjustments. He appreciates the immediate application of his increased speech proficiency. He comes to the classroom, or, for that matter, to any situation in which he must employ speech behavior, with problems, interests, and abilities which are peculiarly his own. These, most of them habits of long standing, must be *evaluated* so that he will know which should be retained, which modified or supplemented by new learnings.

The teacher must be capable of making the necessary appraisal of these potentialities so that the four principal parts of his job may be carried forward efficiently. These four functions are: (1) to formulate wholesome and desirable attitudes toward speech performance; (2) to provide information and theoretical principles needed for speech development; (3) to correct and improve the personal speech habits of the pupils with whom he works; (4) to develop in his students greater skill and proficiency in all types of speech activity. These can be divided into *basic* skills in speech and *specialized* types of performance.

The teacher who carries out these responsibilities makes a vital contribution to the personal growth of his students. The four functions in the basic job are the underlying objectives of the *teacher* in all kinds of speech instruction. They are not confined to beginning speech courses only. These teacher functions exist in courses in public speaking, in discussion and debate, in interpretative reading, in the theater, in radio, or in corrective speech. To be sure, the skills and techniques become more specialized as these particular areas of instruction are undertaken, but the teacher should never lose sight of the four parts of his basic job, no matter what the area of his teaching.

TYPES OF POSITIONS

Because of local conditions and the wide range of possibilities for teacher activity in the field of speech, there are many types of jobs in secondary school speech. The teaching situations that offer full-time or "all speech" positions in high schools are extremely few. The one exception is in the field of speech correction, where special education laws of the states restrict, and at the same time insure, full programs of activity for persons trained in clinical service. In midwestern universities only 20 to 25 per cent of the graduates trained to teach speech are placed in beginning positions calling for speech exclusively. Most jobs require speech plus English or social studies. Often the teaching load may consist of four classes of English to one of speech. Only occasionally will the entire teaching program be made up of speech classes. Very often the speech work is extraclass in character; it includes declamation, oratory, debate, theater, interpretative reading, or radio. Classroom instruction covers many possibilities: speech correction and improvement, fundamentals of speech, public speaking, debate and discussion, interpretation, theater, and radio are the most common.

College positions are more specialized. Occasionally a speech position will include English. There are also jobs in integrated programs (basic communication skills) combining speaking, writing, and so on. However, speech departments usually hire people to teach an entire speech program. Beginning college instructors with an M.A. or a Ph.D. degree may be surprised to find how many positions ask for a combination of teaching in the basic course with specialized assignments in public address, theater, interpretation, as only part of the load.

Secondary School

1. *Speech and Hearing Therapy; Improvement*

Although the correction of speech and hearing disabilities is most often conducted in individual conference or clinical situations, this duty falls within the responsibility of many secondary school teachers of speech. Persons who undertake this special type of work should be trained specifically as clinicians or speech and hearing therapists under requirements of state law. The person with a *general* speech training should not attempt cases that are too difficult. He should refer them to those who have the training to handle them. Specifically, the work necessitates the diagnosis, treatment, and follow-up of persons whose speech is so noticeably different from the normal as to call attention to itself and to interfere with the success of those individuals in their daily living. Consequently, provisions in the special-education laws of most states encourage the employment of individual correctionists by elementary and secondary school systems. Because this type of work must be undertaken as early as possible, the larger proportion of it is done in the lower grades. States with certification requirements indicated for speech correction or the rehabilitation of persons with defective hearing usually pay a part or all of the salary of such teachers so that all school districts may have equal opportunity in the care of children handicapped in these categories.

Persons who wish to become speech correctionists should be guided closely by the requirements of the American Speech Correction and Hearing Association,[1] as well as by certification requirements in the various states in which they desire to teach.

[1] Martin F. Palmer, "American Speech Correction Association Membership Regulations," *Journal of Speech Disorders*, VIII (March, 1943), 41–51; also, "The New Requirements of the American Speech Correction Association," *Quarterly Journal of Speech*, XXIX (April, 1943), 196–99.

2. Fundamentals of Speech, Public Speaking, and Interpretation

In the secondary school this work consists of teaching general speech classes in which these fields are usually combined. Occasionally, separate courses are offered; often a course in fundamentals of speech may precede a course in public speaking and/or interpretation. The local organization of the speech program determines the sequence. Frequently, the teacher handling course work of this kind is responsible for various extraclass speech activities, which have been listed above.

3. Debate

Although debate is an extraclass activity in many schools, the instructor may be so fortunate as to have an actual debate course, particularly in those areas where participation in state forensic programs is customary. Here he can teach theory and practice in argumentation, discussion, and debate, which will either prepare students for the extraclass program specifically and will supplement such an organized activity, or will be offered as an advanced course in a public-speaking sequence.

4. Theater

Positions in this field have often combined theater with interpretation or public speaking. Recently there has been some demand for combinations of theater with radio. Some schools offer regular course work in theater, which includes history, acting, directing, and technical production. Where school theater is highly developed, greater job specialization exists. For example, two teachers may handle history, dramatic literature, acting, and directing. A full-time teacher may be hired for technical work and costuming. Certain schools with many programs using the auditorium employ a director of auditorium activities to administer the program. He usually also teaches in the theater area.

5. Radio and Television

As in theater, the number of schools having course work in radio is quite small. The local school and community conditions usually affect this kind of instruction. FM radio, with school and community broadcasting stations, and closed-circuit television are giving considerable impetus to instruction in specialized techniques. These include knowledge of the background in the field, announcing, script and continuity writing, acting, and production. Very frequently a workshop plan is instituted in a school in order to allow this activity to flourish in after-school time. It is not uncommon for local commercial stations to give time to the high school in the town so that speech class or radio or television workshop productions can be aired. All of these possibilities are stimulating to student interest and encourage students to seek instruction in this area. The teacher who desires to pursue work in this field should have good training through commercial stations or experience in college broadcasting as a part of his regular teaching preparation.

Representative College Positions

The number and kinds of college positions vary greatly, depending upon the needs and departments of the schools. Personnel is hired at any of the various ranks—instructor, assistant professor, associate professor, or professor—subject, of course, to professional qualifications and job specifications. Below are listed descriptions of representative positions posted with a placement service:

Midwestern college: Instructor for basic course or beginning public speaking; five 3-hour classes weekly. Will accept M.A. without experience. $4,800.

California—state college: Assistant professor for argumentation, discussion, advanced public address, and directing forensic program. Activities counted as part of course load; strong tournament program. Ph.D. required. $6,500.

University: Assistant professor to teach theater-production, including lectures and laboratories, plus technical work on four major productions a year. M.A. degree with experience required. $6,000.

Teachers' college: Associate professor to head teacher-training program in speech. Teach methods courses; administer student teaching in speech; direct service course in speech for all teacher candidates. Ph.D., experience required, $8,000.

Liberal arts college: Assistant professor to teach fundamentals, interpretation, discussion. Coach debate squad and direct two plays. M.A. accepted; experience preferred. $5,300.

University: Professor for classical rhetoric, British and American public address, persuasion, graduate seminars, supervise graduate work. Ph.D., experience, research publications required. Salary open for desired person.

DESIRABLE TEACHER QUALIFICATIONS

Secondary

Personal Characteristics

Because of the important personal demands in the field, the speech teacher can never be a mine-run, stodgy individual. He should have a sincere interest in teaching; he should be a well-adjusted person emotionally; he should have the ability to keep his head when pressures build up; he should understand the problems of the adolescent and should have a desire to help him; he should know how to organize a job and follow it through; he should be willing and able to work hard; he should be intelligent and have good judgment as well as confidence in himself; he should be vital and optimistic; he should possess a sense of humor; he should know how to get along well with people; he should be neat and clean in person and dress.

Speech Proficiency

The prospective teacher of speech should have good voice and articulation plus the ability to use them. He should have had experience in high school and college in a variety of speech activities. Experience in debating, interpretation programs, plays, assemblies, radio or television programs, operettas, and variety shows is extremely valuable in teaching. He should be proficient in several of these performance areas if possible.

College instructors should have greater specialization and skill if they are expected to appear on special programs or conduct demonstrations.

Academic Training

A. Speech
  1. At least a major in the field is desirable. This varies, depending upon the institution, from 30 to 40 semester hours. The total amount should:
      a. provide adequate preparation in subject matter;
      b. meet state certification requirements. (These should be checked carefully by the candidate through official pub-

lications or by writing directly to the department of public instruction of the state whose requirements are desired.);

c. allow opportunity for taking work in minor and related fields necessary for certification and teaching.

2. Key course work for high school teachers:

a. In *general speech positions:* Voice and Phonetics; Fundamentals of Speech; Debate and Discussion; Interpretation; Play Production, including organization, design, construction, lighting, and make-up; Directing; Dramatic Literature; introductory work in Acting; Speech Correction or Improvement; Radio Production. These last three can be altered or amplified to fit the interests and needs of the prospective teacher. Courses in Play-writing, Radio Writing, and History of the Theater would be useful, but are not quite so vital to the high school teacher.

b. In *speech correction and audiology* (not confined primarily to high school: See the latest state requirements available through the Special Education Division of the State Department of Public Instruction. Write the Executive Secretary of the American Speech and Hearing Association, 1001 Connecticut Ave., Washington 6, D.C.).

3. Methods of teaching speech in the high school:

This should be a strong, practical course organized around the problems the teacher meets in secondary schools. It is also credited as an education course in special methods. See B2, below.

B. Education (15 to 24 semester hours, depending upon the state requirements)

1. Introduction to Education, Philosophy, Principles, Psychology, Measurements, General Technique of Teaching and Administration, as required.

2. Methods:

a. Special course in teaching of speech.

b. Special course in teaching minor is desirable.

3. Student teaching (5 to 8 semester hours).

a. Observation of skilled teachers in action.

b. Planning and organizing units for instruction in cooperation with an experienced teacher.

c. Actual classroom teaching under supervision.

d. Experience in the direction of extraclass activities in speech from the following: declamation, interpretative reading, extemporaneous speaking, oratory, debate and discussion, dramatics, radio, and so on.

e. Individual cases and small group work for speech-correction teachers.

f. The use and operation of all types of teaching aids: tape-recording equipment; public address and/or radio apparatus; motion picture, filmstrip, opaque, and overhead projectors; playback equipment; and so on. (California requires an audio-visual course of all teachers.).

C. Related Fields (in many states two minors are required or a second major)

1. English (a minor is suggested; a major is advisable, especially for prospective dramatics and interpretation teachers).
Beginning and advanced courses in Composition; survey courses in American and English Literature, Dramatic Literature, Contemporary Literature.

2. Social Studies (a minor is recommended; a major is desirable, especially for public speaking, debate, and discussion students). Economics; Economic Geography; Sociology; English and American History; Political Science; History of Special Periods, Movements, etc.; World Geography and Politics.

D. General Education (in addition to course work in C)

1. The speech teacher especially needs a broad background. His work utilizes much from cultures throughout the ages, and necessitates his having close touch with contemporary ones.

2. Philosophy, Religion, the History and Appreciation of Art and Music are especially important.

3. Science and Mathematics should not be overlooked. State certification requirements in these fields are being increased.

4. Foreign Language is a valuable cultural and practical study.

College Instructors

College instructors and secondary school teachers need many of the same qualifications. This is true of personal characteristics and proficiency in speech. However, their academic training, while quite similar in many respects, may show certain differences. Like the high school teacher, the college instructor (1) needs a bachelor's degree from a four-year college or university; (2) should have a broad *general* education; (3) should present a speech major of considerable strength. He may also have developed definite special interests or areas of study important in college teaching. On the other hand, unlike his secondary school colleague, (1) he is not required to take professional courses in education, including student teaching, although he may have done so; (2) he must complete a master of arts degree in speech to get started in college teaching; (3) he will have to complete a Ph.D. degree or an Ed.D. if he is to make a career of college teaching.

The college teacher moves to greater depth and specialization in his teaching field than does the high school instructor. Through the college courses he conducts, he may ultimately train or direct many students entering the field of speech or the various careers or occupations that use speech significantly in their operation.

Research is another important duty of every college teacher. Closely allied to this is the writing of scholarly articles, periodical articles, books, and so on, which are published for use in the speech field or by interested groups outside it.

Service on university committees and accepting college offices, active participation in the professional organizations in speech, lecturing to lay and academic groups—all these are added to the basic job of a classroom instructor.

PROFESSIONAL EXPERIENCE

The teacher of speech, either in training or in service, should take advantage of opportunities for additional professional training. These include participation in radio and theater as actor, director, and technician; in public speaking and lecturing; and in platform reading. They afford the advantages not only of additional experience but also of financial return. Professional training can also be gained through the observation of productions in the educational and commercial theater, network radio and television shows, lectures and recitals, and distinctive or representative motion pictures. Interested teachers of speech living in outlying communities often visit metropolitan areas to enrich their backgrounds, to preview contemporary plays, or to note techniques in professional productions useful to their teaching. Finally, these experiences may ultimately lead to development and contacts which will help the speech teacher also achieve a professional career in lecturing, radio, television, or theater, if he desires one.

PROFESSIONAL ASSOCIATIONS

Membership and *activity* in professional associations aid teacher development. Membership in the National Education Association and state teacher organizations identifies the teacher with general educational associations. He receives their publications and can attend their meetings in order to keep abreast of new information and activities which affect the speech field.

The Role of Professional Organizations

Importance to Teachers

Membership and activity in professional associations aid teacher development. First, affiliation with such groups gives the teacher a sense of "belonging" and creates unity among the members of a profession. Next, these organizations are a means of supplying important knowledge of new developments in materials, methods, programs, equipment, and so on, through both their professional meetings and conferences and their publications. Third, such groups are a source of professional contacts and friendships that are very stimulating and useful to teachers. Fourth, they provide for the teacher member an arena for professional status that will strengthen his leadership in his own school. Fifth, they inform teachers of vacancies and expansion in the field that provide opportunities for advancement. Finally, they may be the means for subsidizing important professional ventures in research, publication, or deliberation so strongly needed for enriching education.

General Professional Associations

The National Education Association represents the broadest professional group of classroom teachers in the United States. Similar in purpose and activity are numerous state organizations to which high school teachers and elementary teachers belong. A similar college group is the American Association of University Professors.

Professional Organizations for Speech Teachers

There are a number of important groups with which persons in the speech profession may affiliate. All offer the advantages mentioned at the beginning of this section. The payment of the nominal sums asked as dues by these organizations is a wise professional investment. When one considers the large dues paid by members of trade unions and business groups to help promote their work, educational organizations have a very modest financial program.

1. *The Speech Association of America.* This association, which might be called the parent group in the field, was organized in 1914 under the name of the National Association of Academic Teachers of Public Speaking. Rapid growth of the field broadened the base of its membership and moved it to choose its present name. Its members include elementary, secondary, college and university teachers in all fields of speech: public speaking, debate, discussion, communication, interpretation, theater, phonetics, voice science, communicative disorders, radio, television, and semantics. Membership is open to any person. Members in the speech field number in the thousands.

The Speech Association publishes three journals quarterly: the *Quarterly Journal of Speech,* which serves the whole field, but leans somewhat to college level materials; the *Speech Teacher,* developed for elementary and high school teachers in particular, with extensive consideration of pedagogical problems; the *Speech Monographs,* a research and bibliographical journal.

The association also publishes annually a *Directory of Members.* This includes names, addresses, school affiliations, and brief professional data on each member. It also contains the organizational structure of the association, its committees, its officers, its interest groups, the officers of regional and cooperating associations, and a list of speech departments with their chairmen. A bibliography and list of equipment is also there. The SAA also operates a placement service for members on a nonprofit basis.

The annual conventions of the association, held ordinarily in August or December, in major cities, attract between 1,000 and 2,000 members, who can choose from fifty or more sectional meetings.

The national headquarters of the association are located at Indiana University, Bloomington, Indiana.

2. *The American Educational Theatre Association.* For teachers with special interests in educational, commercial, and community theater, the AETA is the professional group. Organized in 1936, it provides for its members services and programs very similar to those of the SAA.

Membership is open to anyone interested in theater. Special interest groups include acting, directing, playwriting, technical activities, children's theater, puppetry, radio, television, and film.

Recent development of the Secondary School Theatre Conference and the Children's Theatre Conference within this organization has given more emphasis to these two areas.

Its publications, the *Educational Theatre Journal,* the *CTC Newsletter,* and the *Secondary School Newsletter,* are available to all members. An annual *Directory of Members* is also published.

National conventions are held annually, usually in August.

The executive secretary-treasurer is located at Northwestern University, Evanston, Illinois.

3. *The American Speech and Hearing Association.* Another organization, serving teachers interested in professional work with communicative disorders—speech correction, audiology, speech pathology, language development, and the like—was founded in 1925. Members serve their field in hospitals, clinics, public schools, colleges, and universities.

This group maintains its own permanent national headquarters at 1001 Connecticut Avenue, N.W., Washington 6, D.C. It publishes two journals, the *Journal of Speech and Hearing Disorders* and the *Journal of Speech and Hearing Research.* It also issues a *Directory of Members,* maintains a placement service, and supervises certification of its members in the field.

Its national conventions are held annually in the fall.

4. *The National Society for the Study of Communication.* Organized on a broader basis of interest, this group was founded in 1949 by persons interested and working on problems of communication. Members come from colleges; universities; secondary and elementary schools; the fields of speech, English, journalism; radio and

television; film; linguistics; personnel departments; and other fields.

Its publication, the *Journal of Communication*, deals with subjects relevant to this wider emphasis in study and practice. Its national convention, usually held in conjunction with that of the SAA, is supplemented by a summer conference. Membership is open to all interested persons.

5. *The National Association of Educational Broadcasters.* This group is interested in uniting for study and service all individuals concerned with educational broadcasting in radio and/or television. It offers eight classes of membership to institutions, individuals, companies, and agencies interested in the field.

Among its services to its members are its publication, the *NAEB Journal*, and the NAEB Radio Network tape exchange. The latter provides a wide service of taped productions, which can be rented or purchased for use by educational stations. A placement service is also available for persons seeking positions in broadcasting.

6. *The American Forensic Association.* This organization, somewhat recently founded, is composed of teachers and directors of forensics in high schools, colleges, and universities. Its aims are the study, improvement, and promotion of work in debate and other forensic events. Its meetings are held jointly with SAA. Four times a year, it publishes the *AFA Register,* which contains a calendar of events, a membership directory, and reports of interest.

7. *Regional and State Associations.* National organizations are important. However, smaller groups can often deal with sectional or local problems more quickly and directly. There are six regional speech associations in the United States. Each holds an annual convention and four publish academic journals. The Western Speech Association includes the Pacific and Rocky Mountain states. Its publication is *Western Speech.* The Central States Speech Association serves the Midwest, including North Dakota, South Dakota, Nebraska, Kansas, Oklahoma, Missouri, Iowa, Illinois, Wisconsin, Minnesota, Indiana, Michigan, and Ohio. It publishes the *Central States Speech Journal.* The Southern Speech Association covers Arkansas, Texas, Louisiana, Mississippi, Tennessee, Kentucky, North Carolina, South Carolina, Alabama, Georgia, and Florida. Its publi-

cation is the *Southern Speech Journal.* The Speech Association of the Eastern States includes West Virgina, Virginia, Delaware, Maryland, Pennsylvania, New Jersey, New York, and the New England States. Its journal is *Today's Speech.* The New England Speech Association serves the six states in its region, and the Pacific Speech Association includes Hawaii only.

There are also approximately forty state associations, each doing professional service through a wide variety of activities. Recently, their efforts have produced numerous excellent curriculum guides. (*See* Chapter V.)

8. *Honorary and Service Organizations.* In this group are three high school organizations—The National Forensic League, National Thespian Society, and Masque and Gavel—and numerous college groups, which include: Phi Beta and Zeta Phi Eta (women's honorary and professional); Delta Sigma Rho, Pi Kappa Delta, Pi Kappa Alpha, Phi Rho Pi (all honorary forensic); Sigma Alpha Eta (speech correction and audiology); Alpha Psi Omega, Theta Alpha Phi, and National Collegiate Players (drama).

HOW TO GET A JOB

Every teacher is interested in getting a good job. This is the goal of preparation and the hope for a professional future. These suggestions should prove helpful.

Find available positions.

The first step is to discover what positions exist, where they are located, and important details about them. *Your college placement service* is your first channel. List your name, fill out the required papers, giving your courses, activities, experience, recommendations, personal data, the kinds of positions you wish, and the salary desired. Pay the modest fee involved and wait for notices of vacancies. There is usually no charge beyond this for the use of this service. You can *join a commercial teachers' agency.* The procedure for listing and setting up your file is similar. However, these agencies charge a commission, a certain percentage of your salary for their help, in addition to their registration fee. *Registration with the Placement Bureau of SAA, AETA, or ASHA,* or other professional organization,

is another method, and very usable. *Word of mouth notice* is a common method. Your friends, former teachers, book salesmen, school officials, and school board members may all be potential sources. *Newspaper listings, advertisements and notices in professional journals* are another means of getting such information. Finally, *direct inquiry by letter to schools or administrators* is very effective. It is important that you write a good, tactful, attention-getting letter if you use this method. The sample below should help you:

LETTER OF INQUIRY

1725 Orrington Avenue
Evanston, Illinois

January 2, 1963

Mr. A. J. Smith
Superintendent of Schools
El Paso, Texas

Dear Mr. Smith:

For some time, I have been interested in obtaining a teaching position in Texas. Upon inquiry, I have learned of the excellence of your school system and, in particular, of your high school speech program. I am wondering if there will be any vacancy in your system for a speech teacher for the coming school year.

I will receive the Bachelor of Science degree in June, 1963, from Northwestern University. My academic major, in which I have completed sixty quarter hours, is in the field of speech, with particular emphasis in the area of speech education. My primary interest is in public speaking, and I have had work in argumentation and debate, persuasion, discussion, speech composition, and group leadership. I also am qualified to teach English, which is my minor field of study; I have completed thirty-two quarter hours in this area. My student teaching

experience consisted of one quarter of regular classwork on a full-day basis in a combined speech and
English course for high school juniors and seniors
at Evanston Township High School, Evanston, Illinois.
This preparation has enabled me to fulfill the
requirements for Teacher Certification in the State
of Texas.

In addition to academic preparation, I have
had experience working with high school students
through the Evanston YWCA as a counselor for Y-Teen
groups for two years. This consisted of club
activities and helping in the production of their
annual operetta.

A set of my credentials is on file at the Northwestern Placement Bureau, Pearsons Hall, Northwestern University, Evanston, Illinois. I will be
happy to provide you with additional information
or meet with you for a personal interview, should a
vacancy exist.

Sincerely yours,

Doris Doe

Prepare a strong set of credentials.

When you make inquiry or application for a position by mail, the
only acquaintanceship the employer has with you is through the
letters you write and the set of credentials you prepare for him.
Therefore, you should have the best set of papers possible. They
should be carefully prepared well in advance of the time you plan
to use them.

Credentials consist of *personal data:* name, address, age, telephone
number, sex, height, weight, nationality, religion, health record or
medical history, interests, hobbies, and so on; *formal education:*
high school, college or university work, including undergraduate and
graduate work, with a list of courses, number of hours, and a summary according to departments; *outside employment:* summer jobs,
work done during schooling; *organizations:* honorary, professional,
social, with which you are affiliated; *activities:* offices, committees,

campus activities, appointments, honors, and so on; *teaching experience:* location, schools, subjects, grades; *administrative or supervisory experience:* in general activities, speech contests and plays, special projects; *recommendations:* personal, high school, college, graduate school, previous employers in or outside of educational work; *an excellent photograph:* natural pose, in good taste for employer to view, recent, good print.

All of these materials should be nicely organized, neatly and clearly typed, with clean type and a new ribbon, on bond paper or on forms provided by the placement service.

Apply for the position you desire.

(By letter) After securing listings of available jobs, select the one or ones in which you are interested. Make formal application for the job. A sample application letter appears below. As a rule you do not send your credentials with the application, but allow the prospective employer to request them. If in reply to your letter you are sent an application *form* to fill out, complete it promptly and return it. This is customary procedure when time permits.

LETTER OF APPLICATION

1725 Orrington Avenue
Evanston, Illinois

January 2, 1963

Mr. John Jones
Superintendent of Schools
Baton Rouge, Louisiana

Dear Mr. Jones:

The Placement Bureau of Northwestern University has informed me that there is a vacancy in speech and English in Baton Rouge High School for the coming school year. I should like very much to be considered as an applicant for this position.

In June, 1963, I shall receive my Bachelor of Science degree in speech from Northwestern University. My academic preparation in the field of speech education consists of extensive courses in all phases of speech work, with particular emphasis on public speaking. I have had work in argumentation and debate, persuasion, discussion, speech composition, and group leadership. I have completed sixty quarter hours in my major area of study. In addition, I have completed thirty-two quarter hours in my minor field of study, which is English. My student teaching experience consisted of one quarter of regular classwork on a full-day basis in a combined speech and English course for high school juniors and seniors at Evanston Township High School, Evanston, Illinois. This preparation has enabled me to fulfill the requirements for Teacher Certification in the State of Louisiana.

In regard to extracurricular activities, I have participated in intercollegiate debate for three years. At the present time, I am a member of the varsity debate team. I have also participated in the annual Kirk Oratorical Contest. In the field of dramatics, I have done extensive work in the Theatre Workshop, in which experimental plays are produced. I have experience in both acting and technical work.

In addition to academic preparation, I have had experience working with high school students through the Evanston YMCA as a counselor for Hi-Y groups for two years. This consisted of club activities and directing their annual sports program.

A complete set of my credentials is on file at the Northwestern Placement Bureau, Pearsons Hall, Northwestern University, Evanston, Illinois. I shall be happy to supply you with any additional information you may require. I shall be glad to arrange a personal interview with you either in Baton Rouge or in Evanston at your convenience, should you wish such an interview.

Sincerely yours,

Keith Smith

(In person) Under certain circumstances, when time is limited or in particular geographical situations, you may hear of a position and make immediate personal application. This corresponds to an employment interview but is held early and perhaps before placement papers have been viewed. They may be requested later, as well as a formal application letter. Some school systems invite candidates to apply in person, whether or not papers have been submitted. Such a procedure may act as a personal screening device for administrators.

Pass a successful interview.

Customary procedure indicates that administrators will first ask for credentials, then evaluate them, following which they will call or write candidates to come for interviews. In this way, top-ranking teachers are selected and the others eliminated. The desirable persons are asked to come for a conference which explores their papers and personal qualities more fully. The conference also permits the applicant to see the school, check the job and facilities, get acquainted with the prospective employer, and meet possible colleagues. Suitable dress, proper social courtesies, straightforward questions and answers, and a basic rapport are desired in this situation if it is to be successful.

Agree on terms and sign a contract.

If the candidate is successful and has had a favorable interview, he will have an indication of salary, rank, duties, housing, and other factors relating to the job. The contract may be offered at the time of the interview or be mailed for his final consideration and signature. In either case, details must be agreed upon and the signed document returned at the proper time. Usually a signed copy is given the teacher for his file after the contract has been approved by the board of education or trustees.

Obtain the proper certification.

Secondary school teachers of speech are concerned with the mechanics of certification. These procedures vary with schools and states. In some cases, diplomas and certificates are given at commencement. In others, certificates are obtained by application through the superintendent and county in which the teacher is employed. Still another practice is to require each teacher to make individual application on forms provided by the state department. Whatever the practice, the teacher should inform himself and promptly proceed to obtain the certificate to which he is entitled.

SUGGESTIONS FOR PROFESSIONAL ADVANCEMENT

After obtaining a position, you are anxious to succeed and move ahead in your career. These suggestions may help you to advance in your school situation or may lead you to a better position:

1. Build strong professional ties in your faculty and with your administration. Identify yourself with constructive development of the general program being conducted.

2. Do an outstanding job in your field, bringing distinction and credit to your school. Superior teaching, strong work in activities, and careful attention to routine duties will help you.

3. Develop and maintain strong community relations through your work with students, parents, and organizations.

4. Continue with your professional growth through advanced study, travel, or graduate degrees.

5. Join and be active in professional organizations such as the NEA, state teachers' association, the SAA, AETA, or one of the others. Serve with distinction on committees and programs on which you appear.

6. Develop a program of research, writing, and publication which will mark you as an active scholar and professional person in your field.

Should you desire to move to another position, examine carefully the situation in which you are and compare it with the prospective one on these points: nature of the job, the classes taught, the load, the activities conducted; the professional opportunities in each situation; the facilities and plant in which you work; the faculty and administrators; the salary, now and in the future; the geographical location, climate, cultural and recreational opportunities; the housing; the cost of living; your happiness and personal satisfactions.

These are some of the considerations in building a professional success; you will discover others as you continue to teach.

EXERCISES

1. Outline what you believe should be required courses in speech and in general education for individuals preparing to teach speech, giving a justification for such requirements.
2. List the certification requirements for a teacher of speech in the state in which you intend to teach.
3. Construct a check sheet dealing with personal and professional qualifications for teaching, then proceed to rate yourself in terms of each item you have included.

REFERENCES

BARR, A. S., and OTHERS. "The Measurement and Prediction of Teacher Efficiency," *Review of Educational Research*, XXV (1955), 261–69.

BARZUN, JACQUES. *Teacher in America*. Boston: Little, Brown and Co., 1945.

BERRY, MILDRED F. "A Liberal Education for the Teacher of Speech," *Quarterly Journal of Speech*, XXXII (October, 1946), 287–91.

BURNS, KENNETH. "A Report on Teacher Training in Speech," *Speech Teacher*, IX (September, 1960), 192–99.

HABERMAN, FRED ERICK. "Toward the Ideal Teacher of Speech," *Speech Teacher*, X (January, 1961), 1–12.

HENNING, JAMES. "Current Credit-Hour Teaching Load Practices in Selected American Colleges and Universities," *Speech Teacher*, VIII (September, 1959), 237–41.

HITCHCOCK, ORVILLE. "How to Get a Job as a Teacher of Speech," *Speech Teacher*, IV (November, 1955), 225–30.

KELTNER, JOHN. "Salary and Employment Trends in Selected College and University Speech Departments," *Speech Teacher*, IX (January, 1960), 49–60.

LAASE, LEROY. "A Survey of Instructional Loads in University Speech Departments," *Speech Teacher*, VIII (September, 1959), 304–9.

PALMER, MARTIN. "The New Requirements of the American Speech Correction Association," *Quarterly Journal of Speech*, XXIX (April, 1943), 196–99.

PHILLIPS, DAVID. "Graduate Study and Teacher Supply," *Speech Teacher*, VII (January, 1958), 104–9.

RASEY, M. I. *This Is Teaching*. New York: Harper & Bros., 1950.

REID, LOREN. *Teaching Speech*. Columbia, Mo.: Artcraft Press, 1960. Chap. XVIII.

ROBINSON, KARL F. "Recent Trends in Certification of High School Speech

Teachers and the Report of the SAA Committee to the North Central Association," *Speech Teacher*, VIII (March, 1959), 114–19.

Tarver, Jerry, and Owen Peterson. "Specialization in College Teaching," *Speech Teacher*, X (November, 1961), 304–8.

Trauernicht, Maxine. "The Training of High School Teachers of Speech," *Speech Teacher*, I (January, 1952), 29–36.

Tucker, Raymond. "The Speech Teacher in American Industry," *Speech Teacher*, IX (September, 1960), 232–36.

CHAPTER FOUR

Important Factors in Speech Instruction

Basic educational goals, a distinguished academic tradition, and the role of the teacher have already been discussed as important factors in speech instruction. This chapter develops others equally essential: the students, the attitude of the administrator, the facilities, the community pattern, and relationships with other departments in the school. Each is significant and will be explained as it affects the speech program.

THE STUDENTS

All speech training is directed toward the development of the student. The instructor who accomplishes most in his speech class is the one who thoroughly understands the general behavior characteristics of his students and has a clear insight into their speech needs. He also knows that significant progress is directly related to his adjusting instruction to their individual interests, needs, and abilities. High school and college students have many characteristics that are similar. Both groups display some of the characteristics of adolescence evident in the period from thirteen to twenty-three.

General Behavior

Physical Characteristics

First and probably most obvious is the marked growth of the body, its functions, and its organs. Sex functions develop and reproductive organs share in this growth. There is a definite increase in height and weight. Growth of bones and muscles is prominent.

Hands, arms, and feet seem very noticeable parts of the high school anatomy, although they are somewhat less conspicuous in the college student. Rapidity of growth causes lack of coordination in the early years. Change of voice also occurs during the adolescent period.

Tremendous energy characterizes young people at this age. Desirable use and control are needed. Training is therefore of great value in developing ease and physical power. Adolescents also have amazing "bounce," or ability to recover from exertion or injury.

Not infrequently there is some instability in health during this period. Imperfections in complexion, huge appetites, and emotional upset are sometimes associated in this pattern.

Social Characteristics

These persons are gregarious. They like to be "with the gang," the club, or the fraternity. They are extremely sensitive to group pressures. They seek social recognition, or *status*. They are therefore susceptible to fads in dress, activities, food, even vocabulary. They have strong likes and dislikes, coupled with an extremely wide range of interests. These include a definite awareness of the opposite sex, with concern about dress and personal appearance. In the speech class these qualities provide useful subject matter and motivation.

Self-Interests

A strong drive in high school and college students is their great interest in *themselves.* They desire to have the independence and treatment given adults. They reach out hungrily to try to be what they have not yet quite become. Thus they sometimes flaunt rules, parental supervision, and authority on the campus. Quite often they turn to teachers, believing them more capable of understanding than members of their own family.

Intellectual Interests

Students have much intellectual curiosity. Proper motivation "touches them off." Under these conditions they will tackle almost anything in their pursuit of knowledge. The recent motivation of comparison with Soviet students, honors courses, ability grouping, and the keen competition for college entrance have whetted the intellectual interests of students as never before. In high school this hits the upper 25 per cent hardest, but appeal to intellectual interests is there in the majority, if the right channels are tapped.

Ideals

They are usually very positive and straightforward in their expression of opinions. Surveys show that they are honest in big things, but as a group do not have too many scruples about lesser events such as copying the work of other students, or making changes in papers they may be marking. They place a high premium upon fair play and loyalty; in general their ideals are high. They are, however, influenced by the things which appear to them to be the marks of adulthood. This accounts for adolescents copying the behavior of older men and women with respect to smoking, drinking, or extremes in dress. Although they adhere closely to the patterns of their own group, they do not revere established conventions which clash with temporary interests or with what they consider expedient or desirable.

They are extremely sensitive to ideals of fairness, good sportsmanship, and decency, ideals which make them individuals who can readily welcome a code of moral principles incorporated in religious teaching. Hero worship, characteristic of this age, causes them to admire the older individual who embodies the good qualities they seek. This may be a parent, an adult friend, a minister, a baseball player, an actor, or, very often, a teacher.

Emotional Characteristics

Their emotional behavior is characterized by some insecurity resulting from rapid skeletal and physiological development. It may also cause young people to be extremely sensitive with regard to their position in the social group. Many high school students and some in college look like adults physically and approach the intellectual capacities of an adult, yet they lack the emotional stability of older people. They are sometimes timid and retiring; they may be nervous or "jittery," by their own statement. On the other hand they may be boisterous and loud, simply as compensation for their insecurity. In certain instances, emotional difficulties may assume the form of stubbornness or sullenness as a defense mechanism for this same insecurity.

Speech Needs and Problems

The general behavior characteristics of students are of utmost importance to the teacher. They provide the basis for interest and motivation which are the lifeblood of successful teaching. Through a knowledge of these characteristics, the teacher develops the attitude of understanding and sympathy so necessary to the job of teaching speech. The teacher should also be aware of a number of specific considerations which directly concern speech instruction and the pupil. First, because of his tendency toward uncoordination, the adolescent is frequently gawky and awkward in speech work. Careful training in bodily control is helpful to the individual during this period. As stated earlier, a change of voice occurs in boys; girls are not usually thus affected. This is an important factor in voice training. The emotional patterns which have been described above also affect the classroom work. Cases of nervousness or stage fright must be handled in the instructional procedure. Overcompensation by the pupil may produce exhibitory vocal or physical behavior. His desire for social recognition drives him to use all methods at his disposal to secure leads in plays, to make the debate team, or to belong to the dramatic club or radio workshop. Contest speech activities have a strong appeal because they provide new experiences and stimulating competitive activity.

Boy-girl relationships are considerations in high school group work. Care must be exercised in handling love scenes in plays and in the distribution of male and female roles. Such activities may be strong motivating forces; however, some shyness or even refusal to participate may result if the "right" members of the opposite sex are not included. Fads in dress, reading, and entertainment may also help to determine interest in related speech activities, such as costume and period plays, operettas, variety shows, or minstrel programs.

Among studies of individual speech needs of high school students, the following appear as important problems to be met: vocal control and flexibility, smoothness in rhythm, attention to the development of careful articulation and pronunciation, suitable adjustment both mentally and physically to the speaking situation, mastery of the technique of choosing ideas, and organization of material. These studies also point out the willingness of the secondary school student to cooperate in developing greater speech ability. However, the teacher will find among his pupils *some* severe cases of speech deficiency such as stuttering. He should refer these to a speech therapist. He will have to deal with numerous minor speech deviations in his regular classroom work. Skillful use of motivation and assignments planned to meet individual needs in voice and articulation will produce results in classroom groups.

College freshmen have many of the same individual speech problems as high school students. Also, their emotional or social adjustment is influenced by their being away from home and by the pressures of a new campus environment. Some feel the competition of superior talented students in speech classes, in other subjects, or in activities. Some may need encouragement; others may need tactful suggestion to temper their aggressiveness. Teachers can help set them straight on goals and values. They can directly aid them in meeting college standards in basic speech skills or specialized performance.

As students reach the sophomore year, they are better adjusted. They seek greater knowledge of speech theory and opportunities for performance in their fields of talent and interest. They start to crystallize their plans for major study and perhaps for professional careers in teaching, acting, radio-television, or public address. The speech faculty has a major role in such development.

Upperclassmen continue these trends; they also become leaders in intercollegiate forensics, theater, campus shows, interpretation, and so on. They find more applications for speech theory. They develop more specialized speech needs. Some have interests in research and graduate study. Speech professors with a wealth of experience and knowledge of such students challenge them with rich experiences.

THE ADMINISTRATORS

In any school the speech instructor must have the support and cooperation of the administrative head if he is to develop a successful program. The secondary school principal has a place of distinctive importance in the school and community. The college department head or dean has a similar role in higher education.

Importance of the Principal

The principal is an educational leader. He is directly responsible to the superintendent of schools, to the board of education, and to the parents of the pupils for the activities in his school. Because he has this administrative responsibility, he must see that the school functions smoothly and efficiently. Consequently, he is very sensitive to parental and other community pressures which affect the school. Within the institution he is the highest authority; his ideas, attitudes, and decisions set the pattern for all instruction and for school policy. Of primary importance to the speech teacher is the attitude of the principal toward speech education. This attitude, a part of his educational philosophy, inevitably colors his thinking on routine matters.

The principal organizes the curriculum of the school, and thus provides for the various subjects to be taught, new courses which may be added, and others which may be reorganized or discontinued. He also plans the class schedule, which includes the subjects taught by each teacher, the number of classes, class size, hour of meeting, and room assignments. He designates all extraclass duties. Depending upon the school, these may include such possibilities as study-hall supervision, hall duty, sponsorship of clubs, class advisory jobs, personnel of faculty committees, and the direction of special programs or activities. He also determines the scope of extraclass activities by giving permission for groups to organize and carry on their programs. Although many of these seem to be routine matters, all have implications for the teacher of speech.

Careful planning in conferences with the principal can help the speech teacher to be sure of class load; to get rooms for speech classes and activities; to avoid conflicts with speech electives; to develop a workable schedule for plays, debates, assemblies; and to gain a "clear title" to the use of the auditorium for rehearsal and performance.

In large high schools the teacher may have to clear such details with a department head (Speech or English) as well as with the principal.

Furthermore, the principal is responsible for the school budget and usually directly controls all expenditures through the need for his signature on requisitions. Thus, he supervises all money spent for equipment, library books, supplies, transportation, and services of all kinds. He also allocates the use of funds earned by various school projects and organizations such as the dramatic club, theater group, debate, the minstrel show, or the variety program. A sound and workable financial arrangement between speech teacher and principal is needed for all speech activities in the school.

Such desirable cooperation can be strengthened if the speech teacher understands the principal's point of view. Balcer, a former principal and a speech teacher, presents his position with this list of qualities in the person he would hire:

1. *He should see the relation of speech to the total school program.* . . . The speech teacher should realize that his program is an important and integral part of the school's total program, but that it is not more important than that total program. . . . The speech teacher must be willing to cooperate with the band director, the choir director, the newspaper, athletic coaches, etc.

2. *He should have a definite philosophy of speech and the ability to express that philosophy.* . . . Also, he has a right to ask the administrator *his* attitude towards speech.

3. *He should be well prepared in speech.* He needs a broad background in all aspects of speech.

4. *He should possess good speech habits and serve as a model to his students.*

5. *He should maintain excellent pupil-teacher relationships* and should take advantage of opportunities for guidance.

6. *He should be able to handle extra-class activities efficiently.*

7. *He should know how to handle money properly.* The speech teacher should be a competent bookkeeper and record-keeper.

8. *He should organize the speech program effectively.* Administration, students, and teachers should know where they are going.[1]

The Role of the Department Head or Dean

In a college or university, the instructor has a department head, a dean, or both. Together they perform all the functions of the principal in the high school. The department head handles administrative matters within the speech area. He *recommends* courses, schedule, load, appointments, budget, and so. The dean has *final approval* of these details. He also serves in determining educational policy. He

---

[1] Charles Balcer, "The High School Principal and the Teacher of Speech," *Speech Teacher,* IV (September, 1955), 183–87.

makes decisions on departmental programs throughout the school. The speech instructor should be in close touch with his department head. His conferences with the dean are by appointment or upon the dean's request.

Typical Administrative Attitudes

Wherever the speech instructor teaches, the favorable attitude of his administrator is vital to his program. Many different attitudes exist. These are explained and evaluated below:

1. *We definitely favor a strong speech program.* This first attitude follows closely the pattern for speech training given in Chapter I. The school head sees speech instruction as a significant educational need for *every student.* He reinforces that belief by providing remedial work for the speech and hearing handicapped; requires curricular speech for all; sponsors advanced elective courses, coordinated with extraclass activities, for those with special interests and abilities. The teacher who finds this type of administrative support will be a busy but very happy person. Pierre Tracy, a high school principal, expresses this position, applicable as well to a college program:

There are certain concepts of public education which seem self-evident. Among them are: (1) we must educate *all* American youth, (2) we must adjust our curriculums to provide a "general" education, which shall include all that every high school boy or girl should learn in order to fit him to become a good citizen in a free democracy, and (3) we must adapt that instruction to the individual's specific needs and abilities. No such general education for life can properly leave speech instruction out of the picture.

That the average citizen speaks more words in his daily life than he writes or reads cannot be contested. That the school should devote a proportional amount of time to this skill should certainly follow. That the administrator has long sensed the importance of speech training in personality development has been universal, but his uncertainty about its place in the curriculum has retarded its development.

Speech is too complex an act to be passed over lightly. The assumption that instruction in reading and writing also assures instruction in speaking is a fallacy. To teach a student to read, write, and compute is by no means instructing the whole child. If young Americans are to be fully prepared for this complicated social life we now live, more and more they must be given opportunities to participate in speech learning activities in the schools.[2]

Not all attitudes are favorable. Misunderstandings and lack of information contribute to produce beliefs that can seriously curtail or warp a school program.

2. *Speech is a frill.* This attitude stems from limited information or an outmoded viewpoint. It sees speech as a restricted exhibition for a few students who engage in "piece speaking," "elocution," "spell-binding oratory," and so on. As such it is superficial and impractical education. It is almost always an extraclass program with a small number of students specializing in such activities.

3. *Speech activities are easy ways to make money.* Such an attitude originates in budgetary need, too often serving departments other than speech. It is the result of narrow thinking and faulty information. It may capitalize upon exhibiting a few "stars" in public performance where admission is charged. It may follow the plan of "getting everyone into the act," so that more tickets can be sold to more proud parents or friends. If it is overdone, it will wear out the speech teacher. It will also deprive him of the financial fruits of his labor when the money is diverted to subsidize the school annual, to buy band uniforms, and the like. If the speech department never receives a just portion of the revenues, this attitude is a method of killing the goose that lays the golden eggs.

4. *Speech is a competitive activity.* Here the administrator is probably an ex-athletic coach or an indoctrinated contest man in speech. He measures results principally by the number of cups, plaques, or banners in the trophy cases. He is a twin brother of the "piece-speaking" administrator. Under this plan only the best performers are trained because the goal is the production of highly skilled competitors. Individual or broad development in speech is subordinated to winning decisions. Such an attitude is rather disastrous to sound course development *unless* good planning makes competition an outgrowth of a strong program of speech for every student.

5. *Speech is important, but should be limited.* This position is a

[2] Pierre Tracy, "The Role of Speech in the Secondary School," *Bulletin of the National Association of Secondary School Principals,* XXIX (November, 1945), 6.

"restricted program outlook." The administrator accepts the benefits of classroom instruction, yet holds the amount of such teaching to a minimum. Typical thinking insists that speech should be an elective, wherever it can be fitted in. A common practice has been to place it in the senior year in high schools requiring only three units of English. In college degree programs speech becomes an elective. The administrator does not wish to disrupt the traditional sequence of instruction. With pressures from all sides for more curricular time in science, mathematics, social studies, *and* English, the restricted outlook can squeeze speech out of the curriculum, or it may be given *minor* status (two or three meetings per week). If it permits several quarters or semesters of work with continuity, the second plan can reach *some* students effectively: however, it will never give all students the training they need.

6. *All speech should be taught in English classes.* Here the administrator by academic definition places speech as a part of the work of the English department, to be done by its members in their courses. He opposes any other curricular time for direct, organized speech instruction. This attitude results from certain assumptions and from lack of knowledge of practical teaching problems. The administrator assumes that English (writing) and speech skills (speaking, interpretation, and so on) are alike because they have common elements: they use the same subject matter in some instances for drill purposes; they combine theory, especially on composition, relating to both; and they develop skills which supplement each other. He also assumes, therefore, that the two skills should be taught together.

These assumptions are untrue in practice. As Glen Mills says, "Any consideration of the combined teaching of the two skill subjects should rest upon an examination of the relationships and an answer to the question, 'Are the similarities outweighed by the differences? The answer is needed, and it must be based upon more than armchair theorizing.'" He concludes, after reviewing articles by O'Neill, Seashore, McBurney, and Knower, that the combination of writing and speaking apparently is a "shotgun marriage." He cites Knower's findings that the best index of speech skill when correlated with the best index of writing skill produced an "r" of only −.19. He concludes, "Until better evidence is produced, it seems probable that the

differences of speaking and writing outweigh the similarities." [3]
From a practical point of view there are also problems in the combining of speech and English instruction.

Gladys Borchers, after an experiment at Wisconsin High School, Madison, Wisconsin, concludes that the teaching of speech and English in the same organized course is impracticable. She states, "A careful search for the cause seemed to point to the difficulty of teaching two skill or tool subjects together." [4]

When one examines certain factors in the teaching situation, it becomes increasingly clear that under these *present* conditions the ordinary English teacher cannot do the job successfully. First is the question of *teacher preparation*. Even though the teacher involved is equipped with a strong *minor* in speech or has a wide background of experience in speech activities, he is bound to favor the area of his greatest interest and preparation, English. When one adds the factors of *time allotment* and *required work* in the English program, it becomes clear that certain cherished objectives will be given greatest attention. These include correctness and knowledge of grammatical constructions, the mechanics of written composition with punctuation a prominent goal, required readings of literary classics, and reviews of books read outside class. Accomplishing these goals takes much class and teacher time.

English teachers themselves deplore their inefficiency in teaching writing under present conditions. In a symposium on the teaching of reading and writing, Louis Zahner, headmaster of Groton and a former officer of the National Council of Teachers of English, asks:

With five classes a day of thirty-five pupils each, how can I assign enough compositions, even short ones, to get anywhere with the teaching of writing? A teacher should also say: If my pupils write only one paper a week, I can't honestly read them all. I can only mark the mechanical mistakes like spelling. That isn't teaching. [5]

In the same series Henry Chauncey, former assistant dean at Harvard, adds:

[3] Glen Mills, "Speech in a Communication Course," *Quarterly Journal of Speech,* XXXIII (February, 1947), 40–45.

[4] Gladys Borchers, "An Experiment in High School Speech Teaching," *Quarterly Journal of Speech,* XXXII (October, 1946), 373–85.

[5] Louis Zahner, "Composition at the Barricades," *Atlantic Monthly* (November, 1959), pp. 114–17.

Unquestionably the ability to write is one of the essential goals of education, and the major cause of poor writing is insufficient practice. I am convinced that the lack of practice stems from the extreme shortage of teachers and the increasing number of students. Under present teaching loads, assignments of written work are dwindling, and in the future may be cut even further. The average English teacher meets 175 students daily in 5 classes. If he should assign one paper a week to each class, he would spend four hours a night, seven nights a week and most of Saturday and Sunday afternoons correcting papers.[6]

Just how such overloaded teachers can also teach speech efficiently in a classroom already beset with problems is an interesting question. This is particularly true since speech instruction demands *individual recitation* and effective oral criticism if development is to occur. If the teacher does not wish to take the additional necessary time from the writing for speaking, it is obvious that speech will suffer. Borchers found this to be true in her situation. "Since a large part of the English work was learning to write effectively, the English teacher was forced to ignore the speech program at such times."[7]

These administrative changes are necessary if speech is to be well taught in English classes: hire better prepared teachers, organize courses to guarantee time for speech, have smaller classes (20–25), reduce daily load.

7. *Every teacher is a teacher of speech.* Such an attitude lacks realism, knowledge, or it can be a definite means of bypassing any direct speech instruction. Of course, if this practice is employed *in addition* to providing a planned speech program, and if it is used as a vital part of following through in applying such development in all other subjects, the attitude is a commendable one. However, when it is the *only* provision in secondary school education for oral communication, it is merely a "let George do it" philosophy, and it means that nobody will do the job. It is about as intelligent as saying, "every teacher is a teacher of English," after which the entire English program is wiped out and the development of all skill in written communication is then delegated to every classroom teacher. In the secondary school, teachers of special subjects have all they can do and *wish* to do in teaching their own subjects. Expecting them to teach

[6] Henry Chauncey, "The Plight of the English Teacher," *Atlantic Monthly* (November, 1959), pp. 122–25.

[7] Borchers, *op. cit.*

speech indirectly is the same as not teaching it. This "buck-passing" philosophy is only surpassed by that of the administrator who is completely indifferent to any kind of speech instruction. It is quite obvious that such administrators will never employ a person well-trained in the teaching of speech. They are probably trying to rationalize the need for such training in order to save budgetary appropriations, or, perhaps because of limited information, they are actually opposed to speech training in the secondary school.

There *must be a place and time where these skills are effectively taught by trained instructors. This place is the speech class.* Every teacher should cooperate in the speech program by utilizing this training in his own class.

Causes of Administrative Attitudes

There are various causes for these attitudes toward speech. First is a lack of information regarding the nature of modern speech education and its importance to the individual. Second is the past experience of the administrators themselves with older and restricted types of speech training. Third are the limitations of personnel in secondary schools and colleges. There is no guarantee that all teachers possess proper and sufficient training. Despite rising standards *weak* teachers produce *weak* programs. Last may be the inability of the administrator to organize a speech program in his own school. Factors directly affecting this problem are the local school budget, the teacher supply, the standard pattern of secondary school subjects, college entrance and graduation requirements, the class schedule, the attitude of other departments, and the community. For example, a limited budget can exclude all possibility of classroom speech instruction. This item alone keeps much speech training in the extraclass field. Even when funds are available, it may be difficult to obtain specially trained personnel. This situation may lead to assigning speech duties to English or social studies teachers. Requirements for graduation and college entrance influence an administrator in his thinking about "where" and "when" speech may be taught in the curriculum. This is especially true if his budget and faculty are limited or courses are restricted to standard secondary school subjects. When expansion is possible, the administrator is often torn between demands for speech training and those for additional instruction in other fields. He is also very sensitive to community pressures. The interests and needs of pupils in his town can exert considerable influence upon his thinking regarding changes in school organization, subjects, and budget expenditures.

The same factors affect the attitudes of college department heads and deans. To strengthen his program, the speech instructor should understand and use intelligently the elements in the situation.

Ways to Influence Administrative Attitudes

There are several positive actions the teacher may use to improve such attitudes:

1. *Inform the administrator about speech education.* This can be done by conferences, by the use of published articles, and by memoranda. They should reveal the facts about the nature of speech training, its benefits, the needed time for good teaching, the time and energy demanded by class and activity programs, the financial needs, the present and future opportunities for speech in the school, and should emphasize the relationship of speech to the whole school program.

A brief note inviting the administrator to special events will sometimes pay dividends. Asking him to participate as a presiding officer may give him a chance to observe speech activities. Short, modest summaries of student achievements may also help. Facts about other schools will introduce constructive, yet mild competitive motivation.

2. *Make a substantial contribution to the school.* The speech teacher is very fortunate in this respect. The nature of his department opens wide opportunities for school service. It can aid students in other courses in school; it can build school leaders; it can develop students specially trained in speaking, theater, and radio. Through the efforts of speech-trained students, school events can be publicized, community projects served, ticket sales promoted, conferences organized and led. In the interscholastic field, sound programs can build a fine reputation for the school and can develop favorable community and professional relationships. Many of these activities can be cooperative efforts with the school administrator.

3. *Run an efficient, well-organized program.* Classwork, special programs, assemblies or convocations, radio programs, debates, plays—all elements of the speech program—should be so well planned

that they do not demand special consideration in student time, adjustment of classes, or change in schedule for their achievement. Financial details should be accurately and punctually administered. Nothing pleases a school official more than work that is well managed. Similarly, careless work can kill a program very quickly.

4. *Use publicity wisely*. In all relationships of the speech program with the administrator, the students, the faculty, and the community, publicity plays an important role. The school and town newspapers, radio and television stations, and alumni journals are useful vehicles to the speech program. Tactfully placed news items, short accounts of speech activities containing the names of students, human interest stories about leaders in speech and drama—all help school officials, parents, and students to know and be well disposed toward the speech program. By intelligent planning and wise use of publicity the speech teacher can continually strengthen his position.

SCHOOL FACILITIES

School facilities and equipment do not *determine* the speech program; however, they do *influence* its nature and scope significantly. It is a fact that public speaking and interpretation *can* be taught in an ordinary classroom with little more than standard equipment. To be sure, certain additions to these minimum essentials would be very desirable, but it is possible to teach without them. It would be extremely difficult, however, to develop a theater program without an auditorium or a suitable room containing a usable stage, basic lighting equipment, and at least some rudimentary scenery. Similarly, radio instruction should have a public-address unit as essential equipment for announcing, or for simple types of acting. Radio production or aired shows demand a studio with turntables, a control panel, and devices for sound effects.

These examples merely indicate that the teacher must recognize not only the relationship between school facilities and the *kind* of speech program which can be developed, but also that there is great *variation* among the facilities of secondary schools in which he may be employed. Community interest, the budget, the administrator's attitude, among other things, influence the purchase of equipment in a school. It is particularly necessary that the beginning instructor recognize the limitations of his teaching situation. He should appreciate that the college or university in which he has been trained may have had facilities which are more complete or more elaborate than those in the school in which he does his first year of teaching. At times he may find a position in a school which surpasses his alma mater in its physical facilities.

In either case he should be intelligent in his selection of class assignments, his course plan, and his program of extraclass activities. He must not let his ambition for achievement go beyond the limits of the facilities with which he has to work. He should temper his ambition with sufficient realism to make his job relatively simple and his chances for success reasonable.

The Teacher's Part in Improving Facilities

If equipment and facilities are inadequate, there is no reason why a resourceful and energetic teacher cannot improve conditions. Through his own skill he can do whatever his time, energies, and materials permit. Many schools have speaking stands, scenery, properties, electronic equipment, flannel or bulletin boards, display shelves, and bookcases, to mention only some items, which were added by a practical speech instructor.

His second method is to enlist the help of other persons on the faculty or staff to improve facilities. Engineering or manual arts personnel, science teachers, home economics, music, or art teachers are the most probable helpers because many of them have interests in theater, radio, or television. Students also have interesting potentialities in the various areas of speech. In one college, students built the entire radio transmitter, planned the studios, painted and sound-treated them. In another school, students and faculty built two sets of scenery for a new auditorium. With much cooperation, it is not impossible for a speech department to improve facilities considerably.

Desirable Facilities and Equipment

Fundamentals, Public Speaking, and Individual Interpretation

1. *Basic classrooms:* designated for speech, with movable recitation chairs rather than desks; ample size with available space in front; good lighting; attractive decoration, and so on.

2. *Minimum room furnishings:* a small platform; a lectern; a large chalkboard; a flannel board; a bulletin board; a large wall mirror; appropriate pictures relating to speech; shelves for books, trophies, and so on.

3. *Room or school library facilities:* ample supply of periodical literature, general reference works with specialized sources in social science and literature; a reference shelf for the various speech areas including titles in public address, discussion, debate, parliamentary law, interpretation, stagecraft, acting, make-up, puppetry, radio, television, film, and so on.

Suitable cooperation with the school and public librarians will make it possible to shift such materials to the speech classroom when desired.

4. *Audio-visual materials:* wall charts and models on the speech mechanism and theory as needed; a library of transcriptions, recordings, and tapes of speeches, readings, debates, discussions, scenes from plays, and so on can be augmented by tapes made by the teacher and classes; slides and film strips, with a slide projector or viewer; a portable screen; motion picture films—silent and sound —with suitable projection equipment; a tape recorder with numerous blank tapes (*a must for basic course work*); a playback or turntable for transcriptions; collections of clippings, flat pictures, printed speeches, for related speech units.

These facilities may be called minimal for basic work in the areas of fundamentals, public speaking, and interpretation.

Discussion and Debating

Certain additions will greatly help in teaching these two areas: two small tables with straight-back or folding chairs to seat eight persons; two water pitchers and four tumblers; a metal evidence card file (4 x 6) for squad use; a letter-size file, preferably metal; a gavel and striking block; several sets of painted or printed time cards; duplicating equipment—ditto or mimeograph—either in the room or in the central office; a typewriter with a two-color ribbon.

All of these added items are especially useful in debate and discussion for preparation of outlines, evidence cards, letters, and so on.

Dramatic Arts [8]

It is difficult to state specifically the required facilities for theater work because a play can be performed in a number of situations. The kind of equipment varies widely among schools, some of which do extensive productions or difficult shows and have standards and facilities approaching those for professional performance. Others are satisfied with very ordinary work and their equipment is meager. Most schools have auditorium or stage facilities. A speech teacher with a strong theater preparation can adapt or develop facilities to meet his needs. However, when new auditoriums are built or purchases of new equipment undertaken, it should be with the close consultation of the speech or drama teacher. Other specialists also can be utilized in planning a functional theater plant.

Radio and Television

Facilities of a very definite type are needed for school radio and television programs. If the institution plans to broadcast from its own studios with its own equipment, professional knowledge and consultation is essential in planning and building the layout. If commercial facilities are to be used with programs taped or filmed for broadcasting, the school is relieved of the expense and effort of building equipment. Local conditions will determine the action taken.

COMMUNITY COOPERATION

The relationship between community resources and speech programs is a reciprocal one. This means that speech instructors and students make numerous contributions to the life of the community, but the many local resources can provide an invaluable training ground for practical speech experience.

The high school in any town always commands great interest from townspeople. It is an obvious fact that practically all of the students enrolled come from within the boundaries of the municipality. They carry to their dinner tables each evening the latest "news" from school, which in turn is discussion material for the

[8] See specialized references at the end of this chapter and after Chapter XXIII.

family circle. As a rule, the parents have attended the high school and, in many cases, have received diplomas from it. Thus, school activities have become a *community* interest because, through the relationship described above, they have become *community* activities. The use of the school plant as a center for many types of social and educational gatherings has helped to develop this situation, and the things that occur at the *school* in many localities are the principal *town* events. This relationship has laid a foundation for a mutual exchange of services between the high school and the various organizations in the community.

Colleges and universities with active speech programs share a similar relationship in a community situation. As a rule, many local students attend such schools, whether or not they are municipal institutions. Thus the life and relationships of the school and the community are inevitably interwoven.

In expanding these possibilities it is feasible to discuss them under two headings: (1) contributions which speech programs can make to community life; and (2) contributions which the community can make to speech work in the school.

Contributions of the Speech Program

The speech program provides numerous services for the community. The most useful of these is the training of students for community leadership. Youth organizations of many kinds provide application for speech skills. These include the Hi-Y and Girl Reserve clubs, the 4-H Junior Farmers, Boy Scouts, Campfire Girls, Epworth League, Christian Endeavor, Catholic Youth Organization, B'nai B'rith, Junior Red Cross, and a host of similar groups in which leadership and participation depend upon speech ability. Interest in these clubs is transferred later in adulthood to the Chamber of Commerce, Rotary, Kiwanis, Lions, Exchange, Red Cross, American Legion, Veterans of Foreign Wars, American Veterans organizations, labor and fraternal groups, as well as to many business and professional clubs, and to numerous political organizations. All provide opportunities for functional speech experience which develop essential skills for community leadership.

Other services include furnishing speakers for many kinds of school and community functions—United Fund, Red Cross, lecture courses, concert and musical events. Frequently student speakers furnish programs for dinner clubs and professional women's groups.

Closely related to this service is that of furnishing educational entertainment programs in the community. Teachers and students appear as masters of ceremonies, readers, or actors in community enterprises.

Another significant contribution in some cities is the development of community and school theater programs. These are expanding in an interesting way. Often they are the only "live" theater existing in certain towns. They provide stimulating programs for audiences and an outlet for persons interested in directing, acting, and technical work. Their work is aided by faculty and students from high school and college theater departments. Large cities may have several companies. The Cain Park Theatre at Cleveland, Ohio, the Shorewood (Wisconsin) Community Theatre, and the Community Theatre at Kalamazoo, Michigan, are notable examples.

Another service originating in speech programs is the adult education program. Evening classes in discussion, play-reading, effective speaking, and parliamentary practice are frequent offerings.

Other significant services include providing consultation and clinical assistance to the handicapped in speech and hearing, organizing school radio and television programs broadcast to the community, and developing educational assemblies and convocations to which townspeople are invited.

All of these activities enrich the life of a community.

Contributions of the Community

The other side of this cooperative venture includes the various aids which the community provides for the speech program. In some respects they parallel those of the speech department.

The first is the use of additional auditorium or stage space. When school facilities are inadequate, church auditoriums, club rooms, lodge halls, and similar locations are valuable sources of help.

Speech departments always turn to the community for assistance in procuring properties, furniture, and costumes for certain drama work. The rental or loan of these items should be done on a responsible, businesslike basis. Definite agreements should be made for rental fees, prompt return, good care, cleaning and repair of articles used. In addition, credits on the program help to recognize these services and promote good relations between the donors and the school.

Townspeople are often very generous in helping the program to obtain new equipment. Parent-teacher organizations and luncheon clubs may purchase needed items; business houses frequently give reduced prices to schools to make the acquisition of equipment possible.

Financial assistance in the purchase of awards and trophies, in setting up scholarships or other prizes, and in underwriting the expenses for the trips of speech organizations is another fine community service. Many young people can credit their stimulating experiences in speech activities to such generosity from community sponsors.

Probably the most extensive service is one inherent in community life itself. The many communication situations serve as a speech laboratory for high school and college students. Here they find action and realistic application for their classroom training. Debaters, orators, discussants—all have many opportunities to try their skills before live community audiences. Similarly, school theater projects are viewed and evaluated by community audiences. Their reactions and standards are instrumental in shaping the kind of plays given, as well as in appraising directing, staging, and acting.

Other possibilities lie open to school drama students by watching professional or stock companies that play the community. These include regular theater, opera, musical comedy, and ballet. Larger population centers are more fortunate in this respect. They often organize theater parties, attend the shows, and make arrangements for talks by outstanding performers after the final curtain. Often students are invited backstage to see particular technical methods employed.

University theater departments also present invitational performances to serve a large number of high schools or colleges on a clinical basis. After viewing the play, the students take part in a backstage tour and question period to help them in solving their own theater problems.

Where none of these experiences is available, the motion picture has something to offer theater students. The speech teacher can use observations of scenes, dialogue, interpretation, acting, directing, and staging to stimulate interest in this medium, as well as to set better standards for appreciation of films.

Finally, many communities serve speech departments through their local educational or commercial radio and television stations. These stations frequently donate time for school programs each week. They are also a wonderful laboratory for observation of the techniques of broadcasting. Some stations employ students on a part-time or full-time basis. Many persons in radio and television today owe their start to the interest and assistance of persons in such stations.

The many aspects of the community speech laboratory offer a rich motivation and training ground for young people interested in speech.

RELATIONSHIPS TO OTHER DEPARTMENTS

Speech Useful to All Departments

The speech teacher cannot work in an academic ivory tower nor pursue a policy of isolationism with respect to other school departments. Speech training, by its very nature, is a development which enables those who possess it to use it in every class recitation in the school. In short, it aids in implementing every other subject. Moreover, it is an important factor in all kinds of pupil activities within the school or in the community at large. The speech courses, then, are ultimately *service courses* for every other department or teacher in the school organization.

The personal speech habits of students affect their work in every subject, and speech fundamentals directly affect good recitation. Also, skills in oral reading, public speaking, discussion, debate, simple dramatization, certain kinds of radio performance, and many special kinds of speech performance are usable in the regular stream of classroom instruction. They aid in implementing the work in political science, history, sociology, science, art, English, commercial subjects, music, and languages. The first important relationship of speech to other subject matter lies in its ability to make facts and information *vital* and *functional* in the lives of students. Through the experience of communicating, this information becomes more pur-poseful and meaningful to the speaker, and a source of influence upon those who hear him. Conversely, in the speech classroom, facts, principles, and problems from every field are utilized; they become the content for numerous types of platform assignments and exercises. From an informational point of view, the speech teacher must deal with and know, to some extent at least, almost every subject taught, as well as many things not included in the classroom studies. By its very nature, speech integrates all subject-matter areas.

Cooperation Invaluable

The teacher of speech should see clearly the significance of his work; he should know that all other instructors in the school will look to him as an expert in all problems of oral communication whether he qualifies for that title or not. To him they may send speech defectives, students inadequate in oral reports, the inaudible and timid in class recitation, those weak in discussion, or those poor in reading aloud. He should regard this relationship as an opportunity, not as an added chore. He can make a real contribution to the individuals whom he helps. He should strive to aid those whose problems are within his knowledge and ability. However, he should admit his limitations honestly and seek help or refer difficult cases to speech clinicians, audiologists, or those with clinical training. These contacts give him the chance to strengthen his department in the school by means of the services he can contribute to the entire educational scheme. He should become aware of the many important results stemming from his willingness to help students in developments so fundamental that they affect the students' success no matter where they go. Through such cooperation many students may also be directed into the speech program. They may enroll for regular class instruction; they may be improved in personal speech habits through individual appointments or conferences; or they may participate in the varied extraclass activities which the speech department conducts within the school.

If he wishes to supplement these avenues of instruction, the teacher of speech can organize and conduct a follow-up program which takes him into every classroom at the request of other teachers who desire his services or advice for individual or group projects. Such an opportunity should not be overlooked. Failure of speech teachers to consider the applications of their teaching to circumstances in other classrooms has left a weak spot in the instructional

scheme in speech. The teacher of speech should develop such opportunities so that basic and specialized skills in speech are carried over and utilized intelligently in every possible aspect of school life. Interesting programs of this kind are in operation in Wisconsin High School, at Madison, Wisconsin, and in the high school at West Bend, Wisconsin.[9]

In colleges and universities most of the same relationships exist. However, interdepartmental ties are not so close. The speech department in a college would not follow up individual students in other departments unless requested. Physical separation of departments often makes cooperation in a university more difficult. Numerous effective working arrangements exist between speech and certain departments on undergraduate and graduate programs.

Thus it seems clear that from a practical point of view the teacher of speech should know and use the many relationships which exist between his work and that of other teachers in the school. Such knowledge is the basis for cooperation between the speech teacher and those other teachers whose work relates specifically to the success of his program. Furthermore, possibilities for the coordination or integration of instruction in speech with that in other fields rest upon compatible conditions in the local situations.

Specific Relationships

Among the many interesting specific relationships with other departments are those developed below.

1. English

Traditionally, there are two areas in which speech and English come together. One is what we know as composition or rhetoric; the other is literature. Common ground exists between English and speech in the following areas of composition: subject selection, investigation of sources of information, selection and arrangement of materials, methods of development, organization, and use of language and style.

The great difference between speech and English is in the *emphasis* and *use* of these operations. English teachers are interested

[9] See Gladys Borchers, "Basic Issues in Integrating Speech with Other Subjects," *Bulletin of the National Association of Secondary School Principals,* XXXII, No. 151 (January, 1948), 169–78.

principally in a writer-reader relationship, while speech teachers consider the speaker-listener aspect. Speech teachers stress the implications of speech as a unit of social experience in which there are more considerations than those of literary structure. As a result, speech teachers must consider the emotional adjustment of the speaker in a speech situation and also his purpose with respect to his particular audience. They must stress the analysis of this group, the selection, choice, and arrangement of materials to secure from it the response desired, and finally the effective *delivery* of the talk so that it will carry out the intended purpose. These matters are too often disregarded by teachers of English, who emphasize literary excellence as the goal of their writing or who may not have time to include speech instruction in a crowded course.

The second general area of common ground lies in literature. Both English and speech draw heavily upon it for study. Many plays from dramatic literature are produced in the theater; courses in play writing and dramatic literature are often found in both English and speech departments. Interpretation draws upon *all* types of literature for its material. Poetry often receives a major share of attention. In many classes, ballads, narrative poems, sonnets, lyrics, and monologues provide a rich body of material. Other types of literature are also used for interpretation. These include the essay, humor, fiction, adventure, and biography, all of which provide the interpreter with an inexhaustible storehouse of material. The selection, analysis, appreciation, and delivery of these by a platform reader require a thorough study of the author, his philosophy and background, his content, style, and technique, and so on. Oral interpretation makes literature a realistic, stimulating experience for the student.

Radio and television use principles of writing, speech skills, and special techniques of announcing, acting, and interpretation. They combine much that is closely related or common ground to both speech and English. They are excellent examples of a combination of skills and materials from English and speech, all developed to meet the needs of broadcasting.

The speech teacher can capitalize upon these significant interrelationships between the two fields. While the seemingly common problems in the teaching of the two skills of writing and speaking

suggest a possible academic union, it is yet to be established that such a marriage is an efficient and compatible one.

2. Social Studies

The information, principles, and problems of social studies material are the informational content of many speeches. Public speaking, debate, and discussion draw heavily upon political science, history, economics, and sociology. Persons who teach these courses see the important relations involved here. Similarly, the teachers of social studies rely upon speech techniques and activities to implement the content of their field. Proficiency in public speaking and discussion enables individuals to make their information *function* in society. The social sciences provide essential *knowledge* of contemporary problems; speech provides the necessary *methods* of social action and participation in democracy. The drama, radio, and motion picture, also, make extensive use of contemporary problems in social studies. Their strength as a medium for enlisting social action is well known. Through them the personalities and events of history live for high school students as they see and hear the events of history. As an example, students in class who listen to the Columbia recordings of the "You Are There" program which describes the signing of the Magna Charta and the Battle of Gettysburg gain a living picture of these events.

The speech teacher will find teachers of social studies interested and willing to cooperate in projects which mutually strengthen the work in the two fields of study.

3. Education

Professional courses for the training of teachers find college speech work basic to classroom instruction. Voice and diction, effective speaking, discussion, parliamentary procedure, persuasion, interpretation, story telling, dramatization, radio and television become areas of importance to all teachers when used as classroom methods.

4. The Sciences

Interesting relationships exist between the sciences and speech. Physics has a close tie through the study of the principles of sound and acoustics. One of the most vivid approaches to voice instruction is a demonstration by the teacher of the production of sound through the use of vibrators and resonators; the analogy is simple to carry into the study of the human speech mechanism, the attributes and characteristics of voice, and the factors which lead to voice defects. Such equipment of the physics laboratory as tuning forks and resonators can be used in demonstrations with various kinds of recording machines to explain and analyze voice and articulation problems. From the areas of light and electricity the theater technician draws his craft in stage lighting.

Psychology has a number of relationships with speech. These exist in the areas of audience analysis, motivation and persuasion, learning and the formation of speech habits, the study of the emotional attitudes of the speaker, certain underlying causes of speech defects, the testing of speech performance, and speech and hearing rehabilitation.

Biology and physiology have important sections of knowledge which are also common to the field of speech. These include the development and growth of the human organism; its structure and anatomy; the functioning of various parts of the body as a "speech mechanism" as well as for the primary bodily functions for which these structures were intended; the study of the hearing mechanism; understanding of the structure and function of the nervous system, and so on. These are only some of the areas closely related to the field of speech.

5. *Foreign Languages*

The chief relationships between speech and foreign languages lie in the use of phonetics as a basis for pronunciation and in the study of speech sounds. The international phonetic alphabet provides a common denominator for the pronunciation of sounds in any language. The description of sounds, ear training, pronunciation, and the development of fluency in utterance are common objectives in language study and in speech. Language teachers require students to drill in order to develop proficiency and accuracy in pronunciation; speech teachers make similar demands upon students in the improvement of voice, articulation, and pronunciation.

The development of suitable techniques for practice has made necessary and desirable the use of recording equipment employing discs or tape. Often language and speech teachers can cooperate in the purchase of recorders or in the use of language laboratories which will enable both to improve their teaching.

6. Music

Teachers of vocal music also have problems similar to those of the speech teacher. Since many of the operations in voice improvement for singing and speaking are much the same, it is quite easy for cooperation to be established. Another common area is in the many special programs that become the combined responsibility of speech and music instructors. Operettas, assemblies, convocations, and dramatic productions are some of these.

7. Commerce and Business

These fields have considerable interest in speech as an important vocational tool for all persons trained to enter business. Success in sales operations, in personnel work, and in the many types of public-relations programs place a heavy responsibility upon the student entering such fields. He must be thoroughly competent in informal speaking situations, in public speaking, in conference and discussion, in the ability to read effectively, in techniques of dramatization in advertising, and in commercial radio and television, for which many businessmen have the highest regard as a sales medium. The many opportunities for in-service training programs for employees in commercial and industrial concerns make challenging applications for many speech methods. Both men and women working in business occupations realize the important relationship of speech proficiency to their professional success. Many of them take evening school courses in speech to increase their skills. Commercial teachers are interested in the speech programs because they see the immediate and practical use of the training they provide.

8. Engineering, Manual Arts

These fields have many applications in the technical areas of speech. Production work in theater, including design, building, painting, and the lighting of scenery; sound effects; designing and making costumes; printing of programs; and recording of speech performance are some of these. Radio and television engineers have a close tie with speech also.

There are direct benefits to the speech program from this cooperation. The speech instructor needs the help of persons in these fields.

9. *The Fine Arts*

Active working relationships with this field are not uncommon in speech instruction. Theater is the chief area. The study of color, design, balance, perspective, and grouping enter here, with specific use in dressing the stage, costuming, make-up, and lighting.

10. *Physical Education and Health*

General health as it relates to speech, emotional poise, physical control and coordination, structural deviations in the body are some of the common areas. Also involved are projects in dance, fencing, gymnastics, track, and other sports. Both fields of study can work together for the improvement of students.

The speech department can also be of direct assistance in the school and public-relations programs in physical education. This is evident in pep meetings, award programs, football benefits, ticket sales, and other promotional programs, in which athletic leaders need help from the speech department for effective public appearances.

11. *Counselors, Home-Room Teachers, Deans*

There is no teacher in a school who comes closer to student problems than the speech instructor. The nature of his work is highly personal and individual. Reliable information about students is important to him and to all guidance personnel. Speech teachers and guidance workers alike can share the data gained from observation, tests, and cumulative records. Personal, home, medical, academic and activity data are invaluable in these administrative areas of education.

Rehearsal schedules and trips should be cleared with official supervisors. Information about required and elective speech courses helps at registration time in planning student programs. Close working relationships with all counseling and guidance personnel are very desirable for speech teachers.

12. *Libraries and Librarians*

Of extreme importance to the speech program are the school librarians. Their conscientious efforts make available to students and teachers supplementary reading materials, standard references, indexes for periodical literature, files of clippings and pictures, bibliographies for debate and discussion subjects, and the facilities of the library itself. Advance conferences between the speech teacher and the librarians can insure smooth, efficient cooperation in all of the investigation that is so necessary in the preparation of materials for speeches, readings, plays, radio programs, debate, and discussion.

13. *The Business Office*

All financial transactions need smooth-working relationships with the cashier, business manager, or purchasing agent. Whether cash advances, new equipment, repair service, or transportation is involved, the speech instructor must know and abide by school business methods. Early contacts with these important school officials are most beneficial.

14. *Custodians and Maintenance Staff*

More than one teacher of speech has failed because he did not have a good working relationship with the school custodians. Many speech instructors have found their work proceeding more smoothly because they took time to cultivate the friendship of these persons. They are concerned with keeping buildings clean and guarding school property. They are potential friends of speech education. The speech teacher should treat them with courtesy and consideration.

Much of the work of the speech teacher and these people is done after school hours. Rehearsals, debate tournaments, dramatic performances—all need a pleasant working pattern with maintenance men. They literally hold the keys to achieving the thousand and one little things demanded by the speech program. Everything from a blown fuse to picture wire or a tricky thermostat in the auditorium needs the personal touch of a custodian. The speech teacher can find in him an indispensable member of the departmental team.

15. *Dormitory and Food Service Supervisors*

Many speech events require rooms for guests, food for special luncheons or dinners, and lounges for convocations or relaxation. Close acquaintance with supervisory personnel in these areas is essential to the success of debate tournaments, play festivals, interpretation programs or dinner meetings.

Through consistent effort and the use of tact in all relationships with other departments in the school, the teacher of speech can secure the assistance of his colleagues in his program. As a result, he will find his work happier, more easily accomplished, and more extensive in its influence in the school. The ability to work with others is a particularly important factor in the professional success of a speech instructor.

Since these many relationships are important to speech education in the school as a whole, certain teachers have organized a speech or speech arts council to aid smooth, efficient operation. Such a body also insures integrating speech training with other subjects and following its application into the work of other departments.

Such a plan is used successfully by Miss Wanda Mitchell at Evanston Township High School, Evanston, Illinois. Representatives of other departments, administration, and counseling divisions form this body, and cooperate in scheduling all-school events, lending their efforts to implement speech services and functions in the school.

EXERCISES

1. Construct a list of adolescent behavior characteristics. Opposite each characteristic, assign a speech activity exercise that will best serve to develop in a positive direction the specific characteristic encountered.
2. Write an analysis of a high school speech program with which you are familiar, indicating the effect that the administrator's attitude had on the total program.
3. Prepare a minimum-essentials list of facilities and equipment that you would like to have in your teaching situation, including the estimated cost for each item, which could be submitted on request of a school administrator.
4. Discuss how the high school speech program and the community can best work together for the benefit of each.
5. Prepare a plan of approach in which you indicate how speech can best serve and work in cooperation with other departments within the school.

REFERENCES

Students

Bohannon, Dorothy. "The Speech Needs and Abilities of Ninth Grade Pupils," *Quarterly Journal of Speech*, XXVII (April, 1941), 182–88.

Cole, Luella. *Psychology of Adolescence.* 4th ed. New York: Holt, Rinehart, and Winston, Inc., 1954.

Crow, L., and A. Crow. *Adolescent Development.* New York: McGraw-Hill Book Co., 1956.

Kellelkamp, G. C. *Teaching Adolescents.* Boston: D. C. Heath and Co., 1949.

Administration

Balcer, Charles. "The High School Principal and the Teacher of Speech," *Speech Teacher*, IV (September, 1958), 183–86.

Miller, Elvena. "How the Principal Can Help All Speech and Hearing Handicapped Students," *Bulletin of the National Association of Secondary School Principals*, XXXIV (November, 1950), 31–34.

Tracy, Pierre. "The Role of Speech in the Secondary School," *Bulletin of the National Association of Secondary School Principals*, XXIX, No. 133 (November, 1945), 6.

Weaver, Andrew; Glen Eye; and Gladys Borchers. "What Speech Can Contribute to a High School Education," *Bulletin of the National Association of Secondary School Principals*, XXIX, No. 133 (November, 1945), 9–18.

Community

Sandle, Floyd L. "Community Relations and Community Recreation through Community Drama," *Speech Teacher*, VI (September, 1957), 229–32.

Tacey, William S. "Community Speech Programs," *Speech Teacher*, VIII (November, 1959), 310–15.

Facilities

Barrows, Alice, and Lee Simonson. *The School Auditorium as a Theater*, Bulletin 1939, No. 4, U. S. Department of Interior, Office of Education. U. S. Government Printing Office, Washington, D.C. 51 pp. Price $.10.

Fuchs, Theodore. "Equipment for School Dramatics," *American School and University*, VIII (1936), 267–76.

———. *Home-built Lighting Equipment for the Small Stage.* New York: Samuel French, 1940. Pp. vii-39. Illustrated. $3.00.

————. "Planning a School Theatre," *Theatre Arts Monthly*, XXII (October, 1938), 760–65.

————. "The Shorewood High School Auditorium," *American School and University*, X (1938), 345–55.

————. *Suggested Layouts for Stage Lighting Equipment for Typical Large, Medium-size, and Small Non-commercial Stages.* Copyright 1939. Evanston, Ill.: Theodore Fuchs, School of Speech, Northwestern University, $.50.

Gillette, A. S. *Planning and Equipping the Educational Theatre.* Cincinnati: National Thespian Society, 1945. 30 pp.

Plette, Frederic. *Directory of Stage Equipment and Supply Houses.* Cincinnati: National Thespian Society, 1948.

Other Departments

Borchers, Gladys. "Basic Issues in Integrating Speech with Other Subjects," *Bulletin of the National Association of Secondary School Principals*, XXXII, No. 151 (January, 1948), 169–78.

Bryant, Donald. "Critical Responsibilities of the Speech-English Program," *Speech Teacher*, X (November, 1960), 180–89.

Mennes, Arthur, and Donald K. Smith. "A Follow-up Program in Speech Education," *Bulletin of the National Association of Secondary School Principals*, XXXII, No. 151 (January, 1948), 157–65.

Mills, Glen. "Speech in a Communication Course," *Quarterly Journal of Speech*, XXXIII (February, 1947), 40–45.

Phelps, Waldo. "Integration of Speech with English and Social Studies," *Bulletin of the National Association of Secondary School Principals*, XXXVI, No. 187 (May, 1952), 79–88.

Robinson, Karl F. "Speech—The Heart of the Core Curriculum," *Quarterly Journal of Speech*, XXVI (October, 1940), 374–76.

Smith, Dana. "A Curriculum in Language Arts for Life Today," *English Journal*, XL (February, 1951), 79–85.

Wiksell, Wesley. "Integrating Speech with Other Subjects: I. Reports on Integration," *Bulletin of the National Association of Secondary School Principals*, XXIX, No. 133 (November, 1945), 125–33.

CHAPTER FIVE

Planning Speech Courses and Curricular Programs

The first chapters of this book have discussed the broad factors that affect the teaching of speech in the high school or college. Whether speech instruction is organized as courses in the regular curriculum pattern, is conducted in activities outside the classroom, or, as usually happens, is a combination of both patterns, these seven *general* factors influence it: (1) a clear understanding of the goals and objectives of speech training in the secondary school; (2) a thorough knowledge of the needs, interests, and abilities of the students; (3) a trained teacher with suitable personal qualities to handle the program; (4) the cooperation of the administrator; (5) facilities that at least meet the minimum essentials; (6) satisfactory community–school cooperation; and (7) compatible relationships with other departments in the school.

Before the teacher can proceed to plan a program or deal with classroom problems, he must have a basic approach to instruction upon which courses, activities, and methods of teaching depend.

BASIC APPROACHES IN TEACHING SPEECH

Since a *mastery of fundamentals* of speech underlies success in any speech situation, no matter what the type of speech may be, *a sound teaching approach must insure such mastery.* In addition it must *follow up such fundamentals,* stressing them in activities and more specialized types of performance; further, it must *allow the addition of theoretical principles and techniques necessary in meeting the more complex speech situations.*

Three basic approaches are possible; all are in use in high school speech instruction. Predominance of any one over the others depends upon the character of the speech courses and the local conditions affecting them. These three approaches will be designated as (1) the *elements* approach, (2) the *activities* approach, and (3) the *combination* approach.

The Elements Approach

In the elements approach the mastery of fundamental processes is considered so important that it is made the *end* of speech instruction, rather than merely the *means* of meeting various types of speech situations.

In this text these fundamentals are treated in Part Two, and include poise and emotional adjustment, communicativeness, bodily action, voice and articulation, language, speech preparation, and listening. Becker and others [1] found that 100 per cent of Michigan high school speech teachers include such fundamentals as their basic course content with the use of talks the chief exercise for teaching them. Evelyn Konigsberg,[2] formerly Chairman of the Department of Speech, Jamaica High School, and now Principal, Washington Irving High School, New York City, supports an elements approach through the use of functional drill in the teaching of voice and articulation. She attacks the stress upon merely "communicating ideas" and "practicing speaking in functional situations" as ways of insuring effective speaking. "Voice and articulation are two very basic elements of communication through speech," she states, and indicates that they must be *taught directly* by the teacher of speech.

The elements approach requires goals, units, and methods to be planned so that fundamentals are taught through drill, talks, oral reading or any other suitable vehicle, but with stress upon the mastery of the element or fundamental habits to be developed. In no case, however, should this approach be used without a satisfactory synthesis of the element with the whole act of speech.

An elements approach is also found in many college beginning

[1] Albert Becker, Charles Brown, and Jack W. Murphy, "Speech Teaching in Michigan High Schools," *Speech Teacher,* I (March, 1952), 137–45.

[2] Evelyn Konigsberg, "Making Drill Functional," *Speech Teacher,* I (March, 1952), 128.

courses. Jones [3] in his study of the basic course in colleges and universities in the United States, reported many schools which organized their fundamentals or voice and diction courses on this basis.

The Activities Approach

The activities approach rests upon the selection of an experience (activity) such as conversation, discussion, and so on, as a vehicle by means of which the fundamentals are taught. The emphasis is upon the theory and technique of the activity as an end. Fundamentals are involved as *means* of performing the activity. Such activities are developed later in this text.

Quite often the particular techniques of the activity dominate such work, any emphasis upon the basic elements of speech being by-passed in the stress upon successful communication in the activity. The activities approach has much to recommend it: it is an accepted educational approach through everyday speech experiences; it is easily motivated; it *can* be used successfully to teach fundamentals. However, unless the teacher is on his toes, the total activity and its techniques will crowd out the individual pointing-up and repeated experience (drill) necessary to set desirable speech habits. No teacher should delude himself that he is doing his basic job if he teaches activities *only*, and never "nails down" the fundamentals upon which they depend for successful oral communication.

In the majority of basic college courses, public speaking is the principal activity used, according to Jones.[4] A greater variety of activities characterizes the standard high school course.

The Combination Approach

Most usable in high school speech instruction and in many college courses is a *combination* of these two. *Motivation* for development in speech fundamentals and mastery of everyday speech situations can be secured readily through activities. Diagnosis of needs in fundamentals, pin-pointing areas for work, and repeated experience on particular basic skills in order to build *new habits* are best served

[3] H. Rodman Jones, "The Development and Present Status of Beginning Speech Courses in the Colleges and Universities in the United States" (unpublished doctoral dissertation, Northwestern University, 1952).

[4] Jones, *ibid.*

by the elements approach. The desired synthesis can be secured through activities. Both approaches can serve in teaching techniques of an activity. The intelligent teacher must learn when and how the goals of his instruction are best served by the two approaches.

In this text, the fundamentals are studied with a careful analysis of elements and suitable culminating exercises in Part Two, the principal vehicle being talks or public-speaking experiences. The forms of speech are treated in Part Three as extraclass or classroom activities. They can be taught *within* regular classroom work, as well as in extraclass programs of speech instruction without any emphasis upon contest speech. Necessary adaptations should be made by the teacher. Course outlines suggested in this chapter rest upon a combination approach with fundamentals or elements stressed first and activities following.

FACTORS UNDERLYING ORGANIZATION

In addition to the *general* factors influencing the speech program in any school, the instructor must consider certain *specific, organizational* factors that determine the exact courses, their content, sequence, and relationship in the whole program. A discussion of these follows.

1. *Adequate Class Time for Speech*

High school and college speech instruction invariably stresses improvement of personal speech habits and development of speaking skills. To achieve these ends time is needed for (1) individual performance, (2) careful evaluation and criticism by the teacher, (3) repeated performance under supervision to allow application of suggestions given. The student must *do* the thing he wishes to develop. Reading books, hearing lectures, or writing *about* speech is not enough. Each student should have as many actual performances as possible in every course.

Skills courses meeting every day are best. They allow wide participation, keep interest high, and permit benefits of cumulative experience. If a five-hour course per week is not possible, a three-hour plan is next best. Teaching efficiency and results go down in the two-hour or one-hour per week class. This is especially true when enrollments run thirty to forty pupils in a class. In a one-hour class, especially, ten to fifteen students is a top figure. Even then a teacher needs careful planning to achieve his goals. A better plan usually is to have a shorter course with more frequent meetings.

2. *Optimum Class Size*

As noted above, class size directly affects efficiency in teaching speech, more than in other subjects, because individual performance is essential. Large classes and short teaching time frustrate both pupil and teacher. Administrators not acquainted with the nature of speech instruction often use the same measuring stick for speech classes that they employ in social science or English classes; the result is overcrowding and ineffective work. Speech teachers who inadvertently or deliberately admit too many students jeopardize their program.

Best results in basic skills courses are achieved when classes do not run over twenty-five students. A three-hour or five-hour class permits a given assignment to be covered in about three periods, assuming eight recitations are heard daily. The teacher must see that maximum class size limits are respected.

Experiments with closed-circuit television and/or team teaching have shown it is possible to instruct larger speech classes, sometimes of sixty to seventy students, using lectures and demonstrations of skills assignments. However, all such experiments employ smaller groups of about twenty students when individual pupil performances are conducted and teacher critiques are given to each person.

3. *Length of Performance*

Length of performance is another important variable. Beginning assignments usually are short, running one, two, or three minutes. Standard course patterns indicate longer performances as pupils develop and as projects become more difficult or principles of composition are applied. If speeches averaged three minutes in a five-hour semester course with an enrollment of twenty students per class, each student might have a total of ten appearances. This would be most desirable. Gardner [5] found a combination of three, six, and nine minute speeches a popular one in beginning college classes.

[5] Wofford Gardner, "The Relationship of Improvement in Public Speaking Skill to the Length and Frequency of Classroom Performance" (unpublished doctoral dissertation, Northwestern University, 1952).

Most instructors prefer more frequent, short talks to few, long ones.

4. A Class Schedule Permitting Students to Program Speech

Regardless of time, class size, or speech length, the teacher must reach as many students needing speech training as he can. If speech is *required*, class schedules will be organized to permit students to take it. However, when speech is an *elective subject* it must compete with other subjects which are required. The speech instructor should always clear schedule with the principal or department head to see that there are no such conflicts. He should also try to avoid scheduling against other popular electives.

5. Full Accreditation of Speech Classwork

Speech classwork taught as an elective or requirement should always be accredited on the same basis as any other academic subject. Any other plan penalizes the student and teacher. Noncredit speech, either as a requirement or as an elective, places an unfair burden of motivation upon speech instruction.

6. Sufficient Instructional Budget

The speech teacher should never hesitate to make his budgetary needs known. Texts, equipment, supplies, library materials—all these are standard curricular items. They affect course sequences, teacher planning, and classroom work. The speech teacher should consult with his administrator regarding his needs and budget practices.

7. Application beyond the Classroom

Speech training must function beyond the class assignments and exercises. It should be applied in school and community life. The teacher should survey these two fields for possibilities that affect the courses he teaches, the subject matter of speech assignments, audiences to be met, and so on. Thus he lays the foundation for a broad and functional program.

8. Suitable Coordination with Extraclass Speech Activities

A reciprocal relationship should exist between classroom instruction in speech and activities outside the classroom. A knowledge of the *whole* school speech outlook permits carefully planned courses that will help to feed the extraclass program and provide basic training and specialized skills useful to both. Similarly, these activities can serve the courses in speech. They introduce students to speech, they let them taste the benefits and enjoyment of participation, they motivate them to desire more work in the field presented in a continuing, organized form in class. Activities are often the beginning of an organized classroom program growing from a demand for more speech education.

Thus speech classes and activities serve each other. Intelligent organization and planning of the *total* program make for good coordination and effective work.

All of these factors underlie sound organization of speech instruction. They are fundamental to the more detailed planning of course outlines and lesson plans that follow.

BASIC PRINCIPLES UNDERLYING PLANNING AND TEACHING

Realistic and successful planning of speech instruction rests upon certain basic principles of teaching. The list below and the subsequent teaching pattern furnish such a foundation for the beginning teacher.

1. He must know (through diagnosis) the speech interests, needs, and abilities of his students.
2. He must realize that speech is a complex form of behavior, that it is habituated, and that the speech habits he observes are of long standing.
3. He must provide suitable motivation for students if they are to make the desired changes in speech behavior.
4. He must set up the long-term or remote goals (objectives) that he wishes the students to achieve in the course.
5. He must determine the immediate, tentative, readily achievable goals for the various steps in development leading to the remote goals of the course.
6. He must provide satisfactory theory and training experiences for the accomplishment of both immediate and remote goals. These experiences should not be isolated drills used only as exercises for teaching fundamentals or basic skills. They should be chosen to permit elements to be *taught* and *synthesized* in relation to the *whole* configuration of speaking.

7. He must guide the students toward goals through his criticism and suggestions, tactfully and effectively given.
8. He must allow sufficient time for maturation in the learning process, and repeated performance to permit the "setting" of the new habits.

A TEACHING PATTERN

In practice these principles indicate a teaching pattern or "instructional ladder," which characterizes high school speech instruction:

I. LONG RANGE OR REMOTE ← VI. CONTINUED UNTIL, *COURSE* GOALS
(Determined by teacher in terms of the desired information, attitudes, personal speech habits, basic and specialized speech skills to be developed in the *course*.)
↓

II. NEEDS, INTERESTS, ABILITIES OF STUDENTS
(as related to I above. Revealed through testing and diagnosis by the teacher.)
↓

III. IMMEDIATE GOALS FOR CLASS AND INDIVIDUALS (tentative)
(Based on II, within limits set by I. Set by the teacher for the particular class and pupil to achieve.)
Achieve via IV: *organized* units of instruction in course.

VI. CONTINUED UNTIL, IDEALLY, EACH REMOTE GOAL IS REACHED BY EACH STUDENT
(Within the limits of his abilities.)
↑

V. NEW IMMEDIATE GOALS
(Set by the teacher after III goals are reached. The goals in V are tentative, also, more difficult of achievement, always moving towards I, the long range course goals.)
Achieved by using suitable units such as in IV, suited to the *new* goals.
↑

IV. UNITS IN THE COURSE including
A. *Suitable motivation*
B. *Selected individual and group experiences and activities, needed theory*
C. *Evaluation: suggestions and criticism by teacher and class*
D. *Application of criticism and suggestions*
E. *Repeated experience* (until first immediate goals [III] are reached)

PLANNING THE BASIC COURSE

The first course is the most important and most common course in the secondary school or college. Since it is often the only speech course offered in high school, it necessitates careful planning. As has been noted earlier, it is peculiarly subject to conditions in the local situation. However, certain general trends and patterns are helpful to the teacher as a plan that can be adapted to meet conditions in a given situation. A guide of this type is useful in the statement of objectives.

Objectives in Basic Speech Skills

The speech program should be based upon a comprehensive set of objectives. In Chapters I and II we have discussed the broad aims of secondary and higher education and the needs of students. The list of goals [6] that appears below is designed to meet student needs. It indicates the possible scope of a program in basic speech skills and reading that is the chief concern in a first course in speech. Additional and more specialized courses, quite obviously, have more specialized objectives.

1. The speech needs and abilities of every student should be tested and diagnosed.
2. Students who possess speech defects such as stuttering, lisping, dialects, or speech maladjustments should be provided opportunities for correction.
3. *The large group having "inadequate" and normal speech should be given the chance to profit from systematic education in such fundamental speech processes as:*
   a. Adjustment to the speaking situations of everyday life so that social adaptions of this type can be made without fear and with confidence and poise.
   b. Development of a speaking personality characterized by attitudes of sincerity, friendliness, and communicativeness.
   c. Skill in developing a subject, in using one's ideas and in

[6] Karl F. Robinson and W. Norwood Brigance, "The Program of Basic Skills in Speaking," *Bulletin of the National Association of Secondary School Principals*, XXIX, No. 133 (November, 1945), 19–29.

knowing the sources of information to supplement them with ample and relevant materials.

d. Analysis of the audience which is addressed.

e. Organization and arrangement of content to insure the desired response from the audience.

f. Mastery of an effective technique of delivery.

g. Expressing one's ideas in simple, acceptable, and effective spoken language.

h. Articulating and pronouncing words intelligibly.

i. Using the voice effectively.

j. Communication of ideas with expressive and well-coordinated bodily activity.

k. Ability to select and arrange content for reading aloud.

l. Effective use of fundamental processes in reading aloud ordinary material from the printed page.

m. Cultivation and acquisition of suitable listening habits that will enable the individual to give respectful attention to speakers for purposes of learning, evaluating, and criticizing.

4. Students who are superior in basic speech skills should be given opportunities to develop special skills directly associated with their life interests and in keeping with their needs and abilities.

5. Basic speaking skills should be implemented through a balanced program of functional speech experiences. These should be directly related to school and community problems, practical situations, and educational experiences which form a framework for participation in a democratic society.

6. Evaluating the growth and development in basic speech skills.

A Simplified Plan for Constructing Courses of Study in Speech

Knowing the goals of the basic speech course gives an orientation to the teacher who is planning the courses of study for a particular situation.

The average speech teacher who undertakes to build a course of study or to construct a curriculum in speech faces an unusual predicament. Logically, such a teacher may turn for help to readings on curriculum building in textbooks on education, but in them he will find little specific help. For the most part, they concern themselves with building the curriculum for an entire school system, or with the reorganization of courses of study in the school as a whole.

Too often they suggest a series of detailed steps in procedure that makes the process complicated and confusing for one seeking a comparatively short and easy solution.

The following plan, which has been evolved from years of teaching summer and regular term courses in problems and methods of teaching speech in the secondary school and college, is presented as a suggested practical procedure. It has been employed by thousands of teachers. The steps are set down in order below:

I. *Determine the philosophy of speech education, stating it in terms of broad objectives.*

The question to be here decided is what one believes to be the broad objectives of education and what place speech has in the objectives of education. One's philosophy may be stated in terms of them.

II. *Determine the specific course objectives.*

These will be refinements of the broad objectives and in many cases will be the result of analysis of them. The objectives for a basic course have been stated above.

III. *Choose the content: speech experiences and activities that will accomplish the objectives.* These can be listed in outline form.

A. Content should always be selected with respect to the objectives and the student needs, etc. (see IIIB below and II above).

1. A knowledge of available sources of platform assignments, information, materials, teaching aids, and equipment is essential to proper selection. (Consult methods books, speech texts, bibliographies, textbook reviews, course notes, personal experience, and issues of the *Quarterly Journal of Speech* and *The Speech Teacher* for assistance.)

2. Examine and note the content of courses of study and curricula in speech that are available.

a. Courses of study published by various states and municipalities.

b. Curriculum projects in colleges and universities.

c. Courses of study in English and the language arts often include usable speech materials.

d. College and university courses may be summarized

in catalogues of the particular department or school. They are available in the school or public library. Catalogues may also be obtained from the registrar of a college or university.

3. List *all of the content* that might be included in the program.

B. *Select, refine, and restrict that which fits the local situation* (most of these factors have been developed in Chaps. I–III).

1. *The training and preparation of the teacher,* including particular abilities and weaknesses.

2. *The students to be enrolled in the class.*
   a. Age; year in school; grade or class.
   b. Elective or required subject.
   c. Mental, physical, racial, social, and emotional characteristics; their nationality.
   d. Interests and abilities in speech, as well as in other areas.

3. *Facilities in the school for speech work.*
   a. Classroom: furniture, lighting, equipment.
   b. Auditorium; stage—its size, shape, usability; lighting; paint shop; amplifying system and sound equipment.
   c. Library facilities.
   d. Recording apparatus.
   e. Transportation: school bus, cars, railroads, etc.

4. *Attitude of the administrator.*
   a. His ideas about speech education.
   b. The budget for speech work.

5. *Attitude of other departments in the school toward speech.*
   a. English.
   b. Languages.
   c. Science: Physics, Chemistry, Biology.
   d. Music.
   e. Commercial.
   f. Athletics.
   g. Manual Arts.
   h. Social Studies.

   i. Art.

   j. Counselors and home-room teachers; deans.

  6. *The attitude of the community toward speech.*

   a. Parents.

   b. Church groups.

   c. Dinner clubs: Kiwanis, Rotary, Lions, etc.

   d. Community resources: recreation center, theater, etc.

   e. Services expected by the community.

  7. *Extraclass speech activities and contests.*

   a. Forensics.

   b. Plays.

   c. Operettas.

   d. Assembly programs; convocations.

  8. *The textbook to be used* (if one is used).

   a. General textbook in speech.

   b. Specialized or supplementary books.

  9. *The course or courses to be offered.*

   a. Relationship to all points above must be considered.

   b. Relationship to the extraclass program in particular.

   c. Number of semesters.

   d. Number of meetings each week.

   e. Number and kind of speech performances.

   f. Year offered.

   g. Elective or required; credit.

IV. *Organize the content as units, having specific objectives for each.*

  In the first course, representative units might be Introduction and Orientation, Voice and Articulation, Bodily Action, Speech Composition, Discussion, etc.

V. *Determine the teaching order, or the arrangement of the unit.*

  Consider the logical and psychological factors that will affect the *arrangement* of the units.

  Check principles that should govern:

  1. Simple to complex.

  2. Part to whole.

  3. Chronological.

  4. Easy to difficult.

  5. Immediate to remote developments.

VI. *Plan the units specifically.*
VII. *Break down the units into daily lesson plans. Carefully develop the lesson plans.*
VIII. *Provide for evaluation of the work taught and the course of study as planned.*
    A. Recordings, tests, rating scales, other methods.
    B. Descriptive evaluations of course content and organization by teacher and students.

How to Plan a Unit of Work

A further important consideration is the organization and planning of the content of the units that have been selected for the course. The unit outline should be carefully conceived and should precede the daily lesson plans in a course syllabus or curriculum guide. Below are some suggested steps for planning the units:

1. Write the specific objectives of the unit.
2. List the subject matter sources from the textbook or from reference books. State exact chapters and pages to be used.
3. Write such materials as will be needed to supplement textbook information. If no text is used in a speech course, lecture notes should be prepared.
4. List the activities of the students; include
    a. Facts and theory to be learned.
    b. Performance activities.
5. Prepare any guide or study sheets needed to aid the student in the preparation of his written work or platform performance. Be sure to distribute these well in advance for speaking assignments.
6. Indicate the plan of procedure or method by which the theory and practice are to be developed.
7. List any special equipment or facilities that are needed.
8. Plan any test, evaluation, or criticism scheme for appraising the work to be taught. In the case of an evaluation scheme, be sure that it is understood by the students and has been previously used successfully in a teaching situation.
9. Indicate the estimated time in days or hours for the unit.

So that the teacher may note applications of these principles, a sample of a unit plan prepared by a teacher in the field is included.

Unit Two [7]

Bodily Action (Time: 7 days)

I. *Specific Objectives*
  A. To give the students an understanding of bodily action and the importance of action in communication.
  B. To develop free, spontaneous, and abundant action that springs from inner impulses.
  C. To provide situations that demand the use of bodily action.
  D. To show the relationship of body and voice as an integrated part of speech presentation.
  E. To develop through lecture and discussion an understanding of the principles of bodily action.

II. *Evaluation of Unit Work*
  A. Class participation in discussion.
  B. Evaluation of speeches presented.
  C. Effort and interest shown in bringing in and presenting outside materials.
  D. Teacher's observation.
  E. Speech activities showing use of bodily action as a whole.

III. *Student Activities*
  A. Read chapters 5–6 in Sarett and Foster.
  B. Outside reference reading.
  C. To determine what good bodily action entails from the use of pictures brought to class.
  D. Discuss phases of bodily action (gesture, movement, posture), arriving at good definitions as well as understanding and use.
  E. Reading of paragraphs to demonstrate movement.
  F. Round-robin story telling.
  G. Speeches of demonstration.

IV. *Sources of Material for the Student*
  A. Text: Sarett, Lew, W. T. Foster, and J. H. McBurney. *Speech—A High School Course.* Boston: Houghton Mifflin Co., 1956.
  B. Outside readings:
    1. Griffith, Nelson, Stasheff. *Your Speech.* New York: Harcourt Brace and Co., 1955, pp. 132–35.
    2. Adams, H. M. and Thomas Pollock. *Speak Up.* New York: The Macmillan Co.; 1956, pp. 436–42.

[7] This unit outline and the lesson plans that follow were prepared by Miss Elizabeth Hubbs, Highland Park (Ill.) High School.

    C. Newspapers.
    D. Magazines.
    E. Radio and TV.
    F. Personal experiences.

V. *Supplementary Materials*
    A. Lectures.
    B. Additional text references.
       1. Griffith, Nelson, Stasheff.
       2. Adams and Pollock.

VI. *Special Facilities*
    A. Round-robin stories.
    B. Reading of paragraphs from magazines.

VII. *Plan of Procedure*
    First day—Definition of bodily action and what it includes.
    Second day—Application of bodily action to pictures and stress on posture.
    Third day—Study of movement.
    Fourth day—Study of gesture.
    Fifth, Sixth, and Seventh day—Demonstration speeches.

Preparing the Lesson Plan

In order to reach the final stage of implementing a course of study, the units should be broken down into daily lesson plans. These are the teacher's blueprints for daily class instruction. In order to aid the teacher, the following suggestions are given for the organization of daily work:

1. Know the *criteria* for a good lesson plan:
    a. It has a definite aim or goal.
    b. It includes specific questions designed especially for the class to be taught.
    c. It states specifically what facts, skills, or attitudes are to be learned.
    d. It allows for and makes necessary correlation of the day's lesson with previous work and with pupils' out-of-class experiences and interests.
    e. It provides for a variety of motivations, approaches, methods, drills, exercises, etc.
    f. It is designed to evoke *pupil activity.*

2. Prepare the *content* and *form* of the plan carefully:
   a. Indicate the *date, subject,* and *classroom.*
   b. List the *specific aims* for the day's work.
   c. *Link the new work to the old,* or to the students' previous experience and background.
   d. *Include the materials for instruction* (texts, charts, models, pictures, references, etc.).
   e. State specifically the *knowledge, skills,* and *attitudes to be taught.* This can be outlined carefully and clearly.
      (1) Determine a teachable order for the content.
      (2) Prepare adequate examples, illustrations, models, sketches, etc., to support main ideas.
      (3) Write out and develop key questions that will determine or unify activities for the day.
      (4) Try to individualize the work as much as possible.
   f. Develop *practical procedures* and methods for teaching the content. Include:
      (1) Approach and motivation.
      (2) A sequence of questions.
      (3) Drills and applications.
      (4) Summary.
   g. Plan the *evaluation* of the day's teaching.
   h. Give the *next day's assignment.* Make it clear and definite. Present it early in the hour, as a general rule.

Using Sources of Motivation in Teaching

A vital part of the teacher's planning and teaching rests upon his motivating the students to learn. This is especially true in a speech class where both knowledge and skill must be mastered. Although this step need not be written into the lesson plan, it should be carefully developed by the teacher in relation to the interests, abilities, and needs of his students. The speech class and activity program have many distinctive sources of motivation:

   a. The personality of the teacher. He should be friendly, fair, enthusiastic, sympathetic, and understanding. Often his personal attitude is sufficient to insure the success of a lesson. His skill, learning, and experience also enter in.
   b. The goals and objectives of the student: his personal improve-

ment and skill, professional career, grades, credit, basic drives for action. One or all of these may be utilized in an assignment.

c. The content of the unit or lesson: a particular platform assignment or theory.

d. Special methods or unusual procedures in teaching content. Class programs, student planned lessons, and mild competitive methods are examples.

e. The classroom atmosphere that is created by the teacher and students.

f. The physical conditions in the classroom. The traditional desk setup may be modified by the use of movable chairs, tables for conference, and so on; soundproofing, restful wall color, and attractive decoration of the room also help. Sometimes classes are held in the auditorium, on the stage, in a radio studio or recording room. Students look forward to class time because of the room.

g. Special awards including credit, honor roll, medals, letters, trophies, scholarships, money, and certificates.

h. The use of special equipment such as a public-address system, recording apparatus, motion pictures, television, slides, films, charts, or models.

i. Special trips or public appearances in other communities.

j. Approval of the class; praise, favorable comment, or constructive criticism by the teacher.

k. Publicity in the school or local newspaper, play programs, over radio, television, or public-address system.

l. Pictures of school representatives, play casts, festival and contest winners, and so on. These can be displayed in the speech classroom or hall.

m. Participation and public performance in speech activities, plays or contests—local, state, national.

n. Particular responsibilities in the speech program: director, program chairman, presiding officer, discussion leader, etc.

o. Membership in speech or drama clubs or societies.

A Sample Daily Lesson Plan

To further the understanding of the teacher regarding the relationship between the unit plan and the daily lesson scheme, daily lesson plans are included below. Here it will be seen clearly that the teacher is concerned with how much content can be covered in a single class period. One can see easily the greater detail, specific questions, methods and procedures, motivation, the provision for pupils' activities in future assignments, and teacher activity through questions, lecture, and criticism.

Lesson Plans for Unit Two [8]

First day: Time: 40 minutes
Aims
1. To explain what is meant by the term bodily action and to familiarize the students with the vocabulary in relation to it.
2. To show why bodily action is important to good speaking.
3. To explain why the body must work as a whole.
4. To get as many of the class participating as possible to stimulate interest.

Materials
1. Textbook assignment: Sarett, Foster, and McBurney, Chapter 5.
2. Magazine and newspapers with pictures of speakers who are examples of good and poor bodily action.
3. References:
   a. Weaver, Andrew T., and Gladys Borchers. *Speech.* New York: Harcourt Brace and Co., 1946, Chapter II.
   b. Elson and Peck (See unit outline.).

Knowledge to Be Taught
1. Bodily action is any motion that helps the speaker in expressing an idea.
2. Random activity is nervous action and does not aid the speech.
3. Bodily action includes:
   a. Posture.
   b. Gesture.
   c. Movement.
4. Parts of the body used in bodily action are:
   a. Hands, arms, and shoulders.
   b. Legs and torso.
   c. Head.
   d. Facial expression.

Procedure
1. The teacher will discuss what is meant by bodily action with examples to clarify it in the student's mind.
2. After explanatory material the teacher will ask class about observa-

[8] These plans cover the first four days of the unit outline on p. 113.

tion of any TV speaker or friend that they believe uses good bodily action.

3. From class discussion she will develop on the board a list of qualifications for good bodily action.
4. She will also show pictures and ask students to determine meanings from bodily action used.

Evaluation

1. Class participation.
2. Ability of students to develop awareness of bodily action.
3. Teacher's observation and comments.

Assignment

1. Bring to class pictures that represent good bodily action. These will be placed in the speech notebook.
2. Read Sarett, Foster, and McBurney, Chapter 6. Emphasis on posture.

Second day: Time: 40 minutes
Aims

1. To evaluate and recognize good bodily action through use of pictures.
2. To stress good posture and show its importance in speaking.

Materials

1. Chapter 6 in Sarett, Foster, and McBurney.
2. Pictures from newspapers and magazines brought in by students.

Knowledge to Be Taught

1. Good bodily action stems from inner impulses.
2. Facial expressions in pictures show emotions.
3. Good posture is a position of the body that is comfortable for you and for the audience.
4. Stress good posture in relation to speaking both for the audience and the speaker.

Procedure

1. Students will show pictures exemplifying bodily action to the class, and the teacher will lead a discussion concerning free unrestrained bodily action. Class will discuss the integration of bodily action and voice.
2. As bodily action is being discussed special attention will be paid to the posture of the speakers and how it affects presentation. The teacher will then demonstrate some poor speech postures such as the "limp rag" for general criticism of the class. The class will arrive at a stance that would be acceptable for speaking and then build a definition of good speaking posture for their notebooks.

Evaluation
1. Interest and response of the class.
2. Choice of materials brought to class.
3. Teacher observation and comments.

Assignment
1. Continue study of Chapter 6 in Sarett, Foster, and McBurney. Stress material on movement.
2. Prepare exercise No. 2, page 72, in text for presentation before the class.

Third day: Time: 40 minutes

Aims
1. To explain and define what is meant by movement.
2. To show how movement can help the speaker in gaining poise, lack of stiffness, and ease.
3. To show times when movement can be used advantageously.
4. To provide opportunities for the students to use movement.

Materials
1. Reading in Chapter 6 of text in Sarett, Foster, and McBurney.
2. Exercise in text, No. 2, page 72.
3. Paragraphs from various magazine articles will be given to the students and they will read before the class with an attempt to move to get away from the "frozen position."

Knowledge to Be Taught
1. Movement or moving the body from one place to another is an advantage to the speaker.
2. Aimless movement is distracting.
3. Movement serves many purposes:
   a. Shows lapse of time.
   b. Shows change of idea.
   c. Relaxes the speaker.
   d. Gets attention.
   e. Stresses a point.
   f. Walking to and from the platform gives first and last impressions to your audience.

Procedure
1. Teacher will lecture on the definition and use of movement, showing how it can be used advantageously with emphasis on walking to and from the platform.
2. After the lecture the students will be asked to participate in a discussion the object of which will be to get as many purposes of movement as possible listed by the class.

3. Several students will be asked to read paragraphs from the exercise in the text or others given by the teacher and they will be asked to use movement at least once. This may look planned at first, but it will get them out of the idea of standing "frozen." Comments concerning movement from the class will follow.

Evaluation
1. Response from class.
2. Reaction and use of movement in exercises.
3. Teacher observation.

Assignment
1. Chapter 6 in Sarett, Foster, and McBurney. Stress on gesture.
2. Outside reading:
   a. Griffith, Nelson, and Stasheff, pp. 115–32.
   b. Adams and Pollock, pp. 436–42.
3. Prepare a three-minute demonstration speech for the fifth day.

Fourth day: Time: 40 minutes

Aim
1. To give the students an understanding of gesture and its use in effective speech.
2. To give an understanding of the various types of gesture and their use.
3. To provide opportunities for the students to use gestures.

Materials
1. Chapter 6, Gesture. Sarett, Foster, and McBurney.
2. References:
   a. Griffith, Nelson, and Stasheff, pp. 132–35.
   b. Adams and Pollock, pp. 436–42.
3. Round-robin story for exercise in gesturing.

Knowledge to Be Taught
1. What is meant by gesturing?
2. The parts of the body that take part in gesturing.
3. The types of gestures:
   a. Emphatic.
   b. Descriptive.
   c. Suggestive.
4. The value of gesturing.

Procedure
1. A lecture will be given by the teacher on gesturing, explaining the meaning, value, and types of gesture. She will demonstrate occasions when the various types could be used.
2. The students will be asked specific questions orally to determine their knowledge of the reference reading done.

3. The teacher will begin a round-robin story calling on any students who have not thus far participated in the specific daily activities. The class will comment on types of gestures upon completion of the story.

Evaluation

1. Observation of class when story is presented.
2. Class knowledge on reading assignments.

Assignment

1. Three-minute demonstration speech demanding use of action.
2. Practice speech before mirror to observe action.

Further assistance in planning speech courses can be obtained from a study of the publications of the Speech Association of America,[9] the Secondary Schools Principals Association,[10] and the American Educational Theatre Association, as well as numerous state curriculum guides.[11] They contain representative descriptions and outlines of courses.

The pattern of the more common first course is as follows:

Unit Headings

BASIC SKILLS (Individual approach through public speaking materials, primarily)

Orientation; First Steps in Speech Preparation

Poise and Adjustment

Directness and Communicativeness

Bodily Action

Voice and Articulation

Language

Speech Preparation (detailed treatment)

Oral Reading (optional)

Listening

[9] See "Fundamentals of Speech: A Basic Course for High Schools," written by the Secondary School Interest Group of the Speech Association of America in *Speech Teacher*, VIII (March, 1959), 93–113.

[10] See especially Chap. XII, "Speech Programs in Large High Schools," and Chap. XIII, "Speech Programs in Small High Schools," *Bulletin of the National Association of Secondary School Principals*, XXIX, No. 133 (November, 1945); also Part IV, "Representative Speech Programs," *Bulletin of the National Association of Secondary School Principals*, XXXII, No. 151 (January, 1948), 179–99; also Part II A, "Types of Experiences in Public Speaking, Discussion, and Debate-Courses," *Bulletin of the National Association of Secondary School Principals*, XXXVI, No. 187 (May, 1952), 27–79.

[11] Study the list at the end of this chapter.

SPECIAL ACTIVITIES (Group approach)
Group Discussion
Parliamentary Procedure
Debating
Oral Interpretation of Prose and Poetry
Choric Speaking
Theater
Radio

PLANNING SPECIALIZED COURSES

In many secondary schools speech training has been developed so that courses are offered beyond the basic or first course. The advanced work usually assumes a character that is developed from local demand because of pupil interests and needs, class training and outside speech activities desired by the administration and community, insufficient time to provide such specialized training in the first course, and the foresight of the teacher who knows that his most efficient means of training for all purposes is through classroom instruction. As a rule, the teacher gets along as best he can in a situation, including short units in his first course as an introduction or as "samples," until he can develop a new area in an advanced course to meet the needs.

In college departments specialized courses exist in greater numbers. The character of these courses is determined by the goals of the program, the nature of the school, the scope of the program (major or minor in speech), possible ties of the program with professional training, teaching, and graduate study.

Among the most frequently organized advanced courses are Discussion and Debate, Theater, and Radio. Listed below are objectives and unit headings for possible courses in these areas.

Discussion and Debate [12]

Objectives

1. To learn the essential theory and principles of debate and discussion.

2. To develop skill in reasoned discourse in both discussion and debate.

[12] For a complete unit outline see Karl F. Robinson and John Keltner, "Suggested Units in Discussion and Debate," *Quarterly Journal of Speech*, XXXII, No. 3 (October, 1946), 385–90.

3. To develop skill in reflective thinking.
4. To develop an understanding of, and a consideration for, the opinions of others.
5. To develop the ability of the student to work cooperatively with others in discussion groups and on debate teams.

Unit Headings

I. Preparation for Argumentation
   A. The Place of Debate and Discussion in a Democracy
   B. First Steps in Discussion; Selection of Problems; Investigation
   C. Analysis of the Basic Problem (using discussion methods)
   D. Analysis of the Debate Proposition
II. Construction of the Debate Case
   A. Methods of Outlining
   B. Development of the Case from the Issues
   C. Methods of Support
   D. Affirmative Case; Negative Case
   E. Development of Cases Using Methods of Support
III. Refutation
   A. Methods of Refutation
   B. Fallacies
   C. Demonstration and Practice in Refutation
IV. Oral Language and Delivery
   A. Methods of Delivery
   B. Methods of Delivery and Style

Dramatic Arts [13]

Objectives
1. Through participation in dramatic activities the individual should gain in poise, ease of manner, and charm of personality. His emotional and imaginative powers should be enriched and he should acquire a respect for the theater through an appreciation and understanding of its arts and techniques.
2. Through the cooperative effort necessary in producing plays, the pupil should learn to work successfully with other people

[13] For the complete outline see "A Suggested Outline for a Course of Study in Dramatic Arts in the Secondary School" (American Educational Theatre Association), *American Educational Theatre Journal,* II, No. 1 (March, 1950), 15–31.

and to practice the methods of democratic procedures. He should gain a better understanding of human behavior and of life.

3. Through the study of dramatic literature and the observation of dramatic performances the pupil should gain an appreciation of the influence which the theater has upon civilization. He should develop personal standards of taste that will make him a more discriminating part of an audience.

Philosophy [14]

Education in general is directed toward an integration of a child's personality which will result in satisfactory adjustment to his environment. Integration, the ideal of mental health, requires a harmonious balance between the intellect and the emotions. Since the emphasis in education has been for so long on the development of the intellectual factors of personality, there is a present need for greater stress on the developing and training of the emotions through experiences both real and imagined. Actual experience in all forms of life situations is neither desirable nor possible. The study and production of drama affords vicarious experience in a variety of social situations and thus offers opportunity for the development of insight into problems of living. Such study is most useful in providing an outlet for emotional expression, for its content is primarily the interpretation of human reactions with regard to life situations.

The principles of dramatic study are the principles of integration. If, through participation in the production of a play (as actor, artist, builder, or musician) an adolescent experiences aesthetic proportion, integration of personality is materially advanced. The truer the aesthetic experience, the deeper the educational effect. If this approach is sound, the educational theater and the course in dramatic arts are not to be judged by the popularity of the play with the high school audience, nor by the box-office receipts. Rather they are to be judged by the measure and value of their contribution to the intellectual and emotional life of the pupils participating as evidenced by their increased maturity, judgment, poise, understanding, independence, and leadership.

[14] Marion Stuart, Lauren Brink, Dina Reese Evans, and Robert Seibert, "Materials, Methods, and Special Projects for a Course of Study in Dramatic Arts in the Secondary School," *Bulletin of the National Association of Secondary School Principals,* XXXIII, No. 166 (December, 1949), 87–156.

Unit Headings

I. Exploring the Field; Investigating the Broad Field of the Theater
II. The Play
   A. Dramatic Forms
   B. Structure of the Play
   C. Evaluation of a Play in Production
III. The Actor
   A. Fundamentals of Acting
   B. Characterization
   C. Bodily Action
   D. Voice
IV. The Director
   A. Play Analysis
   B. Cutting and Adapting a Play
   C. Blocking a Play
   D. Tryouts
   E. Conferences on Production Details and Business
   F. Rehearsals
V. The Technician
   A. Backstage and Front-Office Organization
   B. Scene Design
   C. Lighting
   D. Stagecraft
   E. Costumes
   F. Make-up
VI. History of the Theater
   A. Greek Period
   B. Roman Period
   C. Middle Ages
   D. Elizabethan Period
   E. Restoration and Eighteenth-Century Period
   F. Nineteenth-Century Theater
   G. Twentieth-Century Theater

Radio

Objectives

1. To develop the student's appreciation of the significance of radio as a means of communication and education.

2. To acquaint the student with the structure of broadcasting.
3. To give the student an appreciable understanding of public service in radio.
4. To introduce methods of audience measurement and present its effect on programs.
5. To point to new developments in the communication field.
6. To present the organization and management of stations, independent and affiliated, and of networks.
7. To provide a knowledge of the fundamental techniques and some opportunity for practice in the specific areas of:
   a. Announcing.
   b. Writing.
   c. Production.
8. To develop desirable standards for radio performance for the participant and the listener.

Unit Headings [15]

(An Introductory Course, I)

    I. Introduction to the Course
   II. The Significance of Radio
  III. The Radio Studio and Equipment
  IV. The History of Radio
   V. Broadcasting Systems
  VI. Control of Broadcasting
 VII. Organization of Radio
VIII. Allied Service Agencies and Sales Organizations
  IX. Technical Aspects
   X. Program Planning
  XI. Public Service in Radio
 XII. Education by Radio
XIII. New Developments in Radio
XIV. Vocational Opportunities

(An Introductory Course, II)

   I. History of Broadcasting
  II. Microphone Technique
 III. Sound Effects and Radio Music

[15] Taken from course outlines of teachers in the secondary school.

IV. Radio Writing
V. Radio Acting
VI. Radio Production

PLANNING CORRELATED AND INTEGRATED COURSES

In both secondary school and college, speech training is sometimes combined with other areas of subject matter. Such combinations are called "integrated" or "correlated" courses. The most common subject-matter areas with which speech has been combined in secondary schools are English, history, and social studies.

Some of these programs have been experimental, and have been dropped. However, one of the most successful correlated programs has been conducted for many years by Rowena Roberts [16] at the William Palmer High School, Colorado Springs, Colorado. In this program every one of the students (over 2,300 in 1957) receives training in speech once a week for four semesters. A staff of three speech teachers meets pupils enrolled in second semester sophomore English and in first semester junior English, as well as each American history (senior) class in the one day a week sessions. Each regular subject-matter teacher accompanies his class to the speech classroom. The speech teacher plans the assignments in speech skills, correlating the content as much as possible with the work being done in the other subjects.

The sophomore speech assignments include giving directions (recorded on tape), panel and symposium discussions, radio newscasting, announcements of school events in the auditorium, personal anecdotes, parliamentary procedure, and pantomimes. The junior course consists entirely of public speaking with speeches to inform, to convince, to actuate, and to entertain; training in outlining; and use of the motivated sequence in speech preparation. The senior course includes work in group dynamics; a required fifteen-minute senior research speech on a social studies subject approved by the cooperating teacher. Students speak in other classes and in community situations.

A cumulative speech record is kept of each student with the written evaluation and critique sheets for four years being assembled in individual pupil folders by the speech teachers. Teachers in the

[16] See Rowena Roberts, "Speech through Correlation," *Speech Teacher,* VI (November, 1957), 292–97.

other subject-matter fields and the guidance teachers use these records and cooperate in the total program.

In addition to the correlated course for all students, the speech program includes two-full time classes in stagecraft, two in dramatics, and extracurricular work in debate and radio.

Although certain disadvantages of the correlated course exist, these are pointed out as the chief advantages: (1) it deals with the student at different stages in his development; (2) it is administratively convenient in programming—no special classes, no conflict; (3) the "carry-over" from speech into other classes is greater because speech and other teachers work together; (4) the course can be adapted easily to ability groupings; (5) the school board is favorable to purchasing equipment, such as recorders, audio-visual aids, etc., for the large number of pupils; (6) pupil motivation is high in this type of program; (7) the other teachers in the correlation welcome the lighter load and the help of the speech teacher.

Other secondary schools have used integrated or correlated courses with success. These include Alhambra and Pasadena, California; Downers Grove and J. Sterling Morton (Cicero), Illinois; and some New York City schools.

The most notable examples of integrated courses at the college level are those in basic communication skills in which speaking, writing, listening, and sometimes reading have been combined. These courses have usually been taught by a single teacher, who handles the instruction in all of these areas, generally being able to call upon specialists for particular problems in remedial reading, speech, and hearing, where necessary. Although many colleges have claimed they are doing "basic communication skills," the number following the specific organization described above is not as large as it was ten years ago, according to Ziemann.[17] Schools employing this pattern at present include the University of Minnesota (St. Paul), Stephens College, Western Michigan University, Grinnell College, and the Air Force Academy.

As a rule this course is a school requirement for graduation and replaces the usual separate courses in beginning speech and English.

[17] See Norman Ziemann, "A Study of the Basic Communication Skills Course in Selected Colleges and Universities of the United States" (Unpublished doctoral dissertation, Northwestern University, 1960).

In order that the teacher may develop a full-scale plan for a speech program in a secondary school, the following sequences of courses are listed. It may be that all these courses will never be organized in a secondary school situation. However, they present possibilities for the teacher who wishes to look ahead a bit.

REPRESENTATIVE SPEECH PROGRAMS WHICH CAN BE ORGANIZED

I. Varied Course Sequence
   A. First Course (required)
      1. Speech fundamentals (one semester)
      2. Introduction to group speech activities (one semester)
         a. Discussion, parliametary law, interpretation, choric speaking, dramatics, radio
   B. Debate and Discussion (one semester)
   C. Theater (one semester)
   D. Interpretation (one semester)
   E. Radio (one semester)
II. Public Speaking Course Sequence
   A. First Course in Fundamentals of Speech (required)
   B. Discussion (one semester)
   C. Debating (one semester)
   D. Speeches for special occasions (one semester)
III. Course Sequence in Theater
   A. First Course in Fundamentals of Speech (required)
   B. Dramatics I
      1. History of the drama
      2. Types of drama
      3. Technique of the playwright
      4. Interpretation of the character through pantomime, voice, diction, characterization, and acting.
      5. Dramatic criticism
   C. Production Techniques
      1. Design
      2. Construction
      3. Make-up
      4. Properties
      5. Costuming

IV. Radio Sequence
  A. First Course in Speech Fundamentals (required)
  B. Radio Announcing and Continuity Writing
  C. Radio Acting
  D. Radio Writing and Production
V. Course Sequence in Interpretation
  A. First Course in Fundamentals (developed through basic skills in oral reading)
  B. Advanced Interpretation
    1. Individual work in poetry
    2. Individual work in prose
  C. Group Interpretation Techniques
    1. Choric interpretation
    2. Reader's theater; chamber theater

Time divisions for these courses may be modified to fit local situations. Many teachers will combine fundamentals and activities in the first course into one semester; they may combine interpretation with theater in the varied course sequence; some may not even be allowed the time to have basic speech courses, but may have to rely upon the integration of speech with English, with social studies, or incorporate it in core programs.

STATE COURSES OF STUDY IN SPEECH

CALIFORNIA: Although no state course of study exists, various publications are available: *Speech Correction in The Elementary School,* Vol. XVII, Bulletin No. 1, 1948, .25; *English Language Arts* in the California Public High Schools, Vol. XXVI, Bulletin No. 7, 1957, .35; and various bulletins in special education, including *Information for Parents of Cerebral Palsied Children,* 1948, .25; *Handbook of Information for the Hard of Hearing,* 1947, .50. Write California State Department of Education, Bureau of Textbooks and Publications, Sacramento 14.

COLORADO: *Speech and Dramatics—A Guide for Secondary Schools in Colorado* (1960). Write: Leo Black, Colorado State Department of Education, Office of Instructional Services, Denver, Colorado.

FLORIDA: Bulletin 34A, *A Guide to Teaching Speech in*

ILLINOIS:

INDIANA:

IOWA:

LOUISIANA:

MICHIGAN:

MISSISSIPPI:

MISSOURI:

Florida Secondary Schools, revised 1954, .55. Write: State Department of Education, Tallahassee.

Communication in the High School Curriculum-Speaking and Listening (1961), Bulletin D–1. Also available: *English Language Communication* (Kindergarten–VI), Bulletin C–Six. Write: Dr. Woodson Fishback, State Co-ordinator of Curriculum, Office of the State Superintendent of Public Instruction, Springfield, Illinois.

The Source Guide for the English Language Arts (1958). Covers elementary and secondary school program. Write: State Department of Public Instruction, Indianapolis, Indiana.

Communication series, *Speech*. Iowa Secondary Schools, January, 1949. Contains: "A Course of Study in Discussion and Debate," "A Course of Study in Interpretation and Drama." Write: Department of Public Instruction, Des Moines.

See *Course of Study in Speech*, State Department of Education, Baton Rouge; also Bulletin 881, *Basic Assumptions, Supported by Suggestions for Language Learning*, 1958, .30. Write: Department of Education, Baton Rouge 4.

Five *Curriculum Guides in Speech:* "Drama," "Interpretation," "Discussion-Debate," "Intermediate School," "Basic Speech for High Schools," published in 1959 by the Michigan Speech Association, 3501 Administration Building, University of Michigan, Ann Arbor, .35 each. Each pamphlet covers a full semester, and contains bibliography, course objectives, activities, teaching procedures, audio-visual materials.

See: *A Suggested Program of Oral Communication for Mississippi Schools*, and *Communication Series: English, Grades 7–12*. State Dept. of Public Instruction, Jackson.

A Guide for Speech, Dramatics, Radio and Television. Publication No. 118–G (1959), Tentative Report. Write: Hubert Wheeler, State Department of Education, Jefferson City, Missouri. Also available: *A Guide for Language Arts, Grades 7, 8, and 9*, from the same office.

MONTANA: See the tentative outline for *A Study Guide in
                    English: Grades 9 and 12*. Written by the State
                    Committee on the Curriculum in English. The sec-
                    tion for each of the four grades contains five or six
                    pages of outline material in speech. Write: De-
                    partment of Public Instruction, Helena.

NEW MEXICO: See *Speech and Drama: Tentative Guide for High
                    School Teachers*. Bulletin No. 14, 1951, $1.25.
                    Write: Superintendent of Public Instruction,
                    Santa Fe.

NEW YORK: *The Syllabus in English, Grades 7 to 12*, (1950),
                    contains a section on oral English. See also *Eng-
                    lish-Speech Language Arts for Senior High
                    Schools*, Curriculum Bulletin 1955–56 Series, No.
                    12, 1956, Board of Education of the City of New
                    York.

NORTH DAKOTA: No state course of study. *A Speech Handbook for
                    Teachers*, .25. See *English Language Arts Course
                    of Study*, 1953. Order from: Dept. of Public In-
                    struction, Bismarck.

SOUTH DAKOTA: See the series of bulletins on *Language Arts for
                    Secondary Schools*, 1947. Bulletin 8C is the most
                    helpful for the teacher of speech. Write: Depart-
                    ment of Public Instruction, Pierre, S.D.

TEXAS: *The Teaching of Speech in the High Schools of
                    Texas*. Write: State Dept. of Public Instruction,
                    Austin, Texas.

VERMONT: New bulletins on *Language Arts in Vermont Ele-
                    mentary Schools* and *Language Arts in Vermont
                    Secondary Schools* are in process of publication.
                    For information write the Division on Instruction,
                    State Department of Education, Montpelier.

WASHINGTON: The Supervisor of Curriculum Guides and Courses
                    of Study writes that the Curriculum Committee is
                    working on Speech for the regular 12th Grade pro-
                    gram. For information write the Superintendent of
                    Public Instruction, Olympia; also Dr. Oliver Nel-
                    son, University of Washington, Seattle.

WISCONSIN: Curriculum Bulletin No. 18, 1948, *Basic Consid-
                    erations in a Functional Speech Program*. Write:
                    Dept. of Public Instruction, Madison 2.

EXERCISES

1. Review sample copies of state courses of study issued by the individual state departments of public instruction. Select a course of study of a particular state and write a critical analysis of your findings.
2. List and describe, with objectives and unit headings, a sequence of courses you would like to see taught in your situation or in a school with which you are familiar.
3. Plan a course of study for a first course in speech on the high school level and include the following material:
   a. Analysis of the situation in which the first course in speech is to be taught.
   b. Broad objectives of the total speech program.
   c. Specific objectives of the first course in speech.
   d. Unit headings arranged in proper teaching order.
   e. Daily lesson plans to be included within each unit of work, with each lesson plan developed as fully as possible.

REFERENCES

ALEXANDER, FRED, and GORDON THOMAS. "The High School Speech Teacher in Michigan," *Speech Teacher,* IX (September, 1960), 189–92.

BORCHERS, GLADYS. "An Experiment in High School Speech Teaching," *Quarterly Journal of Speech,* XXXII (October, 1946), 373–84.

———. "A Reaffirmation in Support of Essentials in Secondary Speech Education," *Speech Teacher,* VIII (November, 1959), 300–303.

COMMITTEE OF THE AMERICAN EDUCATIONAL THEATRE ASSOCIATION. "Dramatics in the Secondary School," *Bulletin of the National Association of Secondary School Principals,* XXXIII, No. 166 (December, 1949).

CRANDELL, S. JUDSON. "Teaching of Public Speaking in High School," *Quarterly Journal of Speech,* XXVIII (December, 1942), 477–83.

FRIEDERICH, WILLARD. *The High School Drama Course.* Cincinnati: National Thespian Society, 1956.

HANCE, KENNETH. "The Character of the Beginning Course: Skills and/or Content," *Speech Teacher,* X (September, 1961), 220–25.

HARGIS, DONALD. "A Selected Bibliography on the 'First Course,' " *Speech Teacher,* III (November, 1954), 252–54.

———. "The First Course in Speech," *Speech Teacher,* V (January, 1956), 26–33.

KENNER, FREDA. "Speech in Messick High School," *Speech Teacher,* VI (November, 1957), 298–99.

KERIKAS, E. J. "Current Status of Speech Education in the Public Secondary Schools of the Intermountain States." Unpublished Ph.D. dissertation, Northwestern University, 1962.

KNOWER, FRANKLIN. "Source Materials for Speech in the Secondary Schools," *Quarterly Journal of Speech,* XXXIV (February, 1950), 94–100.

JONES, H. RODMAN. "The Development and Present Status of Beginning Speech Courses in the Colleges and Universities in the United States." Unpublished doctoral dissertation, Northwestern University, 1953.

McNESS, WILMA. "An Orientation Course in Creative Skills for First Year Junior High School Students," *Speech Teacher,* I (November, 1952), 279–87.

NATIONAL COUNCIL OF TEACHERS OF ENGLISH. *The English Language Arts in the Secondary School.* Committee on the English Curriculum, Curriculum Series No. 3, 1956.

NELSON, OLIVER. "An Evaluation of High School Speech Training in Washington," *Speech Teacher,* IX (September, 1960), 180–89.

NICHOLS, RALPH. "Material for Courses in Communication," *Quarterly Journal of Speech,* XXXVIII (December, 1952), 465–69.

REID, RONALD, and RAYMOND ROBERTS. "A Survey of Fundamentals of Speech Courses in Missouri Public High Schools," *Speech Teacher,* VII (November, 1958), 320–23.

ROBERTS, ROWENA. "Speech through Correlation," *Speech Teacher,* VI (November, 1957), 292–97.

SANTIAGO, FLORENCE (compiler). *Inexpensive or Free Materials Useful for Teaching Speech: A Source List for Secondary Schools.* Ann Arbor, Mich.: Braun-Brumfield, Inc., 1959.

SECONDARY SCHOOL INTEREST GROUP OF SAA. "Fundamentals of Speech: A Basic Course for High Schools," *Speech Teacher,* VIII (March, 1959), 93–113.

CHAPTER SIX

Developing Cocurricular Activity
and Contest Programs

Most total programs of speech education include organized courses in the regular curricular pattern plus cocurricular activity and contest programs. This chapter will develop the place of such types of speech training and show their relationship to the materials discussed in Chapter V.

Present estimates are that approximately 50 per cent of all speech training in secondary schools is done through activities and contests, with a somewhat smaller percentage in colleges. Therefore, it is of great importance that teachers know the scope and nature of these areas and possess a sound point of view as a basis for planning and administering such programs.

THE NATURE OF ACTIVITIES AND CONTESTS

Speech *activities* include *all* organized, group, or individual speech performances conducted *in* or *outside* the classroom. Conversation, interviewing, and storytelling are more typically classroom experiences than others which occur as extraclass experiences as well. Extemporaneous speaking, discussion, interpretative reading, choric interpretation, parliamentary procedure, debating, and one-act plays are in this group. Activities also *may be interscholastic* in character, when schools agree to hold conferences or festivals which promote their practice. Interpretative reading, plays, and discussion are frequently so organized. The speech activities developed in Part Three provide rich experiences useful in basic courses for teaching or supplementing fundamentals of speech. The teacher will be able to adapt these materials readily to his situation.

135

Almost any speech *activity* can become a *contest* if the *element of competition for a decision or award* is introduced. A contest then is a speech activity organized with the goal of winning local, district, regional, state or national honors. Certain activities traditionally have been so conducted, debating being a good example. Others occur as festivals *or* as contests. Interpretation and one-act plays are of this type.

The resourceful teacher includes many activities in his classroom program; he employs others as extraclass experiences or contests as local philosophy, interest, or tradition indicate. In many schools such activity-contest phases are more extensively organized and more strongly supported than the curricular speech program. In others they *are* the program, no classwork being in existence. A thorough knowledge of this field is therefore invaluable to the high school and college teacher.

Speech contests are as old as mankind. Aristotle mentions disputation and debate as teaching devices in ancient Greece. Syllogistic and forensic disputations, early forms of debate, were in use in the United States as early as 1716 at Harvard, as outside-class and commencement exercises. Other colleges, including Yale, Brown, Rhode Island, and Princeton, also used these forms. Orations were included in colonial training. Debate and literary societies were also a chief source of forensic training for many years.

According to Trueblood, the first intercollegiate debate was held in 1892 between Yale and Harvard. However, records show that Northwestern University debated Chicago on October 10, 1873.[1] Other midwestern activity in forensics took place in 1881 between Illinois College and Knox College. Illinois won the debate, but Knox was victorious in essay, declamation, and oratory.[2]

From these beginnings a great variety of activities has developed.

PURPOSES AND VALUES

Activities and contests have three similar general purposes: (1) to arouse interest in speech; (2) to give training in speech performance; (3) to contribute to the general education of high school stu-

[1] James McBurney, J. M. O'Neill, and Glen Mills, *Argumentation and Debate* (New York: The Macmillan Co., 1951), p. 265.

[2] David Potter (ed.), *Argumentation and Debate* (New York: Dryden Press, 1954), pp. 12, 13.

dents. In addition, *contests* have one more: (4) to motivate speech development to a high level of skill among participants because of *competition*. An activity program widens the base for participation by removing competition which tends to restrict members in the effort to train fewer persons more intensively. There should be less pressure in activity programs; all can take part and learn through a desire to enjoy and do well. Most schools combine activity and contest programs.

Training in activities and contests provides these specific values to students who participate:

1. Of the extraclass possibilities, among the most practical are extemporaneous speaking, debating, and discussion. A case can be made for oratory and for oratorical declamation, but certainly they are less functional in the lives of students than are the three above.

2. Specifically, training through experiences can:
   a. Contribute to the total growth of the student.
   b. Insure increased speaking skill in the individual.
   c. Provide essential theory and specialized techniques of debate, discussion, and conference that are directly useful in our democracy.
   d. Develop skill in reflective thinking, reasoning, and the use of evidence.
   e. Stimulate an understanding of and consideration for the opinions of others.
   f. Develop the ability to work cooperatively with other people.

3. In addition to these basic goals, forensic programs can realistically meet the demands of our society through providing both special techniques for *cooperative* deliberation in seeking solutions for problems and *competitive* techniques including the tools of advocacy which are essential in meeting situations in which cooperation *alone* does not suffice. Furthermore, such speech contests can and should provide a code of ethics and sportsmanship with respect to the use of these techniques in school situations and later in life situations.

4. Interpretative activities, dramatic work, and radio or television performance are useful means of developing taste and appreciation for good literature and are suitable vehicles for sharing it through oral presentation in small groups, from the school stage and/or

studio. They also help to provide criteria by which students may judge plays in the commercial theater, pictures at the local movie house, radio and television programs heard in the home and school. The evaluation and criticism of performance to which participants in the interpretative, dramatic, and radio or television activities are inevitably subjected make them keenly aware of the weaknesses existing in these related commercial media. Through the demand of performance and production, interpretative activities also develop initiative, responsibility, and cooperativeness in human relationships. They can also serve as professional and vocational orientation for many pupils who participate.

A POINT OF VIEW TOWARD ACTIVITIES AND CONTESTS

A practical point of view underlies sound philosophy regarding activities and contests. Every teacher needs to establish such a basis for his program.

Speech contests and activities are a definite part of the total program of speech education because of the possibilities expressed in the objectives above. However, contests serve *best* the purpose of training students with superior *ability* and *interest in speech. They are in no sense a substitute for an integrated, well-coordinated program of speech instruction in the secondary school or college on the curricular basis.* Sound educational philosophy does not indicate the expansion of contest programs merely to give more training to more students. The logical solution for that point is to provide adequate classroom and course work for the great majority of "normal" students in speech who need increased proficiency and to allow those in the special-interest and ability group to be the principal recipients of further instruction via contest programs.

Speech contests or activities are not the *sole end* of speech instruction. They are merely *one* of the possible agencies by which schools can reach a relatively small proportion of the total school population which needs and wants training. They should be only a *part* of a well-planned and integrated speech program. The bulk of instruction belongs in the speech classroom. As course work is expanded in the curricular scheme, speech contests should serve *principally* as a training ground for the specially talented students and as a source of interest and motivation for the whole program. Activities can be sponsored for special-interest groups. However, until the cooperation of pupil, parent, teacher, and administration furnish *time in the regular classroom schedule, money for facilities and equipment, and trained personnel to teach the courses,* speech contests will *of necessity* have a more prominent place than would otherwise be indicated. Until these possibilities are realized, schools cannot hope to achieve the type of speech education that will be of service to the greatest number of students in the secondary school or college.

KINDS OF ACTIVITIES AND CONTESTS

Forensic Activities

1. *Extempore Speaking*

Since 1926 extempore speaking has been a part of many speech programs. It consists of the preparation and delivery of an extempore speech varying in length from six to ten minutes, depending upon local regulations. The speech is based upon a previous period of wide reading by the student; the specific speech is prepared in a relatively short period of time just previous to the contest. The time interval for preparation is usually not in excess of one hour. The topics upon which the individuals speak are drawn from the reading of the speaker. Two methods have been most common in the assigned reading. First, a general subject of interest has been selected. For example, the question of conservation of national resources was used at one time. On another occasion, the subject of federal world government was taken. The most common method is to designate subjects taken from the daily press or from particular news publications during a selected period of time preceding the contest. When the contest is held, each student usually draws three topics by lot from a large number of specific subjects prepared by the coaches' committee or the state headquarters of the speech organization conducting the contest. The contestant takes his choice of one of these subjects and prepares his talk. During this period of preparation he is free to use the library or his own notes. In the actual delivery of the final speech, contestants are judged on standard criteria with respect to composition and delivery for a good extempore speech. A strict check is also maintained upon time limits. In some instances, a minimum, as well as a maximum, time is set, with penalties established if either limit is violated. In certain states, contestants question each other after the speech and a rejoinder is required to these questions. Both the prepared talk and the question period are included in judging the contest.

Extempore speaking is popular both as an activity and as a contest with high school and college students. It has excellent potentialities in the development of speaking ability in real communicative situations. It is equally useful in a class in public speaking or as a club or after-school activity for training students in quick organization of materials and adaptable delivery. This activity, developed as a protest against the standardized type of old-time oratory, is the heart of basic speech training.

2. Oratory

Oratory is an activity in which the student writes, memorizes, and then delivers a persuasive speech arising from his personal feelings, convictions, or a "source of irritation" about some problem. In best practice it is not a display of exhibitory speaking, although this unfortunate concept has often been held by laymen. Oratory which is well-handled gives the student an opportunity to investigate a problem about which he feels deeply. It necessitates careful organization of his information. It requires skillful writing in order to achieve desirable oral style. It demands straightforward, sincere, communicative delivery that is not artificial or burdened with ornamentation. To the extent that the student has attempted to follow such a formula, oratory is an exceedingly profitable experience. To the extent that the oration becomes a coach-written project, the only motivation for which is accurate memorization and mechanical delivery, it loses its value. Oratory can also be handled as an activity; as persuasive speaking it is often taught in the classroom in advanced work in public speaking.

3. Analysis of Public Address

This new event, used successfully in Oklahoma, is an attempt to train students in analyzing and criticizing outstanding speeches. First, it demands much research in the library in finding and selecting suitable examples of public address. Next, it requires careful analysis of organization and content. Then the student must evaluate or criticize the selection. Finally, he prepares a ten-minute speech in which he presents his findings to the audience. He is judged on his choice of speech, background information, the composition of his analysis, and his delivery of his analysis. Guides to this event are available in the *Official Handbook of the Oklahoma High School Speech League:* James Robinson, Director, University of Oklahoma, Norman, Oklahoma.

4. Debating

Debating is a group speech activity. The original purpose in the development of debating was to provide a technique for training students in argumentation. The present orthodox or traditional high-school debate is a direct, oral contest on a given proposition between two teams, usually in the presence of judges. *The debater in school and in life starts with a proposition and, in an effort to win a decision, organizes his arguments as skillfully as possible to support his position.* The standard number of speakers on each team is two. Most debates have constructive speeches of eight to ten minutes in length, rebuttals from three to five minutes.

There are many variations of the standard debate described above. Lahman [3] lists some twenty-one types, to which others have been added. Among these are the cross-question, direct clash, split-team, and heckling debates. The most popular has been the cross-examination or Oregon-style debate. The original plan provided that a member of one team be permitted to cross-examine a member of the opposing team. Usually the debate proceeds through three phases: (1) constructive speech for each side; (2) cross-examination of opening speakers by opponents; (3) rebuttal-summary by the two cross-examiners.

Newer variations include the jury-trial debate and the problem-solving debate.

Because of its team aspects and the wide use of extempore speaking in debate, this activity has become one of the most valuable in the development of individuals who are analytical and discerning in their thinking, thoroughly conversant with techniques of argu-

[3] Carroll Lahman, *Debate Coaching* (New York: H. W. Wilson Co., 1936), pp. 21–65.

mentation, and particularly skilled in adaptation to meet the arguments of their opponents.

5. *Discussion*

Discussion is becoming a popular activity in secondary schools and colleges today. There are a number of reasons for this popularity: first, the problem can be considered from a variety of points of view, not from the affirmative and negative alone; second, the "final decision" or competitive factor of debating is avoided; third, it is an important method of solving problems and of sharing information and opinions.

In discussion the participants start with *a problem* for which they are seeking the *best solution.* In debating the speakers start with a *proposition* for which they seek *acceptance and a decision.* The organization of group discussions or tournaments follows quite closely John Dewey's five-step analysis of reflective thinking. A standard pattern uses this sequence: (1) statement of the problem; (2) analysis; (3) proposal of solutions; (4) evaluations of solutions and selection of one; (5) specific recommendations for putting the solution into action, which are presented in a final session of all participants.

Discussion activities have followed such patterns as the symposium, the intercollegiate forum, the discussion progression, and the panel discussion. A current plan provides for study of a discussion problem ahead of regular contest debating. Students also prepare three suggested debate questions on the same problem. One is selected as a proposition for tournament competition. This directs more emphasis to discussion as a complementary activity for debate. Many high schools have used this plan. There are some attempts made to combine discussion with debate and parliamentary procedure in such meetings as the Student Congress of the National Forensic League, the Delta Sigma Rho Congress, and the convention plan of debating. The essence of this plan is that several debaters from each of a large number of schools organize themselves along the lines of the United States Congress or a state legislature. They usually meet for a period of two to three days. During that time several problems are discussed, debated, and acted upon. Students first attack problems in committees where, after discussion, bills are formulated. Committee bills are reported to the whole assembly, where they are debated under parliamentary rules, possibly amended, accepted, or rejected.

Because the various forms of discussion and debate provide practical tools for use by the average citizen in communication situations, these activities have been increasing in popularity. Discussion on the radio, or television, or in forums increases community interest and is an extremely useful method in adult education.

6. *After-Dinner Speaking*

After-dinner speaking is another common type of speaking activity, although it is not quite as extensively developed as extempore speaking. It is often treated in the regular course in public speaking as one type of occasional speech. In the contest or activity program, it becomes a specialized kind of performance. In a forensic tournament or festival, schools are invited to enter their representatives, who speak at a general dinner session. The usual method is to assign a general theme or subject. The speeches are all related to this theme. Judging is done by coaches of the schools entered or, occasionally, by outside critics.

When organized on a local basis, after-dinner speaking is usually employed at dinners or banquets held for special school occasions, as a part of holiday celebrations, or at certain community functions. Under these conditions, there is no formalized judging, but the audience response is an indication of the success of the speaker. This type of speaking activity is popular with high school and college students because of the humorous touch it involves and the association with food, which is always appealing. Therefore, it is frequently a part of classroom instruction.

Interpretative Activities

1. *Declamation*

Some persons are inclined to classify declamation as a "forensic activity," but it is merely the delivery of content, written by some other person, which has been memorized by the speaker or reader. There is no great stress placed upon the compositional aspects of the work. The performer's first interest is in making an effective delivery or interpretation of the content he selects.

There are three standard types of declamation used primarily in secondary school speech activities: (1) the *oratorical declamation,* which requires the selection of a public speech, careful memorization, and delivery (This type of declamation is sometimes classified as a forensic activity because it utilizes public-speaking material); (2) the *humorous declamation,* which necessitates the selection of a piece of prose or poetry regarded as funny by the contestant and his coach or teacher (This, like the oratorical declamation, is memorized and delivered with appropriate interpretation); (3) the *dramatic declamation,* which demands the choice of a piece of prose material or a cutting from a play and has certain essential dramatic qualities that the contestant strives to convey to his audience. Declamatory contests are carefully organized with definite restrictions on length of time of the selections and specific judging requirements on the delivery of a selection. In cases where the choice of material is poor or preparation has merely stressed the mechanistic aspects of delivery, performances are highly exhibitory and artificial.

The declamatory contest is highly organized in some localities: contestants move through a series of subdistrict and district contests to a state, regional, and national final performance. Thousands of students participate annually. Efforts are being made to raise the quality of declamatory selections presented by participants so that materials from good works of literature will be used, such as cuttings from short stories, plays, novels, or essays, rather than commercialized, oversentimental selections written for the commercial market. On the activity level, declamation and "elocution" have been with us a long time. Unless the work is unusually well done, it is an exhibitory activity lacking the motivation of good communication. Under such conditions, it exists only because of the patience of the audience, the enthusiasm of a somewhat misguided teacher, and the naïve trust of the "piece-speaker." From the point of view of speech education, declamation is a technique of training people in delivery. If the materials used do not stimulate or enrich the background of the student, it is obvious that training in speaking can be obtained more effectively by other speech activities.

2. *Individual Interpretation*

Individual oral reading or interpretation has many similarities to declamation. It involves choosing a literary selection and reading it so that the audience re-creates the content. In some localities memorization of this material is permitted. In many other sections of the country, interpretation requires a *reading from a manuscript.*

This activity has been organized both on a contest and a festival basis. In the contest situation winners are chosen after the selections are prepared, presented, and judged on their delivery. These may proceed through a series of subcontests to a final state contest. The festival type of organization also allows students to read their selections and receive an evaluation on their performances which is based on the standards of good interpretation. But in these events no winner is picked. A considerable number of students may be rated as *superior, excellent, good,* or some other designation. The emphasis is placed upon the sharing of literature by oral interpretation rather than upon winning. The University of Iowa, for example, holds an annual festival for high schools in which each contestant reads a prepared selection of poetry and a prepared selection of prose. Each student then reads *impromptu* a selection from an anthology designated by the state association. Participants first read their materials before groups of five to eight persons, and a critic appraises each individual. At the conclusion of this, all evaluations are tabulated and a general program is held in which students who have received superior ratings read for the entire group. In Illinois, students can participate in verse reading, prose reading, serious reading and comedy reading, and original monologue. State winners are chosen. Other states such as Texas and Oklahoma declare state winners in these events.

3. *Choric Interpretation*

This is a group form in which more than one person interprets the same piece of literature at the same time. Large groups are common, but duets, trios, and quartets may be used. In ancient times it was used extensively in Greek drama. From the time of its contemporary popularity in England, it has gained interest among school and adult groups. It is a method of developing an appreciation of good literature, of motivating speech improvement, and of teaching skills in interpretation. The material is usually poetry, although other types of literature are read. The teacher either chooses selections or consults with students on the literature used. The selections are then arranged for choric reading with suitable parts for types of voices, for solos, and for ensemble reading.

Choric interpretation allows large numbers of students to take part in interpretation, helps them to improve personal speech habits, and aims at a high quality of performance. Audiences also enjoy this activity.

4. Reader's Theater

Another group form of interpretation now becoming well known and accepted is reader's theater, in which several interpreters present a work of literature so that each performer does only one role. The most common types of literature used are drama and poetry, although prose is sometimes employed.

The methods of reader's theater are essentially dramatic, but differ from acting in that the characters and situations are merely *suggested* by each reader. The lines need not be memorized but the reader should be familiar enough with his material so that the script does not hinder his suggestion of character.

The emphasis in reader's theater lies upon the language of the play, plus the voices of the readers. Thus a play with exceptional dialogue and good interpreters should be a suitable vehicle. Usually reader's theater productions are presented without the aid of properties. However, reading stands or high stools are often used and help to establish the importance of the various characters. Dark-colored notebooks appropriately cover the scripts in order not to distract audience attention from the presentation. Costumes, as such, are not needed although dress should suggest the characters. Color is important in setting mood or feeling. Straight make-up is used.

Using this form of interpretation, an entire play or suitable cutting may be presented simply, quickly, yet effectively by a group of readers. Reader's theater is a very usable speech activity because it permits the use of a number of students, is low budget, needs no properties, costumes, or lights. It employs fine literature; it can be done with less rehearsal than a fully staged dramatic production; and it is very much enjoyed by audiences.

5. Chamber Theater

Another group form somewhat in the experimental stage has been developed by Professor Robert Breen of Northwestern University.[4]

[4] See Wallace Bacon and Robert Breen, *Literature as Experience* (New York: McGraw-Hill Book Co., Inc., 1959).

Chamber theater utilizes several interpreters to present a piece of nondramatic prose literature (a portion of a novel or a short story) in *dramatic form*. Dialogue taken directly from the text or edited suitably for this vehicle is employed. The readers interpret lines and carry out, rather than merely suggest, action. However, there is the added possibility, in this form, of exploring the internal motivation of the character (much as the prose author would do with his comments and description) through a narrator or "central intelligence" who ties together the action and lines of the other characters. He acts as a sort of thinking camera who "sees all and knows all." As part of a chamber theater production he can bring his observations and images to the audience, either through narration or acting.

Rules and guides are very flexible. Those using this form must be willing to sacrifice conventions in production, giving attention to verbal presentation, plus the action the director considers appropriate to the characterization. This experimental form is gaining definition and popularity as it develops.

Like reader's theater, chamber theater is a group activity that has numerous similar advantages for speech training because of its characteristics in preparation and performance.

Dramatic Activities

1. *The One-Act Play Contest (or Festival)*

The principal dramatic vehicle employed for contest or festival purposes is the one-act play. Schools entering this activity select a play which they believe has good possibilities (in some states a list of approved or recommended plays is provided by the state interscholastic organization). They then cast their piece; rehearse it; prepare properties, lighting, and scenery; and develop the best dramatic production of which they are capable. The show is then taken to the contest, where it is judged by experts in theater upon such qualities as acting, characterization, dialogue, lighting, setting, and total effectiveness. The judges may declare a winner or merely give the production a quality rating. In either case, it is possible for superior shows to be selected for the next round in contest or festival procedure.

In many localities the contest has given way to the festival plan in order to remove the need for designating only *one* production as worthy of top ranking or of presentation in a subsequent meeting. In either case the one-act play activity may be, and frequently is, carried as far as the state or national meeting where winning or highest-rating productions are presented, evaluated, and given suitable recognition for superior work in the various aspects of theater.

Among the states holding such activities are Texas, Illinois, Tennessee, and Oklahoma, to mention only a few. Schools participating in the one-act play competitions may do this in lieu of course work in drama or in addition to it.

2. *Three-Act Plays and Other Full-Length Productions*

Thousands of secondary schools and colleges present three-act plays as part of the speech activities program. These are done for school and community audiences. In many places these are the only live theater available to the public. There is scarcely a person, recalling high school days, who is not familiar with the senior class play, or more recently, the all-school production.

Some idea of the tremendous scope of this activity can be gained from this quotation from Rufus Jarman:

Not more than 2,000,000 Americans see professional plays of Broadway caliber regularly, and only about 5,000,000 see them occasionally. When Broadway numbers its actors by the hundreds, the huge amateur theater counts its performers by the hundreds of thousands and its audiences by the tens of millions. Its playwrights, unknown to the Great White Way, sometimes turn out a play that has 10,000 or more performances, which is more than Rodgers and Hammerstein ever did. Last year an estimated 100,000,000 Americans, counting repeaters, attended between 350,000 and 500,000 plays by amateur groups. The largest single group in this field of play givers was the nation's high schools, which, during 1950, produced about 75,000 full-length plays. These were viewed by between 18,000,000 and 25,000,000 persons.[5]

In 1960–61, with 1,560 of 2,221 schools reporting, the National Thespian Society recorded 2,871 full-length plays, 251 children's theater productions, 1,443 musicals, operettas, pageants, and 3,773 one-act plays. Projected *modestly* to all schools, these figures could

[5] Rufus Jarman, "To Heck with Broadway!" *Saturday Evening Post* (April 28, 1951), pp. 22–23.

each be multiplied by *ten* to give estimated totals. A very conservative total could be close to 100,000.

Some schools have no organized dramatics program. In such situations, the theater work is on an activity basis. In schools having an organized drama program, it is the usual practice to do most of the production of plays as after-school activities, with course work providing training for persons who take part in these shows.

Radio and Television Activities

Although these media have unusual possibilities for motivating and training students in speech, relatively few high schools have *courses* in radio; even fewer have television *courses*. The reasons for this situation are the same: the cost of equipment, limitations of time in the curricular pattern, the scarcity of available teaching personnel, and the greater priority of other less complicated activities in the speech program.

Because radio and television have great appeal to students, there has been a development of them as extraclass experiences that are achievable in club or workshop programs or station projects.

One possibility open to a great many schools is to secure time on a commercial radio or television station near at hand, thus providing an outlet for training and programs. Another, especially in radio, is the building of a school FM station. At times, in school systems using newer methods of teaching, closed-circuit television equipment is available. A third, confined to radio, is the use of a public-address system of some sort for in-school broadcasting. This involves the school hookup or may employ a tape recorder used to tape programs, and a playback through the unit for class or school listening.

Colleges face a somewhat different situation. If their plans in communications or speech training include radio and television, they will have radio or television equipment used for *course* instruction and available for a variety of activities. If they have no such facilities, they will move toward the types of programs mentioned in high schools without equipment.

At present the contest field shows rather limited development in these areas.

1. *Individual Performance*

Some localities conduct an activity designated as radio speaking, announcing, or newscasting. The National Forensic League uses this in its national meet. Illinois uses a newscast containing an event broadcast "on the spot" with commercials prepared by the contestant. Iowa has asked the participant to prepare an original expository manuscript not more than three to four minutes in length. This presentation of the prepared copy constitutes one part of the performance for the individual, whose work is evaluated by critics who listen to his reading in another studio. The second part of his responsibility is to "read cold" a two-minute section from the teletyped news dispatches. In recent years, these performances have been put on closed-circuit television. All of these are heard or viewed by critics and are judged according to appropriate criteria and standards.

2. *Prepared Shows*

The prepared radio program, usually a dramatic show, is also entering the contest field in college and university broadcasting. In organization, this competition somewhat resembles the one-act play contest. Time of the shows is restricted, usually to fifteen or thirty minutes. Schools write and produce their own scripts. These are recorded on disc or tape. Shows are judged on script, continuity, music, sound, acting, direction, and other elements in radio production by critics listening over a studio speaker system. Best-performance awards are given or winners designated.

While this activity has not, as yet, been taken up by secondary schools, it may be a possibility in the future. National and local script-writing contests are held for secondary school students.

3. *FM Station Activities*

Schools having their own stations utilize the broadcasts as community service and public-relations vehicles. They have been found useful in interpreting the work of the school to the public, at the same time providing training to students in broadcasting and station operation. Elgin, Illinois, and New Trier High School at Winnetka, Illinois, are among the schools having such activities.

To the person reading the preceding pages, speech contests and activities will appear to be numerous. This is true, but certain facts regarding their development and status should be noted. Regardless of rapid expansion in some areas, the field of speech is still in the process of development. Administrators often find strong community interest and demand by students for training in speech skills. Usually school executives have chosen to "go easy," making use of existing faculty and facilities. As a result, the *only* speech instruction given in certain schools has been via speech contests (or activities). This is still true in many localities. Many extraclass programs have proved to be the starting point for curricular speech programs. The interest aroused among the students, plus their genuine realization of the benefits of speech training, has produced a demand for classes in speech capable of reaching larger numbers than could be accommodated in the competitive speech activities. However, from the point of view of the administrator in the high school, speech contests and activities have become an expedient method of giving training to certain students on extraclass time. Relatively moderate demands were made on school budgets because the director of these programs did not receive additional compensation, even though it was merited; he did this work in addition to classroom teaching. Also, such programs often became useful public-relations devices in schools where administrators desired to emphasize winning or to exhibit talented students. All of these considerations have tended to keep much speech activity on the extraclass rather than on the curricular level.

SECONDARY SCHOOL PROGRAMS

State Organizations

From this kind of development has come nationwide expansion to the point where there are now forensic or speech leagues in approximately forty-four states, most of them under the direction of officials in university extension divisions. The National University Extension Association (NUEA) has for many years been instrumental in the development of state forensic and speech organizations. Its attention was first directed to the educational possibilities of this work in 1928. At this time debaters from Suffolk High School in Virginia, who had won the championship of Virginia, met debaters from Hartshorne High School, Oklahoma, who were the champions from their state in a national championship before the House of Representatives in Washington, D. C. Influenced by this, Professor Ted Beaird of the University of Oklahoma Extension Division presented to the NUEA the idea of a national championship high school debate tournament.

He was placed in charge of this project and ran it for several years. The National Forensic League, an independent speech organization, added other speech events which it still sponsors.

The headquarters of the NUEA Committee on Debate Materials and Inter-state Co-operation is located at the office of the Extension Division of a major university. This helps to explain the sponsorship of the greater number of speech organizations by extension divisions. Examples of such leagues are those in Michigan, Wisconsin, Oklahoma, Texas, and Kansas. In other states, sponsorship of speech work is included with all other high school activities such as music and athletics. This situation exists, for example, in Minnesota, South Dakota, and Illinois.

Membership in these leagues is quite large. Texas, which has the largest, had a membership of twenty-eight schools in 1910 and over six thousand just previous to World War II. Present membership runs between two thousand and three thousand schools, the reduction being the result of consolidation of school districts. This league has competition in debating, extemporaneous speaking, declamation, and one-act plays in the high school speech field. It also has contests in storytelling, spelling and plain writing, number sense, slide rule, typewriting, shorthand, journalism, band, orchestra, vocal music, baton twirling, music appreciation, football, basketball, tennis, volleyball, track and field, playground baseball, and baseball. These additional activities are mentioned to illustrate the scope and development of the Texas League. Many states such as Wisconsin and Michigan have two to three hundred member schools each year.

Typical speech activities in most leagues include debating, oratory, declamation (humorous, dramatic, and oratorical), extempore speaking, interpretative reading, and one-act plays.

Each association has a printed or mimeographed publication which describes its organization. In it are the constitution and rules, which cover purpose, membership, officers, types of activities and contests, regional and district divisions, dates of meets and tournaments, eligibility requirements, regulations for conducting the contests, selection of judges, judging, financial arrangements, awards, names of member schools, previous winners and top-ranking schools, and suggestions for the preparation and training of students. These are distributed to affiliating schools, with library materials supplied by the state and national extension associations.

Privately Sponsored Organizations

In addition to the state associations, there are three high school speech organizations, privately sponsored, which function in the contest and activity area. These are the National Forensic League, the National Thespian Society, and Masque and Gavel.

1. National Forensic League

The National Forensic League is a society whose purpose is "to train youth for leadership through developing their skill in effective speech." It was organized in 1925 as an honor society to recognize achievement primarily in the field of contest speech. At that time it had a membership of twenty-four chapters in fifteen states. Today it has an organization of over 150,000 active and alumni members. It added approximately 15,000 new members in 1962. A quota holds its active chapters to 1,000, with 200 affiliate chapters standing by for charters. It recognizes attainment of students through a point system with degrees of Honor, Excellence, and Distinction, each having awards of a key and a certificate. It holds state or district tournaments in debate, extemporaneous speaking, original oratory, and oratorical, dramatic, and humorous interpretation. The National Speech Tournament held annually includes debate, original oratory, extemporaneous speaking, dramatic interpretation, radio, and poetry. The NFL Student Congress is held concurrently, giving training in all the aforementioned forms of public speaking, as well as in discussion and parliamentary practice. Increasing interest and expansion is reported in debate and student congress.

A local chapter of NFL pays a fee for a charter, which is renewable every three years. Members pay single life-membership fees and the cost of the honor keys they earn. The society furnishes guides for chapter organization, materials for contestants and coaches, keys, cups, banners, and certificates, and the working plan for its contest organization. A system of state chairmen and an elected district committee provide the operational personnel. The association is headed by an executive council of which the Honorable Karl E. Mundt, senator from South Dakota, is president. Professor Bruno Jacob, Ripon College, Ripon, Wisconsin, is the executive secretary. Its official publication, *The Rostrum,* contains chapter news, standings, announcements, and occasional articles.

2. *National Thespian Society*

The National Thespian Society is an educational organization of teachers and students, established for the advancement of dramatic arts in the secondary schools. The aims of the society are twofold: (1) to establish and advance standards of excellence in all phases of dramatic arts, and (2) to create an active and intelligent interest in dramatic arts among boys and girls in the high schools. The society was established in the spring of 1929 and today has an active and alumni membership of over 411,000. The active working unit in the organization is the chapter or troupe, of which there are 2,221 (1962) in the fifty states, Panama Canal Zone, Canada, Greece, and Okinawa. The society is an "honor" or "recognition" society in the sense that students are granted membership for having performed meritorious work in dramatic arts and for having met the membership qualifications and standards of their respective troupes. However, the National Thespian Society is, in the truest sense, a service organization. Through a board of expert advisers it provides without charge to its members services on all phases of play production: play selection, casting, rehearsals, acting, lighting, stagecraft, make-up, costuming, publicity, and handbills. It also provides expert advisory service and materials on all phases of dramatic-arts work at the secondary school level: (1) how to teach high school dramatics; (2) suggested courses in dramatics; (3) organization of the dramatics club; (4) organization of the play production staff; (5) organization of drama festivals; (6) participation in drama festivals; (7) equipment for the high school stage; (8) play lists. Finally, the society aids in effecting savings in the play-production budget in high school; royalties on plays are reduced; a free library loan service is maintained; discounts are secured on stage equipment and supplies; and complimentary publications are distributed to all troupes. The secretary-treasurer and editor of its publications, Leon C. Miller, has his office at College Hill Station, Cincinnati 24, Ohio. Students pay only a single life-membership fee. The official publication, *Dramatics*, is published eight times yearly. It contains chapter notes and pictures of interest as well as many articles of service character for the secondary school teacher. The advisory board of thirteen editors contributes these articles.

3. Masque and Gavel

The third society, Masque and Gavel, has stressed participation and an activity-program approach rather than competition as the basis for its organization. Its slogan, "Speech for use—nationally recognized," epitomizes the principle for which it stands. Organized in 1941, it has among its honorary founders Edgar Bergen, John Mason Brown, H. V. Kaltenborn, and Lew Sarett. Its membership has grown to approximately three hundred chapters. It gives points and awards for all-school activities, class and home-room participation, community service, and interschool performance. All types of speech activities are recognized. Members pay a single life-membership fee with no dues or assessments. Its publication is *Masque and Gavel,* which contains chapter news and service articles for students and teachers. The national president is Mary Blackburn, Community High School, Granite City, Illinois. Harold Green, Evanston, Illinois, is the permanent executive secretary.

Summer Institutes and Annual Workshops

A significant influence upon secondary school speech training has been the increasing number of summer institutes. Some are national and some statewide in their membership. Northwestern University, which originated the plan in 1931 on a national basis, has had thirty-two consecutive programs. It now serves 200 high school juniors each summer. They live on campus for a period of five weeks. During this time they get a preview of college, devoting their full time to a mastery of basic speech skills and one special area of their choice—debate and public address; theater; radio-television-film. Classwork and terminal projects are done in each field as demonstrations for university students and the public. Institute members also gain general cultural enrichment through trips, lectures, contact with leaders in the field, musical and dramatic productions in the metropolitan area. On returning to their local high schools, students are in a position to provide leadership in speech education and in other school activities. This pattern is typical of institute programs.

There are now over fifty summer institutes from Florida to California. Individual schools have developed their own special programs.

Other schools having institutes of long standing include the State University of Iowa, Denver University, Kent State University, Baylor University, the University of Illinois, the University of Colorado, Montana State University, and Florida State University.

Workshops and conferences held during the year at various schools provide another important service. In general, these may be distinguished from regularly scheduled tournaments or festivals in state leagues, NFL, or other privately sponsored agencies. The principal purpose of the workshop is to help students learn the theory and skills of speech activities and gain an orientation to the place they occupy in secondary education. Many conferences of this type are slanted to help beginning students. However, others emphasize and study the special problems of experienced participants. Colleges and universities organize their workshops on a convenient time schedule to permit large numbers of students to attend. Areas covered may include debate and discussion, individual forensic events, interpretation with both individual or group forms, theater, and radio or television. A typical program consists of lectures by experts in the field with question periods following, demonstrations by university students or professional performers, critiques and discussions of the performances, and sometimes performance by high school students attending, which are evaluated by specialists in the speech field. An added feature of such workshops may include an outstanding university speech event such as an international or varsity debate, a university theater performance, a lecture recital by an outstanding interpreter, a reader's theater or choric interpretation program, and so on.

Used to supplement the usual tournament or organized festival programs in a region, workshops provide valuable aid to speech education. Teachers and students should attend them.

All these organizations, both state and privately sponsored, contribute a great deal to the training of students in speech through the contests and activities they promote. They represent a part of speech education that reaches thousands of secondary school pupils each year. In the majority of localities they are administered efficiently for the benefit of the schools, teachers, and students involved. However, it is very important that the teacher see them and their work as part of a total speech program. The next section sets forth a similar description of college programs.

COLLEGE AND UNIVERSITY PROGRAMS

State Organizations

Many states have intercollegiate speech organizations. These are not sponsored by NUEA or by a particular institution. They are usually independent leagues organized under a constitution and bylaws specifying the events, procedures, and rules agreed upon by the members. Standard events are debate, discussion, extemporaneous speaking, oratory, and various forms of interpretation. In oratory especially, state winners compete for regional or national honors in such organizations as the Inter-State Oratorical League.

Most recent figures indicate expanding programs at the state level as the number of institutions and students grows. Wilson [6] found twenty states had no leagues, but there were nineteen in active operation in the United States, principally in the Midwest. The chief activities were debate, discussion, extemporaneous speaking, oratory, after-dinner speaking, and dramatic interpretation.

Privately Sponsored Organizations

Other patterns of college and university activity programs are developed through private sponsorship. These fall into various classes: (1) forensic fraternities, (2) individual institutions, (3) regional organizations, (4) other national organizations, and (5) international agencies.

1. Forensic Fraternities

Three honorary forensic fraternities sponsor tournaments and conferences. Tau Kappa Alpha and Delta Sigma Rho hold annual regional or national meetings in the spring. Pi Kappa Delta has a national tournament every two years. Events include debate, discussion, student congress, and extemporaneous speaking.

2. Individual Institutions

Many colleges and universities hold debate tournaments, forensic meets, conferences or speech festivals. One of the most highly regarded is the West Point National Debate Tournament. This is a

[6] L. L. Wilson, "A Study of State Intercollegiate Speech Associations" (Unpublished graduate paper, Northwestern University, 1961).

culmination of state and regional competition in debate, and is held in April at the United States Military Academy. The Owen Coon Memorial Debate Tournament, held at Northwestern University in February, is a distinctive national invitational tournament. Kansas University, Nebraska, Louisiana State, Dartmouth, Harvard, Florida State, Mississippi, Ohio State, and Arkansas are among the schools offering fine debate tournaments.

The Chicago Branch of the University of Illinois sponsors annually the National Discussion Contest, in which 25-minute tapes of discussions on the national question may be submitted for judging. Regional and national winners are chosen.

3. Regional Associations

Among the regional associations conducting forensic events are the Western Speech Association, the Southern Speech Association, the New England Forensic Conference, the Pacific Forensic League, the Southwest Conference Debate League, the Rocky Mountain Forensic League, and the Atlantic Coast Conference. Events held are similar to those mentioned earlier.

4. Other National Organizations

The American Forensic League is an important professional organization whose members are directors of forensics in colleges, universities, and high schools. Its functions are to promote forensic activities, improve standards and procedures, and serve as a clearinghouse for schedules, a calendar of events, and professional problems. In cooperation with the Speech Association of America, it holds national meetings for directors and all speech teachers.

5. International Agencies

The Institute of International Education sponsors two important events, which reach beyond the boundaries of the United States. The first is the annual tour of foreign debate teams, principally British, to the United States. This project has been conducted almost every year (except during the war) since 1921. The other is the tour of a selected team of university debaters from the United States to European centers of learning. These speakers, chosen each spring by tryout, have done distinctive work in the speech field.

All these programs of speech contests and activities constitute a significant portion of speech education at higher levels of learning. Often one of the principal means of continuity between secondary school and university training in the field is through these numerous avenues of cocurricular speech training.

EXERCISES

1. Obtain copies of state bulletins dealing with activity and contest work in speech from the various state high school speech organizations. List the activities and contests sponsored by one particular state of your choosing, noting rules for membership in the association, method of organizing the program, provision for materials, securing of judges, financial arrangements, and all other relevant details.
2. Write a paper on the pros and cons of speech contests in speech education, giving your own personal views on this subject.
3. Investigate the purposes, organization, and activities of the various speech organizations, such as the National Forensic League, the National Thespian Society, Masque and Gavel, Delta Sigma Rho, Pi Kappa Delta, Theta Alpha Phi, the National Collegiate Players, or any other privately sponsored organizations.

REFERENCES

Barber, G. Bradford. "An Analysis and Evaluation of Forensic Contests as Conducted in the Secondary Schools within the Area of the North Central Association," *Speech Teacher*, III, (January, 1954), 20–22.

Bavely, Ernest. "Dramatic Arts in Secondary Education," *Quarterly Journal of Speech*, XXXII (February, 1946), 40–47.

———. "Suggestions for Improving Drama Festivals and Contests," *Quarterly Journal of Speech*, XXVIII (October, 1942), 327–32.

Blyton, Gifford. "Whither the Speech Activities Program?" *Speech Teacher*, II (January, 1953), 55–57.

Carmack, Paul A. "The Development of State High School Speech Leagues," *Speech Teacher*, III (November, 1954), 264–68.

Dietrich, John. "Dramatic Activity in American Colleges: 1946–1947," *Quarterly Journal of Speech*, XXXIV (April, 1948), 183–90.

Ehninger, Douglas. "Six Earmarks of a Sound Forensics Program," *Speech Teacher*, I (November, 1952), 327–41.

Fest, Thorrell B. "A Survey of College Forensics," *Quarterly Journal of Speech*, XXXIV (April, 1948), 168–73.

Hunsinger, Paul. "Festivals and Changing Patterns," *Speech Teacher*, VII (March, 1958), 93–98.

LARSON, P. MERVILLE. "Some Suggestions for High School Forensics," *Speech Teacher*, I (January, 1952), 52–54.

MURPHY, RICHARD. "Festival or Tournament?" *Quarterly Journal of Speech*, XXVII (October, 1941), 392–97.

SPEECH ASSOCIATION OF AMERICA. "A Program of Speech Education," *Quarterly Journal of Speech*, XXXIII (October, 1951), 347–58.

WALSH, GRACE. "Tournaments: For Better or Worse?" *Speech Teacher*, VI (January, 1957), 65–67.

WEIR, CLARA B. "Extracurricular Problems and Their Solutions," *Speech Teacher*, V (November, 1956), 277–84.

CHAPTER SEVEN

Selecting a Textbook

BASIC CONSIDERATIONS

Although there are many educators who claim that the adoption of a textbook for classroom use leads to "textbook teaching," the textbook holds an important place in modern American education. From kindergarten through university, the textbook has become the most popular tool in teaching.

Although textbook selection in public schools is generally under the control of the board of education, in cooperation with the superintendent, supervisors, principal, and teachers, the recommendation of a text is usually initiated by the teacher. Sometimes considerable thought may precede such a recommendation in an attempt to answer two major questions: (1) Should a textbook be used? (2) Which text shall be used?

In answering the first question there are numerous arguments against the use of textbooks: (1) teachers often become overdependent on textbooks to the point where originality and creativity give way to a mechanical approach; (2) textbooks are often dull, meaningless, and sometimes difficult to understand; (3) textbooks, unless replaced regularly, lose their value in terms of current educational thought and practices; (4) it is impossible for any one textbook to deal adequately with all the material it attempts to cover; (5) one standardized textbook for classroom use often fails to meet the individual differences in reading comprehension and interest that may exist among a group of students with varying mental capacities; (6) it is often impossible for a textbook to fit into a specific curriculum as set up by local school administration.

The following reasons support the use of a textbook: (1) many teachers do not have the skill, time, or energy to undertake the overwhelming and complicated task of organizing teaching materials as they are assembled and presented in modern textbooks; (2) since textbooks are written by authorities in the field, a more accurate compilation of facts concerning the subject matter is presented than if the task of compilation were assigned to the average inexperienced teacher; (3) realizing that with each new generation a gradual evolution of new theories and practices occurs, textbooks are constructed to reflect current trends in educational thought and practices; (4) textbooks are invaluable to students, since they serve as a ready reference to the basic material necessary to understand and appreciate all phases of the subject matter under consideration.

Unless the speech teacher is an extremely capable, well-trained individual with considerable experience and a depth of knowledge in his field, the elimination of a textbook can prove hazardous. There are those individuals who, because they are limited in budget or dissatisfied with existing textbooks, find the guide sheet or mimeographed content and assignment sheet the answer to the textbook problem. There is much to commend this attack upon the organization of information, theory, and platform work. For the teacher whose budget does not permit the purchase of a textbook, this is the only possible approach. For the teacher who finds no book perfectly geared to his needs, this approach is really only part of the solution. The more practical approach is the one taken by the intelligent teacher who, realizing that the textbook serves as a focal point for the teaching pattern and the learning process, will adopt the one textbook that comes closest to meeting the needs of the program and, when necessary, reinforce weak aspects of the textbook with supplementary materials.

In answering the second question, "Which text shall be used?" the next section develops some detailed guides that should assist the speech instructor.

GUIDES IN SELECTING A TEXTBOOK

Every teacher should know the textbook literature of his field. He should be able to answer straightforwardly, intelligently, and quickly when the administrator says to him, "Mr. Johnson, which book would you like to use for a text in your first course in speech?" He should not have to fumble, apologize, or weakly ask for more time so that he can check his notes from his college courses. Furthermore, he should keep abreast of the new publications in the field so that he can request a new text that better meets his needs. This knowledge is even more important in school systems or states in which there is a state adoption or a minimum time period for the use of books purchased by the system. If the teacher adopts a text under these conditions without really knowing the book, it may turn out like some marriages that are hastily contracted—he may discover that he is stuck with it. Therefore the teacher should obtain and carefully examine, page by page, all the available books for his particular course. This is a standard assignment in those teaching-of-speech courses that realistically meet the problems of the teacher. Each text is listed, inventoried, and evaluated by the prospective teacher. At the time, such a task may seem to be somewhat boring and time-consuming. It is, however, an excellent time investment for the teacher. Later he need not take the word of another person for the merits of a book; he will have seen them all, know their individual merits, and will have chosen a textbook long before the principal asks him to make his recommendation.

Such an examination of secondary school textbooks in speech will reveal certain things to the teacher. First, that no one book has everything the teacher desires for a given situation. There is wide variation in teaching situations and course plans. Books are printed and sold for two major purposes: (1) to serve the needs in the field, and (2) to make money for the publisher. The publisher must have a market wide enough to make the publication pay; the author must adjust his content to the needs of the majority and must make his book extensive enough and sufficiently varied to be used by many persons. Otherwise, author and publisher face the dilemma of an intensive treatment of a limited area for only a restricted market.

What effect do these factors have upon speech texts? The most noticeable result is in the quality of the treatment of the content by the author. Very few are as extensive, thorough, or balanced as the teacher may desire. Too often he is persuaded by one outstanding feature of a book—the exercises, the pictures, or a section that is currently popular.

The bibliography and the book review are excellent aids for the speech teacher who is looking for either a listing or a critical analysis of textbooks in his field. The bibliography, which is a compilation of books, articles, journals, bulletins, and pamphlets on a particular subject, is found in nearly every textbook and is a basic tool for further study. The book review is indispensable to the speech teacher who seeks an authoritative guide in evaluating textbooks in the various areas of speech. Book reviews are an important segment of such professional speech journals as *The Speech Teacher, The Quarterly Journal of Speech, Educational Theatre Journal,* and others. They furnish brief, critical comments, usually by an expert in the field, on works published within a recent period of time. The best book review is the one that judges a textbook on the basis of both its merits and its failings. It deals with such items as the subject matter covered, the author's purpose in writing it, and the extent to which this purpose was achieved. Frequently, a textbook is compared with others in the same area. Realizing that the book review is merely a condensation, the speech teacher should seek out the actual textbook before making any definite decisions concerning the material under consideration.

To avoid errors in selection, the teacher should survey the whole book, note its coverage and the quality of its content, and evaluate the text in terms of his needs. The book he selects should be the one that meets his needs on the greatest number of points.

As an aid to selecting texts the check list for general textbooks (p. 166) may be of some help; the scope of the book can be noted, and brief comments placed opposite each section in the space to the right. For more extensive analysis, a total impression can be written on the back of the sheet, using the following list of criteria for evaluating general textbooks. It is suggested that these methods be employed in an effort to secure the most satisfactory estimate of a book.

Criteria for Evaluating Introductory Textbooks in Speech

Each new year seems to multiply the number of new textbooks designed specifically for the beginning course in speech. The speech teacher usually finds himself in a state of bewilderment as he listens to an endless number of textbook salesmen "pushing" their particular product. In order to avoid the unsatisfactory selection of a weak textbook, the teacher needs suitable standards and criteria for textbook selection.

Perhaps the two most important questions facing the speech teacher as he prepares to select a textbook are: (1) What are the elements of a good textbook? (2) What makes one textbook better than another? Possibly some answer to these questions is found as one considers the following criteria:

Author; publisher
1. The author should have a recognized reputation based on knowledge and experience in the field of his writing.
2. The publisher should have a reputation as a distributor of scholarly material.
3. Dates of publication and revisions must insure against obsolete material and indicate modern educational thought and practice.
4. The price of the textbook should not have precedence over the ultimate educational value derived from a particular textbook.

Philosophy; purposes
5. The author must set forth a definite philosophy of speech education, usually in the preface, and actually implement this philosophy throughout the entire textbook.
6. The speech teacher should decide to which of the following philosophies of speech education the textbook conforms most closely in regard to the beginning course: (a) it is devoted to the fundamental speech processes; (b) it is a survey course; (c) it is a public-speaking course; (d) it is a speech arts course; (e) it is devoted to functional speech activities; (f) it is concerned with the development of the individual person; (g) it has some other special point of view.

Grade; age level
7. The textbook should be appropriate for the general age or grade level, the needs of a particular group of students, a particular sequence of units or course arrangement, and a particular type of school curricular organization.

Content; exercises
8. Some attempt should be made within the textbook to be systematic in the treatment of the content of various areas of speech, such as the fundamental processes, creative and interpretative speech activities, and speech for special occasions.
9. The quality of the content in the various areas treated in the textbook should be strong, reliable, and accurate, and the speech teacher should decide in which areas the content appears to be weak.

10. The textbook must be well balanced in content for training in the fundamentals of speech and should not overemphasize one particular area to the sacrifice of another.
11. Exercises in the textbook should be clear, interesting, functional, motivating, numerous, graded, adequate for various areas, and adaptable to individual needs.
12. Exercises should be selected and organized on the basis of clearly indicated principles of curricular organization or learning procedures.
13. The textbook must clearly present facts and principles, establishing their significance and application; it must be written in clear and effective style, have stimulating pictures and illustrations, well-organized content, and acceptable printing.
14. Methods of diagnosis and evaluation of achievement, as found throughout various sections of the textbook in the form of tests, self-evaluation, audience evaluation, and critic evaluation, must be adequately presented.

Organization
15. The textbook should contain such helpful aids as a table of contents, plans for course organization, methods of using audio-visual aids, exercises, bibliographies and references for both teacher and students, sources of supplies, and an index.

Physical make-up
16. The mechanical construction of the textbook should be sound. Artistic balance should be maintained in an attractive and durable binding, the quality of paper, an attractive and eye-appealing jacket, and the general page make-up as evidenced in the size of type, length of line, spacing, and margins.

General evaluation
17. The speech teacher should evaluate the contributions made by the content and organization of the textbook to his understanding of the field.
18. The textbook should conform in general to the aims set up in accepted school curricula.

CHECK LIST FOR CONTENT OF SPEECH TEXTBOOKS

Author:
Title of Textbook:
Publisher:
Date of Publication and Revisions:

Content

1. General Information
   a. Definition of Speech
   b. History of Speech
   c. Importance of Speech
   d. Word Roots and Origins
2. Speech Preparation and Composition
   a. Determining the Purpose
   b. Analyzing the Audience and Occasion
   c. Gathering Material
   d. Wording the Speech
   e. Making an Outline
3. Poise and Self Confidence
   a. Explanation of Problem
   b. Methods for Controlling Stage Fright
4. Language
   a. Vocabulary
   b. Pronunciation
   c. Phonetics and Speech Sounds
   d. Diction: Word Usage and Style
   e. Semantics
5. Voice
   a. Anatomy and Mechanism
   b. Mechanics of Speaking
      1) Respiration
      2) Phonation
      3) Resonation
      4) Articulation
   c. Attributes of Voice
      1) Quality
      2) Pitch
      3) Intensity
      4) Rate
   d. Exercises for Improvement
6. Bodily Action
   a. Types of Action
   b. Posture
   c. Movement
   d. Gesture
   e. Visual Directness and Eye Contact
   f. Distracting Mannerisms

7. Listening
    a. Definition and Concepts
    b. Types and Uses
    c. Techniques and Processes
    d. Methods for Improvement
8. Forms of Speaking
    a. Classroom Discussion and Recitation
    b. Conversation
    c. Telephone Techniques
    d. Interviewing
9. Public Speaking
    a. Extempore Speaking
    b. Persuasive Speaking
    c. Speeches for Special Occasions
        1) Announcements
        2) Introductions
        3) Presentations
        4) Acceptance
        5) Welcome
        6) Farewell
        7) Dedication
        8) Eulogy
        9) Goodwill
        10) Campaign Speech
        11) Commencement Speech
        12) After-Dinner Speaking
    d. Original Oratory
    e. Declamation: Oratorical, Humorous, **Dramatic**
    f. Group Discussion
    g. Argumentation
    h. Debate
    i. Parliamentary Procedure
10. Interpretation and Oral Reading
    a. Prose
    b. Poetry
    c. Dramatic Literature
        1) Monologue
        2) Dialogue
    d. Storytelling
    e. Choric Interpretation
    f. Reader's Theater
    g. Chamber Theater

11. Theater and Dramatic Arts
   a. History
   b. Dramatic Literature
   c. Forms and Types of Play Production
   d. Staff Organization
   e. Business Management: Advertising, Box Office, etc.
   f. Principles of Pantomime and Acting
   g. Rehearsal Techniques
   h. Play Production and Direction
      1) Directing
      2) Scene Design
      3) Set Construction
      4) Painting the Set
      5) Lighting
      6) Properties
      7) Costuming
      8) Make-up
12. Radio
   a. Speaking, Announcing, and Broadcasting
   b. Production, Direction, and Writing
13. Television
   a. Speaking, Announcing, and Broadcasting
   b. Production, Direction, and Writing
14. Motion Pictures
15. Puppets and Marionettes
16. Assembly Programming and Programs
17. Bibliographies

EXERCISES

1. Select a textbook that you would use in teaching the first course in speech and evaluate it, using the check list found in this chapter.
2. Select and write a review of the specific textbook you would use in teaching each of the specialized areas of public speaking, debate, theater, interpretation, and radio and television. Defend your choice in each case according to the appropriateness of the textbook for your specific grade level, secondary or college.

A SHORT BIBLIOGRAPHY OF TEXTBOOKS DEALING WITH GENERAL SPEECH AND PUBLIC SPEAKING °

ANDERSCH, ELIZABETH G., and LORIN C. STAATS. *Speech for Everyday Use*. Rev. ed. New York: Holt, Rinehart and Winston, Inc., 1960.

BAIRD, A. CRAIG, and FRANKLIN H. KNOWER. *Essentials of General Speech*. 2nd Ed. New York: McGraw-Hill Book Co., Inc., 1960.

———. *General Speech: An Introduction*. 2nd ed. New York: McGraw-Hill Book Co., Inc., 1957.

°BARNES, HARRY G., and LORETTA W. SMITH. *Speech Fundamentals*. Englewood Cliffs, N.J.: Prentice-Hall, Inc., 1953.

°BARRICK, AUGUSTA I. *The Power of Effective Speech*. New York: Bookman Associates, 1959.

BLACK, JOHN W., and WILBUR E. MOORE. *Speech: Code, Meaning, and Communication*. New York: McGraw-Hill Book Co., Inc., 1955.

BRADEN, WALDO., and MARY LOUISE GEHRING. *Speech Practices: A Resource Book for the Student of Public Speaking*. New York: Harper & Bros., 1958.

BRIGANCE, WILLIAM NORWOOD. *Speech Communication*. 2nd ed. New York: Appleton-Century-Crofts, Inc., 1955.

———. *Speech: Its Techniques and Disciplines in a Free Society*. 2nd ed. New York: Appleton-Century-Crofts, Inc., 1961.

BROWN, CHARLES T. *Introduction to Speech*. Boston: Houghton, Mifflin Co., 1955.

BRYANT, DONALD C., and KARL R. WALLACE. *Fundamentals of Public Speaking*. 2nd ed. New York: Appleton-Century-Crofts, Inc., 1953.

———. *Oral Communication*. 2nd ed. New York: Appleton-Century-Crofts, Inc., 1954.

°BUEHLER, E. C. *You and Your Speeches*. Rev. ed. Lawrence, Kan.: Allen Press, 1957.

CROCKER, LIONEL. *Public Speaking for College Students*. 3rd ed. New York: American Book Co., 1956.

DICKENS, MILTON. *Speech: Dynamic Communication*. New York: Harcourt, Brace and Co., 1954.

EISENSON, JON. *Basic Speech*. New York: The Macmillan Co., 1950.

°ELSON, E. F., and ALBERTA PECK. *The Art of Speaking*. Rev. ed. New York: Ginn and Co., 1957.

GILMAN, WILBUR E.; BOWER, ALY; and LOREN D. REID. *The Fundamentals of Speaking*. New York: The Macmillan Co., 1951.

GRAY, GILES W., and WALDO W. BRADEN. *Public Speaking: Principles and Practice*. New York: Harper & Bros., 1951.

° High school textbooks.

————, and CLAUDE M. WISE. *The Bases of Speech*. 3rd ed. New York: Harper & Bros., 1959.

*GRIFFITH, FRANCIS; CATHERINE NELSON; and EDWARD STASHEFF. *Your Speech*. 2nd ed. New York: Harcourt, Brace and Co., 1960.

*HEDDE, WILHELMINA G., and W. NORWOOD BRIGANCE. *The New American Speech*. Philadelphia: J. B. Lippincott Co., 1957.

*IRWIN, JOHN V., and MARJORIE ROSENBERGER. *Modern Speech*. New York: Holt, Rinehart and Winston, Inc., 1961.

LAASE, LEROY. *Speech Project and Drillbook*. Dubuque, Iowa: William C. Brown and Co., 1954.

LOMAS, CHARLES W., and RALPH RICHARDSON. *Speech: Idea and Delivery*. Boston: Houghton Mifflin Co., 1956.

*MARKERT, EDWARD E. *Speech for All*. Rev. ed. Boston: Allyn and Bacon, Inc., 1959.

McBURNEY, JAMES H., and ERNEST J. WRAGE. *The Art of Good Speech*. New York: Prentice-Hall, Inc., 1953.

————. *Guide to Good Speech*, 2nd ed. Englewood Cliffs, N. J.: Prentice-Hall, Inc., 1960.

*MASTEN, CHARLES H., and GEORGE PFLAUM. *Speech for You*. Evanston, Ill.: Row Peterson and Co., 1955.

MONROE, ALAN H. *Principles and Types of Speech*. 5th ed. Chicago: Scott, Foresman and Co., 1962.

MURRAY, ELWOOD; RAYMOND H. BARNARD; and J. V. GARLAND. *Integrative Speech*. New York: Dryden Press, Inc., 1953.

*NELSON, THEODORE F., and W. KIRTLEY ATKINSON. *Speech and Your Personality*. Chicago: Benjamin H. Sanborn and Co., 1955.

NICHOLS, RALPH G., and THOMAS R. LEWIS. *Listening and Speaking*. Dubuque, Iowa: William C. Brown Co., 1954.

NORVELLE, LEE; RAYMOND G. SMITH; and ORVIN LARSON. *Speaking Effectively*. New York: Dryden Press, Inc., 1957.

OLIVER, ROBERT T., and RUPERT L. CORTRIGHT. *Effective Speech*. 4th ed. New York: Holt, Rinehart and Winston, Inc., 1961.

————, DALLAS C. DICKEY, and HAROLD P. ZELKO. *Communicative Speech*. Rev. ed. New York: Dryden Press, Inc., 1955.

*PAINTER, MARGARET. *Ease in Speech*. 3rd ed. Boston: D. C. Heath and Co., 1954.

*RAUBICHECK, LETITIA; ROBERT L. DAVIS; and L. ADELE CARLL. *Your Voice and Speech*. 3rd ed. New York: Prentice-Hall, Inc., 1953.

SANDFORD, WILLIAM, and WILLARD H. YEAGER. *Effective Speaking*. 5th ed. New York: Ronald Press, 1950.

*SARETT, LEW; WILLIAM T. FOSTER; and JAMES. H. McBURNEY. *Speech:*

* High school textbooks.

A High School Course. Rev. ed. Boston: Houghton Mifflin Co., 1956.

———; ———; and SARETT, ALMA. *Basic Principles of Speech.* 3rd ed. Boston: Houghton Mifflin Co., 1958.

SOPER, PAUL L. *Basic Public Speaking.* 2nd ed. New York: Oxford University Press, Inc., 1956.

THOMPSON, WAYNE N., and SETH A. FESSENDEN. *Basic Experiences in Speech.* 2nd ed. Englewood Cliffs, N. J.: Prentice-Hall, Inc., 1958.

THONSSEN, LESTER, and HOWARD GILKINSON. *Basic Training in Speech.* 2nd ed. Boston: D. C. Heath & Co., 1953.

*WATKINS, RHODA, and EDA B. FROST. *Your Speeches and Mine.* 2nd ed. New York: Lyons and Carnahan, 1956.

*WEAVER, ANDREW T.; GLADYS L. BORCHERS; and DONALD K. SMITH. *Speaking and Listening.* Englewood Cliffs, N. J.: Prentice-Hall, Inc., 1956.

———, and ORDEEN G. NESS. *An Introduction to Public Speaking.* New York: Odyssey Press, 1961.

WHITE, EUGENE E. *Practical Speech Fundamentals.* New York: The Macmillan Co., 1960.

*WILLIAMS, JOHN H.; FRED M. HENLEY; ROBERT E. MURRAY; and THOMAS C. SAVAGE. *Correct Speaking. Adult Speaking. Effective Speaking. Planned Speaking.* Chicago: Loyola University Press, 1958. A series for secondary schools.

* High school textbooks.

CHAPTER EIGHT

Audio-Visual Materials

FUNDAMENTAL PRINCIPLES

Audio-visual materials are not new. They have been a part of the instructional process for centuries. The only change that has taken place has been in the method of employing these teaching materials in accordance with modern principles of teaching. The ancient Greeks and Romans used games, pageants, and festivals to instruct their youth. Many references relating to the observation method and object lessons can be found in educational literature. John Amos Comenius, a Moravian bishop, wrote the first textbook containing pictures, *Orbis Sensualium Pictus*, which gave impetus to visual materials as a part of teaching.

Audio-visual materials are those objects, or their representation, used to help make the learning experience more vivid for the student by giving reality to words, ideas, and principles. Audio-visual education is based on the psychological principle that an individual gains a better conception of something he actively does or sees than of something he reads or hears from someone else.

A half century ago, the pioneers of audio-visual education devoted much of their time to disproving many misconceptions concerning the educational values of audio-visual materials. Today, few, if any, educators oppose the use of audio-visual materials in education, and nearly all schools either own or have access to this type of material. There is much to commend the use of audio-visual materials. They not only broaden the students' experience by having them participate actively, but also intensify impressions they receive by appealing to more than one sense. Whereas verbalization tends to decrease the interest of the students, audio-visual materials create interest by adding variety to the teaching situation and giving the class something to see, to examine, and to handle. Audio-visual materials save valuable classroom time, because they tend to focus the attention of the class on information directly related to the lesson, eliminate unnecessary questions due to abstract verbalization, and prevent confusion by establishing a uniform mental image among the group.

In recent years, the value of audio-visual materials has been demonstrated by both research and actual use in classroom teaching. Certain basic principles have evolved, which the speech teacher should use in developing his audio-visual materials: (1) audio-visual materials are not a substitute for the classroom teacher but are a supplement to classroom activities; (2) audio-visual materials are a means to an end rather than ends in themselves; (3) when used intelligently by a skillful teacher, audio-visual materials can be effective tools in teaching; (4) audio-visual materials are not a cure-all or a magic formula for inept teaching; (5) each form of audio-visual material has its particular strengths and weaknesses; there is no one superior form; (6) best results are achieved when audio-visual materials are used in combination; (7) audio-visual materials should not be used if there is a more satisfactory way to enhance and insure the learning process; (8) there should be a definite relationship between the audio-visual material used and the content of the lesson; (9) before he introduces audio-visual materials, the teacher must prepare the students for active learning rather than passive entertainment; (10) the teacher should be familiar with all facets of the audio-visual materials for classroom use; (11) audio-visual materials should be used to achieve the objectives and purposes of the lesson being undertaken; (12) the method and timing for the use of audio-visual materials in the lesson are important; (13) audio-visual materials help to enrich and extend the values of various classroom experiences; (14) audio-visual materials provide a reality of experience that helps to make learning more permanent.

The most successful audio-visual materials are simple in nature and presentation, realistic in giving a true picture of the activity being encountered, accurate in subject matter, legible and colorful to attract attention, and manageable by those who deal with them.

Audio-visual materials can be obtained in a variety of ways. Speech teachers can resort to their own creative instincts and either make or collect them. Students can be motivated into constructing them as a part of the classroom assignment or encouraged to contribute them from personal endeavors. In addition, there are several agencies from which the speech teacher can rent, purchase, or receive free for the asking the audio-visual materials desired.

The speech teacher has a great variety of audio-visual materials at his disposal. These materials can be placed on a continuum, ranging from the direct experiences of daily living to pure abstractions of verbal symbols. Edgar Dale [1] presents this concept in a pictorial device which he calls the "Cone of Experience." This cone shows the interrelationship of the various types of audio-visual materials and their individual positions in the learning process. "Direct, purposeful experience" is the broad base of the cone and represents the type of experience that makes for the most effective learning. As the cone tapers toward the top through the stages of decreasing directness, the "experiences" become more abstract, more verbal, more remote, and potentially less effective.

Dale's "Cone of Experience," which should be read in an upward direction, is as follows:

toward abstractness	Verbal Symbols Visual Symbols	Involves SYMBOLIZING in order of increasing abstractness
	Recordings, Radio, Still Pictures Motion Pictures Television Exhibits Field Trips Demonstrations	Involves OBSERVING in order of decreasing directness
toward concreteness	Dramatized Experiences Contrived Experiences Direct, Purposeful Experiences	Involves DOING in order of decreasing directness

Unfortunately, too much teaching is on the level of abstract verbalization, which often fails to make learning permanent. It is desirable, therefore, that the speech teacher make learning concrete by providing experiences, through audio-visual aids rather than words,

[1] Edgar Dale, *Audio-Visual Methods in Teaching* (New York: Holt, Rinehart & Winston, Inc., 1954), p. 43. Reprinted by permission of the publisher.

as a basis for the building and learning of proper concepts, principles, and attitudes.

APPLICATION TO THE TEACHING OF SPEECH

If audio-visual materials are to be of value, the speech teacher must select wisely the proper material for each situation. Below is a list and description of audio-visual materials that might be included under each division of Dale's "Cone of Experience," with suggested application to teaching speech.

I. *Direct, Purposeful Experiences.* These involve participation in an activity on the direct, concrete, and sensory level. Because of the nature of speech instruction and the active participation of the student, many of the speech activities can be considered as direct, purposeful experiences.

A. *Audio-Visual Materials:* All of those elements in reality that are experienced directly and involve all the senses of sight, hearing, touch, smell, and taste.

B. *Suggested Application to Speech:* Include various types of speechmaking, group meetings using parliamentary procedure, group discussion, debate, oral reading and interpretation, play production and direction, and radio and television production.

C. *Basic Principles for Use:* Take every opportunity to involve students in direct participation in these various curricular and cocurricular speech activities.

II. *Contrived Experiences.* These are simplified or rearranged imitations of the real experience and are used when the real thing cannot be perceived because of its size or complexity. It is often impossible for the speech teacher to bring to class in their natural state many of the items that he wants his students to see and to experience. When this is the case, he must resort to contrived experiences.

A. *Audio-Visual Materials:*

1. *Model.* An imitation of the real object in every respect except size.

2. *Mock-up.* Designed to show only specific parts of the

original complex system or process to the exclusion of other parts not under consideration.

3. *Object.* A tangible item that is complete in itself as a tool in teaching. It is a real thing that has been removed from its natural setting.

4. *Specimen.* A part of a total thing, it is representative of a group of similar objects.

B. *Suggested Application to Speech:* Use models of stage sets, properties, radio and television studios, anatomy of the speech and hearing mechanisms. Develop mock-ups of electrical circuits and devices for the technical aspects of theater, television, photography, radio. Use objects, such as stage tools and equipment, stage properties, costumes, speaker's podium, prompt book, microphones, manuscripts for oral reading. Employ specimens of human skeletons to aid in studying speech science and anatomy, a page out of a drama book, a collection of patterns for costuming.

C. *Basic Principles for Use:* Construct materials large enough and situate them in such a position that they can be viewed easily. Give students the opportunity to handle and examine them closely. Establish the correct concept concerning size in order to avoid misunderstanding about the actual size of material. Give students a clear understanding of the relationship between these materials and the total part or setting.

III. *Dramatized Experiences.* These are substitutes or reconstructions of the actual experience in which participants and observers are involved. The speech student becomes either an active participant or an observer in this two-way communication process. The spectator identifies himself with persons and situations.

A. *Audio-Visual Materials:*

1. *Plays.* Formal plays have predetermined plots, memorized parts, and cued action. Informal plays do not involve memorization or rehearsal, and sequences depend upon imagination and sensitiveness.

2. *Pantomime.* The total effect depends on the performer's

ability to express himself through action rather than words.

3. *Psychodrama, Sociodrama, and Role-Playing.* All of these involve spontaneous dramatization, yet are distinct in nature. Psychodrama is avoided by some speech teachers, since it deals with the inner conflicts of individuals. Sociodrama is much less personal in nature and deals with social problems. Role playing places the emphasis on the role being played rather than on the problem itself.

4. *Pageant.* This is usually associated with special occasions or historical events.

5. *Tableau.* A picturelike scene, complete with background and appropriate scenery, in which the participants do not move or speak.

6. *Puppetry.* The main types are hand, string, and stick puppets. They give the individual the opportunity to identify himself with specific characterizations.

B. *Suggested Application to Speech:* Teach basic skills; have therapeutic value in helping the individual understand himself and others; also help him to overcome emotional handicaps by offering an outlet for feelings and motives, relieving tensions, etc. They also stress cooperation in achieving group goals; involve the student in activities, such as informal speaking situations, interviewing, telephone conversation, the dramatic and interpretative arts.

C. *Basic Principles for Use:* Select meaningful material for presentation. Establish the appropriate atmosphere for both participant and spectator so that a true learning experience evolves. Permit students to be as original and creative as possible in presenting characterizations. Use follow-up in permitting students to express new insights gained from dramatizations. Incorporate as much as possible general ideas and knowledge pertaining to the problems and conflicts basic to living.

IV. *Demonstrations.* These are visual experiences used to clarify ideas or processes.

A. *Audio-Visual Materials:*

1. *Live Demonstrator.* This is in the form of the teacher

or some other person who is in direct communication at all times with the observers.

2. *Apparatus and Mechanical Devices.* All audio-visual materials that can be either heard or seen are included herein.

3. *Chalkboard, Blackboard, or Writing Board.* The most widely used of the demonstration media and a vehicle for visual materials rather than a visual material in and of itself. It takes up most of the wall space in a classroom and is green, white, or yellow in color, satin-surfaced, and glareproof.

4. *Felt Board, Flannel Board, or Flannelgraph.* A rough or fuzzy surface, usually of felt or flannel, on which are placed several items with felt or flannel backing.

B. *Suggested Application to Speech:* Use as aids in clarifying techniques, principles, and assignments concerning speech; as substitutes for the actual experience encountered in interviewing, speechmaking, and acting; as vehicles for analyzing speech organization, phonetics, stage design, anatomy, and interpretative material.

C. *Basic Principles for Use:* Keep the demonstration simple, unhurried, and accurate so that the experience being demonstrated is clear, vivid, and meaningful. Be sure that apparatus and mechanical devices used in demonstrations are in excellent working order so that there is no interference during the demonstration period. Arrange carefully and legibly materials written on boards. Aid contrast and emphasis of materials by using various colors of chalk. When writing on the board, speak to the audience and not to the board. Prepare complex material before the class convenes. Tilt felt board, flannel board, and flannelgraph with the bottom slightly forward; carefully organize and select the material to be used before the demonstration is begun; do not place so many materials upon it that it appears cluttered; include figures and symbols that are in contrasting colors; have a demonstrator who can point to it often and not block the material placed upon it; suggest the principle of perspective through the use of both large and small objects to indicate distance; include progressive explanations.

V. *Field Trips.* Trips can be taken by speech students to gain practical information by viewing real-life situations and activities. They are often the forerunner of the student's actual participation in a related activity.

    A. *Audio-Visual Materials:* All of those real-life situations related to the subject under consideration.

    B. *Suggested Application to Speech:* Attend play productions, view performances by outstanding speakers and poets, visit radio and television studios, attend meetings held by state and government authorities exercising elements of discussion and parliamentary procedure.

    C. *Basic Principles for Use:* Make preliminary preparations by getting the consent of school administration, making arrangements for suitable transportation, constructing a detailed schedule of activities from starting to finishing time, agreeing on standards of discipline to be followed by students, and contacting all individuals in charge of places involved in the field trip.

       Conduct preliminary discussion to stimulate interest in the trip, to acquaint students with purposes and objectives of the trip, to give students a background and basic understanding of what is to be viewed, and to establish what particular points should be noted. During the field trip, students should be encouraged to ask questions, to look for answers to predetermined questions set up during the preliminary discussion, and to take notes.

       Conduct a follow-up discussion and evaluation to determine the value of the trip, to secure student reaction, to answer questions arising from the trip, to pool student observations, to check students for newly developed concepts, and to test the students to determine the amount of information gained. Conclude with follow-up projects related to the field trip undertaken.

VI. *Exhibits.* These are a collection of related items arranged in a meaningful display to inform, interest, or influence the observer.

    A. *Audio-Visual Materials:*

        1. *Display.* An arrangement of either flat or three-dimensional material.

2. *Bulletin Board or Tackboard.* Made of a material such as cork, composition board, softwood, veneer, or Celotex, which will take tacks, pins, or adhesive material.

3. *Poster.* A placard, with its principal feature a picture.

B. *Suggested Application to Speech:* Permit viewing of prompt books, theater programs, types of microphones, samples of speech outlines, pictures of historical actors and poets, samples of briefs for debate, costume plates, make-up charts, pictures of speech and hearing mechanisms, clippings of play reviews, perspective drawings of stage settings, information dealing with such items as club meetings, debate schedules, special projects, rehearsal calls, and other important notices.

C. *Basic Principles for Use:* Establish a purpose and theme for the exhibit. Construct a plan or blueprint showing measurements, placement of materials, lettering, color, and other necessary information. Strive for a dramatic and attractive arrangement of materials, keeping the design and arrangement simple, uncluttered, and attractive to the eye. Use color wisely to give proper emphasis to the specific elements involved. Provide adequate lighting to keep all the elements in proper focus. Change the exhibit often to ensure interest. Permit student committees to maintain the exhibits under the direction of the teacher.

VII. *Television.* In very simple terms, this is a means of converting a scene into an electronic image. This image is sent through space, picked up on an antenna, and translated into a duplicate scene on the surface of a picture tube or, to use the correct name, a kinescope.[2]

A. *Audio-Visual Materials:*

1. *Commercial Television.* Commercial television stations are required by the Federal Communications Commission to devote portions of their time to public service programs; thus, educational programs are often given the opportunity to be presented over commercial channels.

2. *Educational Television.* Nonprofit educational televi-

[2] Walter Wittich and Charles Schuller, *Audio-Visual Materials: Their Nature and Use* (New York: Harper & Bros., 1957), p. 432.

sion stations are being established by many communities, which concentrate on the telecasting of programs produced by educational institutions.

3. *Closed-Circuit Television.* A closed-circuit television link can be established to permit telecasting from colleges to public schools, from public school to public school, or from one central place to any desired number of classrooms within a school, mainly for teaching or training large numbers of individuals.

4. *Kinescope.* A sound motion picture record of a television show which is made in the television studio during the telecast performance for purposes of re-showing or preserving the original program.

5. *Video Tape.* Electronic recording on magnetic tape of video *and* audio parts of a television program. Can be replayed immediately after recording.

B. *Suggested Application to Speech:* Commercial and educational television provides opportunities either to participate in television which is planned, produced, and broadcast at school or to view television which has sound instructional material. Programs useful to speech include United Nations proceedings, newscasting, special news conferences, special reports by government officials, city council meetings and conferences, presentation of legitimate theater. Closed-circuit television provides experience for students in dealing directly with the elements of planning, programing, directing, producing, and camera operation; the ideal situation exists for original student speeches, discussions, debates, oral reading and interpretation, newscasting, and teacher lectures and demonstrations.

C. *Basic Principles for Use:* Check the reputation of the program producer, participants, and past performances, since preview of a live telecast is impossible. Preview kinescopes and telefilms when possible. Provide the classroom with a satisfactory television set for viewing. Select television material with great care so that it will educate rather than merely entertain. View only television material that contributes to the learning situation and is related to the subject matter under class discussion. Prepare students for the telecast, kinescope, or video tape to be viewed. Conduct a general follow-up discussion and evaluation of the program viewed.

VIII. *Motion Pictures.* Briefly stated, a motion picture is a series of still pictures taken in rapid succession, developed, and finally projected again as a series of still pictures but under such conditions as to give the viewer an illusion of motion. The addition of a coordinated sound signal or track results in a sound motion picture.[3]

A. *Audio-Visual Materials:*

1. *Motion Picture Projector.* A mechanical device used for projecting the motion picture film and reproducing any element of sound that might be included.

2. *Motion Picture Films.*

a. *Educational, Instructional, or Teaching Film.* Related to the content and subject matter found in various curriculum areas; its chief purpose is to inform through exposition.

b. *Documentary Film.* Deals directly with realities of life and gives factual information concerning a subject in its natural setting.

c. *Sponsored Film.* Deals with the product of a particular manufacturer and yet has educational value because of its contribution to the learning process.

d. *Entertainment Film.* Produced by the motion picture industry for entertainment purposes; however, many of these Hollywood films have educational value and 16 mm. versions of them are condensed and released on a nonprofit basis by TFC (Teaching Film Custodians).

3. *Motion Picture Screen.* The surface upon which the motion picture is projected.

B. *Suggested Application to Speech:* Motion picture films can be used in instructional presentations to show: principles and concepts in the basic processes and fundamentals of

[3] *Ibid.,* p. 363.

speech; fundamentals of speech and voice production; anatomy and function of the speech and hearing mechanisms; parliamentary procedure in action; discussion in process; all aspects of bodily activity, including posture, movement, and gesture; techniques and illustrations of interpretative reading; radio and television techniques; visible processes of dramatic arts, including dramatic productions of literature, acting, make-up, stage business, scene design, directing, costuming, principles of lighting, etc.

C. *Basic Principles for Use:* Purchase a motion picture projector which can be handled easily (light in weight), threaded and operated without difficulty, has a good sound system and amplification unit, possesses an adequate light source, is sturdy in design and construction, and has a service guarantee.

Select film for its appropriateness to the subject under discussion, its authoritative information, its intellectual level of comprehension, its general organization of material, and its physical qualities concerning sound, photography, and color.

Preview film to decide if it serves the intended purpose, to anticipate and to prepare for questions that might arise from students who view the film, to check difficulty of language and terminology that might need to be defined before viewing, to note specific scenes to which students should pay particular attention, and to construct questions that will help to guide the students' viewing. Prepare students for viewing the film by creating an interest in it.

Show the film under ideal conditions, which include proper seating arrangement so that all students can see easily, satisfactory ventilation to insure a comfortable setting, strategic placement of the amplifier for good sound reception, adequate darkening of the viewing room, and use of a room that will be free from interruptions and outside distractions.

Discuss and evaluate the film after its viewing to determine its effectiveness, to answer questions arising from the film, to permit students to express their reactions to what they have learned, and to determine the necessity for further study.

Provide for follow-up activities that stem from the film viewing.

IX. *Recordings, Radio, Still Pictures.* These are visual or auditory devices that usually require the use of mechanical aids. Whereas radio and recordings involve only listening, still pictures involve only seeing.

A. *Audio-Visual Materials:*

1. *Radio:*

   a. *AM Radio.* Typical commercial radio broadcasts transmitted a considerable distance through the air by amplitude modulation. Most radio sets receive this type of broadcast.

   b. *FM Radio.* Radio broadcasts transmitted a fairly short distance through the air by frequency modulation. This type of broadcast is not commonly found in the typical radio set, although there has been an increase in the purchase of radios that receive both the AM and FM broadcasts.

   c. *Educational Radio.* Handled through FM radio stations established by school systems and universities for the purpose of broadcasting educational programs in their areas with complete freedom in program and time scheduling. FM broadcasting has its advantages in that it almost guarantees static-free and high-quality reception.

2. *Recordings:*

   a. *Disc Recording.* A disc or phonograph record that has a diameter ranging from 7 to 16 inches and is designed to rotate at one of four speeds: 78 rpm (revolutions per minute), 45 rpm, 33⅓ rpm, 16⅔ rpm.

   b. *Magnetic Tape Recording.* A recording made on magnetized tape, which is usually ¼ inch wide, comes in various lengths, and has a speed of 3¾ ips (inches per second), 7½ ips, and 15 ips.

   c. *Magnetic Wire Recording.* A recording made on wire instead of metallic-coated tape.

3. *Recording Equipment:*
   a. *Playbacks or Record Players.* The machine on which the disc recording rotates; it rotates at various speeds to reproduce the proper sound.
   b. *Tape Recorder or Wire Recorder.* The machine through which the magnetic tape or wire passes; it should include the necessary tape speeds for accurate reproduction.
4. *Still Pictures.* These are reconstructions of real life, photographed or drawn, which are nonprojected or projected depending on the size of the group doing the viewing.
   a. *Photograph.* A picture obtained through the act of photography, which produces an image on a sensitized surface by the action of light.
   b. *Illustration.* The reproduction of an image through drawing rather than photography.
   c. *Slide.* A transparent picture or image either black and white or in color, individually mounted on cardboard or between pieces of glass; standard size is either 2 x 2 inches or 3¼ x 4 inches.
   d. *Filmstrip.* A strip of 35 mm. film on which is placed a related sequence of transparent pictures or images.
   e. *Stereograph.* Two three-dimensional pictures of the same subject, each viewed separately but simultaneously by the right and left eye through a specially designed device.
   f. *Microfilm.* Printed matter reproduced on 35 mm. or 16 mm. film.
5. *Still Picture Equipment for Individual Viewing or Projection:*
   a. *Opaque Projector.* A projector that can throw any nontransparent picture on a screen by means of a very intense reflected light; nontransparent material might include book illustrations, flat pictures, sketches, maps, pupils' work, and even certain objects and specimens.
   b. *Slide Projector and Filmstrip Projector.* A projector that can handle either a 3¼ x 4 inch slide or both

2 x 2 inch slide and filmstrip; slide carriage and filmstrip fittings are interchanged in the projector designed to handle both.

c. *Overhead Transparency Projector.* A projector that throws the transparency on a screen located behind the instructor, who is facing his students; the instructor is able either to write or draw on a plastic material, which is then thrown on the screen, or to build up his material through means of the overlay technique.

d. *Stereoprojector.* A projector that throws a pair of stereographic transparencies on a screen. A pair of specially designed glasses must be worn by the viewer to receive a clear three-dimensional image, since both pictures of the stereograph become blurred when seen by both eyes.

e. *Microprojector.* A projector that can project microscope slides so that the entire group can view a specimen at the same time.

f. *Tachistoscope.* A diaphragm-type shutter that is attached to an overhead slide projector so that the material thrown on a screen can be controlled in exposure periods ranging from 1 to 1/100 of a second.

B. *Suggested Application to Speech:* Radio can provide the immediate experience of listening to speeches, reports, discussions, debates, interviews, and dramatic productions as they occur, thus permitting the listener to feel the realism and emotional impact of the situation.

Recordings can provide models in public speaking by presenting the voice, style, and speech composition of excellent speakers of reputation; demonstrations of classroom speeches, discussions, oral readings, and speech problems for analysis and evaluation; presentation of great pieces of dramatic literature and poetry as read by recognized actors and interpreters to illustrate principles and techniques of writing and interpreting.

Still pictures and slides can provide visible aspects of the principles and concepts of speech performance dealing with posture, movement, gesture, and facial expressions; stage settings; make-up, both straight and character; properties; lighting effects; costumes of various eras; sequence of scenes and highlights of dramatic productions.

C. *Basic Principles for Use:* When using radio, determine the relationship between the selected program and the subject matter under discussion in the classroom. Create a desire within students to listen. Construct guide sheets or evaluation forms to motivate students into accurate listening habits. Check physical conditions for listening, which include room ventilation, proper placement of radio so that all students can hear without strain, and elimination of a crowded audience. Tune in and check reception of the radio program prior to the listening experience. Take notes during the broadcast as a basis for follow-up discussion. Write any necessary or complicated material that might arise during the broadcast on the blackboard for the purpose of clarifying spelling, recording statistical material, and future discussion. Conduct a follow-up discussion to evaluate the learning experience. Engage in activities related to the radio program.

When employing recordings, the same basic principles apply as are listed for radio concerning preparation, listening, and follow-up.

When using still pictures, select them according to their suitability for achieving the desired results, communicating a message without motion, and conveying a message through pictures instead of words. Preview in order to become acquainted with the material, prepare introductory material, and clarify complicated material for students. Prepare students to ensure interest, relationship of material to classroom activity, and elimination of learning barriers. Present material in a smooth and efficient manner by having material ready for use and in a predetermined order for presentation, determining the necessity of discussing each picture or frame and reading any captions that might be included, deciding the length of time necessary for viewing each picture or frame. Follow up with an evaluation to measure the results of viewing and encourage activities that might develop from new interests derived from the still pictures. Remember to select and purchase the mechanical equipment necessary to project still pictures according to the criteria set up for selecting motion picture projectors, which included ease of handling, good amplification and light systems, sturdiness in construction, and service guarantee.

X. *Visual Symbols.* This is an abstract representation rather than a realistic reproduction of the real thing. These are materials that communicate facts, ideas, concepts, and principles through a combination of pictures and written words; they are purchased or created by both teacher and student.

A. *Audio-Visual Materials:*

1. *Chalkboard.* A vehicle for visual materials that offers endless opportunity for graphic demonstrations.

2. *Drawings and Sketches.* Simple or detailed representations of persons and objects whose purpose is to suggest rather than to reproduce.

3. *Cartoon.* A pictorial caricature that deals with situations, ideas, and people and is filled with symbolism and a certain degree of humor.

4. *Strip Drawings or Comics.* A series of closely related drawings that tell a story in a recognizable sequence.

5. *Diagram.* A simplified drawing, void of unessential details, whose purpose is to show interrelationships through lines and geometric forms.

6. *Chart.* A combination of written and drawn material brought together for the purpose of showing relationships between facts and ideas by summarizing, comparing, and contrasting. Types of charts include the genealogy, tree, or stream chart; the flow or organization chart; the chronological, time, or tabular chart; the comparison or contrast chart.

7. *Graph.* A graphic representation of quantitative data. Types of graphs include the bar graph; the circle or pie graph; the pictorial graph; the profile, line, or curve graph.

8. *Map.* A flat representation of some portion of the earth's surface.

9. *Globe.* A spherical replica of the earth.

B. *Suggested Application to Speech:* Offer opportunity to study tables of motions in parliamentary procedure, phonetic symbols, anatomy of speech and hearing mechanisms, theater production organization, blocking and staging, stage settings, lighting arrangements, make-up plates, costume plates, physical elements of characters for dramatic production, trends in audience attendance and ticket sales during school productions, rehearsal schedules. These also are valuable for publicity and announcements of speech events of all kinds.

C. *Basic Principles for Use:* Teach students to interpret properly the various visual symbols and the forms used to present them. Introduce visual symbols of an abstract nature only after foundation work has been given, since some experience is necessary for students to comprehend and interpret the graphic material. Coordinate proper audiovisual material with graphic material to make the highly abstract visual symbols more understandable. Use visual symbols whenever indicated, as a summarizing device rather than an introduction, since most of them deal with conclusions and relationships. Attempt to keep visual symbols within the realm of student's understanding. Strive for simplicity in visual symbols. Observe basic principles underlying effective design whenever constructing graphic material, color, form, balance, variety, unity, emphasis, line.

XI. *Verbal Symbols.* These are designations which bear no physical resemblance to the objects or ideas for which they stand. These may be words for a concretion (horse), an idea (beauty), a scientific principle (the law of gravity, a formula (H_2O), a philosophic aphorism (Honesty is the best policy), or any other representation of experience that has been classified in some verbal symbolism.[4]

A. *Audio-Visual Materials:*

1. *Spoken Language.* The utterance or articulation of a

[4] Dale, *op. cit.*, p. 53.

group of words placed in combination to express opinions, beliefs, attitudes, feelings, moods, and desires.

2. *Written Language.* A combination of verbal symbols on a printed page which forms words or sentences for the purpose of expressing one's self.

B. *Suggested Application to Speech:* Include all phases of speech, either the spoken or written language or both, whether it be to prepare in a written fashion the material to be presented or to present speeches and read from the printed page.

C. *Basic Principles for Use:* Language, whether written or spoken, is the common mode of communication. Assign meanings to words in accordance with a person's experience; substitute words for the actual experience; involve verbal symbols in almost every other type of audio-visual experience either in spoken or written form.

EXERCISES

1. Obtain catalogues and listings of audio-visual materials from the various manufacturers and distributors and investigate the various sources of free and inexpensive teaching materials. Prepare a list of audio-visual materials that you feel most appropriate for use in the first course in speech, giving specific titles of films, recordings, and others, whenever possible.
2. If you had to make a choice, indicate the one audio-visual material you would choose as the principal teaching aid for your basic course. Defend your choice.
3. Construct, devise, or secure one audio-visual aid and describe its use in teaching a particular unit or lesson in speech.

REFERENCES

DALE, EDGAR. *Audio-Visual Methods in Teaching.* New York: Holt, Rinehart & Winston, Inc., 1954.

SANDS, LESTER B. *Audio-Visual Procedures in Teaching.* New York: Ronald Press Co., 1956.

THOMAS, R. MURRAY, and SHERWIN G. SWARTOUT. *Integrated Teaching Materials.* 2nd ed. New York: David McKay Co., 1962.

WITTICH, WALTER A., and CHARLES F. SCHULLER. *Audio-Visual Materials.* New York: Harper & Bros., 1957.

Periodicals and Publishers

Audio-Record, Audio Devices, Inc., 444 Madison Ave., New York, N.Y.

Audio-Visual Communication Review, Department of Audio-Visual Instruction, National Education Association, 1201 16th St., N.W., Washington, D.C.

Audio-Visual Instruction, Department of Audio-Visual Instruction, 1201 16th St., N.W., Washington, D.C.

Audio-Visual Guide, 2000 Lincoln Park West, Chicago, Ill.

A.V. World, Ver Halen Publishing Co., 6327 Santa Monica Blvd., Los Angeles, Calif.

Educational Screen, Inc., 2000 Lincoln Park West, Chicago, Ill.

Journal of the Association for Education by Radio-Television, 228 North La Salle St., Chicago, Ill.

See and Hear, 812 North Dearborn St., Chicago, Ill. (Ceased publication 1953.)

Visual Review, Society for Visual Education, Inc., 1345 West Diversey, Chicago, Ill. Annual.

PART TWO

Teaching Basic Skills

CHAPTER NINE

Getting Started

The first day of school is filled with thrills and apprehensions for students and teachers. For the beginning speech teacher it is a challenge and an opportunity, a most important occasion. At this time all previous planning, including knowledge of the field, basic teaching principles, and a pattern for procedure, face the test of application. Initial approach and serious motivation for the students must be clearly set forth. The cornerstones of rapport and enduring interest must be skillfully laid. Success in getting started underlies the development and skill in speech which both pupils and teacher seek. Certain purposes are basic to this outcome.

BASIC PURPOSES AND PRINCIPLES

1. *Get to know your students as soon as possible.*

To his general knowledge of young people the teacher should add as much *specific background information* as possible. The information blank on page 197 indicates the minimum essentials he should have. Such facts are of great help in planning work, in conferences, and in motivating students through specific appeals to their interests. Other useful data are available in the principal's office or in the files of guidance teachers: scores on standardized tests; health, hearing, eye examination records; economic and family status, and so on.

A written autobiography from each student may also be employed to gain much useful personal information. Such papers are written by the students and read by the teacher with the understanding that all material will be confidential.

To this information the teacher adds his individual, specific knowledge of each pupil's *speech needs, interests, and abilities.* Such

material results from early analysis and diagnosis of oral performance.

2. *Establish a favorable classroom atmosphere.*

Such an atmosphere reduces the tensions of students unused to
speaking before an audience and encourages their desire to participate. It helps each student feel that his teacher and classmates
are interested in the common objective of his own growth and
development. The teacher can promote this atmosphere by establishing rapport with the pupils. A friendly interest in their problems plus constructive handling of criticism are good tools with
which to begin. A slightly less formal procedure will also help, but
one should be careful to adjust the degree of informality to the
group and to its ability to maintain speaking and listening conditions that will insure the greatest possible success for all members
of the class. The teacher can further aid the establishment of such
an atmosphere by getting students acquainted so that they are
interested in each other's speech problems and are mindful of the
effort and progress made in overcoming them.

3. *Select beginning assignments wisely.*

There are many types of beginning assignments, and all teachers
have their favorite ones. Often these are based upon sentiment; in
other cases they are used because they have been successful; less
frequently they reflect serious thinking upon the conditions to be
met. Opening assignments should do more than just *start* the course.
At the least they should fulfill these essential purposes:

a. Provide an opportunity for the instructor to know the student
—background information and specific facts about his speech needs,
interests, and abilities.

b. Enable students to become better acquainted.

c. Furnish an initial speech performance in which they can succeed with the knowledge, speech habits, and skills they possess at
the start of the course.

d. Aid students in becoming better adjusted to the oral communication situation because they will enjoy and understand better
the experience of speaking to an audience.

e. Motivate interest by providing a basis for future work.

SPEECH INFORMATION BLANK

Name_____ Address_____ Phone_____

Age_____ Class in School_____ Adviser_____

Course_____ Other subjects now scheduled (besides speech):

Subject   Hour   Days of Week   Room   Instructor

Schools attended previously _____

_____

Extraclass activities in which you are interested _____

_____

In which of these do you participate regularly? (Give days and place, also) _____

_____

Are you employed after school? _____ No. of hours weekly _____

Hobbies, interests, etc. _____

_____

Newspapers you read regularly _____

_____

Magazines you read _____

_____

Best books read in the last year _____

_____

Favorite movies, radio or television programs _____

_____

Previous training or experience in speech _____

_____

What do you hope to gain from this course? (List any particular goals, interests, or problems you wish) _____

_____

The various types of beginning assignments that follow have been observed in use over a period of years. The preceding purposes will be used as criteria by which they will be evaluated.

TYPES OF BEGINNING ASSIGNMENTS

1. A Short Announcement

This is a simple assignment. The content involves only the place, time, and occasion. Practically everyone can handle it successfully. However, it is too short to permit the instructor to make a satisfactory analysis of needs and abilities. The materials have no particular interest value and would rarely serve as a basis for work to follow.

2. Conversation

As an opening project, conversation has many good things to recommend it. It creates an informal situation which almost every person can meet with respect to content, problems of adjustment, and techniques. It can serve as a basis for further work in informal speaking situations which can lead to more formal work later. However, it is difficult to teach effectively with a group situation unless the situation is carefully planned in terms of subject matter, organization of desirable situations, assignment of partners, and so on. Because of the group character of this work, it allows only a limited opportunity for the teacher to diagnose abilities and needs. It is also sometimes regarded lightly by students if not properly motivated. It presents only a limited opportunity for work on the organization of ideas for speaking. Its chief value is as a method of gradual adjustment to speaking situations and as a basis for teaching more specifically the techniques and principles of informal speech.

3. Interviewing

This has all the advantages of the conversation project and is conducted so that all can observe each interview. Also, it permits somewhat greater analysis of speech needs. Only a restricted use of body could be checked, however, since most of the work would be done while the students were seated. Like conversation, interviewing needs careful planning and some special instruction on procedure. Furthermore, one person is likely to do most of the talking. It would probably be better as a sequel to number 2 above than as an opening assignment.

Interviews can also be used to gather information important to introductions of other members of the class. (See *b*. in the next starting assignment.)

4. Introductions

a. Introducing One's Self

This kind of assignment, like the interview, is useful as a get-acquainted device, especially in those high schools where students do not know each other. If they are all well known to one another, it may seem a bit silly to them. It provides a familiar content and gives a chance for an adjustment situation that most can master. However, boys and girls sometimes feel embarrassed when they talk about themselves before a group. In some cases it may be too short a speaking performance for adequate diagnosis.

b. Introducing Other Members of the Class

The advantages of this assignment are the same as those in 4.*a*. Moreover, it makes for a more normal situation in getting acquainted than does the first of these two. The disadvantages are essentially the same as they are for the first in the matter of analysis of speech needs.

5. Group Discussion

Like numbers 2 and 3 above, discussion is valuable in aiding emotional adjustment. It also provides interesting and significant content, furnished by stimulating subjects, for oral communication. Such material has greater intellectual appeal than much of that usually handled in conversation assignments. It offers only a limited use of certain fundamentals, however, and thus restricts the teacher in finding out what student needs are, particularly in the area of posture, movement, and other aspects of bodily action. The group nature of the project makes careful analysis by the instructor almost impossible. If anything more is wanted beyond the mere opportunity for all to participate, the teacher will probably have to lead the discussion, or at least make some provision so that retiring, quiet individuals have a chance to speak; however, it does make an excellent starter.

6. Reading Aloud

a. Selections of the Student's Own Choice

This type of assignment should give an accurate sample of the student's reading habits. It tends to reduce the complexity of the adjustment problem before the group by having a content furnished. Further, it gives some opportunity for the teacher to become better acquainted with the interests of the students.

By itself, however, it does not provide a complete picture of the speech habits of the student. It should be supplemented by a speaking assignment.

b. Selections Chosen or Prepared for Reading by the Teacher

This possibility has all of the advantages of 6.*a.* above and allows the teacher an opportunity to control the nature or the difficulty of what is read. It does not give an indication of student taste, however. It has the additional benefit of allowing the instructor to load the piece to be read with particularly selected sounds so that a broad screening of voice and articulation difficulties can be accomplished. Disadvantages are the same as those in 6.*a.*

7. Memorization of a Portion of a Speech or Literary Selection

This provides an opportunity for the teacher to check habits of delivery on *memorized* materials. It places no burden upon the student to compose or organize ideas or choose language. It does involve the burden of remembering, however, and this may more than offset any gain in the problem of adjusting to the speaking situation secured by a prepared content. If this kind of material is used for analysis, the question can be raised of the accuracy of the diagnosis if a sample of ordinary speaking habits on unmemorized, spontaneously developed materials is desired. Although this selection can be used handily for drill on delivery during the course, there is some question about the transfer of this learning to other experiences in speaking and reading later in the course.

8. Choric Interpretation

This is another opening *group* assignment that offers the beginning student an easy situation for adjustment. It gets him into the swing of things in a fashion similar to that of assignments numbers

2, 3, and 5. As a result, it does not permit careful analysis of student needs until after the process is reduced to individual participation unless each student is given "part" reading to do. It has the advantage of stressing delivery and does not bother the student with preparation of the content of his selection. It could be used to build toward certain types of subsequent assignments, particularly those in interpretation, for which type of work it would appear to be more definitely suited.

9. *Pantomime*

This is frequently used as an ice-breaker because it demands no spoken communication. It also provides a situation in which the need for bodily action is an outgrowth of a situation. Most students can have fair success in this assignment, particularly in broad or gross bodily movements. Too often the pantomimes used demand more technique than students possess at this point, if the meanings demanded by the exercise are to be conveyed accurately or completely. They often fall into patterns of action suggesting unsuccessful attempts at doing something, followed by success, and so on. Because the assignment demands no speaking, it does not offer an opportunity for diagnosis of needs in the fundamentals of the use of voice, articulation, and so on. It is doubtful, also, how much carryover or basis is included here for later assignments unless one should work on bodily activity as an early unit. Even then the problem of transfer is involved.

10. *Voice and Articulation Test*

Although this type of beginning project provides an opportunity for a very careful, specific, and individualized check on voice and articulation, it does not give the student the experience of speaking or reading before an audience. It does not give the teacher an opportunity to diagnose habits in continuous speech. It would be valuable as a starter, but more satisfactory as a supplement to one of the other assignments.

11. *Voice Recordings*

Voice recordings should be made from carefully prepared materials such as speeches, readings, or interviews. There is no question of the value of recordings as a device for enabling the student to hear himself, to listen to his voice while the instructor analyzes it, and as motivation for improvement. But if recordings are made too early in the course, they are not likely to be an accurate reproduction of the normal speech because of an undue emotional tension at this stage of development. If made later, the normal student will be more at ease, and the result will more nearly reflect the student's normal speech.

12. *An Original Speech on a Hobby, Interest, or Recent Personal Experience*

This assignment offers advantages that follow closely the purposes and qualities set up for opening projects. It draws upon materials familiar to the student; it enables him to speak before the audience and be sure of success; it enables the teacher to make an estimate of the student's speech needs and abilities; it acquaints class and instructor with his interest; it places a minimum of tension upon him because of the nature of the task; it can serve as a basis for other subsequent work.

Such an assignment necessitates some preliminary and elementary instruction in speech composition, a thing which the teacher can do in preparation for the first platform appearance.

13. *Best (or Worst) Speaker I Ever Heard*

This talk asks the student to describe the characteristics of the best or worst speaker he ever heard. Thus, to the various purposes of the beginning assignment it adds a consideration of speech standards to be achieved in the course. This is a useful basis for future work. In addition, this assignment sets up suitable motivation when successful speakers are analyzed as models.

14. *The Problem-Solution Speech*

Because of its provocative nature, this talk has been rated most popular among beginning assignments by many college students.[1] It requires that the student select a problem, explain it clearly, and offer a reasonable solution (which he supports) to get at the causes of the problem. The speech encourages originality, substantial speech

[1] See Wilmer Linkugel, "A Student Evaluation of Assignments in a Course in Fundamentals of Speech," *Speech Teacher*, VI (March, 1958), 154-57.

content, effective organization, and real motivation in proving the solution. It also fulfills other purposes of a starting assignment.

15. A Demonstration Talk Using Equipment or Properties

This speech, similar to some types of hobby talks, satisfies the desired purposes and qualities of the first assignment. It has especial value in focusing the attention of the speaker upon something outside himself, as well as providing him certain manipulative action which will relax him. He should select a subject interesting to the class; the teacher can help by suggesting subjects and organization.

16. The Process-Inquiry Speech [2]

This exposition of a process without blackboard or properties meets the requirements of a very satisfactory first speech. It necessitates direct, communicative delivery suggested for achieving best speaker-audience relationships because of the question-answer feature.

All of these assignments can be used to start a beginning course in speech. A *combination* of reading aloud and an original speech like numbers 12, 13, 14, 15, or 16 reveals most about individual needs. Discussion is an excellent group activity for adjustment; later, individual performances will allow diagnosis of fundamentals. Voice and articulation recordings help after a first talk. With a knowledge of all individual needs in fundamentals, the teacher can adjust his course outline to provide for needed development.

17. A Series of Speech Experiences

However, a carefully planned *series* of speech experiences is a very effective way of getting started. Below is a plan used in the required first course at the University of Kansas. For years Professor E. C. Buehler has administered the program. He points out that the instructor offers no criticism during the first three speeches, but does "identify special merit in a laudatory manner."

First day. (Opening half hour) Key-note the course in your most persuasive and conscientious manner. This is perhaps the most important

[2] See Laura Crowell, "The Process-Inquiry Speech," *Speech Teacher*, I, No. 3 (September, 1952), 167–73.

set of remarks you will offer during the entire semester. Bring the goals of the course into sharp focus, but more important still, picture glowingly the values of speech to the student.

(Second half hour) (1) Assign exploratory reading of the entire text during the first four or five weeks. Comb the book for ideas, hints, clues, which might be helpful. Take notes for your own use. (2) Assign the *autobiographical letter* as follows: "Write a letter to your teacher about yourself, about three hundred words in length, commenting upon four points: (a) your early home, family, and community life; (b) your professional or occupational goals and interests; (c) your experience and training involving speech such as courses, contests, plays, group leadership, salesmanship, etc.; (d) an evaluation of your speech needs and a discussion of what you would like to get out of the course. The letter is confidential. Hand it in at the third class session." (3) Break up the entire class into couples and have students *interview* each other in preparation for a two-minute talk in which he introduces his partner. These should be friendly, informal, good-natured talks to be given at the next session.

Second day. Hear all introductions in pairs from the front of the class. Instructor take notes analyzing student needs, etc.

Next assignment: Divide class into two groups for two-minute speeches. *Group One:* "Rank in importance and give reasons for ranking the six factors of life: (a) friends, (b) education, (c) religion, (d) money, (e) family, (f) health." *Group Two:* "Make the same approach to six professions and evaluate them as to which has contributed most to civilization: (a) the preacher, (b) the farmer, (c) the scientist, (d) the artisan, (e) the politician, (f) the teacher."

Third day. Collect letters assigned the first day. Hear the two groups on "factors of life" and "professions." Speeches may be made by students standing next to their chairs. Instructor keeps diagnostic notes, etc.

Next assignment: Two groups giving two-minute speeches. *Group One:* "You and a companion are to live two years in a lighthouse isolated from the world. You can take only three books other than the Bible and can have sent you for the duration of your stay, two magazine subscriptions. What three books and two magazines would you choose? Support your selections." *Group Two:* "Nine people are stranded on a desert. A helicopter can save only five. The group includes: an army captain, his fiancée, a twelve-year old boy, a wealthy society woman, a noted scientist, the president of General Motors, the governor of your state, a famous movie star, and a little known preacher or priest. Whom would you save and why?"

Fourth day. Hear the two groups on the "Lighthouse" and "Death on the Desert" speeches.

Next assignment: *Demonstration speech* four to five minutes. The assignment for this first major prepared speech should be made with care. Encourage careful planning, much bodily expression, attention to details, specificity, with focus upon clarity plus broad, easy action for description, etc. "No sewing buttons on a shirt!" Insist on objects, physical properties, visual aids, etc. *Divide the class into three sections.*

Fifth, sixth, and seventh days. Hear demonstration speeches. *Begin to make constructive criticism.*[3]

This seven-day approach is currently used in the thirty sections of the beginning course by six hundred students. It was developed after years of experience and study by the course director with the help of student opinion about beginning assignments. Through this sequence the student soon gains the feeling of belonging, of being an important member of the group. Work begins from his point of view and he finds it easy to lose himself in a series of speaking ventures with minimum fear of failure. From the start he is swept into the midstream of enjoyable, successful speaking ventures. He scarcely has time to worry about his feelings of apprehension. Having built a small stockpile of successes, the student is encouraged to apply himself diligently and courageously as the course progresses.

EXERCISES

1. Plan carefully the procedure you feel would be best in starting your course in speech when meeting with your students for the first time. Outline your introductory lecture and remarks and set up a guide sheet to be distributed to the students, making sure that it includes such necessary information as course objectives, name of textbook, reading assignments, platform assignments, observations, special projects and activities, and so on.
2. State which beginning assignment you believe to be best and justify your choice.

[3] E. C. Buehler, "The First Seven Days of the College Beginning Speech Course," *Speech Teacher*, VII (November, 1958), 302–5.

REFERENCES

BUEHLER, E. C. "The First Seven Days of the College Beginning Speech Course," *Speech Teacher,* VII (November, 1958), 302–6.

CROWELL, LAURA. *"The Process-Inquiry Speech," Speech Teacher,* I (September, 1952), 167–73.

LINKUGEL, WILMER. "A Student Evaluation of Assignments in a Course in Fundamentals of Speech," *Speech Teacher,* VII (March, 1958), 154–58.

NILES DORIS. "Notebooks for Neophytes," Speech Teacher, VIII (March, 1959), 129–34.

PHELPS, WALDO. "The Panel Forum as a First Assignment in the Secondary School Speech Fundamentals Class," *Speech Teacher,* I (September, 1952), 162–66.

CHAPTER TEN

Poise and Emotional Adjustment

The problem of poise and emotional adjustment in a speech situation faces both the student and the teacher. The student who is self-conscious, timid, or is apprehensive of failure wishes to overcome his problem. Many students enter a speech class for this express purpose. The teacher has the same earnest desire to see the problem solved; in addition, however, he must plan his part in helping the student to achieve his goal; this necessitates the consideration of a number of questions.

Just how shall the teacher deal with emotional adjustment in a speaking situation? Shall he ignore it completely? Shall he handle it when the problem occurs? Shall he assume that every student is quaking in his boots, and go after the problem completely and directly with the whole class? Shall he approach it indirectly, using various means of reducing tension? Will the aggravated cases finally solve themselves through practice to a point that nothing the teacher does will make any difference? What should the teacher and student know regarding causes, symptoms, and so on? What can the teacher do by his attitude, method, and technique in the speech class to alleviate or eliminate the emotional problems in the speech situation?

TENSION, A COMMON EXPERIENCE

The teacher cannot ignore emotional tension, nervousness, or "stage fright," whatever the label. It is quite common among students as they face speech situations. Many feel that they will fail in speaking before an audience. They also tend to magnify the importance of such things as dress, manners, complexions, social position, family, or economic status. Worrying about such details merely adds to their insecurity as they face an audience.

Studies by Franklin H. Knower [1] at the University of Minnesota indicated that 56 per cent of a group of 210 students and 61 per cent of another group of 277 students stated some form of nervousness was one of their speech problems.

Surveys by Greenleaf [2] of 1,172 college students in a basic speech course indicated that 6 per cent experienced severe nervousness, 45 per cent moderate, 33 per cent mild, and 16 per cent none at all. Studies of high school students showed only 29 per cent to be free of emotional disturbance, while 74 per cent said they were somewhat nervous.

Emotional tension has been a common experience among many persons who have become great speakers or performers. Daniel Webster, Henry Ward Beecher, Prime Minister Nehru of India, and Winston Churchill all had to overcome such a problem. Bing Crosby, Jack Benny, and Ella Fitzgerald also mastered this difficulty to become successful.

In speech classes teacher and pupil have a wonderful opportunity to work together to meet the problem.

The speech teacher especially can note manifestations of emotional reaction in beginning speakers; he is also in an excellent spot to do something for them. Tension and "freezing"; aimless and uncoordinated movements, excessive walking; shortness of breath; inaudibility, lack of variety, harshness, high pitch in voice; avoidance of the audience; breaks in fluency; loss of continuity in content—all are characteristic. Others are less obvious to the teacher, but he knows they accompany emotional tension: cold sweat, spinal shivers, dry mouth, pounding of the heart, and that hollow feeling in the stomach. The teacher must also know the causes.

The practical causes are important: (1) a new and unfamiliar situation; (2) lack of knowledge of what to do; (3) fear of failure, complexity of the situation; (4) lack of preparation; (5) conflict; (6) basic personality deviations; (7) faulty evaluation of psychophysical reactions, and so on.[3]

[1] Franklin H. Knower, "A Study of Speech Attitudes and Adjustments," *Speech Monographs*, V (1938), 131.

[2] Floyd J. Greenleaf, "An Exploratory Study of Speech Fright," *Quarterly Journal of Speech*, XXXVIII (October, 1952), 326–30.

[3] Theodore Clevenger, Jr., and Gregg Phifer, "What Do Beginning College Texts Say about Stage Fright?" *Speech Teacher*, VIII (January, 1959), 1–7.

Basically, it is the body's way to meet an emergency. Typical physiological reactions occur: adrenalin is secreted directly into the blood stream; more oxygen and faster breathing are needed; the heart beat picks up and circulation is accelerated; perspiration cools the body; the gastric juices stop flowing and the stomach feels hollow. In short, the body is "stepped up" to meet the situation.

But, *such a surge of energy is a good thing.* It helps speakers to do a better job than they would ordinarily do; it gives sparkle and drive to a talk. *The important thing is control over the emotion so that it will be a constructive force.* The human organism can develop such control. The brain operates as an intellectual governor over emotional reaction; it can reduce its severity and bring it into line.

DEALING WITH THE PROBLEM

Importance of Experience and Training

Analyses of speakers show that experience is an important factor. First, persons having *had* speech experience have greater confidence and report less tension. Gilkinson's study [4] of fearful and confident speakers supports this conclusion:

	Fearful speakers	Confident speakers
Have had no previous public speaking experience	26	9
Have had no previous speech instruction	41	14
Generally regarded as leaders	24	67
Have had no important parts in plays	52	24
Have been in no interscholastic or major interclass debates	89	55

Next, Edward Robinson concludes that experience is the best method of helping to overcome stage fright:

One answer to the question, "How can I gain confidence as a speaker?" is—Your stage fright is a learned fear response which is subject to conditioning leading to control. The best method of conditioning involves repeated performances. Prepare as adequately as possible and speak as often as possible.[5]

[4] Howard Gilkinson, "A Questionnaire Study of the Causes of Social Fears among College Speech Students," *Speech Monographs,* X (1943), 74–83.
[5] Edward Robinson, "What Can the Speech Teacher Do about Students' Stage Fright?" *Speech Teacher,* VIII (January, 1959), 8–14.

He also cites several experimental studies in which *training* in speech classes improved the emotional control of subjects who participated. In the Leyden experiment they reported "significant improvement in speech performance, speech attitudes, and social behavior," when tested before and after training. Paulson, using a similar method of introspective report and personality inventories, found significant gains in confidence after ten weeks of training with 271 college students. Hayworth concluded that even with differing methods of teaching, stage fright was significantly alleviated in a group of 850 students. He also reports similar results of gains in confidence through repeated performance as found by Garrett, Rose, Moore, Edwards, Eckert, and Keyes.

Importance of Teacher and Class Attitude

In an experiment involving 205 students in a first course in speech, Henrikson [6] endeavored to discover the effects of speech training upon stage fright and to note the factors that influenced reduction of emotional tension or gains in confidence. Using student rating before and after experiences in seven different types of speaking situations, he had these conclusions: (1) speech training promotes confidence in the speaking situation; (2) feelings of confidence apply to situations beyond those in the course; (3) feelings of stage fright are in a constant state of flux; (4) a variety of factors influence a student's stage fright. Those ranking highest are *practice, the attitude of the instructor,* and *the attitude of classmates.* Feelings of having succeeded or failed and analysis of causes of stage fright, contrary to what might have been expected, rank low.

1. *The speech teacher is a counselor.*

The speech teacher has a superior opportunity to counsel students regarding the many worries of adolescence. His whole approach in *knowing* his pupils (Chaps. IV and IX) sets the stage for this function. He can combine his knowledge of students with other data from the home-room director or central records. From these sources he can learn much about individual adjustment problems which are reflected in class. Conferences with students are invaluable to an emotional therapy, which can be carried into the varied activities of a speech program.

[6] Ernest Henrikson, "Some Effects on Stage Fright of a Course in Speech," *Quarterly Journal of Speech,* XXIX (December, 1943), 490–91.

2. *The teacher uses appropriate activities.*

With such an understanding of pupils the teacher can employ the whole range of speech experiences, which will be helpful individually to those in need of confidence and social adjustment. Discussions, class meetings, plays, assembly activities, radio programs, and so on, all provide interesting opportunities for students in situations that will be of benefit to their needs.

Approaches to Teaching

Two major approaches exist that can work successfully. (1) The *direct,* in which symptoms, causes, and cures are explained. Individual problems are talked over freely in class. Methods are identified and are applied to the problems publicly with as much objectivity as possible. (2) The *indirect,* in which symptoms, causes, and cures are *not* discussed. Problems are handled individually, but are not discussed before the class. Suggestions for activities are passed from instructor to the student privately. *The teacher creates class conditions to help reduce tension.* Methods to help the student are set up within this situation.

SUGGESTIONS FOR THE TEACHER

With this in mind the following suggestions are offered to the teacher. They involve *indirect* methods primarily:

a. Cultivate a friendly, positive, and understanding attitude.
b. Build a class atmosphere characterized by an *esprit de corps* that gets students acquainted, makes them feel that everyone is pulling for the success of everyone else, and fosters the ability of each to work for the good of all.
c. Give plenty of opportunities for speech performance with an audience that is interested and an instructor who has helpful suggestions.
d. Put criticism on a constructive basis (see Chap. XI). With beginning students criticize composition first, then delivery. Use conferences and small groups to assist with severe cases of nervousness. Talk over problems.
e. In planning work and making assignments keep the following in mind:

(1) Make assignments well in advance; make them clear and specific; pass out guide sheets to provide a permanent description for study and reference; provide helps on preparation.

(2) Adjust them to the potentialities of the student at a given time in the course (see Chap. IX).

(3) Provide opportunities for individual differences in ability and development with an extensive list of subjects.

(4) Motivate assignments with a definite purpose. Build interest and enthusiasm through your own personal enthusiasm and vitality. Provide experiences that challenge the student.

(5) Require an outline or some similar inventory of preparation.

(6) Plan special performances to take care of factors such as action, directness, and so on (see Chap. XV).

f. Work on individual problems in speech one at a time. Make individual contracts with the students to "achieve this next time for sure."

g. Build the concept that each speech is a new opportunity for growth and improvement; previous failures, if any, are past and done; each student steps up to bat each time with another chance to hit a home run.

h. Do not ignore the problem of nervousness; on the other hand, do not make such a public announcement as this, "I know you are all scared to death." Rather, handle problems as they occur and as the scheme above indicates; do everything to remove the causes in the class; by careful teaching, tactful comment, the springboard of successful experience, raise the level of confidence in each student.

i. Assign readings regarding the nature of emotion and methods of control, if and as they are needed.

A Usable Group Procedure

Another study gives some suggestions the teacher can consider in helping students in their emotional adjustment. Borin [7] conducted

[7] Leighton Borin, *Construction and Evaluation of a Group Procedure Designed to Raise the Confidence Level of Beginning Students in Speech* (Unpublished doctoral dissertation, Northwestern University, 1949), pp. 51–67.

this work with students in a first course in speech. The important steps in his "Group Procedure" were as follows: (1) First Class Meeting: introduced students to each other and the instructor was introduced; the nature of the course was explained carefully; notebooks or "log" books were distributed for recording observations, assignments, and so on; students were asked "Why are you enrolled in this course?" "What would you like to accomplish in the course?"; the assignment was given; a question-answer period was held. (2) Evaluation Sessions (six were held in the ten-week course): used to follow up the assignment of the previous week; students observed real-life speaking situations, their own speech habits, speech situations in class, and their preparation for speaking—all based upon *student* experiences; dynamic aspects were given special attention—group morale, group identification, and group motivation; work methods of each student were discussed and criticized; (3) Laboratory Sessions (three were held in ten weeks): mistakes were corrected by the instructor during the performance of the speaker; he was made to stop, the error was indicated, and suggestions for substitute behavior were made; the speaker then went ahead; these sessions were recorded.

Borin found these sessions significantly helpful in raising the confidence level of speakers in the first course. He also found that regular classroom experiences in public speaking were superior to those in group discussion or interpretation for raising the confidence levels of students. In terms of criticism and general procedure he observed that success accompanied the identification of the teacher as a *member of the group,* and he states that "sessions were planned to permit *active* participation of the student but *passive* participation of the instructor." He also includes a scheme for criticism which he found helpful in the sessions: (1) use brief comments; (2) discuss concepts understood by the student at that point in the course; (3) direct criticism to the speech, not the student; (4) use direct class criticism by other students very *late* in the course; (5) give positive and constructive suggestion; (6) keep it below the student threshold of criticism tolerance; (7) adapt criticism to the sensitiveness of the individual student; (8) emphasize the pleasant and successful aspects of speaking experience.

SUGGESTIONS FOR THE STUDENT

The teacher can also help to bring about certain results by the action of the student. Sarett [8] gives these very valuable suggestions about how the student may reduce his stage fright: (1) by preparation; (2) by the control of his physical machinery; (3) by his mental attitudes.

a. *By preparation*
  (1) Write out the first three or four sentences of your talk and memorize them.
  (2) Prepare a detailed outline in which the sequence of ideas is coherent and almost inevitable.
  (3) Take your outline with you and place it on the speaker's stand.
  (4) Memorize the outline so thoroughly that when you close your eyes you can see every main head and subhead.

b. *By physical control*
  (1) Before speaking force yourself to relax. When you reach the platform take a relaxed posture.
  (2) Keep in mind the necessity of controlling your breath; before you enter the auditorium, breathe deeply for many minutes in order to fill your lungs with fresh air; when you reach the platform, take a deep breath before uttering a word; throughout the speech, pause at frequent intervals to draw a deep breath; and at no time speak at such a rate that your breathing becomes shallow.
  (3) In extreme cases of stage fright, it is helpful to lean on the speaker's stand.
  (4) There are cases of stage fright which may justify a speaker, during the first minute or two of the speech, in handling some unobtrusive object, such as a book from which he plans to read.
  (5) Abundant spontaneous bodily action, properly motivated, will do more than any other single physical factor to help the speaker to acquire self-control and release his powers.

[8] Lew Sarett and W. T. Foster, *The Basic Principles of Speech* (Rev. ed.; Boston: Houghton Mifflin Co., 1946), pp. 51–67.

c. *By his mental attitudes*
  (1) Compensate intelligently for feelings of inferiority.
      (a) Compensate directly by overcoming the defect.
      (b) Compensate by developing other virtues.
      (c) Compensate by helping other unfortunates.
      (d) Compensate by finding a post of authority.
  (2) Cultivate other mental attitudes.
      (a) The all-in-the-same-boat mental attitude.
      (b) The eager-to-share mental attitude.
      (c) The speaking-for-a-cause mental attitude.
      (d) The will-to-fight mental attitude.

Baird and Knower [9] make these suggestions for the student:

1. Reducing the intensity of the emotional reaction
   a. Study the psychology of emotion.
   b. Think and talk about your emotions as an objective fact.
   c. Resolve personal conflicts.
   d. Fight unpleasant frustrating emotions with pleasant stimu-
      lating emotional responses.
   e. Develop habits of voluntary relaxation and control of
      activity.
   f. Use the principle of the Beta hypothesis in learning (nega-
      tive practice).
   g. Do not submit unnecessarily to severe mental and physical
      strain, i.e., control your environment.

2. Increasing the efficiency of intellectual activity
   a. Know what is reasonably to be expected of a speaker.
   b. Prepare as thoroughly as possible for the presentation of all
      organized speeches.
   c. Use devices in speaking which facilitate the memory for
      speech materials.
   d. Use directed movement to keep the mind active.
   e. Develop an effective intellectual philosophy for speaking.

These are two comprehensive methods of helping the student
to overcome nervousness or fear in the speaking situation. He will,
no doubt, have to make the necessary discoveries with the help of

[9] A. Craig Baird and Franklin H. Knower, *General Speech* (New York:
McGraw-Hill Book Co., Inc., 1948), pp. 193–200.

the teacher regarding which particular methods are most successful in his case.

EXERCISES

1. Read a research study that deals with the problem of stage fright and be ready to discuss your findings.
2. List and develop briefly the approaches and techniques used by teachers you know to reduce emotional tensions and problems in performance situations. State your opinion on each of the methods involved.
3. Write a paper in which you answer this question: "Should emotional adjustment be dealt with *directly* or *indirectly* in the basic speech course?" Justify your position.

REFERENCES

BAIRD, A. CRAIG, and FRANKLIN KNOWER. *Essentials of General Speech.* New York: McGraw-Hill Book Co., Inc., 1960.

BRYNGELSON, BRYNG. "Educating the Emotions and Developing Objective Attitudes toward the Self," *Bulletin of the National Association of Secondary School Principals,* XXIX, No. 133 (November, 1945), 39–41.

CLEVENGER, THEODORE, JR. "A Synthesis of Experimental Research in Stage fright," *Quarterly Journal of Speech,* XLV (April, 1959), 134–35.

———, and GREGG PHIFER. "What Do Beginning College Speech Texts Say about Stage Fright?" *Speech Teacher,* VIII (January, 1959), 1–7.

DICKENS, MILTON, and WILLIAM PARKER. "An Experimental Study of Certain Physiological, Introspective, and Rating-Scale Techniques for the Measurement of Stage Fright," *Speech Monographs,* XVIII (November, 1951), 251–59.

GILKINSON, HOWARD. "A Questionnaire Study of the Causes of Social Fears among College Speech Students," *Speech Monographs,* X (1943), 80.

———. "Speech and Personality," *Bulletin of the National Association of Secondary School Principals,* XXIX, No. 133 (November, 1945), 36–39.

GREENLEAF, FLOYD I. "An Exploratory Study of Stage Fright," *Quarterly Journal of Speech,* XXXVIII (October, 1952), 326–30.

KNOWER, FRANKLIN. "A Study of Speech Attitudes and Adjustments," *Speech Monographs,* V (1938), 130–203.

LOMAS, CHARLES. "The Psychology of Stage Fright," *Quarterly Journal of Speech,* XXIII (February, 1937), 35–44.

———. "Stage Fright," *Quarterly Journal of Speech,* XXX (December, 1944), 479–85.

MURRAY, ELWOOD; RAYMOND H. BARNARD; and J. V. GARLAND. *Integrative Speech.* New York: Dryden Press, Inc., 1953.

ROBINSON, EDWARD. "What Can the Speech Teacher Do about Students' Stage Fright?" *Speech Teacher,* VIII (January, 1959), 8–14.

SARETT, LEW; WILLIAM T. FOSTER; and JAMES H. McBURNEY. *Speech: A High School Course.* Boston: Houghton Mifflin Co., 1956. Chap. IV.

———; ———; and ALMA SARETT. *Basic Principles of Speech.* Boston: Houghton Mifflin Co., 1958. Chap. VI.

CHAPTER ELEVEN

Diagnosis, Evaluation, Testing, and Criticism

Successful teaching in any field demands that the teacher know practical methods of testing pupil achievement. In speech it is necessary to measure or test *knowledge* of the field, consisting of facts or theoretical principles. This is also standard practice in other subjects. However, in speech it is also vital to measure much more than information, such as might be done by a pencil-and-paper test. The distinctive and great need is to measure *skill* or *speech performance*. Such changes in behavior are key goals of instruction in all basic speech courses, and in many others specializing in speaking, discussion, debate, interpretation, acting, and so on.

The great problem for the beginning teacher lies in the lack of any effective *single* instrument for the measurement of speech skill. Weaver, Borchers, and Smith observe:

There is no paper-and-pencil test or laboratory instrument known today which will measure, directly or indirectly, the effectiveness of the total act of speech, or the sum of an individual's skills in speaking.[1]

Knower's definition develops the problem in even more detail:

A speech test is the expert use of a great variety of data derived from sound tests, observation of speech performance under controlled conditions, and a review of records of interests and achievements to formulate a critical judgment on the speaking proficiency of the student. To be a speech test, it must measure the achievement of the individual in many speech processes and the integrated use of these processes in functional

[1] Andrew T. Weaver, Gladys Borchers, and Donald Smith, *The Teaching of Speech* (New York: Prentice Hall, Inc., 1952), p. 529.

218

speech activity. None of these processes must be confused with the whole, and the test should be diagnostic as well as evaluative.[2]

The solution to the problem for the teacher lies first in his gaining essential general information about measurement. Then he can proceed to develop satisfactory procedures suitable to him as he applies his basic knowledge to testing speech performance. This learning process underlies the development of materials in this chapter.

ESSENTIAL GENERAL INFORMATION

The Nature of Measurement

All measurement or testing is a type of observation. Devices used in education to measure, such as rulers, tape recorders, microscopes, and so on, help the tester to extend his sense impressions in observation so that they will be more exact, more efficient, or more usable. The standard pencil-and-paper tests help him to observe by getting data from students and by organizing them in some convenient form.

Every observation involves something observed and someone who observes. In each there is a possibility for error. In testing, it is important to know the kind and extent of error that exists. Every observation is also based upon a sample. It is difficult for a teacher to observe *all* of a student's speech performance or to observe it under all conditions. In a pencil-and-paper test, the teacher selects questions covering only *some* of the items that might be tested. He *assumes* that the student's speech behavior or his answers to the questions selected are similar to the responses on all the other questions he might have answered or to the speech behavior he might have exhibited in all the other situations. Such assumptions are subject to error in sampling and in the conclusions drawn from observing the sample. Even the most carefully selected sample is subject to error. The best the teacher (tester) can hope for is to reduce that error and *estimate* that his judgments about the rest of the behavior are accurate. Thus all observations, judgments, scores, and grades are really approximations. In measurement the teacher tries constantly to eliminate any weaknesses in the measuring in-

[2] Franklin Knower, "What Is a Speech Test?" *Quarterly Journal of Speech,* XXX (December, 1944), 492–93.

strument, to understand what they are, and to allow for them in his interpretations.[3]

Qualities of Effective Tests

To understand weaknesses in tests, it is necessary to know *desirable* qualities. Every test should have *reliability, validity, and practicability.*

Reliability refers to the quality of a test to yield consistent results upon repeated performance. In a reliable test, repeated measurement should yield relatively little variation. High reliability alone, however, is not sufficient.

Validity means that a test must measure *specifically* what it is supposed to measure. This quality is most important in testing. As a tester, the teacher wishes to know exactly what he is measuring. If he is trying to diagnose a student's rate of speaking, he does not desire to find that he has measured the loudness of his voice. Similarly, he does not wish to discover that he has tested a student's appearance rather than the information contained in his talk. He must know what is determining the judgments, the scores, or the grades he is getting. Such knowledge is basic to the use of tests in planning or evaluating the content of courses, or to suggestions for improvement given the student.

Practicability concerns the usability of a test. A teacher should ask himself, "Is it worth the energy, time, expense, and results obtained by its administration?" If the answer is "Yes," and the test has reliability and validity, it is worth serious consideration and use.

Purposes of Testing

Three principal purposes of testing are (1) diagnosis, (2) evaluation, and (3) motivation.

Diagnosis means discovering the individual needs and abilities of students. Beginning assignments can serve as diagnostic tests that allow the teacher to establish a *collective* pattern for the entire class, based upon individual needs. Such a pattern can serve as a basis for adapting classwork so that it will meet those needs as closely as

[3] See Jack Douglas, "The Measurement of Speech in the Classroom," *Speech Teacher,* VIII (November, 1958), 309–19, for an excellent summary of problem and method.

possible. Individual diagnoses by testing are also the bases for the instructor's plan of work with each student.

Evaluation means measuring the achievement of each student throughout the course. Each recitation offers a possibility for improvement. In speech, personal habits and skills are evaluated with suitable testing procedures, usually after each performance. Findings are given to the student through appropriate criticism and suggestion.

Motivation is the basic desire or drive to learn provided by intelligent use of tests. By knowing his own strengths and weaknesses the student can direct the effort he will make to improve. Similarly, the teacher will know how to aid the student in overcoming his problems and becoming more effective in performance. Thus the whole learning process becomes more efficient; specific goals are set, individual instruction is facilitated, and classwork is organized to produce results.

THE PROBLEM OF TESTING SPEECH PERFORMANCE

Testing speech *performance* is very different from testing the student's speech *information* or *theory*. It is relatively easy to devise a pencil-and-paper test to use for the latter purpose. However, a test of speech performance presents a number of problems. These include the following: (1) the complexity of the speech performance; (2) the scope of the test or what should be tested; (3) variations and lack of consistency in the behavior of the speaker, either within a given performance or from day to day; (4) the effect of the testing situation upon the speaker; (5) its effect upon the listener-tester; (6) variables affecting the tester in his relationship to the speech performance; (7) the kinds of tests, or the rating techniques used.

The first six of these items will be considered in order. Rating or testing techniques will be treated in the next section. In reference to the first of these problems, Monroe states: "The difficulty in testing speech performance lies primarily in the complexity of the speech act itself." [4]

[4] Alan Monroe, "Testing Speech Performance," *Bulletin of the National Association of Secondary School Principals*, XXIX, No. 133 (November, 1945), p. 157.

THE COMPLEXITY OF SPEECH PERFORMANCE

The truth of this statement is easily seen when one considers the great number of variables involved in the act of speaking. On this point, Monroe continues:

The voice itself is only a small part of the total speech act yet it alone varies in pitch, loudness, timbre, and in the pattern with which these variables change. No two voices are alike any more than are two sets of fingerprints. Add to this the complexity of the visible behavior of the speaker, his posture, his facial expression, the way he moves about, and what he does with his hands, what sort of clothes he wears, and the picture becomes more complex. Nor is this all. The use of language is an important variable, including such things as grammar, choice of words, variety of sentence structure, vocabulary, and the like. In addition, the background of knowledge and experience and the specific understanding of a particular subject seriously affect the speaker's performance, as do the emotional maturity and control which he possesses. These are but a few of the many variables which go to make up the complex performance which we call speaking. Yet all of these variables are present at one time and affect the phenomenon to be tested.

For diagnostic testing this complexity makes more difficult the task of isolating specific variables. It is difficult, for instance, to separate the speaker's control of vocal pitch and loudness since these two variables often occur together; that is, one tends to raise his pitch as he talks louder. Nor is it always possible to determine whether excessive hesitancy arises from poor vocabulary, emotional tension, insufficient knowledge, or all three. The overlapping influence of the many variables in speech performance thus makes their isolation for the purpose of diagnostic testing difficult.

On the other hand, while evaluating testing can be done in terms of "general effectiveness" or the total effect of the performance, the reliability and validity of such evaluation has been found to increase when it is based upon the summation of measurements of separate variables. The derivation of appropriate weights for these variables in the process of summation, however, is somewhat difficult. It is not possible to say, for example, that voice is twice as important as visible behavior and should be given twice its weight. For one speaker this might be true, whereas for another speaker or in another situation it might be completely false. The excellence of an individual in some one variable may be so great as to outweigh or conceal even completely a weakness in several other variables. Weightings of this sort, therefore, while they can be adequately determined for group measurements, may be extremely false when applied to individual speakers.

The difficulties so far listed result from the complexity of a speech performance in the speaker himself, but the actual speech phenomenon involves more than just the speaker; the audience listening to him and the physical conditions under which he speaks are also involved. What might be a good speech at a football rally would not be appropriate at a dedication ceremony. Audiences differ in age, intelligence, prejudices, and many other things. Since the purpose of speech performances, whether conversation, public speaking, or dramatic, is always communication, a proper evaluation or diagnosis must include consideration of the listener as well as the speaker. Thus an entire new set of variables is introduced into the complex which is to be tested. The problem becomes increasingly difficult when, as in the case of rating scales and attitude questionnaires, the listener's reaction is made the index for measuring the speaker's effectiveness. Such procedure is, of course, theoretically the most valid since the ultimate test of the speaker's effectiveness is the information he imparts to the listener or the change of attitude he produces in that listener. Great care must be exercised in the use of this method of testing, however, since the measuring device itself contains so many variables in addition to the thing being measured.[5]

THE SCOPE OF THE TEST

The next consideration is that of the scope of the test. A glance at the preceding paragraphs indicates the number of possibilities for an answer to the question: What shall we test? In many instances a speech test has become only a check on voice and articulation. This is true of the speech tests reported by Mathews [6] in nearly 80 per cent of the educational institutions she surveyed. Moses [7] makes a similar report of types of tests in sixteen of twenty-eight schools he studied.

It is important for the teacher to understand that such tests of a single element or process do not reveal the caliber of the *whole* speech performance. A test of articulation gets at only one part; like-

[5] *Ibid.*, pp. 157–58.
[6] Hannah P. Mathews, "Voice and Speech Examinations in American Educational Institutions," *Quarterly Journal of Speech*, XXVIII (December, 1942), 458.
[7] Elbert Moses, "A Survey of Speech Tests in Thirty American Universities and Colleges," *Quarterly Journal of Speech*, XXVIII (April, 1942), 206–11.

wise, a test of voice is a check on only one process—in fact, if loudness alone were tested, only *one part of a part* would have been
diagnosed or evaluated. Of course, testing *parts* of speech performance is a legitimate technique and can be used to advantage by the
teacher to help a student improve that element. However, any
assumption that such a procedure reveals the *whole* speech pattern
is erroneous.

Proficiency tests surveyed more recently in fifty colleges and universities by Keller [8] and others come closer to Knower's definition of
a speech test. They report almost as many forms of tests as there are
institutions. Among the types used are (1) a recorded interview in
which students respond to general questions and read orally certain
test passages for voice, articulation, and skill in interpretation; (2)
written examinations on principles of speech composition, delivery,
and discussion techniques; (3) a prepared 6–8 minute speech followed by a discussion and question period; (4) a 10-minute original
talk prepared in advance on a subject of the student's own choice,
followed by (5) a 3-minute impromptu speech upon a current topic.
All these tests were used for diagnosis, for screening college students
for courses in basic speech skills, and for purposes of sectioning.

VARIATIONS IN PERFORMANCE

The next problem in testing is that of the variation and lack of
consistency in the performance of the speaker. In commenting on this
fact, Knower states:

> The individual speaker's proficiency in all processes which contribute
> to the total success of his speech is seldom if ever consistent. The values
> of the various processes for accomplishing different purposes may not be
> the same. The effects of speech will vary with the ability and standards or
> tastes of the listeners. The level of achievement in various processes in-
> fluences the effect as a whole in a different manner from speaker to
> speaker and situation to situation.[9]

It is also relevant to note that the performance of an individual
speaker may vary on the various components *within* a given speech.

[8] Paul Keller, William Seifrit, Jr., and John Baldwin, "A Survey of the Use
of Proficiency Examinations in Speech in Fifty Colleges and Universities,"
Speech Teacher, VIII (September, 1959), 242–45.

[9] Knower, *op. cit.*, p. 486.

It is not unusual to observe changes in use of voice, particularly in variation and flexibility, as the speaker overcomes his initial tension in a speech and becomes better adjusted and more relaxed. In a long talk where fatigue may enter and the power of concentration fluctuates, a person testing or judging a speech can readily notice variations in the handling of the elements of the speech performance.

EFFECT OF THE TESTING PROCEDURE

The next consideration is that of the effect of the testing procedure upon the speaker. By its very nature, a testing situation tends to destroy the normal conditions under which speech performance takes place. The knowledge that he is to be tested often changes the behavior of the speaker. He may exert himself, become more tense, or depart from his "normal" speaking performance. If he is aware of certain procedural details, such as the use of rating scales, ballots and pencils, or criticism sheets, the situation may become an artificial one to him. This is noted also when a student is making a disc, wire, or tape recording. He frequently reacts to the equipment and to an unfamiliar situation, so that he is unable to give a satisfactory sample of his typical speech. The situation becomes even more unnatural if the speaker is fitted with laboratory equipment to record breathing, pulse, or other aspects of bodily response for objective testing. This does not mean that such testing is not useful. It does mean that the teacher who interprets the results of speech tests should be aware of the effect that testing procedure may have had on them.

Similarly, the testing situation affects the listener or tester. This is especially true if he is not completely familiar with the method of test administration or if he has any inadequacies in the mechanics of his testing method. The tester himself may find himself concentrating upon the situation to the point of emotional tension, which destroys his own normal receptiveness and attention.

First of all, he has a responsibility in testing to do his best; he must be fair; he must be accurate; he must be as objective as possible; he must give a rating, grade, diagnosis, or criticism after he hears the speaker, sometimes immediately following his performance. He must be tactful in this procedure. All these circumstances make for the tension previously mentioned; they can produce inaccuracy or confusion in an unsophisticated tester.

Similarly, if he is obliged to make notes, check or record his reaction while he listens to the speaker, the normal listener-speaker situation is upset. Further inaccuracy may result from such distractions.

FACTORS AFFECTING THE TESTER

This observation leads to a discussion of the factors that influence the rater or tester. They are all variables in testing speech performance. In commenting upon the attitude of the judge (tester), Simon makes a discerning observation when he states: "A judge is objective or subjective in terms of *his habits,* not in terms of the criteria on the ballot or the items on a criticism sheet." [10] He then adds that these factors may influence judgment:

1. The *attention span* of the listener. How much does he give? How long does he attend at a time?
2. The *knowledge* of the listener; kind of knowledge.
3. The *emotional state* of the listener.
4. The *influence of the preceding speech* or performance.
5. The *perceptual habits* of the tester:
   a. He sees what he wants to see.
   b. He sees and hears what he believes.
   c. The judge or tester tends to evaluate what he sees and hears in terms of his personal likes and dislikes.

In commenting upon the factors that affect the judgment of the listener, Knower [11] lists these: (1) sensory capacities; (2) alertness; (3) concentration; (4) knowing what to look for; (5) lack of bias and prejudice; (6) freedom from fatigue; (7) ability to interpret; (8) ability to record observations quickly.

Thompson [12] lists a number of factors that affect the rater: (1) lighting of the room; (2) acoustics; (3) attention span of the rater; (4) irregular waning of attention; (5) shifting of certain stimuli or elements in the perception; (6) meaning attached to stimuli by the observer; (7) differences in combining evaluation on individual items to reach a total judgment; (8) unusual and varying ideas on what constitutes good speaking; (9) expectation of the observer; (10)

[10] Clarence Simon, professor of Speech Education, School of Speech, Northwestern University, class lecture, in *Psychology of Speech.*

[11] Knower, *op. cit.,* p. 489.

[12] Wayne Thompson, *The Accuracy of Typical Speech Rating Techniques* (Unpublished doctoral dissertation, Northwestern University, 1943), pp. 5–11.

habituation regarding the performance of an individual speaker or different speaker; (11) errors in the particular measuring device which are peculiar to it, e.g., directions, words describing categories of judgment, and so on.

From these lists of factors, it is clear that many things influence the teacher who tests speech performance. From a practical point of view it is desirable for him to learn the particular things that are likely to affect his judgment at any given time and to be able to estimate the extent of their influence in any kind of testing situation. Thus, he can make such adjustments as are needed to move his grading or scoring toward greater objectivity.

This discussion of the problems in testing speech performance is intended to acquaint the teacher with the difficulties in this field so that he may proceed with informed caution in testing. In the field of speech performance we are not so fortunate as are teachers of mathematics, science, or spelling, fields in which achievement can be measured by standardized tests. Despite recent developments, the speech teacher must always face the problem of the complex act of speech performance itself, which takes place before an audience of unpredictable human beings and is judged by still another person with variations in training and ability. As Knower states: "Teachers interested in an exact analysis of speech problems will use testing procedures that enable them to diagnose difficulties as well as to evaluate achievement. The manner of handling these problems is, in fact, one of the most important differences between the well-trained and the untrained teacher of speech." [13] These testing procedures are considered in the next section.

METHODS AND TYPES OF TESTING

In selecting a test, the teacher finds many types from which to choose. In fact, each expert has his own classification of types. Monroe [14] whose classification we shall develop in some detail, lists (1) simple judgment, (2) controlled judgment, (3) audience response, (4) instrumental tests, (5) subjective reports, and (6) subject-matter tests. Knower [15] includes (1) observational, under which he places intuitive, analytically systematic, and instrumental, (2) objective, (3) pragmatic, covering listener comprehension, retention, attitude

[13] Knower, *op. cit.*, p. 487.
[14] Monroe, *op. cit.*, pp. 159–63.
[15] Knower, *op. cit.*, pp. 489–92.

change, changes in listener activity, group balloting, audience meters, photography, and observations and ratings of audience. Thompson [16] bases his list upon types of observer ratings: (1) paired comparisons, (2) rank order, (3) linear scale, (4) letter grades, (5) descriptive letter grades, (6) speaker attitude scales, and (7) rating scales.

Because these overlap considerably, we shall develop only the Monroe list, which is reasonably easy to understand, and provides a scheme under which others may readily be classified.

1. Simple Judgment

This is the most common method of evaluating and diagnosing speech performance. It involves only the judgment of any listener regarding the total effect or quality of the speech or any of the parts of the speech act. The teacher in the classroom uses this method a great deal. To the extent that he is well trained in the analysis of speech performance and is not subject to emotional pressures or other prejudicing factors, his judgment will be reasonably sound. Experimental studies have shown the judgment of the trained teacher to be the simplest and most effective method for day-by-day evaluation and diagnosis of speech performance.

2. Controlled Judgment

In order to enable the tester to be more analytical and systematic in his judgment, rating scales or check lists may be employed. These contain items that direct the rater to focus his attention and make judgments on the criteria listed. These are the result of an analysis of speech performance by the person who devised the scale. In actual use, the tester listens to a speech and makes judgments regarding it in terms of the criteria on the scale. He may assign a numerical rating for each item or merely place a check mark opposite items needing attention by the speaker. It is possible for any teacher to devise a rating scale or check list. Among the very few that have been standardized or checked for reliability is the Bryan-Wilke Speech Profile.[17] This scale has sixteen items. Some teachers find it very usable; others like a shorter scale. Samples of a number of scales appear on pages 229–34.

[16] Thompson, *op. cit.*, pp. 5–11.
[17] Walter Wilke, "A Speech Profile," *Quarterly Journal of Speech*, XXVI (1940), 625–30.

	Poor		Fair		Average			Good		Excellent	
SUBSTANCE	1	2	3	4	5	6	7	8	9	10	11
Choice of subject											
Adequacy of material											
Adaptation of material											
Concreteness											
STRUCTURE	1	2	3	4	5	6	7	8	9	10	11
Introduction											
Clarity of purpose											
Unity											
Emphasis											
Coherence											
Conclusion											
STYLE	1	2	3	4	5	6	7	8	9	10	11
Choice of words											
Sentence structure											
Grammar											
BODILY EXPRESSION	1	2	3	4	5	6	7	8	9	10	11
General posture											
General bodily movements											
Gestures											
Eye contact											
Facial expression											
VOCAL EXPRESSION	1	2	3	4	5	6	7	8	9	10	11
Projection											
General pitch level											
Flexibility											
Quality											
Rate											
Fluency											
Pronunciation											
Articulation											
PERSONAL QUALITIES	1	2	3	4	5	6	7	8	9	10	11
Communicative attitude											
Enthusiasm, vigor, vitality											
Friendliness and good humor											
Poise and self-control											
Freedom from bad mannerisms											

GENERAL COMMENTS: Grade_____

* From Robert T. Oliver and Earl T. Johnson, *Effective Speech Notebook* (Syracuse, N.Y.: Syracuse University Press). Reproduced by courtesy of the authors.

General Speech Performance Scale [°]

Name _____ Date _____ Rater _____

Project _____ Time _____

Subject _____ Grade _____

Criteria	Rate 1–5	Comments
Speech Attitudes and Adjustments Indifferent _____ Antagonistic _____ Tense _____ Apologetic _____ Flustered _____ Posed _____ Irresponsible _____ Immature _____		
Voice and Articulation Weak _____ Loud _____ Fast _____ Slow _____ Monotonous _____ Excess vocalization _____ Poor quality _____ Indistinct _____ Poor pitch _____ Dialect _____ Not rhythmic _____ Mispronunciation _____ Poor phrasing _____ Misarticulation _____		
Bodily Postures and Action Indirect _____ Monotonous _____ Inexpressive _____ Not integrated _____ Random _____ Exaggerated _____ Slovenly _____ Weak _____		
Language Inaccurate _____ Monotonous _____ Ambiguous _____ Inexpressive _____ Wordy _____ Stilted___Technical _____ Colloquial _____ Immature _____		
Content Not clear _____ Inaccurate _____ Insignificant _____ Lacks originality _____ Dull _____ Lacks movement _____ Insufficient _____ Abstract _____ Too much _____ Lacks unity _____		
Organization Poorly purposed _____ Weakly supported _____ Questionable central idea _____ Poor transitions _____ Poorly introduced _____ Poor sequence _____ Poorly analyzed _____ Poorly concluded _____		

Audience Interests and Adaptation
Attention not
   aroused _____   Beliefs not
   considered _____
Interest not
   maintained _____   Obviously
   solicitous _____
Knowledge not
   considered   Confidence not
   secured _____		

General effectiveness		
Total		

° A. Craig Baird and Franklin H. Knower, *General Speech: An Introduction* (New York: McGraw-Hill Book Co., Inc., 1949), p. 494. Used by permission.

CLASSROOM SPEECH RATING SCALE *

1–2, Weak; 3, Average; 4–5, Strong

	Speaker's Name	1	2	3	4	5	6	7	8	9	10	11	12
Rater													
Date													
Project													
Speech attitudes and adjustments													
Voice and articulation													
Bodily postures and action													
Language													
Content													
Organization													
Audience interest and adaptation													
General effectiveness													
Total													
Rank order of all speakers of the day													
Turn sheet sidewise and write in any comments													

* Reprinted from *A Syllabus for Speech 401*, by Franklin H. Knower and Wallace Fotheringham, Department of Speech, The Ohio State University.

SPEECH EVALUATION CHART

Karl F. Robinson

1. Poise and Emotional Adjustment	
2. Subject: Ideas and Information	
3. Organization	
4. Use of Voice	
5. Articulation and Pronunciation	
6. Control of Bodily Activity	
7. Language and Grammatical Usage	
8. Audience Contact	
Total or Grade	

COMMENTS:

Scale values:

5 Superior
4 Above Average
3 Average
2 Below Average
1 Inferior

ACHIEVEMENT IN SPEECH PERFORMANCE *

	Performer
Name	
Grade	
Day of Week	
Period	
Choice of Subject	
Choice of Material	
Arr. of Material	
Language	
Projection	
Body Activity	
Rhythm	
Articulation	
Pronunciation	
Aud. Response	
Total	
Score	

Comments:

* Harry G. Barnes, *Speech Handbook.* Copyright 1941 by Prentice-Hall, Inc., New York.

BRYAN-WILKE SPEECH PROFILE [*]

Speaker: _____ Audience: _____

Date: _____ Number of Judgments: _____ B-W Score: _____

	1	2	3	4	5
1. Opening remarks					
2. Personal appearance	1	2	3	4	5
3. Voice	1	2	3	4	5
4. Distinctness and Pronunciation	1	2	3	4	5
5. Flow of words	1	2	3	4	5
6. Self-control	1	2	3	4	5
7. Degree of energy	1	2	3	4	5
8. Platform behavior	1	2	3	4	5
9. Personality	1	2	3	4	5
10. Sincerity	1	2	3	4	5
11. Command of language	1	2	3	4	5
12. Clarity	1	2	3	4	5
13. Interest	1	2	3	4	5
14. Reasoning	1	2	3	4	5
15. Concluding remarks	1	2	3	4	5
16. Value	1	2	3	4	5

[*] Reprinted with the permission of the authors.

Knower has summarized the values and limitations of such scales very well:

There is no evidence that experienced observers improve their evaluation by use of such scales. They serve such purposes as a guide for the training of inexperienced observers, a convenient form for recording judgments, and a record of the observational evaluation rendered. They also provide a useful means of studying evaluational judgment and analyzing speech performance. Much of the criticism against such scales as evaluational instruments, as we shall explain later, should be more properly directed against the process of rating by the person using the scales. It is essential that the rater thoroughly familiarize himself with any scale before attempting to use it in test situations. If the scale is to work well, the rater must use it easily. If he cannot do this, the accuracy of recorded evaluation is bound to suffer.

To enable the rater to use a scale conveniently it should not contain too many items. The total number of items will depend upon the length of the observation. Moreover, terms used in the scale must be precise and meaningful to the observer. The rater should not attempt to discriminate more than five to seven degrees of difference in traits rated. The attempt to discriminate finer degrees of difference results in a false sense of refinement in the process of observational evaluation.

Graphic scales permit the drawing of speech profiles. Check lists are seldom used to provide numerical records of performance. The rater checks the item if it is to him significant, and omits the check if it is not pertinent. The publication of norms for a rating scale adds little to the usefulness of the scale as such.

The objectivity of observational evaluation is entirely a matter of the objectivity of raters. Although the standards of evaluation in this process are ostensibly subjective, it remains a fact that such judgments may be accurate or even more accurate than an arbitrarily assigned score derived from items on an objective paper-and-pencil test. The conscientious rater will remain constantly alert to factors that influence the quality of his judgments and make every effort to exercise them with care. The *halo effect* in rating involves the tendency to generalize about speech achievement as a whole in terms of the critic's reaction to one or more of its factors. This tendency, when ratings are used merely for general evaluation, is not wholly to be deprecated. Since listeners ordinarily react to a speech performance as a whole, the critic should not always studiously avoid the influence of the halo. However, if ratings are to be diagnostic, then the best of discriminative judgment is needed.

Ratings on the average tend to fall above a theoretical average, although there are marked differences among raters in the central tendency of their ratings to be above the mean. Raters also differ in the range of their scores, although there is a general tendency to avoid use of the extremes on a scale. There is also a danger, in observational evaluation, that optimism or pessimism will cause the finding of achievement, or lack of it, because one looks for it or would like to find it. Some studies of comparative method in teaching where observational evaluation has been used have not guarded against this source of error.[18]

In addition to what has been said above, there are certain pros and cons in the use of rating scales by teachers in classroom situations:

USE OF RATING SCALES

Pro	Con
1. Provide a written (relatively permanent) record of achievement. May be used as a cumulative record of speech.	1. Pyramid the paper work and bookkeeping of the teacher.
2. Useful as motivation in teaching: students like to know their assets and liabilities in order to work for improvement of performance.	2. Dissect or analyze speech performance so that elements are stressed rather than the whole pattern.
3. An administrative help when time is short and oral criticism is restricted. Each person gets a definite instructor reaction.	3. Interfere with complete, courteous listening by the teacher; cause him to give first attention to mechanics of rating.
4. Individualize evaluation, diagnosis, and criticism; each student has a chart.	4. Often cause "overlapping" listening and rating when one speaker finishes and another is called on; otherwise, long class waits may occur.
5. Permit some quantitative basis for comparing students.	5. Inaccuracy is inevitable, especially if too many items appear on the chart. Almost impossible to use well in ordinary time limits of class speeches.
	6. Necessitate a clear understanding by students and teacher of each item or criterion *plus setting of standards* for achievement on each if scales are to be at all helpful.

[18] Knower, *op. cit.*, pp. 490–91.

While these items and Knower's comments seem to indicate a greater number of disadvantages, the individual teacher must decide whether rating scales will be of benefit as teaching helps in his situation. His choice should rest upon the knowledge of their limitations and their potential values to him.

3. Audience Response

Although any individual who evaluates speech performance can be assumed to be a part of an audience and as such establishes an audience testing situation on the quality of a speaker's work, the term "audience test," as ordinarily used, really means audience "reaction" test. Such tests evaluate the effectiveness of the speaker in changing the opinion or attitude of the listener on the subject under discussion; they do not provide for a direct judgment to be made upon the quality of the speaker's performance in relation to a set of standards.

An example of the audience test is the shift-of-opinion ballot, originally devised by Woodward. In using this test, each member of the audience, before the speech or discussion, marks on a ballot the item that most closely indicates his position on the question being considered. This might be *strongly favorable, mildly favorable, neutral, mildly opposed,* or *strongly opposed.* After listening to the speech performance, the listener again marks the ballot, indicating the position he has following the discussion. The effectiveness of the speaker is measured by the totals of tabulated shifts of opinion that have been produced by the speaker. (See Chapter XIX, p. 369.)

The Thurstone Attitude Scales are also used to test the change in attitude of the audience. In this kind of scale the listener marks a series of statements, each having a certain numerical value, which, when scored, will indicate his position on a scale, usually of eleven points. An A form of the test is given before speech performance, and a B form following. The two scores are compared in order to discover the amount of change resulting from the speaker activity; when used by a group of people, the amount, direction, and frequency of shift can be tabulated.

Gains in information and knowledge may also be indications of the speaker's effect upon an audience.

It is comparatively easy to devise a test of information to be used in measuring audience gains on factual material as a result of the speaker's performance. Increases shown by checking scores can serve as a measure of speaker effectiveness.

Audience reaction meters, which can record judgment during performance, push-button opinion machines, and the many kinds of applause and laugh meters are other devices that can be classified as audience tests.

All these instruments for audience testing have uses in research, classroom, and speech activity situations.

4. Instrumental Tests

Many of our commonly known instruments employed in speech testing are merely methods of *preserving* speech performance on recordings; discs, tape, wire, or film are used so that the performance can be replayed, analyzed, or tested by the first three methods listed above. In themselves the voice recorders are not instrumental speech tests. It is possible by their use to control listening conditions; transcriptions permit samples of speech to be played for many selected and varied individuals or audiences; similarly, recordings for study can be obtained from a wide range of speakers.

Direct instrumental testing devices used in voice science, for example, are the pneumograph and the kymograph, which are used to measure respiration, pitch, loudness, and duration during speaking.

Sound film, closed-circuit television, kinescopes, and video tape can also be utilized to permit persons to see and hear their own speech performance or that of others. Another device, the audiometer, is a piece of equipment employed to test hearing, a very important factor in speech development and training.

5. Subjective Reports

In obtaining information regarding the background, training, interest, knowledge, and attitudes of a person before and during speaking, inventories and standardized tests have been utilized. In all of these the subjective report of the person tested is employed. The Knower Speech Inventory and Attitude Scale, the Knower-Gilkinson Speech Guidance Questionnaire, the Miller-Murray Speech Inventory, and similar personality and temperament tests fall in this category. The varied information obtained by these inventories is used to help the teacher individualize his work. Actually, he is able to employ almost a case-study approach to instruction. Often this material helps to explain or to suggest causes for pupil behavior in speech situations; it frequently allows the teacher to build *rapport* with students, which would not be possible without his knowledge of their backgrounds and contemporary problems. Subjective reports are valuable sources of correlative information that cannot be obtained by other methods.

6. Subject-Matter Tests (Written)

Information and theory in speech can be tested in the same manner as the content in other subject-matter fields. The forms of objective tests (true–false, multiple choice, completion, matching tests) with which most teachers are familiar are usable in all speech courses. Essay quizzes and examination are also employed with considerable success. Another variety of the subject-matter test is the situation test in which the student may be called to adapt information and theory to use in a practical speech problem.

Mastery of subject matter as revealed by objective or similar types of tests is not an indication of skill in speech performance. Knowledge of theory must be applied and demonstrated in platform assignments. It should enable the speaker to improve his speech proficiency and conform to accepted practice. As a rule, knowledge is weighted as much less important than performance in beginning skills courses. Here development of individual speech proficiency is the principal goal. Greater emphasis may be placed upon theory in later course work. However, knowledge of the textbook material as revealed by written tests is no substitute for experience in speaking, accompanied by intelligent criticism by the instructor, and hard work by the student in improving skill before an audience.

USING TESTS IN THE CLASSROOM

In classroom work the teacher uses certain of the six types of tests more than others. The *simple judgment* is used on every performance. As a rule, *rating scales* are not used on every talk. Their chief value is to survey needs at the start of a course, at a midpoint to check improvement, and at the end. When so employed, they offer variety and motivation for students. Many teachers reject them because of the disadvantages given on page 236. *Audience* (reaction) *tests* are used for special types of situations to indicate the effect of a talk, discussion, or debate upon audience opinion. *Most instrumental tests* are used in experimental work in a laboratory, not in a class. *Subjective reports* are most helpful at the start of a course to supply personal data to the teacher. *Subject-matter tests* are employed for spot quizzes, hour, and final examinations.

In selecting which types of tests to use, the teacher should heed the conclusions of Thompson's study. His two general conclusions were these: (1) the experiments showed no one speech rating technique to be significantly superior to the others; (2) the training given raters did not increase the rating ability of this particular experimental group.

Certain general interpretations [19] from the findings are included in the study. These are of importance to the speech teacher.

A. The rater should chose his technique upon some other basis than accuracy.

B. The differences among rating methods is less than is believed. Costly devices that actually are no better than simpler procedures may well be eliminated.

C. The fact that raters differ significantly indicates the possibility of eliminating as raters those persons of slight ability. Institutions training speech teachers may use the technique (of this study) to detect and, if possible, retrain persons who give erratic judgments, before those persons become teachers and professional judges.

D. Above all else, the present study indicates that to improve rating, speech educators must devote their time to the individual rater and not to the method by which rating is done.

The conclusions and general interpretations from Thompson's study, the discussion by Knower, and the comments included with the types of tests from Monroe all point to the need for careful training of the teacher of speech in the methods of testing and evaluation. Knowledge of the kinds of instruments in every case has been found to be secondary to the need for competent instruction and experience in testing.

[19] Thompson, *op. cit.*, pp. 65, 66.

CRITICISM—A VITAL TEACHER RESPONSIBILITY

The teacher's skill in diagnosis and evaluation of speech performance becomes functional in the development of the student's ability when the results of the teacher's observations are made known to the student. *Criticism is the process of revealing the findings of diagnosis and evaluation to the student so that he may take the steps needed to improve his work.* Thus, the teacher's criticism underlies all learning in the speech class. His diagnosis of student needs in content, organization, voice, articulation, language, and so on provides the basis for immediate pupil and course goals. His evaluation of pupil achievement is the means of measuring progress in improving speech behavior to reach those goals. But unless the teacher can effectively communicate this information to the student, relatively little learning will take place.

Thus, in all situations where speech skills are taught, *the teacher has squarely before him the vital responsibility of giving each student after each performance a careful, accurate criticism containing specific suggestions for improvement.* He must not only analyze the assets and liabilities of the student, but should tell him how to overcome his weaknesses. Further, he must realize that his comments will shape the education of a human being. He should therefore skillfully use motivation to help that human being achieve his goals.

The teacher's aim may be achieved brilliantly or can be completely lost in the brief period allowed for criticism on each assignment. Here the whole force of his personality is revealed. His entire inventory of speech information and theory comes into play. His grasp of the "how to do it," the practical hints on developing speech skill, are most prominently displayed. Here he shapes values, builds goals, and develops attitudes among the students. Here he can employ serious response, humor, and friendly comment. He must do his job enthusiastically, competently, tactfully, and thoroughly. If he conducts the evaluation period in this way, he will have a room filled with eager students who hang on each word as a signal toward better, fuller endeavor in speech achievement. They will work ceaselessly to carry out his suggestions. If he falters in his job and indifferently spews meaningless, half-turned critical generalities over the classroom, he will surely fail.

Suggestions for Teacher Criticism

General Suggestions

1. Build an atmosphere in the classroom which encourages the student to welcome the criticism as a part of a learning experience.
   a. Be sympathetic, friendly, and enthusiastic in dealing with students.
   b. Explain the important functions of straightforward, tactful appraisal of performance as a necessity in improving speech skill.
   c. Point out that all of us are trying to improve in the course; we should be interested in working together not only for our *own* growth, but also for that of the others.
2. Review the nature of learning speech skills.
   a. Observe that each of us has weaknesses and strengths in his speech skill; most of us are unaware of these characteristics because (1) they are of long standing (13–20 years) and (2) they are habituated; unless some interested person calls these things to our attention, we shall probably do nothing about them.
   b. Stress the fact that friendly, constructive, specific suggestions are the methods by which we become aware of needs so that we can change undesirable speech behavior; emphasize that there is nothing "personal" in criticism: it is not a means of embarrassing the student; it is merely an evaluation, directed toward his improvement.
   c. Explain that new patterns of speech behavior need to be set up and evaluated: these in turn necessitate further evaluation and continued work by the student until the desirable modifications are definitely achieved.
   d. Urge the class to work together in reaching the individual goals each has set; encourage each person to come in for a friendly talk at any time he has a problem that bothers him.
3. Maintain objectivity in criticism; refer to experts or authorities who set criteria and standards for criticism.
4. Make comments definite and express them clearly.

5. Be positive and constructive in attitude and statement. Avoid "don'ts" and negative comment.
6. Concentrate on the speech, the reading, and so on, not upon the student.
7. Word the critique in language that is accurate and tactfully selected.

The Form and Organization of Criticism

Criticism should be clear and well-organized evaluation. It is generally presented orally by the teacher, but written critiques, evaluative comments, or notes of any kind need to meet the same criteria. The following formula has been found helpful in organization:

1. Review the criteria and standards you are using in evaluating the speech assignment.
2. In beginning classes discuss composition and organization first, then delivery. Comment upon the good things first; always find at least one complimentary thing to say.
3. Next, point out the weaknesses and undesirable items. Do this thoroughly and carefully, using an expository, objective approach and manner.
4. Explain specific causes of problems and suggest ways of improving the difficulties.
5. Select one important item and ask the student to work on it in particular for the next talk. As soon as this is improved, proceed to another.

When to Give Criticism

1. Use the first one or two performances for gathering information for actual diagnosis. Introduce criticism on the positive level after the third assignment.
2. Present criticism at the most appropriate time for effective learning. Use these possibilities:
   a. *Immediately after each performance.*

   In general, criticism is most helpful when given as soon after the performance as possible. Then, the teacher, speaker, and class recall what has occurred and can quickly relate suggestions to points needing improvement. Also, the critique can be specific and highly individualized. It can also benefit successive speakers since they will hear or participate in the evaluation given. The instructor can also relate his suggestions for each student to those that have been given earlier.

b. *After each second or third performance.*

This method permits the instructor to compare several speakers before offering an evaluation of them before the class. Similarities, differences, and general behavior patterns can be noted. Some suggestions can be combined if they fit several speakers in the group.

Although all details may not be recalled, it is usually possible to develop the significant, individualized suggestions for each student, also.

c. *At the end of the series for the day.*

The chief advantage of this plan is that it allows the teacher to make generalized evaluations and suggestions about the whole series of performances. These may precede, or may be fitted into appraisals of the work of each student. While some details may be forgotten (if six to eight talks have been heard), important items may be recalled from the notes of the teacher or students. Although the effect of immediate evaluation is lost, it may be balanced by the combination effect of comments under this plan.

d. *During performance; interrupt the speaker.*

Under this method, criticism is given during performance and will interrupt the speaker. When an error is made, or at an appropriate point, the teacher stops him, points out his weakness, suggests ways of improving it, and asks him to try to correct it on the spot.

Some teachers believe this a very effective plan, and certainly it is the most *immediate* method. It assumes the student will accept the interruption without breakdown or embarrassment and be able to continue the talk. It also assumes that the item criticized *can* be corrected on the spot. Certain mistakes in delivery may be handled most successfully by this plan. However, major revisions in composition or content could scarcely be accomplished.

A means of alleviating a "shock" reaction could be achieved by holding periodic "work-out" sessions, in which direct and immediate criticism is the standard treatment, and is expected by the students.

e. *Individual conference outside class.*

Generally used to supplement the methods above, this plan is the most individualized type of criticism. It may become a standard method, as it is in some colleges, but in general is not as frequently used in high schools. Chief advantages are the personal, informal situation, the relaxation from classroom time and administrative pressures, and the opportunity to talk over student problems man-to-man. It offers unlimited possibilities in dealing with students who have special difficulties in the classroom, which need close, personal attention. It is also invaluable to the instructor as a means of getting to know students of all abilities, in the interest of better motivation and rapport between teacher and student. The speech teacher has greater opportunities as a guidance teacher than any other in a school. The personal conference provides a superior educational vehicle.

Suggestions for Criticism by the Class

Criticism by the students in the speech class can be a valuable method when it is used judiciously. It should never be an escape for the teacher from his responsibility. It should be utilized as a means for teaching critical listening to platform assignments, with a view to developing audience responsibility, which is as important as speaker responsibility in communication. It should help students to develop high standards for speech performance. It should help the speaker to know how effective he has been in communicating with his peers in gaining the response he desires.

Student criticism should be used when these conditions exist: (1) the members of the group demonstrate that they know enough about criteria and standards of speech to criticize intelligently; (2) the atmosphere of a constructive learning situation has been established and the class views criticism as a welcome part of it; (3) the students know how to present criticism accurately and tactfully. Then these methods may be employed:

a. Call for volunteers from the class to offer suggestions; use a discussion method.
b. Use the class as a jury, asking them to vote on the accepted items in a scheme for evaluation as the instructor raises the criteria as questions.
c. Select in advance an individual student critic for the day.
d. Appoint an individual student critic for each speaker.
e. Call on individual students as critics without notice and with the understanding that anyone is likely to be selected to give the needed evaluation. This keeps each person on his toes.
f. Provide each listener with an evaluation scale or rating chart for each student speaker; have these handed to the speaker at the conclusion of his performance.
g. Have the students in the class write paragraph criticisms or evaluations of the person in the class. These should be done outside of class, handed in, sorted and assembled, and checked by the instructor before being distributed to the individual student. This device can be used to advantage at midterm or at the conclusion of a semester.
h. Have class members rank the persons reciting each day; require audience members to state reasons for ranking. Occasionally, the procedure can be used to furnish a mild, competitive situation for a group, especially in a high school class, by the award of some inconsequential but original object such as a "certificate of merit," a candy bar, a "speech medal," or similar item.
i. Use a tape recorder to record performance. Conduct playback sessions with each speaker listening. Employ any of the previous class methods to gain suitable audience evaluation.
j. Employ the tape recorder as a public address system (the school system can also be used). Use the class to evaluate specific aspects of audible delivery, e.g., voice, articulation, and so on. Compare written or rating scale judgments in a discussion session.

EXERCISES

1. Give your opinion concerning the effect of testing, evaluation, and criticism on the student's attitude toward the learning process and the classroom situation.

CHAPTER TWELVE

Determining Grades

Every high school or college speech teacher inevitably faces the task of determining grades, either on single performances or on written work, or as final marks in the entire course. Like diagnosis, evaluation, and criticism, this is often a difficult job in skills courses. Research reported earlier has established that no one method of evaluating speech performance is vastly superior to another. The simple judgment of the *trained* teacher using a letter grade system is as satisfactory a method as we have at present. *This fact places the responsibility squarely and inescapably upon the individual teacher.*

Grades are inherently a part of the academic system. With reference to this point Oliver makes these pertinent observations:

Admission to graduate school depends first of all upon grades. Many jobs are secured, or pay levels determined, on the basis of grades. Athletic participation depends on grades—as does entrance into other extracurricular activities. Honor rolls, scholarships, merit awards are determined by grades. Graduation itself depends upon grades. . . .

My own view is that grades are akin to the cash payments that in the competitive areas of business and industry are paid as wages and salaries. Of course, there is a degree of artificiality. "A fair day's pay for a fair day's work" is established even though we know that no two workmen are identical performers or producers. We do try to distinguish those who fail on the job—and are fired; those who do normal work—and receive "average" pay; and those who transcend the ordinary—and are promoted.[1]

With emphasis today upon high achievement, honors courses, and multiple track programs run according to ability, speech teachers

[1] Robert Oliver, "The Eternal (and Infernal) Problem of Grades," *Speech Teacher*, IX (January, 1960), 8–9.

can well examine their standards and grading procedures to ensure that they can face the demands for more rigorous sch͏͏͏. They can begin their work for a solution to the problem computing grades by examining some of the factors underlying it. Some of these have already been described.

In determining grades upon individual performance there are (1) the criteria upon which achievement in speaking, interpretation, and so on are evaluated, and (2) the standards which the teacher holds for satisfactory, superior, or inferior performance on the components or the total speech performance.

In deciding upon grades in the entire course, there are (1) the fundamental bases upon which grading in the course is to rest, (2) the relative weighting or importance of such items as information and theory (written work) in relation to speech performance (oral work), (3) the comparative value of daily work as compared with written or oral tests and examinations, (4) the absence of any norms in speech skill at any given grade or age, such as are found in mathematics, social science, or reading.

The teacher's decisions upon grades for individual platform assignments necessitate clear thinking and adequate description to establish the quantitative bases in (1) and (2) for a letter or number course grade, mentioned in the preceding paragraph. His compilations upon daily work will ultimately determine the course grades he gives. Systematic analysis and sound conclusions on items (2), (3), and (4) for course grades will enter significantly into his scheme. The discussion following attempts to help in his development.

GRADING INDIVIDUAL PERFORMANCES

Since there are no national or established norms for individual performance at a given age or level, the teacher starts with his own criteria and standards. There is quite general agreement upon the criteria or characteristics of a good speech or a good reading. The greater difficulty lies in setting or describing the standards of achievement to be required on these criteria for each grade level in the teacher's grade scheme.

In other words, if he accepts the items (criteria) on a rating sheet for evaluating a public speech (content, organization, style, bodily action, control of voice, personal qualities, audience effectiveness, and so on), just how much or what kind of performance does he expect of each or of the whole performance to award an A, a B, a C, a D, or an F. These are *standards* for grades. Further, does he have varying sets of standards for ninth, tenth, eleventh, twelfth grade students and college level speakers? The chances are that his standards are personal or local, the product of the teacher's habits, training, and experience.

It is nevertheless very important that the teacher know the criteria he will use, be able to explain them clearly, develop his own personal or professional standards for various kinds of speech performance, be able to describe or explain them, and finally *use* them in grading.

In an effort to provide some guidance for instructors, Oliver [2] developed criteria and descriptive standards for A, B, C, D, and F speeches in the basic course at Pennsylvania State University. They may be of assistance in helping others to develop similar patterns for grading.

I. Normally, an "average speech" (C) should meet the following standards:
   A. Conform to type assigned (expository, persuasive, etc.).
   B. Conform reasonably to the time limit.
   C. Exhibit sound organization: a clear purpose adequately supported by main ideas that are easily identified.
   D. Fulfill any special requirements of the assignment—such as, to use three illustrations, or statistics, or authority, etc.
   E. Be intellectually sound in developing a topic of worth with adequate and dependable evidence.
   F. Exhibit reasonable directness and communicativeness in delivery.
   G. Be correct grammatically and in pronunciation and articulation.
   H. Be ready for presentation on date assigned.
II. The "better than average" (B) speech should meet the foregoing tests and also:
   A. Contain elements of vividness and special interest in its style.
   B. Be of more than average stimulative quality in challenging the audience to think or in arousing depth of response.
   C. Demonstrate skill in winning understanding of unusually difficult concepts or processes; or in winning agreement from auditors initially inclined to disagree with the speaker's purpose.

[2] See Robert Oliver, *Effective Speech Notebook* (Syracuse: Syracuse University Press, 1958).

    D. Establish rapport of a high order through style and delivery which achieve a genuinely communicative circular response.

III. The "superior speech" (A) not only meets the foregoing standards but also:

    A. Constitutes a genuinely individual contribution by the speaker to the thinking of the audience.

    B. Achieves a variety and flexibility of mood and manner suited to the multiple differentiation of thinking and feeling demanded by the subject matter and by the speaker-audience relations.

    C. Achieves a demonstrable progression from the initial uncertainty (of knowledge or belief) held by the audience toward the subject, by orderly processes, toward a final resolution of the uncertainty in a conclusion that evolves naturally from the materials used by the speaker.

    D. Illustrates skillful mastery of internal transitions and of emphasis in presentation of the speaker's ideas.

IV. Speeches which must be classified "below average" (D or F) are deficient in some or several of the factors required for the "C" speech.

DETERMINING COURSE GRADES

Closely linked to standards, which form the guideposts for grading, are various factors especially related to determining final grades in speech courses. The teacher needs first to understand the general bases for such grading, and decide which shall govern his compilations.

General Bases for Grading

Among the usable bases are these: (1) *native or initial ability;* (2) *individual improvement* in relation to the student's initial performance and his potential development in the course; (3) *achievement in relation to an absolute or ideal standard* as seen by the teacher for speech performance of this type at a given grade level; (4) *achievement in relation to that of other members of the class;* (5) *effort;* (6) *attitude toward classwork*—e.g., seriousness, willingness, cooperativeness, indifference, antagonism, and so on.

It is possible for a teacher to consider only one of these bases in his grading. It is also conceivable that all of them might be considered in arriving at a final grade on achievement. Probably the more common practice in grading is to employ several of these bases, but to give greater weight to some than to others.

Native or Initial Ability

In considering the merits of these six bases, the teacher cannot escape being impressed by the first, the *native* or *initial ability* of the student. Whether or not it is the best basis for grading, it is always present. High native ability can mean that the student possesses unusual speech proficiency because of (a) heredity or (b) training through other sources before he entered the speech class in question. If a teacher grades on native ability heavily, or exclusively, he removes any motivation for student improvement as a result of his instruction. Students will make little effort to develop greater skill if they know that the teacher gives no recognition to their work. The inferior, the average, or even the superior students, knowing that they are "pegged" on first analysis and can gain nothing more, will lose interest. The superior student really receives a "free ride" in such a course; he can loaf through. The majority of class members will feel that they have lost the one thing for which they entered the course—the chance to improve their abilities. The teacher himself thus removes the necessity for his own existence, save on a recreational level. The real challenge to both student and teacher lies in some evaluation, at least, of improvement as a result of experience and training. Native ability is the foundation on which the student begins his training. It also places a ceiling upon his development in the course; his potentialities for growth are definitely affected by his native ability. It is wise for the teacher to consider initial or native ability in his grading for the course, but not to rest his evaluation upon it alone.

Individual Improvement

Improvement, on the other hand, should play a large part in the grading of speech performance. Successful use of this second basis rests primarily upon accurate diagnosis of initial ability. This pretest is a point of reference for all subsequent evaluations and for the comparison with the final achievement at the conclusion of the course. Consequently, the instructor must be sure that he is not fooled by the sophisticated student, who, having learned that he is to be graded mainly or exclusively upon growth, purposely malingers or does poorly on his opening or diagnostic speech performance. Next, the teacher must have accurate and frequent means of evaluating the progress of the student, including the final product with which he compares the initial performance.

Improvement motivates each student to do his best to develop his own abilities; he tries to move as far up the ladder of achievement as he can. It also motivates the teacher to do all things possible to assist and motivate the student to develop. Through criticism, the individualizing of assignments, and constantly setting up new goals within the potentiality of the pupil, the teacher can aid him in reaching the highest point of which he is capable, and hence the highest reward in terms of grades for his accomplishment. Such a basis necessitates that the teacher be a judge, not only of existing achievement but of the potentiality of each student. The true basis for grading rests not only upon the extent to which the person has improved but also upon how much improvement he was able to make in relation to what he *could* make. The teacher who places too much emphasis on improvement alone may do an injustice to the person of superior ability who actually has less chance for real growth than does the person with little demonstrated initial ability, but who shows great potential growth. The teacher will find that gross improvement is possible in the latter case, while finer, more subtle points of development, which border on the polishing of certain skills, are the case with the pupil of greater initial ability. Differentiation of goals and assignments may also be involved in providing the same relative opportunity to both types of individuals.

Achievement in Relation to Ideal Standard

It is practically impossible for the teacher to overlook *achievement* in relation to his own absolute standards as a basis for grading. It is this factor that is the balance wheel for a grade weighted highly on the improvement basis. This is particularly true if the level of achievement by a student, even though it represents a large gain for him, does not meet standards of adequacy in the mind of the instructor. As has been said earlier, there are no norms widely accepted for speech performance at a given grade or age level. However, the training of the teacher and the standards that have been developed through his background and observation will still play a part in his grading the student in a skills course. The inadequate articulators, the monotonous-voiced speakers, the inaudibles who cannot project beyond the first row, the sloppy thinkers and organizers—all these will be subject to critical comparison with the instructor's absolute standards, regardless of the fact that they may be better at the end of the course than they were at the beginning. They must meet a minimum level of development. Thus, such a basis for grading tends to enter the process to neutralize an overdose of improvement only.

Achievement in Relation to That of Other Pupils

Another balance wheel or counterpoise for too great an emphasis upon the improvement basis for grading comes in the checking of individual achievement in relation to that of other members of the class. It is wise for the instructor to keep a part of this basis in mind as he prepares his final course grades. Students hear all the speakers in the class, note their gains, their shortcomings, and also set up standards for performance. Any grade that the teacher gives will be known before long to all the members of the class. It will be associated with an individual student and with a certain quality of speech performance. While the instructor can justify on the basis of improvement marked deviations from what the class might expect as grades for certain levels of achievement, he cannot escape the necessity for comparing individuals or for ranking individuals within the group. This is a means of checking upon his judgment of, and the final grading of, the work of any given student who is part of the whole participating group. The instructor will be intelligent in his evaluation if he considers the impact of the grade he gives in the class situation, as one student is compared with another. He can often find much help in this process, not only through his own appraisal of this relationship, but also through student comments, criticisms, or written evaluations of the speech performance of class members.

Effort and Attitude

The final two bases, effort and attitude toward classwork, are integral parts of the grading process. They reflect the inner nature of the student and the kind of citizenship he possesses in the class. If they are undesirable or poor, they can completely nullify the effect of native brilliance, a fine voice, or unusual material. They reflect more than anything else the personality and the character of the student. They can make a knight in shining armor of an average or dull stu-

dent whose effort is tireless and whose attitude is sincere, cooperative, willing, and serious. These factors cannot be overlooked and
they should not be minimized.

In concluding this consideration of bases for grading, it should be
made clear that the two outstanding points are *improvement in relation to initial ability* and *achievement in relation to the absolute
standards of the teacher. Initial ability* and *achievement in relation
to others in the class* should influence any grade that is given on
speech performance.

Weighting Other Factors

Other factors to be considered are the relationships between oral
and written work, as well as those between daily performance and
final examinations. In a first speech course the oral work, or speech
performance, should always be weighted more heavily than such
written work as outlines, notes, or even tests. The objective of the
course is the development of proficiency in speech performance. It
follows that achievement in oral skill should be given greater value.
As a rule, such weighting would place twice or even three times as
much weight upon oral work as that placed upon written exercises or
tests. In other words, speeches would be counted as 66 to 75 per cent
of the final grade with written work being given 33 to 25 per cent of
the total. The instructor can determine the exact proportion he desires.

The weighting of the final examination in relation to the daily work
varies considerably with the instructor. In high school or college
courses that permit a large number of platform performances, the
daily work should be rated much more heavily. The final examination, one part of which is oral, can be weighted more than any other
class speech. With a total of ten speeches in a semester, a fair value
for the final oral examination could be one-fifth of the total, or
approximately the equivalent of two daily recitations. The written
part of the final examination, which is usually a check upon textbook
materials, should count in the same ratio to the oral part of the final
examination as other written work in the course does to the oral
performances; that is, roughly 4 to 10. This handling of oral *vs.* written work and daily *vs.* final examination usually gives satisfactory results. However, any instructor may vary these relationships with
justification in his own situation.

Student	Speech 1	Outline 1	Speech 2	Outline 2	Speech 3	Outline 3	Speech 4	Outline 4	Speech 5	Outline 5	Speech 6	Outline 6	Oral Final / Speech 7	Outline 7	Exam. #1	Exam. #2	Written Final / Exam. #3	Speech Observations*	FINAL GRADE** 1	FINAL GRADE** 2	FINAL GRADE** 3	Comments
1	C	√	C−	√	B−	√	B	+	B	+	B	√	B−	+	C	B	C	C	B−	B	B−	Works hard
2	A−	+	B	+	B−	+	C	√	C	√	B−	+	A	+	F	B	C	B	B	B−	B	Lazy; no zip
3	D	−	B	−	C+	−	B−	√	B+	√	A	+	A	+	A	A	A	A	B	A	A	Bookish; has lisp
4	B	+	A−	√	A	√	A	√	A	√	A−	√	A	√	C	C	C	C	A−	A	A−	High IQ; glib
5	C	+	C+	+	C	+	C	+	B−	+	C	+	C+	+	B	A	B	B−	B−	C	C	So-so; talks not motivated; writes well
6	B	+	B	+	B	+	B	+	B	+	B	+	B	+	B	B	B	B	B	F	B	Steady; had previous training
7	D	√	D	−	F	−	D	−	D	√	D	√	ab.	ab.	C	D	ab.	inc.	D inc.	F inc.	F	Not intelligent; cuts when possible
8	A	+	B	+	C	+	C	+	C	√	C	√	B	+	B	C	C	C	C	F	C	Doesn't try hard; "gets by"
9	D	+	C	+	C	+	C	+	C	+	C	+	C+	+	B	A	A	A	C	B	B	Foreign student; Span. accent; sincere
10	C	−	C	−	D	√	D	√	C	√	C	√	F	+	C−	D	D	F	F	F	F	Behavior problem; referred by dean

SAMPLE PAGES OF TEACHER'S GRADE RECORD

* Observations are written reports of five outside speakers (assigned by instructor). Grading Scheme: A, A−, B, B−, C, C−, D, F, *inc* if excused.

Outlines: + (very good); √ (satisfactory); − (unsatisfactory).

** See following pages for discussion.

COMPUTING THE GRADES

These bases and other factors come into perspective when a sample of a teacher's grade record (p. 257) is examined and analyzed. It may seem a bit complicated at first. However, upon examination it is clear that every oral performance grade is listed, including the oral examination, Speech #7; all outline grades; written examination grades on theory, including the final written examination, #3; and grades upon speech observations. Also recorded are short comments on attitude.

In computing grades three methods have been used. A set of grades under the FINAL GRADE column has been compiled for each student using each method in the order below:

1. *Simple inspection* (with oral work weighted 2–1). In this method the teacher has merely run his eye across the record of each student and arrived at a final grade, based upon the greatest frequency of letter grades noted, a "letter grade trend," so to speak. These grades appear in column *one*. Check to see whether you agree with them.

2. *Improvement basis* ONLY (with oral work weighted 2–1; final examination weighted as *two* regular performances). In many instances teachers say, "I grade on improvement *only*." This basis has been discussed earlier in the text. Here is an application of this statement. Recorded grades are assumed to represent a level or quality of work with Speech 1 as a starting point. Subsequent grades that do not show change indicate *no* improvement from this starting point. This may seem a highly artificial condition for teaching purposes, but the final grades are believed to be accurate when computed on this, the one and only basis. Certain students suffer when this basis is applied strictly; others gain. Column *two* contains these grades. Discuss this method thoroughly.

3. *Multiple basis* (weighting the same as in 2; bases used: improvement, achievement in relation to teacher's standards, pupil potentiality, effort, attitude). Here the grades have shifted in several instances, depending upon the teacher's subjective judgment and his individual decisions on applying and weighting the various bases. The grades computed on these bases appear in column *three*.

Some of the cases presented include special problems faced by every teacher of speech in grading. One of these is represented by Student 3. How does the teacher grade the student with a speech defect? Does a lisper with a grade of B or A make a good advertisement for a speech program? Or can the teacher point out that the student is under suitable care, is making good progress, and does B or A work, despite the defect? A similar problem is found in Student 9, who has a second language (Spanish) difficulty. His fine attitude, superior work in theory and written examinations, plus steady but slow improvement have earned him grades of B in columns *two* and *three*.

Questions of attendance, behavior problems, lack of native ability, indifferent attitude—all these exist in the ten students graded.

In facing the computing of final grades the beginning teacher must develop an organized system, be able to explain it, and justify it to his students and colleagues if necessary. Knowledge and experience will make a great difference in the ease and soundness with which he determines his course grades.

EXERCISES

1. Set up standards of work that you will expect for A, B, C, D, and failing work and be prepared to justify these standards.
2. When considering the various bases for grading, select the one on which you would place the greatest emphasis and state your reasons for making this choice.
3. Prepare two sets of course grades using (1) improvement only, and (2) any other combination of bases for a class you are teaching or for a situation given you by the instructor. Justify each grade.

REFERENCES

Braden, Waldo W. (ed.). *Speech Methods and Resources*. New York: Harper & Bros., 1961. Pp. 181–83.

Davis, Frank B. "Speech and Grades: A Request for Further Research," *Speech Teacher*, III (November, 1954), 255–58.

Friederich, W. J., and Ruth A. Wilcox. *Teaching Speech in High Schools*. New York: The Macmillan Co., 1953. Pp. 429–36.

Oliver, Robert T. "The Eternal (and Infernal) Problem of Grades," *Speech Teacher*, IX (January, 1960), 8–11.

REID, LOREN. *Teaching Speech*. Columbia, Mo.: Artcraft Press, 1960. Pp. 228–30.

SAWYER, THOMAS M., JR., "A Grading System for Speech Classes," *Speech Teacher*, IX (January, 1960), 12–15.

WEAVER, ANDREW; GLADYS BORCHERS; and DONALD K. SMITH. *The Teaching of Speech*. Englewood Cliffs, N. J.: Prentice-Hall, Inc., 1952. Pp. 533–39.

CHAPTER THIRTEEN

Effective Listening

The need for better listening constantly emerges as a problem for the attention of educators. As early as 1929, Paul Rankin,[1] then director of research in the Detroit schools, surveyed the personal communication activities of sixty-eight adults in different occupations. For a period of two months he had them keep tab every fifteen minutes of the time they spent during their waking hours in speaking, reading, writing, and listening. A statement of his findings is impressive. He found that on the average, his subjects spent 70 per cent of their day in verbal communication. Also, he learned that they spent 9 per cent of their time in writing, 16 per cent in reading, 30 per cent in speaking, and 45 per cent in listening.

The Columbia Broadcasting Company observes that over 90 per cent of our current events knowledge comes to us by listening to radio and television. People gain the greatest amount of their general knowledge through listening. Group meetings, in which listening plays a major part, are the most frequent means of problem solving in business, industry, and international affairs. Speaking for top management in the City Service Refining Company, Mr. W. E. Bennett stated in a talk before the National Society for the Study of Communication: "We have found that whether any specific problem is in the area of industrial organization or in the field of human relations, in ninety-eight per cent of the cases the root of the problem has been a failure on the part of someone to understand what someone else meant."

Yet how effective are we as listeners? As an integral part of their education, students *listen* to many lectures and discussions, often

[1] See Ralph Nichols and Leonard Stevens, *Are You Listening?* (New York: McGraw-Hill Book Co., Inc., 1957), Chap. 1.

directly to the participants, but frequently over television, or in situations marked by the extensive use of audio-visual aids. Numerous studies show that student listening ability is inefficient and low.

At Michigan State University in 1948–49, listening tests of students revealed that only 6 to 27 per cent could remember the first point of a lecture, about 50 per cent could relate factual detail to the major points of the lecture, and about 60 per cent could answer accurately when asked to draw inferences from materials presented. In 1950–51, Dow and Irvin tested 2,800 students at the same school. They found that 37 per cent comprehended 25 to 60 per cent of the material presented. The great bulk of students had 50 per cent efficiency. The top third, on test scores, averaged 70 per cent efficiency.

At the University of Minnesota, Brown tested college freshmen using a standardized test of listening ability. He found that 49 per cent of the group were able to get the central idea of the selection heard; therefore, they proved slightly less efficient than a group of high school juniors as listeners. Nichols, in 1948, administered a similar test in the St. Paul Branch of the University of Minnesota. He learned that the *average* student listener comprehended about 68 per cent of the materials presented, but some comprehended as little as 20 per cent. After testing large numbers of individuals, Nichols also reported: "Immediately after the average person has listened to someone talk, he remembers only about half of what he heard—*no matter how carefully he thought he had listened.*"

Similar reports on the inefficiency of our listening come from repeated studies in college, high schools, and adult groups all over the country.

TEACHABILITY OF LISTENING

Nichols points out further that listening can be taught successfully. For a period of fifteen years he has given a twelve-week listening course to freshman students scoring in the lowest 20 per cent on a listening test. In nearly *every* class he has found that these low scorers have improved their listening ability to the point where they equal or surpass those who were not required to take the course. Every group has improved at least 25 per cent in its ability to understand the spoken word. Some of the groups have improved as much as 40 per cent.[2]

Similar results are reported by David Krueger at Whittier College where he learned that college freshmen improved in listening comprehension from 18 to 56 per cent after a very brief instructional period. At Michigan State University, in 1950–51, Dow and Irvin reported the *results of instruction* with 2,800 students: "Listening instruction produced improvements in a one-year period of 12 to 25 per cent in better comprehension. . . . students who are extremely poor listeners have made the greatest gains in comprehension, often as high as 50 per cent." [3]

Despite these facts, writing and reading still are stressed more prominently than speech in language arts instruction in most of our schools. Speaking and particularly listening are given much less time. In the Detroit Schools, Rankin learned that 52 per cent of classroom time was given to reading, and to listening 8 per cent. Recent stress upon listening as a general educational skill has found the speech teacher already doing some things about listening, often without *direct* planning or teaching. However, he can assume leadership in this task. His field by nature offers a multitude of natural listening experiences. He can turn many of these into planned teaching situations, either preparing a unit on listening or distributing such training as it applies throughout the course.

The teacher who clearly understands the nature of listening and its purposes, who develops suitable methods and materials, can aid the development of listening skills by his students. This chapter sets forth certain basic information and suggestions to aid the teacher.

DEFINITIONS OF LISTENING

Nichols makes this observation in his definition:

Remembering that *apprehend* means "to become aware of through the senses" and that "comprehend" means "to embrace or understand a thing in all its compass and extent," perhaps one could say that hearing is the apprehension of sound and that listening is the comprehension of aural

---

[2] *Ibid.*, p. 15.
[3] Clyde Dow and C. E. Irvin, *Syllabus Communication Skills* (East Lansing, Mich.: Michigan State University Press, 1954), p. 116.

symbols. . . . Let us assume, then, that in communications work we are primarily interested in listening rather than hearing, and that until a better definition is devised *listening* may be defined as "the attachment of meaning to aural symbols." [4]

Baird and Knower state the following:

Profitable listening requires much more of the listener than his presence. He must recognize the ideas presented, evaluate them, discover relationships among them, and select from what he hears those ideas he finds worth remembering. If a listener makes his listening a thoughtful process, he controls his own thinking; if he does not listen critically, he is little more than a sponge, and often not a very good one. . . .

Listening as we use the word here includes the observation of communication, as well as its audition. To listen well we must listen all over, we must listen to the whole process of communication. That means watching the speaker, and his use of visual aids, as well as hearing what he says. [5]

John Caffrey and Donald Brown are not satisfied with the word "listening" to describe the process. They observe:

Listening has become a portmanteau into which is dumped an endless variety of meanings: paying attention, recognizing grammatical errors, retaining facts, perceiving phonemic variants, comprehending spoken language, and sitting up straight.

No Indo-European language contains a word which denotes . . . hearing, listening to, recognizing, comprehending, AND interpreting spoken language. *Auding* (with the ears) is comparable to *reading* (with the eyes). [6]

They believe the term *auding* to describe more effectively the *total* process of listening to and comprehending spoken language.

These definitions are helpful in clarifying the meaning of listening for the teacher who must explain it to the student. In the speech class listening is specifically related to the development of better personal speech habits, mastering basic speech skills, evaluating and criticizing speech performance, mastering the theory of the speech field, and formulating desirable attitudes toward the speaker before an audi-

[4] Ralph G. Nichols, "Listening: Questions and Problems," *Quarterly Journal of Speech*, XXXIII (February, 1947), 84.

[5] A. Craig Baird and Franklin H. Knower, *General Speech* (New York: McGraw-Hill Book Co., Inc., 1949), pp. 281–82.

[6] See John Caffrey and Donald Brown, "An Introduction to the Auding Concept," *Education*, LXX (December, 1947), 234–39.

ence. All of these are parts of the teacher's basic job in a speech course.

PURPOSES AND FUNCTIONS OF LISTENING

Individuals listen for different purposes. Baird and Knower [7] list three purposes of listening: (1) for enjoyment; (2) for information and inspiration; (3) to improve the understanding and use of principles of communication.

This discussion will consider these purposes of listening in relation to speech instruction: (1) listening in order to recognize and discriminate (speech sounds, especially, but also words, pronunciation, emphasis, inflection, and so on); (2) listening for information: facts, ideas, principles—with recall as a goal; (3) listening for pleasure, entertainment, or enjoyment; (4) listening in order to make an *intellectual* judgment, to criticize, to evaluate ideas; (5) listening to appreciate (to make an *aesthetic* judgment).

TEACHING LISTENING

Most of the studies of listening deal with listener comprehension, or what can be done to understand the activity and to improve effectiveness from the point of view of a member of an audience. In speech instruction this has been very much neglected. There is, however, a need to improve the effectiveness of the *speaker* as a listener as well, if he is to develop his abilities as much as he can. In this section, the teaching of listening will be considered as it affects the audience and the speaker.

In all discussion of listening it will be assumed that the teacher of speech is aware of the possibility of hearing losses among students in the classroom and will check this item as a matter of routine. If this is not the case, it is assumed that he will immediately check it in any specific cases in which listening difficulties exist or effectiveness is not high. In other words, hearing acuity is a matter of fundamental concern in all of this instruction.

The improvement of the personal speech habits of the speaker is directly related to his ability to recognize speech sounds, to discriminate amongst them, and to produce them correctly. He must

[7] Baird and Knower, *op. cit.*, p. 282.

trust his hearing (and listening) to evaluate the accuracy of his production of both vowel and consonant sounds. Again, he has a similar listening function in relation to his pronunciation of the words he uses in speaking. Further, he must be a critic of his own use of voice—elements such as timbre, loudness, pitch and inflection, rate, and duration are all subject to his skill as a listener whose constant function is that of evaluating his own performance. This ability must be developed so that he can realize what he must do in using his speech mechanism to secure the audible results he desires. He must be able to listen with especial care to note changes produced by altered positions or methods that he employs. By this procedure he can become aware of his needs, work to overcome errors, and be satisfied that he has achieved at least some of the improvement he desires. This process all stems from the first purpose of listening to discriminate.

To the Speaker

Use ear training and voice practice as a basic approach.

A. Give practice in discriminative listening.
1. Have students concentrate upon everyday sounds until they can describe them in detail.
2. Have them listen to contrasting sounds, e.g., noise and tone, and note their effect upon the hearer.
3. Have them analyze sounds according to pitch, time, loudness, etc., in order to be able to distinguish among these characteristics.
4. Have them listen to voices of others and study elements that make them pleasant or unpleasant.
B. Develop an appreciation of pleasing voices by listening critically to those of distinguished actors, announcers, lecturers, etc. This will help the students set standards for themselves.
C. Record the students' voices and have them listen repeatedly and analytically as they are played back until they can become conscious of their needs.
D. Develop specific improvement procedures for the errors noted.
E. Record and replay, listening especially for elements stressed in D.

(This program of ear training and discriminative listening can be carried on throughout the course as a means of aiding the speaker in his diction, pronunciation, and vocal work in all the platform work he attempts.)

There is relatively little done in the first course in high school and college in directly teaching students to *listen with discrimination* to themselves and their classmates.

To the Audience—a Single Person or a Group

There is an even greater need for work to be done in emphasizing the development of effective listening among members of the audience. The last four purposes of listening stated—for information, for pleasure, in order to make an intellectual judgment, to make an aesthetic judgment—deal with improving the listening of the student in the audience, either in school, at home, or in the community. In teaching listening for these purposes, there are four principal steps in procedure: (1) the student must be made aware of his need to develop greater listening effectiveness; (2) he must be motivated to improve it; (3) he must be provided with listening experiences that will train him: (a) in the speech classroom or the school; (b) outside the school; (4) his development must be evaluated and suggestions for further work given him.

Many factors affect the listening comprehension and the general listening effectiveness of a member of an audience. Reporting factors that definitely influenced listening comprehension, Nichols [8] lists these: intelligence, reading comprehension, recognition of correct English usage, size of the listener's vocabulary, ability to make inferences, ability to structuralize a speech (to see the organizational plan and the connection of the main points), listening for main ideas as opposed to specific facts, use of special techniques while listening to improve concentration, real interest in the subject discussed, emotional adjustment to the speaker's thesis, ability to see significance in the subject discussed, physical fatigue of the listener, and audibility of the speaker.

There was evidence to suggest, but not to establish, that other factors influenced the listening comprehension of the subjects. These included speaker effectiveness, admiration for the speaker, susceptibility to distraction, sex of the listener, and room ventilation and temperature, to mention only a few.

[8] Ralph G. Nichols, "Factors in Listening Comprehension," *Speech Monographs,* XV, No. 2 (1948), 154–63.

GUIDES TO EFFECTIVE LISTENING

Nichols [9] lists ten universal bad listening habits for which he offers ten guides to effective listening.

1. *Premature Dismissal of the Subject as Uninteresting*

This bad habit is an attempt by the listener to rationalize or find an excuse for his not listening to the speaker. The word "uninteresting" is the basis for his decision not to listen. He fails to realize that much material which seems uninteresting at first may be valuable later. Listeners should not abandon their job because the speaker's title or content do not appeal at once. Guide: *Find areas of interest.*

2. *Criticizing Delivery and Physical Appearance*

Listeners sometimes build an immediate resistance to listening because the speaker's clothes are out of press or are not in style. Also, they may be too critical of the speaker's complexion, make-up, hair styling, voice, or physical mannerisms. There is no question that these details influence a listener's reaction to a speaker. However, they ought not to be used as rationalizations or excuses for not listening to what he says. Guide: *Judge content, not delivery.*

3. *Getting Overstimulated by Some Point in the Speech*

Although members of the audience should and do listen with their emotions, as well as with their minds, they should not become so stirred by something the speaker says that they are diverted from the key ideas of the talk. Listener flights into reflection or undue excitement because the speaker hits an emotional target should be cut short. It is important to keep emotional balance and be able to discriminate. Guide: *Hold your fire.*

4. *"I Get the Facts" Listening*

The listener guilty of this habit may have had an overdose of American television detectives or typical reporters, who must not rest until they get all the facts. Such a principle, applied without

[9] See Ralph G. Nichols and Thomas Lewis, *Listening and Speaking* (Dubuque, Iowa: Wm. C. Brown and Co., 1954).

restriction by a listener, may cause him to miss the central *idea* of a talk and the important message of the speaker. Guide: *Listen for ideas.*

5. *Trying to Outline Everything*

Insisting upon exact and complete outlining of a talk may cause confusion for the listener. Note-taking of this sort is possible with some speeches, in which a logical scheme is evident. However, not all talks are so constructed. The result of trying to apply strict outlining methods to such content may deprive the listener of the important experience of reacting to important *meanings* in content. Within a few minutes the listener can usually tell what situation he faces. He can then adjust his note-taking to fit the need. He should be able to adjust his scheme to the kind of talk being given. He should not try to write everything on paper as the talk proceeds. Short waits help the listener to comprehend and check relationships. He can then record important content. Guide: *Be flexible.*

6. *Faking Attention*

An unintelligent girl in a college lecture was a master of this bad habit. She did everything to make the instructor think she was listening to him—she looked at him with gimlet eye; she smiled occasionally at him; she nodded periodically to indicate her reception of the message. But when the bluebooks were given she flunked them flat. She had done a beautiful job of faking attention. She assumed that if she looked like a listener, she satisfied all the requirements that the professor expected of her. In reality she was only employing *superficial* actions while she let the real message pass her by. She was cheating herself by not giving *complete* attention to the speaker. Guide: *Work at listening.*

7. *Yielding Easily to Distractions*

Nearly every noise in a listening situation competes with the speaker. Such noises should not be convenient alibis for a listener quickly to abandon his mission. A good listener will try to overcome distractions by shutting a window, closing a door, or by moving to a more advantageous location nearer the speaker. Sometimes a listener may help the speaker by notifying him of distractions so that he can help overcome them. If all of these means fail, an effective listener will try mentally to shut out distractions and give his full attention to the speaker. Guide: *Resist distractions.*

8. *Avoiding Difficult Listening*

As in the first bad habit, this one rests upon the listener's rationalization for not listening because the material is too difficult. When he is confronted by such content, he may escape from "sweating out" the experience by "dialing out" the speaker. Many persons would rather turn off a television talk of too challenging material than expend the energy needed to get the content. They simply say, "That's too tough!" and turn the switch. Guide: *Exercise your mind.*

9. *Letting Emotional Words Arouse Personal Antagonism*

Loaded words stir up strong emotional responses. Misunderstandings occur easily because of differing language habits and "trigger-like" reactions touched off by the wrong word. Listeners may lose their concentration upon basic idea content and the speaker's purpose if they experience an emotional explosion, touched off by language, during a speech. The speaker has a real responsibility not to use words that arouse hostility toward him. But the listener has a similar responsibility. He must control his reaction to loaded words so that he will not lose meanings that are more important. Guide: *Keep your mind open.*

10. *Wasting the Advantage of Thought Speed*

As every member of an audience listens, he "talks to himself." This ability to use inner speech is very important to the listener. Studies show that he can talk to himself from four to five times faster than he talks to others, or, in fact, than the speaker can talk to him. Therefore, the listener can do many other things, both relevant or irrelevant, while he is listening. The important issue is how the listener uses these pauses. If he wanders and separates himself from the content of the speaker, he will become an inefficient listener and may ultimately "dial out" altogether. The listener should use the pauses to review points the speaker has already made, anticipate the ideas to come, evaluate and link up evidence and reasoning to key points and the central idea of the talk, and so on. Guide: *Capitalize on thought speed.*

APPROACHES TO TEACHING LISTENING

Nichols [10] and others [11] suggest three approaches to the teaching of listening: (1) the direct; (2) the integrated or coordinated; and (3) the listening laboratory.

1. *The Direct Approach*

In teaching by this method the teacher plans a specific unit or course in listening, depending upon the time available in the curriculum. Speech teachers will probably develop at least one unit in the basic course and then follow the techniques developed throughout this course. Subsequent courses in the speech program may also contain definitely planned units or may be means of following up and strengthening the original material.

Basic steps include: (a) administering a standard test [12] of listening ability; (b) developing through lectures the case for good listening, explaining the gains to be made through increased ability; (c) using group discussion to explore further student problems in making use of listening in learning situations and others needed; (d) holding class discussions of listening skills; (e) employing exercises and materials for applying the skills, arranged in order of increasing difficulty; (f) giving periodic evaluation and progress tests; (g) doing final retesting with standardized tests to measure growth.

2. *The Integrated Approach*

When the teacher cannot organize a specific unit or course in listening because of local conditions, he may find a reasonably effective substitute by integrating or coordinating such instruction with speech, English, social studies, journalism, modern language, and other courses. The language arts area in the lower grades is especially suited for such a plan. Curriculum committees with strong representation from the communicative arts fields can plan with

[10] Ralph G. Nichols, "Listening Instruction in the High School," *Bulletin of the National Association of Secondary School Principals*, XXXVI, No. 187 (May, 1952), 158–74.

[11] Nichols and Stevens, *op. cit.*, Chap. 16.

[12] *The Brown-Carlson Test of Listening Comprehension* (Yonkers-on-Hudson: World Book Co., 1951). Others are also available. See the bibliography at the end of Chap. X.

other teachers suitable ways of integrating instruction in listening skills throughout the school program. Recent textbooks [13] can also be of considerable help.

There is an increasing amount of material and suggestion for this sort of organization. One of the earlier plans, used with success over a number of years in a speech program was developed by Mercer [14] in the Senior High School at Amarillo, Texas:

A. *Objectives*
  1. To "get across" the fact that responsiveness to communication determines to a great extent the competency of communication.
  2. To make a speech class a genuine speaking situation rather than just a class in which the student recites for the benefit of the teacher.
  3. To develop for use, in school and out, habits of listening that are characterized by quietness, discrimination, and reflection.

B. *General Method and Approach*
  1. The work is carried on simultaneously with the speaking activities, rather than as a separate unit.
  2. Listening is introduced as a counterpart of speaking.
  3. In preparation for speaking, students are also advised of their responsibilities as listeners.

C. *Making Students Aware of the Need*
  Two simple devices are used to impress the students with their need for training in listening:
  1. Have someone who is a fair speaker—probably an advanced student—talk to the class. Let the class write a précis of the talk at the conclusion. Do not warn the students beforehand that they are to do so. Have the papers checked by the speaker on the following points: grasped the idea effectively, failed to get the idea, elaborated on the idea with facts and judgments of his own.
  2. Read a poem to the class, preceding the reading with facts of the life of the writer that have no bearing on the content of

[13] See Marion Monroe, Ralph G. Nichols, W. Cabell Greet, and Helen M. Robinson, *Listen, Speak, and Write* (Chicago: Scott, Foresman and Co., 1961).

[14] Jessie Mercer, "Listening in the Speech Class," *Bulletin of the National Association of Secondary School Principals*, XXXII, No. 151 (January, 1948), 102–7.

the poem. Have the class summarize the contents of the poem. Check them on their ability to grasp and give the content of the poem rather than the facts of the life of the author.

D. *The Importance of Listening in the Speech Situation*

The first phase of the work is concerned with the discussion of listening. Here it is hoped that the student will realize that for him to devote all his available time and thought to speaking is erroneous. Just as the speaker prepares, so should the listener prepare. Problems considered include:

1. Is the high school student an effective listener?
2. Should the high school student accept a responsibility for becoming an effective listener in the classroom, at church, in assembly, at club meetings, and over the radio?
3. Why should the high school student listen?
   a. Can he be taught more effectively?
   b. Can he develop an ability to listen critically?
   c. Can he evaluate what he hears and thereby determine the good and the bad?
   d. Can he add to his information?
   e. Will he receive pleasure and inspiration?
4. What should be the attitude of the high school student toward listening?
   a. Do his friends and superiors deserve respectful listening?
   b. Should his classmates expect courteous listening?
   c. Will critical listening aid the student?
5. How should a high school student listen?
   a. Should he observe as well as hear?
   b. How should he express approval or disapproval of a speaker?
6. What part does listening play in the speech course?
   a. Should a student be expected to listen to members even though he is not interested?
   b. Why should he not be allowed to study when he is not speaking?
   c. Should he always be listening in order to criticize the speaker?

E. *Motivation for the Work*

Grading and criticism based upon performance as members of an audience are added motivations for improvement. Judging is done on the basis of (1) how effectively they understand, (2) how respectfully and attentively they listen, and (3) how appropriately they approve or disapprove of the speaking of their classmates (general reaction and evaluation they give). Best speaker AND best *audience* member are selected at each session.

F. *Preparatory Instruction for Classwork*

Students are informed on the purposes of listening, what to listen for, and how to listen to the various types of speech performance included in the course.

G. *Outline of In-school Listening Activities*

An outline of the listening activities of the fundamentals course may be illustrative of what can be done. In the unit *Everyday Speech,* involving conversation, introductions, group discussion, and etiquette talks, the students are told that their listening will be checked by:

1. Discussion of what took place in the conversation groups:
   a. What was the topic?
   b. Did you solve a problem?
   c. What type of people: big talkers, quiet, courteous?
   d. Who was the best participant?
2. Test on introductions:
   a. Questions on facts learned.
   b. What errors were heard?
   c. What person did the best job of introducing?
   d. What did you learn that you had not previously known?
3. Forums following etiquette talks in which class members may ask questions or offer comments.

In the unit on *Parliamentary Procedure,* the students may be asked to:

1. List errors made because of ineffective listening.
2. List cases of poor audience attitude:
   a. Discourteous people.
   b. Inattentive people.
3. List cases of good audience attitude:
   a. Good thinking.
   b. Fair-mindedness.
   c. Attentiveness.

In the unit on *Action* in which much of the understanding is dependent on what is seen, the student learns that listening in speech requires observation as well as hearing. Here he may be expected to tell what he understood by:

1. Imitation of members of the class, pointing out:
   a. What he liked.
   b. What he disliked.
   c. What was wrong.
2. Telling stories pantomimed by the group.
3. Describing, in words, characters "acted out" by groups.
4. Retelling the instructions given in chalk talk. Students may be assigned particular persons to follow.
5. Following instructions given in "How-to-do-it" talks. The students should be told they will be expected to carry out instructions given.
6. Helpful criticism of action of speakers.
   a. Were they sure of action?
   b. Were the actions spontaneous?
   c. Was there enough action?

In the unit *Oral Interpretation,* the material includes stories, poetry, and declamations. The presentation of the selection is usually preceded by a short analysis. By this time the class is able to do some critical evaluating. Their purpose in listening has become threefold: for pleasure, for criticism and evaluation, and for ideas. Their activities include:

1. Expressing opinions about interesting information.
2. Helpfully criticizing classmates:
   a. Asking questions about analyses of poetry and prose.
   b. Making suggestions concerning voice, action, or feeling.
3. Selecting the best readers of prose and poetry:
   a. Setting up standards for evaluation.
   b. Selecting best boy and girl in each division.

The *Public Speaking* unit, which is the last in the semester, consists of panel discussions, impromptu and extempore speaking, and special-occasion speeches. By this time the students have usually developed an interest in listening and need little motivation. The speaking of the students has improved, thereby making the audience response more spontaneous and easier. The purpose varies according to the type of speech.

1. Panel discussion:
    a. To evaluate ideas presented on the panel.
    b. To take part in the forum.
2. Special-occasion and after-dinner speeches:
    a. For pleasure.
3. Impromptu and extempore speaking:
    a. For information.
    b. To evaluate.
    c. For entertainment.

Here the effectiveness of the student's listening is most often checked by methods that may include:

1. Class discussion of ideas.
2. Response in forums.
3. Appropriate applause.
4. Attentive attitude.

H. *Outline of Out-of-class Listening Activities*

The third phase of the work is out-of-class listening. This may be carried on through the semester or limited to a brief period. Generally the decision is governed by the availability of material. The activity is threefold in nature:

1. Mapping out a program of listening:
    a. Choosing a variety of types of public speaking—church, lectures, radio and television.
    b. Choosing everyday speech—conversation, telephone, salesperson.
2. Determining what to listen for:
    a. Public speaking—ideas and facts, challenges, emotional appeals.
    b. Everyday speech—fads, opinions, humor.
    c. Choosing a legitimate stage production.
    d. Choosing a radio drama, interview, or discussion program.
3. Reporting on material heard:
    a. Classroom discussion of talks heard by all.
    b. Individual reports on talks heard by student.
    c. Reports on listening to conversations or interviews.

The teaching of listening for the improvement of the speaker and the greater effectiveness of members of the audience is a challenge that speech teachers must meet through their study, experimentation, and resourcefulness in planning their work. It should not continue to be neglected.

3. *The Listening Laboratory*

Nichols describes his recommendations for a school listening laboratory [15] under the following headings:

Facilities

A partially soundproofed room, acoustically treated if possible. The room, if budget allows, would have acoustically treated cubicles for individual use. Such facilities are now available to schools or have been constructed for teaching modern languages. The initial expense could therefore be distributed or justified because of use by more than one department.

Equipment and Materials

A library of spoken-word recordings (tape, disc, or both) and playback equipment. The recordings would include as many commercial spoken-word records as the budget permits: authors reading their own writings, actors reading classical literature, famous speeches, instructional recordings on a variety of subjects, children's stories, drama and the *Hear It Now* type of recording. The library might also include discs or tapes made by teachers, guest speakers, student groups or individuals, and others, assuming that the school has recording equipment.

A tape recorder for use in making recordings and in playing back tapes obtained from commercial or educational sources. Numerous possibilities exist for such service.

A radio, and, if possible, a television set, for "controlled use" limited to programs selected by teachers for educational purposes.

Objective and/or standardized tests constructed by the teachers to cover a portion of the recorded material, especially the instructional records. Also *a file of published standardized tests* for listening is desirable.

Indexing and filing facilities for recorded materials; arrangement should be according to difficulty of material.

Schedule and Use of the Laboratory

At scheduled times the laboratory should be available to students

[15] See Nichols and Stevens, *op. cit.*, pp. 211 ff.

who care to listen to spoken-word records for pleasure, or instructional records for academic reasons. During such hours a competent attendant should be on hand to operate the equipment. For the remainder of the time, the laboratory would be available to teachers. They could use it in conjunction with listening-improvement activities and to supplement other classroom studies. Teachers, for instance, might make assignments requiring students to use the laboratory as they now use a library of books.

This plan and schedule is not uncommon in schools of music and in connection with courses in music appreciation and analysis.

Approach and Procedure

After reaching agreement upon an approach to listening and the use of the laboratory, faculty members can use their imagination and creative ability to produce a program that will do much to remedy current listening deficiencies. Pupils will benefit from the motivation and training provided by such planned experiences.

Exercises and "Things to Do"

A list of forty-four things to do is set forth by Nichols. These exercises are taken from work in progress in such school systems as Nashville, Phoenix, Minneapolis, Cincinnati, and others, as well as from educational journals and college listening courses. Selection from this list, plus adjustment and adaptation, is indicated for the speech teacher desiring to develop a successful listening laboratory to be used by the speech department or the entire school.[16]

EXERCISES

1. State what you consider to be the most effective approach to teaching listening and support your opinion by drawing upon personal experience, outside readings, or research in the field.
2. Examine various state courses of study. Note the amount of emphasis placed on listening in the classroom and recommended approaches to the problem.
3. Select two contemporary basic speech textbooks. Note the amount and kind of materials on listening and evaluate this content, comparing and contrasting the two treatments.

[16] See "Forty-four Things to Do," in Nichols and Stevens, *op. cit.*, pp. 212–22.

REFERENCES

BIRD, DONALD E. "Teaching Listening Comprehension," *Journal of Communication,* III (November, 1953), 127–30.

BLEWETT, THOMAS T. "An Experiment in Measuring Listening at the College Level, *Journal of Communication,* I (May, 1951), 50–57.

BROWN, DON P. "Auding as the Primary Language Ability." Unpublished Ed. D. dissertation, Stanford University, 1954.

———, and JOHN CAFFREY. *California Auding Test, Form F. Revised.* Redwood City: Council on Auding Research, 146 Columbia Ave. 1952.

———. "Teaching Aural English," *English Journal,* XXXIX (1950), 128–36.

BROWN, JAMES I. "The Construction of a Diagnostic Test of Listening Comprehension," *Journal of Experimental Education,* XVIII (December, 1949), 139–46.

———. *Manual for Brown-Carlsen Listening Comprehension Test.* New York: World Book Co., 1953.

———. "The Objective Measurement of Listening Ability," *Journal of Communication,* I (May, 1951), 44–48.

———. "How Teachable Is Listening?" *Educational Research Bulletin,* XXXIII (April 14, 1954), 85–93.

CAFFREY, JOHN G. "Auding Ability as a Function of Certain Psychometric Variables." Unpublished Ph.D. dissertation, University of California at Berkeley, 1953.

———. "An Introduction to the Auding Concept," *Education,* LXX (1949), 234–39.

IRVIN, C. E. "Evaluating a Training Program in Listening for College Freshmen," *School Review,* LXI (1953), 25–29.

KRAMAR, E. J., and R. LEWIS. "Comparison of Visual and Nonvisual Listening," *Journal of Communication,* I (1951), 16–20.

LODER, J. E. "Study of Aural Learning with and without the Speaker Present," *Journal of Experimental Education,* VI (1937), 47–60.

NICHOLS, RALPH G. "Listening Instruction in the Secondary School," *Bulletin of the National Association of Secondary School Principals,* XXXVI, No. 187 (May, 1952), 158–74.

———. "Factors in Listening Comprehension," *Speech Monographs,* XV (1948), 154–63.

———, and LEONARD STEVENS. *Are You Listening?* New York: McGraw-Hill Book Co., Inc., 1957.

CHAPTER FOURTEEN

Speech Preparation

The teacher's role in treating speech preparation is to help his students meet successfully the problems they face. Anticipating these, the teacher may lay down certain basic preparation procedures very early in the course. He can later build upon them as he makes specific speech assignments. He will probably be wiser to organize a specific unit in speech preparation, placing it at the appropriate point in his course sequence to ensure a solid treatment of this area.

GENERAL PROBLEMS IN PREPARATION

1. *Analyzing the Audience and the Occasion*

Each speech is given to a particular audience. Essential to sound preparation is a knowledge of the occasion, the time limits, and the kind of audience to be addressed in school or community. The details of such an analysis appear in step A on page 284.

2. *Finding the Subject and Content of the Talk*

Among student speakers and adults the choice of a subject plus the development of its content is a major problem. In the first group the problem may spring from an inadequate background of knowledge and experience. Shallow-minded students in high school or college may channel their speeches along lines of superficial interests, such as recent movies or television shows, popular music, comparative scores in athletic contests, or their next romantic interest. These persons may not comprise the majority in speech classes, but they present a challenge to their teacher. No speech teacher should be satisfied with trivial or weak subjects or content. Neither should he accept careless preparation based upon such limited information. Young people can readily be awakened to their responsibility in choosing provocative subjects demanding their best thinking, combined with a depth and variety of knowledge. Great political issues and serious social problems surround them. The speech class should be a sounding board for their attitudes, knowledge, and opinions. The teacher should not be satisfied with less than a high quality of content in the talks he accepts in class.

3. Gathering Materials

The efficient use of sources of information can be a critical problem among students. Library skills are important to all fields of study. The job of teaching such skills, however, is often neglected unless specific teachers are given the responsibility. In some secondary schools, the English department has a unit on library skills as a required part of the work in the freshman year. Most colleges assume the skills have been taught earlier. Yet it is not uncommon for the speech instructor to find some uninformed pupils. It is a wise precaution for him to check this matter either through direct questioning or by observing the students' study habits. He may decide to place such training in one of the early sections of the speech course, often as a part of a unit on speech preparation. Good treatments of these skills appear in many basic high school and college texts. Other compact, helpful materials may be obtained from the H. W. Wilson Company [1] and from the Reader's Digest Association.[2] Best results are obtained from class sessions held in the library so that knowledge of sources may be applied on the spot.

Accurate recording and documenting of information should also be a part of this training. It is essential if materials found are to be useful to the speaker as he develops his talk; such training pays large dividends in speech courses.

4. Organizing and Outlining Speech Content

A fourth problem that the student faces after finding materials is

[1] *Time Savers: The Periodical Indexes,* prepared by the Junior Members Round Table of the American Library Association (New York: H. W. Wilson Co., 1936).
[2] Frank H. McCloskey, *The Library,* No. 7 in a series of Reader's Digest College Department Aids to Composition (Pleasantville, N. Y.: Reader's Digest Association, 1945).

proper arrangement or organization. This process is closely related to the notes or outline he makes as a guide for his speech. The making of such a "blueprint" is basic to good composition and successful delivery of his talk. Should students lack such knowledge or skill, the speech instructor again must assume the responsibility for teaching them. He should be certain that student speakers are familiar with (1) ways of organizing ideas; (2) outline types; (3) proper form, with correct use of subordination and coordination of points; (4) types of outlines best suited to particular needs in speaking. Every student must realize that outlining is an exercise in *thinking;* it is much more than merely jotting down a series of sketchy notes on a piece of paper.

5. *Wording the Talk*

Using oral language effectively is another definite problem in speech preparation. It is closely related to the making of notes and to the types of delivery employed. It is most vitally linked, however, to the demand of the speaker's ideas and feelings as he seeks to verbalize them effectively for his audience.

Initial selection of language to word the talk occurs as the speaker develops his notes or outline. Short phrase outlines require less amplification in language. Complete sentence outlines, when carefully detailed, move the speaker very close to complete wording of the talk or near manuscripting of his ideas. If he adheres to extemporaneous method in delivery, he will make less choice of language *before* the time he practices delivery and "sets" the oral language for performance.

An extensive treatment of teaching oral language appears in Chapter XVII.

6. *Delivering the Talk*

The final problem facing the person preparing to speak concerns the type of delivery he will use. Speech instructors generally advocate the extemporaneous method. Thus, they encourage the student to prepare his materials carefully, to organize them clearly, to outline them systematically, and to practice the talk aloud before coming to class. This method takes some time to develop, but it is worth the effort. Writing out parts of the talk will help the student in his sentence structure, transitions, and choice of language. However, it is advisable for the student to destroy any manuscript copy used in preparation and work from an outline in performance. The outline should be firmly fixed in mind so that it will not be overused in delivery. Too frequent reference to notes breaks communication with the audience and loses attention.

Memorization of speeches, word for word, is undesirable. It destroys spontaneity, makes communication a mechanical process, and places such a heavy burden on a speaker that he often forgets his material.

Reading from manuscript is a method that all persons should know how to employ effectively. In our modern world there are many occasions when this type of delivery is required. Radio and television, for instance, demand exact timing for a speech, and a manuscript can be written and read to fit this time limit. Also, when censorship exists or exact quotation is necessary, manuscript preparation and reading protect the speaker against inaccuracy or misquotation. It is preferable, however, not to read a speech as an established practice, but rather to learn to read well aloud so that these special types of communication situations can be met. Good, extemporaneous speaking, in which the use of notes or outline is held to a minimum, insures the best delivery.

These problems must be met in the course of any instruction in the preparation of speeches. The teacher must be aware of them and should develop suitable methods to meet them in his teaching situation. In addition to this, he needs to formulate a specific procedure for teaching speech preparation and composition. The sequence below contains workable suggestions for this type of teaching.

A SUGGESTED PLAN FOR TEACHING SPEECH PREPARATION

I. *Use a textbook that contains a strong treatment of this unit for the basic information on composition.*

Such a guide makes the theory easily available to the whole class. It relieves the instructor of developing this material in other ways, such as by lecture or mimeographed sheet. It allows him, however, to supplement it with special devices of his own, as well as to provide more detailed reference materials on particular types of speeches.

II. *Make sure that students understand the essential steps in composition and the reasons for their place in the scheme.*

Although there are variations in procedure in composition, depending upon which textbook is studied, the list below includes the principal steps common to most books.

A. *Analyze the audience.* Before selecting a subject, gathering materials, considering language or methods of delivering the speech, the speaker must know the audience. This is not difficult in a classroom situation in which one becomes acquainted with the group. At least, it is less of a problem than it would be if a new and different body of listeners were present at each occasion. In each case the speaker should make an initial audience analysis with respect to (1) size, (2) age, (3) sex, (4) occupation, (5) educational background, (6) previous knowledge of the subject, (7) interests, (8) attitudes and beliefs, and (9) attitude toward the speaker as a person. Such an analysis will serve as a basis for the further preparation of the talk.

B. *Select the general subject for the speech.* The speaker should choose a subject in which he is interested and on which he has some information. He should select a subject which has possible interest for the audience (the class). He should be sure that the subject is appropriate to the occasion. He should choose a subject which will meet the established time limits. To this end he should move toward the specific rather than the general in his choice. For example, he should speak about income taxes or sales taxes rather than the general subject of taxation. The speaker in a class situation should use subjects suggested by the teacher only when he "gets stuck" or is required to conform to a certain topic; it is desirable for the student to develop his own list of subjects.

C. *Determine the general end or purpose of the speech.* The purpose will be one of the commonly recognized purposes or ends of the speaker, e.g., to inform, to entertain, to convince, to actuate, to stimulate, and so on.

D. *Restrict the subject and word the central idea with the particular audience and occasion in mind.*

E. *Make a preliminary analysis of the central idea, blocking out its principal subdivisions.* This analysis is facilitated by the speaker's information and thinking on the subject.

F. *Consult available sources of information to supplement the speaker's basic knowledge.*
  1. Begin with your own experience.
     a. List points on which no further information is needed.
     b. List points which need further investigation.
  2. Use observation to gain information.
     a. Pictures often supply ideas.
     b. Trips are very informative.
     c. Experiment with things that might be used in the talk. If a process or mechanical device is to be used, it should be "run through" and carefully observed.
  3. Get help from others.
     a. Converse with informed people.
     b. Arrange formal interviews with known experts.
     c. Write letters to persons, organizations, or agencies that have materials.
     d. Attend lectures; listen to radio and television.
  4. Read about the subject. Consult—
     a. Encyclopedias and general reference works.
     b. Special books.
     c. Magazines, newspapers, pamphlets.
     d. Clippings and other library materials.
G. *Record information accurately and systematically in a form that is usable for the speaker, being sure to note sources.*
  1. Make notes on interviews and observations.
  2. Copy quotations from written sources that are read.
H. *Collect more material than will be used in the final draft.* Organization is easier if one has plenty of material. The result will be a better speech.
I. *Select and organize the materials.*
  1. Check the specific purpose and the preliminary analysis of the subject.
  2. Revise materials in the light of new information.
  3. Choose the two or three main ideas that will constitute the body of the speech. Arrange them in an effective order, taking into consideration—

    a. Time order.
    b. Space order.
    c. Climactic order.
    d. Topical order.
    e. Logical order.
    f. Problem-solution order.
    g. Particular point of view.
    h. Psychological order.
    i. Basic principles of operation.

4. Fit in the subheadings, descriptive illustrations, statistics, quotations, and so on, under each main heading. In (3) and (4) keep the audience analysis in mind.

5. Outline these materials in an appropriate form. Keep in mind the audience analysis in section A, and use the order selected in I,3, above. Also choose an outline *form* that gives the greatest amount of help in wording the speech and delivering it, such as—
    a. Topical outline.
    b. Phrase outline.
    c. Sentence outline.
    (See sections IV and V below for special methods of teaching outlining.)

6. Plan the conclusion and the introduction; include these in the outline.

J. *Consider the wording of the speech; experiment silently, orally, and in writing with those parts that need careful choice of language.*

K. *Practice the talk orally at least twice from the outline.* Do not memorize or set the language; keep it flexible and alive.

L. *Select an appropriate title for the talk.*

III. *Employ helpful procedures to teach basic steps.*

  A. To aid students in improving choice of subjects:

    1. Analyze their interest, both long-range and temporary.

    2. Develop a list of possible speech subjects for every assignment based on these interests (A, 1). Make this extensive and suggestive; do not confine the students to these topics. Encourage them to choose and develop their own subjects.

3. Let pupils make lists of their own. This can be done by asking each to bring to class a list of ten to twenty subjects that interest him. These can be pooled, organized into general categories by a student committee, edited, dittoed, or mimeographed, and distributed to the entire class as supplementary student suggestions. Thus, within a short time, some five hundred potential suggestions can be developed. If the class interests and contemporary events make some obsolete, additional materials can be added.

B. To assist students in making a *preliminary analysis* and in stating the *central idea* clearly:

1. Assign written exercises based on these subject lists to give the students practice in stating the various central ideas and main headings that might be used to develop these subjects.

2. Stress the idea that analysis and good speech preparation demand clear thinking and an understanding of relationships. This approach can be used in the outlining of materials.

C. To strengthen the ability to use sources of information:

1. Encourage students to read more widely as an independent activity for information, recreation, and appreciation.

   a. The student's reading should be purposeful, careful as he seeks details, exploratory as he looks for new concepts and points of view, enthusiastic as he seeks to solve problems, and discerning if he seeks quotations and evidence.

   b. List materials, such as book reviews, bibliographies, and clippings, on the bulletin board in the space for new books, interesting articles, and so on. Obtain copies of stimulating, attractive publications for display and loan in class.

   c. Help to make attendance and study time in the library an interesting experience to be enjoyed without red tape.

   d. Have a speech reserve shelf in the library to make things more accessible.

2. Help the students to become better listeners and observers so that they may enrich their backgrounds.

    a. Post, in the classroom, program schedules of major networks and local programs such as talks, discussions, and dramatic shows. The public-relations division of the radio and television industry will furnish these schedules in advance.

    b. Study and analyze tapes and pamphlets of radio and television programs, such as *Meet the Press,* and Northwestern University's *Reviewing Stand* and *Your Right to Say It.* These are current, well produced, and will yield interesting materials.

    c. Announce lectures and local events of educational character early so that students may attend. In some instances, the class can attend as a body.

    d. Get movie and theatrical reviews that will give an evaluation of productions coming to the community. Encourage attendance at those that are helpful and deal with issues of importance to students.

    e. Urge pupils to converse, discuss, and interview persons who can supply interesting, vital, and usable information for talks. Urge students to participate in community enterprises, such as forums, panel discussions, play reading and book clubs which will build their store of knowledge.

    f. Assist in planning trips to points of interest that will give them first-hand knowledge through observation.

3. To strengthen library skills, take students to the library and teach them how to use it. Both public and school librarians are, as a rule, most cooperative in such projects. (This item has been covered more extensively above.)

IV. *Use a laboratory session to meet individual problems.*

  A. *General procedure.*

    Assign a speech in advance. Have each student choose the general subject, formulate his purpose, state his central idea, and break it down into logical subdivisions. Tell the class that they are to read widely upon the subject after these preliminary steps and to take adequate notes on their reading.

Also assign the pertinent chapters in the class textbook for careful rereading and study. Emphasize, especially, the various types of introduction, ways of organizing and supporting the body, and kinds of conclusions. Ask each student to use this material in projecting a plan for the talk to be organized in the laboratory session.

Then have them bring all their information, notes, and writing materials to class. Devote class time to a definite laboratory on the organization of their materials into the introduction, the body, and the conclusion of the speech. The end product should be a highly developed outline.

B. *Special methods for teaching outlining.*

   1. Use a fill-in outline form. This method helps the student in his arrangement of ideas by providing a spatial layout for the speech. Using his collected materials, he fits them into the scheme. He is able to see thought relationships as they occur in the scheme he has developed with the fill-in form as a guide. (See the following form.)

OUTLINE FORM

Specific Purpose: (Copy here the sentence suggested in II, C. You may not use this sentence in your speech, but it will serve to remind you of what you want to do.)

Introduction

  I. Your "attention getter" goes here. Write it out quite completely and memorize it, so that you can get off to a good start.

 II. Any necessary background information goes here. Sometimes you may not need this step in the introduction.

Body

  I. Your first *main point* goes here (remember the order you decided on).

  A. *Supporting material* for first main point.

 II. Second *main point.*

  A. *Supporting material.*

(Continue until you have listed all main points—one per roman numeral.)

Conclusion

I. Write your conclusion here, word for word, and then memorize it. In that way you are sure when you are through, and you leave the audience feeling that you have done a good job.

    2. Collect copies of all outlines; ditto them. Thus, every student will have copies of all outlines prepared in the session. Ditto work will require at least a day to complete. However, the next session can then be devoted to a careful study of the scheme for each talk as prepared by each student. Basic ways of arranging ideas, supporting materials, and relationships of points in the body of the talk; introductions; conclusions, and so on, can be studied carefully and discussed. Class and teacher suggestions will be freely yet tactfully given.

    3. Use the opaque projector to show outlines. For immediate use in sharing the work done by each student with the class, the opaque projector is a valuable aid. As each outline is projected upon the screen, the teacher, the class, and the writer of the outline can engage in productive discussion and helpful suggestions. The immediacy of this method in the laboratory session makes it a sure-fire evaluative technique to teach and reinforce all principles of form, content, support, and organization being taught.

    4. Follow-up to the delivery session. In all these methods specific follow-up is possible at the time the speeches are given in order to establish the utility of the outline in the speaking situation. Of the three the most tangible is the ditto method because the talk can be followed by each student, using his duplicated copy of the speaker's notes.

       Interesting relationships are thus established between preparation methods, spoken language, vocal and physical delivery.

Such a procedure may take two or three class periods, but it is worth the time. It enables the instructor to (1) check on the work habits of students; (2) evaluate their ability to select their information; (3) note their ability to think and organize ideas. It also provides an opportunity for individual and group instruction in planning the various parts of the speech, and it enables the student and teacher to face certain language problems in a preparation session rather than on the platform.

V. *Analyze written or printed speech models by other students, by lecturers, and by persons in public life.*

Here the students come into contact with examples of good and successful practice in composition. It helps them to build standards for their own work. This aspect of the study of speech organization can also be handled in a laboratory situation or in a class discussion. The best method is to utilize texts of relatively short speeches that are within the understanding of the class. In many instances these can be dittoed or mimeographed by the instructor for use by the entire class, with appropriate study questions to direct analysis and understanding of composition principles. On-the-spot study can be made possible by the use of slides with parts of the speech or by employing the opaque projector to show larger sections of text from a book or manuscript, or even the speaker's notes and outline if they are available. Collected speeches are available in books and in *Vital Speeches*, a magazine which also supplies study guides.[3] Compilations of college orations such as those published by the Northern Oratorical League or the Inter-State Oratorical League can also be used. The chief objection to these sources is that the speeches are often too long and too difficult for class study. Teachers can profit from collections of student speeches and others of suitable length and content. A useful teaching device is a skeleton outline indicating the divisions of the speech, with space for main points, subpoints, illustrations, and so on. Such a form (p. 289) can serve as a guide in analysis and enables the student to see the structure of the speech with its various parts in proper relationship, the use of compositional devices such as forms of support, examples, evidence, as well as particular ways of developing the introduction and conclusion.

VI. *Observe and analyze the composition of outside speakers in assemblies, church, lectures, and meetings.*

This activity is a good sequel to IV and V. It challenges the student to make note of the essential items in a speaker-

---

[3] *Vital Speeches* is published by City News Publishing Company, 33 West 42nd St., New York 18, N. Y.

listener situation and affords him a practical opportunity to check upon the effectiveness of organization. Students may take notes which can be followed by pointed class discussions immediately after assembly talks, political speeches, or radio talks of various kinds.

It is wise to require that a series of such observations be made, written up with critical analysis and comment, as a part of pupil activities in the course. These observations can become a part of a speech notebook to be kept by each student. They can serve as a basis for class discussion on composition, delivery, and total effectiveness. A representative list includes (1) an assembly speaker, (2) a classroom lecturer, (3) a minister, (4) a radio speaker, (5) a community lecturer, (6) a political speaker, (7) an after-dinner speaker, (8) a presiding officer.

A report blank for these observations is relatively easy to develop and furnishes a guide for the observations themselves. An example of such a blank appears below.

NORTHWESTERN UNIVERSITY
Department of Speech Education
SPEECH OBSERVATION BLANK

Name of Student _____ Type of Speech _____

Name of Speaker _____ Subject _____

The Speaking   A. Place _____ Occasion _____ Time _____

Situation   B. The Audience (Size, composition, etc.) _____

The Speaker's Specific Purpose or Thesis _____

Brief Outline of Talk:

    Introduction

    Body

    Conclusion

Observer's Comment: (Criticize the speaker specifically, using items on the speech chart we employ in class.)

(Use the back to conclude your discussion.)

VII. *Employ transcriptions and recordings of famous speakers of the past and present.*

Through collections of transcriptions and recordings the teacher can demonstrate various principles in speech composition, distinctive points in composition and delivery of outstanding speakers, various types of speeches, and the particular treatment and development of issues in the speeches played for the students.

This method gives the teacher control over the kinds of model speeches used, allows class analysis and discussion and repeated playing if desired. The teacher may use the commercial records and transcriptions available and can develop other items in such a library through his own recordings of radio speeches.

Still pictures of some speakers, plus sound films of more recent personalities, can be utilized in this study also. In the first case motivation is the principal interest; with the audiovisual materials it is possible to study the occasion, the audience situation, the speaker's appearance and delivery as well as the compositional aspects and perhaps the total effect of the speech on the audience if that is filmed.

VIII. *Have students check upon organization, materials, and all aspects of composition in subsequent recitations by class members.*

Here the criticism of the class is directed to the results of the laboratory session described earlier; it also makes use of principles learned through observation of live speakers and records. Each individual is asked to note the general subject, central idea, principal subpoints, supporting information, organization, language, and general effectiveness of the composition of each person speaking. Such a process focuses the attention of all listeners upon the structure of each speech; it helps to develop standards for composition work and encourages a high quality of preparation. This device can be used as often as the instructor desires in order to meet individual needs.

Again, the teacher may use commercial records and transcriptions available and can develop other items in such a library through his own recordings of radio speeches.

These suggestions reveal many possibilities in methods of teaching composition. Their effectiveness will be judged by the influence they have upon the end product of such a unit of study—improved speech preparation by the students.

EXERCISES

1. Observe a number of speakers in a variety of situations. Make an outline of each of the talks you hear and analyze carefully the composition and content of their material.
2. Assemble a list of recordings and transcriptions that could be used to emphasize good speech preparation. Explain or demonstrate how you would use such teaching material.

REFERENCES

BAIRD, A. CRAIG, and FRANKLIN KNOWER. *Essentials of General Speech.* New York: McGraw-Hill Book Co., Inc., 1960.

BRIGANCE, W. NORWOOD. *Speech Communication.* New York: Appleton-Century-Crofts, Inc., 1955.

————. *Speech: Its Techniques and Disciplines in a Free Society.* New York: Appleton-Century-Crofts, Inc., 1961.

CROCKER, LIONEL. *Public Speaking for College Students.* New York: American Book Co., 1956.

CROMWELL, H., and ALAN MONROE. *Working for More Effective Speech.* Chicago: Scott, Foresman Co., 1955.

DOWLING, FRED. "Teaching Impromptu Speaking," *Speech Teacher,* VI (September, 1957), 205–8.

HANCE, KENNETH. "Public Address in the Secondary School," *Bulletin of the National Association of Secondary School Principals,* XXXVI, No. 187 (May, 1952).

HEDDE, WILHELMINA G., and W. NORWOOD BRIGANCE. *The New American Speech.* Philadelphia: J. B. Lippincott Co., 1957. Chap. VIII.

LARUSSO, DOMINIC. "Paperbacks: The Teacher's Friend. IV. Public Speaking," *Speech Teacher,* V (September, 1956), 202–4.

LAASE, LEROY. *Notebook for Public Speaking.* Dubuque, Iowa: William C. Brown Co., 1950.

MCBURNEY, JAMES H., and ERNEST J. WRAGE. *Guide to Good Speech.* Englewood Cliffs, N. J.: Prentice-Hall, Inc., 1960.

MILLER, N. EDD. "Speech Introductions and Conclusions," *Quarterly Journal of Speech,* XXXII (April, 1946), 181–83.

Monroe, Alan. *Principles and Types of Speech.* Chicago: Scott, Foresman and Co., 1958. Chaps. VII-XVIII.

Robinson, Karl F., and W. Norwood Brigance. "The Program of Basic Skills in Teaching," *Bulletin of the National Association of Secondary School Principals,* XXIX, No. 133 (November, 1945).

Sarett, Lew; William T. Foster; and James H. McBurney. *Speech: A High School Course.* Boston: Houghton Mifflin Co., 1956.

———; ———; and Alma Sarett. *Basic Principles of Speech.* Boston: Houghton Mifflin Co., 1958.

Wallace, Karl R. "More Than We Can Teach," *Speech Teacher,* VI (March, 1957), 95–102.

CHAPTER FIFTEEN

Developing Effective Bodily Action

Although bodily action is often taught as a part of speech delivery, many speech teachers face certain problems because they lack a satisfactory procedure for developing it. Many of these problems originate because of teachers' misconceptions about what should be taught and how it should be done. Oftentimes, bodily action is looked upon merely as a set of techniques or tricks that enable the speaker to embellish an exhibitory delivery. Fundamentally, this mistake is based upon failure to see action as a basic, integrated part of good communication. With a desire to build techniques quickly, teachers often impose a mechanical system of gesture, stance, and movement on the beginning student. Before he has been properly motivated, the unhappy student is practicing hand positions, stroke, and return. The results are soon evident: stilted machinelike action, which lacks motivation and calls attention to itself, little integration of action with vocal communication, an absence of ease and freedom often ending in a "freezing up" in later speech situations.

In short, the student is inhibited by the very teaching procedures employed. Instead of developing speakers whose action is natural, free, spontaneous, animated, pleasing, varied, appropriate, and purposeful, teachers sometimes produce those so obviously mechanical in their activity that they resemble the product of the old schools of elocution.

NATURE AND PURPOSES OF EFFECTIVE ACTION

Contemporary teachers understand that *action is itself communication through visible symbols.* They know that its effectiveness with *an audience* when used by a speaker rests upon the principle of empathy. Empathy is the tendency that human beings have to reflect the muscle tones or "sets" and the expressions of persons whom they observe, or with whom they associate. Members of a crowd watching a football game strain, lean forward, and even reach out, as they observe a halfback leaping desperately to catch a pass. They undergo an empathic response; they "feel themselves into" the situation. Similarly, an audience watching the actions of a speaker, actor, or reader reflects his facial expression, his gestures, or his movements. In this situation there is also a mental or imaginal counterpart. Knowing the speaker's ideas, the listeners project themselves into his mental state as well. Consequently, their attention is gained and held, and their responses achieved through *empathy*, which involves them mentally and physically.

In addition, teachers must comprehend that action is a necessity to the speaker. Lew Sarett [1] develops five important benefits to action: (1) it helps to break down stage fright; (2) it is an outlet for nervous energy; (3) it generates fervor; (4) it stimulates rapidity of thinking and fluency of utterance; and (5) it reveals the personality of the speaker.

Teachers must realize further that set mechanical rules regarding posture, walking, and gesture have gone by the board. This has been caused by the success of speakers who communicate ideas and feelings and win responses from the audience through *self-motivated action*, not by techniques learned by rule. In addition, teachers should know the guiding principles and basic techniques for developing desirable habits of posture, facial expression, movement, and gesture. They should understand and apply such principles in their true proportion and relationship to the total job of helping the student (1) achieve freedom in action, and (2) develop physical control suitable to his purposes as a speaker. These "techniques" should always be ways of refining and improving the natural, spontaneous activity that the speaker feels impelled to employ. They are not an end in themselves.

OBJECTIVES IN TEACHING BODILY ACTION

The major objectives in teaching bodily action in a first course are: (1) to define action and explain its functions in communication;

[1] Lew Sarett and William Foster, *Basic Principles of Speech* (Rev. ed.; Boston: Houghton Mifflin, 1946), pp. 130–50.

(2) to motivate the student to improve his use of action; (3) to free him from inhibitions so that he can have effective natural physical behavior in communicating with an audience; (4) to aid him in developing bodily *control* so that he will have ease, coordination, and vitality; (5) to assist him in understanding and acquiring suitable techniques of action for oral communication; (6) to help him further to polish and perfect his techniques for specialized performance, if necessary. A first course in speech should succeed in carrying out the first five and should lay a suitable foundation for the last.

WHEN TO TEACH BODILY ACTION

In the development of the human being, the mastery of body precedes the control of the vocal apparatus. The child gains control of the various parts of the body, such as arms, legs, face, and neck, much earlier than he learns to control and use his muscles for speech production. It is also a fact that a controlled body is basic to effective speech. It is closely related to emotional adjustment. It is essential to good use of the mechanism for vocal production and careful articulation. Therefore, bodily action should precede work on voice in the beginning course.

Although many college courses in speech include work in action as a part of a general treatment of delivery, the instructor should know how to deal with the needs of students who do not possess freedom, control, and technique in using action. Beginning high school courses usually deal with the problem directly in a unit constructed to serve such ends, or develop a series of activities to accomplish suitable control of action.

A METHOD OF TEACHING BODILY ACTION

A sound method of teaching bodily action must *create the conditions for physical response, rather than teach the response.* Using a public speaking approach primarily, the instructor can plan a series of situations moving from simple, gross activity to specific, complex action.

Some fundamental principles follow.

1. *Teach essential information* regarding action as a *means of communication.* Students should be aware of its influence upon the

speaker and the audience, and its relationship to meanings they wish to convey. Encourage them to think of their present reliance upon action to convey those meanings.

2. *Motivate students to improve.* This can be done by their developing the desire to improve; they should also realize their own inadequacies.

3. *Break down restraints and free students from inhibitions.* Get everyone "into the act." Individuals feel less self-conscious in a group. They will also learn the power of the empathic response as they watch others, respond to them, and in turn observe the effects of action upon their listeners.

4. *Work first for abandoned, energetic action.*

5. *Next, develop physical control and conscious purpose in the speaker's response;* this should be built upon awareness, readiness, and the ability to employ action meaningfully in a communication situation.

6. *Then strive for specificity, definiteness, and the more subtle, polished movements.*

7. *Provide means for evaluating improvement.* The teacher, the class, and the student himself can participate in this appraisal.

With these principles in mind a suggested teaching sequence is presented.

I. *Provide information regarding the importance of action in communication.* (Lecture, readings, and discussion.)
   A. Explain what it includes; indicate that it is a fundamental means of communication. Use flat pictures, sketches, television, and available teaching films.
   B. Develop the importance of bodily action to the speaker and to the audience.
   C. Use an observation assignment so that students can note uses and effect of action in communicating; introduce photographs showing communication that uses activity of whole body, face, hands, arms, and so on.
II. *Motivate students to improve by (1) making them aware of inadequacies, (2) stimulating their desire to do better.*
   A. The strongest motivations are *self-motivations.* If students realize that their appearance is unsuitable and that they

communicate undesirable things by their action, such inner motivation can be created.

B. Use a full-length mirror for individual observation of posture, walk, gesture, facial expression. Allow the student to observe himself in an act of pantomime, speaking, or reading. Ask him for his judgment.

C. Supplement his opinion by teacher evaluation.

D. If appropriate, ask for judicious class reaction, thus trying to objectify each student's appraisal of his own physical activity.

E. Take short footage black-and-white motion pictures of students in both unrehearsed and planned platform speech situations. Use them for motivation and diagnosis of needs in using action. Some beginning college classes use sound motion pictures as standard diagnostic methods. Closed-circuit television is also employed in certain situations. Schools having sound-on-film or video-tape equipment can do this easily. Thus voice *and* action can be recorded simultaneously.

III. *Free the body from inhibitions; develop free, spontaneous action that proceeds from inner motivation.*

A. Build simple situations that necessitate a total response; get the student to utilize postures, walking, facial expression, hand and arm movements, and activity of the head and other parts of the body. Have the student freely react to the situations you create.

EXAMPLES:

1. You see a classmate dozing in class; walk over to him and rouse him with a slap on the back.
2. Your friend, standing on the curb, starts to cross the street in the path of an oncoming car. Stop him.
3. Your mother is ill in bed and is sleeping. You are seated in the living room at some distance from the phone, which starts to ring. Get up and move to the phone in time to prevent its ringing a second time.
4. You are carrying a large folder filled with papers. It slips from your hand and the papers scatter in spite of your efforts. Pick them up quickly and rearrange them.

    5. The chairman calls your name to come forward for a recognition-introduction. Respond to his invitation and then return to your seat.

B. Develop situations that demand response of a more complex nature.

EXAMPLES:

    1. You are fishing from a boat on a lake. Row into position, check the depth of the water, set your bobber, bait your hook, and start fishing. At first, you catch little ones, which you throw back. Then activity ceases for a while. You grow bored, then drowsy. Suddenly you get a terrific strike, which rouses you. After a lively time you land your fish and sit there limp and shaking.

    2. You are late for an engagement with a gentleman. You hurry last-minute dressing and "make-up" preparations. As you prepare to go downstairs you snag your stocking and start a run. You hasten to repair the damage and then depart to meet your friend.

    3. Play the game of charades in which each person has to act out alone a sequence of meanings, such as a book title, place, proper name, or slogans. Concentrate the attention on the process of pantomiming an idea.

C. Have students impersonate or mimic the actions of interesting personalities they have observed.

D. Develop situations in which body and voice are integrated in a speech presentation.

    1. Use a simple demonstration or gadget talk with properties or objects.

    2. Similarly employ a talk using blackboard, chart, or other visual aid.

IV. *Develop through lecture and discussion principles of bodily activity from these exercises.*

A. Expand the underlying information and analyze action.

    1. Explain overt and covert movement.

    2. Audience response.

    3. Physical control (tension-relaxation).

    4. Rhythm.

        a. Timing.

         b. Emphasis.

         c. Follow through.

      5. Relationship to ethical appeal of the speaker.

      6. Coordination.

   B. Give supplementary reports on:

      1. Walking to and from the platform.

      2. Posture and stance.

      3. Movement on the platform.

      4. Gesture: face, hand, arm.

   C. Individualize these points according to observed class needs.

V. *Assign demonstration speeches, designed to further the integration of voice and action, which more specifically demand definite responses without properties or objects. Check them according to the principles evolved.*

   A. Use the complex expository speech.

   B. Employ the vivid or detailed and expansive description talk.

   C. Tell a story or narrative with exceptional animation.

VI. *Smooth up and polish the action with reference to specific suggestions which will introduce techniques if needed or desirable.*

   A. Discuss such problems as:

      1. Movement as a transitional device.

      2. Planes of gestures.

      3. Types of hand gesture.

      4. Stereotypes of poor posture.

      5. Movement as an aid to building a climax.

      6. Individuality of movement.

   B. Use pictures, drawings, television, and films of polished speakers. Have the students collect materials and prepare exhibits showing uses, principles, and techniques.

   C. Utilize a forceful argumentative or persuasive talk as an end-product assignment incorporating all that has been taught and learned.

VII. *Follow through on individual needs on every assignment, using suitable evaluation.*

   A. Use constructive, specific oral and written criticism to accomplish these ends.

   B. Have the speaker or reader check his own responses against
       the desired characteristics of effective action. Emphasize
       his own reaction to empathy as it affects him and as he sees
       it revealed by audience response.
   C. Use aids such as mirrors, still or motion pictures, closed-
       circuit television, to check improvement.
   D. Employ members of the class as evaluators of gains made
       in platform experiences and to make further suggestions.
   E. If the teacher desires, III, IV, V, and VI can move into the
       theory and practice of acting rather than speaking, if
       drama is to be stressed.

ACTIVITY APPROACHES TO BODILY ACTION

Although a systematically planned development of experiences
stressing bodily action (as given above) is most effective, some
teachers may wish to employ various activities designed to obtain
response from the student. These can be followed by individual
work on technique, or students can be expected merely to evolve
their own without planned classroom help. Such activities as these
are most usable with, or after, II in the previous sequence, or as special activities later in the course: (1) group pantomimes: a card
game, dinner party, movie audience; (2) impersonations of types:
celebrities or popular figures, historical characters; (3) short scenes
from plays, two or more parts; (4) shadow plays; (5) individual interpretations; (6) readings with characterizations enacted by other
pupils; (7) choric interpretation; (8) parliamentary meeting or
dramatized Senate session; (9) dramatization of historical debate;
(10) mock or simulated television program or radio show.

BODILY ACTION AND DIRECTNESS IN DELIVERY

A speaker's delivery involves not only overt, well-motivated action.
It includes a related component, *directness,* sometimes called audience contact. This means that he speaks *to,* not *at* or *in front of,* the
audience. The most obvious evidence of directness is physical—the
speaker looks at the audience. His eyes hold their eyes attentive to
him. He also observes their facial responses and minutest reactions.
Other components of directness, or "being on the beam," are *mental*

aliveness or awareness of the significance of each word uttered, and *vocal* "focus" or concentration suited to the meaning desired. A speaker is genuinely direct when each member of the audience feels that the speaker is reaching him *individually*—physically, mentally, and vocally.

Important Factors

Certain underlying factors help the speaker to be more communicative. The first are his *earnestness* and *sincerity* as a person. These two qualities are part of his personality; they affect his attitude toward his subject and his desire to reach his audience. They are closely connected with a *definiteness of purpose* about what he says. To be direct and communicative, he must relate purpose to the central idea of his talk, his ideas, and his information. These must also be in a form easily followed by his audience. These qualities increase his chances to be direct.

Further, he will be more direct if he understands his function as a speaker. If he shows off, thinking that he must "strut his stuff" to be successful, he will also fail to reach his listeners. He will be more interested in the mechanics of exhibiting himself than in communicating with his audience. The indirectness will also appear in his voice, his physical presentation, and his mental concentration. He must objectify self in the speaking situation, and use his talents as a *means,* not an *end,* if he would really succeed in being communicative.

Finally, a speaker's fear or timidity may weaken his communicativeness. Physical avoidance or withdrawal from a situation because of emotional tension is expressed among beginning speakers, especially, by their failure to look at the audience and by speaking in a voice that is monotonous and flat. Because they are worried about the details of the speaking situation they often seem disconnected in ideas and frequently make long pauses commonly filled with "uhs," all in an effort to organize their thinking and formulate the language they wish to use. Most of the indirectness of the early part of a speech course springs from these causes.

The Teacher's Responsibility

The teacher must devise assignments that will cause the student to (1) be thoroughly convinced of his function as a communicator and not a showman of platform tricks; (2) be able to face the situation by reducing emotional tensions rather than withdrawing from it; this will help the speaker to meet the eyes of the audience; (3) have the talk fully prepared with a clearly defined purpose and central idea, adequate content, and a suitable organization for extemporaneous delivery; (4) present his talk more ably: (a) be fully aware of each idea and its importance in achieving the purpose; (b) be able to concentrate fully upon the delivery of his material; (c) be competent in utilizing voice so that it carries conviction and is focused upon the individual listener; (d) be physically direct through effective eye contact.

METHODS FOR TEACHING DIRECTNESS

First Method: Talking to Individuals

This practical method teaches physical, mental, and vocal directness through public speaking.

1. Have the student select a subject that shows a strong personal conviction; it should involve the need for straightforward exposition of his belief and the desire to share that conviction with others. Make this assignment after the course has been under way approximately three weeks and at a time when the student has been on the platform at least twice previously. Tell him to prepare it carefully, making an outline, speaking it outside class so that he can be as independent of notes as possible. Samples of such subjects are:
   a. Secondary school students today are better educated than those of ten years ago.
   b. Social standards of students.
   c. The athlete I most admire.
   d. Science—a blessing or a curse?
2. Explain to the class that the goal of this round of talks is to achieve direct, communicative speaking in delivery. Other matters will be subordinated to this assignment. Also make clear that the class period is to be a "work-out" session on this point because of its importance in speaking. With this purpose in mind, point out that it may be necessary and desirable to stop a speaker if he is indirect, give him constructive sugges-

tions, ask him to continue with a more communicative delivery.

3. During class time set up this situation for the student:

   a. The approach and opening remarks in the introduction will be checked particularly to see that the speaker is direct, physically and vocally.

   b. During the delivery of the talk the speaker sees and works with his audience as individuals. He selects one person, addresses him by name, and looks him in the eye. As he concentrates on the idea he wishes to convey, he focuses his voice directly on the one addressed. In his place the listener meets the glance of the speaker and holds it until he feels that the speaker is vital, direct, and "on the beam." He then nods to him. At this signal the speaker turns to another classmate, addresses him by name, and continues the talk. This process is followed until the speaker has succeeded in reaching a large number of his listeners.

   c. Appoint a questioner for each speaker. This can be done automatically by designating the current speaker as the questioner for the speaker following him in each case. The functions of the questioner are to (1) put one question to the speaker, a question that is relevant and grows out of the purpose and content of the talk; (2) make the speaker aware of the definite interest and response of the audience to what he is saying; (3) cause the speaker to break any vocal, physical, or mental pattern that exists in his prepared talk and communicate directly with the questioner.

   d. After the speaker has made the rounds of the class, using the "direct address and recognition method" (perhaps halfway through his talk), the questioner raises his hand and on recognition from the speaker asks his question. The speaker handles the inquiry on the spot, returns to his planned material, and continues to the end of his speech or until the instructor stops him.

   e. Check the conclusion for directness and note especially the speaker's physical and vocal performance at this point, often a very weak part in the delivery.

4. Encourage movement and mastery of the elements of the

speech situation that might restrict or interfere with the speaker's ability to reach his audience.

5. Make a careful explanation of the need for inconspicuous and skillful use of notes so that the speaker will preserve all the elements of communicative speaking.

6. Conclude the speech experience with a jury vote by the class on the success of the student in accomplishing the purpose of the assignment; add your suggestions and specific recommendations for continued work in future speeches.

Progressive Method: Individual to Groups

A second method that can be utilized is as follows:

1. Assign a speech of the type suggested in the first exercise.

2. Ask the student to plan to discuss it in three units, each a part of the body of the talk which develops his central idea.

3. Have him make an outline and prepare his delivery to meet these three situations:

    a. Present the first part of the speech to a single individual in the class, adjusting it to him and emphasizing all the elements of communicative delivery.

    b. Present the second part of the speech to the speech class as it is, a group of some twenty-five to thirty individuals.

    c. Present the third part of the speech to the school assembly, imagining the existing conditions, making the needed adjustments, but keeping all the elements of good, direct speaking that have been stressed in the first and second units.

These are two workable methods for teaching directness. In both, the element of directness has been made the *end* or *goal* of each pupil. Gains in communicativeness should be carried over into every subsequent performance. An alert teacher sees that this is done.

Directness through Other Speech Activities

For follow-up or for an *indirect* attack upon directness, the teacher can find other activities very useful. These include an individual prose reading having vivid or exciting content; a short narrative told to achieve suspense; a panel-forum discussion in which questions require direct answers; a class debate with a forum following; or a round of persuasive talks stressing personal conviction with direct, forceful action.

EXERCISES

1. From magazines and newspapers, clip pictures usable in teaching bodily action. Bring them to class, show them, and explain your use of them.
2. Observe a speaker and be prepared to describe the elements and techniques of delivery employed to aid in the communication of content and your response to the speaker's approach.
3. Prepare a list of exercises or platform assignments that could be used to teach bodily action.

REFERENCES

BAIRD, A. CRAIG, and FRANKLIN KNOWER. *Essentials of General Speech*. New York: McGraw-Hill Book Co., Inc., 1960.

DENSMORE, G. E. "The Teaching of Speech Delivery," *Quarterly Journal of Speech*, XXXII (February, 1946), 67–71.

DRUSHAL, J. GARBER. "An Objective Analysis of Two Techniques of Teaching Delivery," *Quarterly Journal of Speech*, XXV (December, 1939), 561–69.

GRIFFITH, FRANCIS; CATHERINE NELSON; and EDWARD STASHEFF. *Your Speech*. New York: Harcourt, Brace and Co., 1960.

HEDDE, WILHELMINA G., and W. NORWOOD BRIGANCE. *The New American Speech*. Philadelphia: J. B. Lippincott Co., 1957. Chap. IV.

IRWIN, JOHN V., and MARJORIE ROSENBERGER. *Modern Speech*. New York: Holt, Rinehart and Winston, Inc., 1961. Chap. XIV.

McBURNEY, JAMES H., and ERNEST J. WRAGE. *Guide to Good Speech*. Englewood Cliffs, N. J.: Prentice-Hall, Inc., 1960.

MONROE, ALAN H. *Principles and Types of Speech*. Chicago: Scott, Foresman and Co., 1962.

NELSON, THEODORE F., and W. K. ATKINSON. *Speech and Your Personality*. Chicago: Benjamin H. Sanborn & Co., 1955. Chap. VI.

PARRISH, W. M. "The Concept of 'Naturalness,'" *Quarterly Journal of Speech*, XXXVII (December, 1951), 448–54.

SARETT, LEW; WILLIAM T. FOSTER; and JAMES H. McBURNEY. *Speech: A High School Course*. Boston: Houghton Mifflin Co., 1956. Chap. V.

——; ——; and ALMA SARETT. *Basic Principles of Speech*. Boston: Houghton Mifflin Co., 1958. Chap. X.

CHAPTER SIXTEEN

Handling Voice, Articulation, and Related Problems

SPEECH IMPROVEMENT AS A GOAL

One of the principal goals in a first course in speech is to improve the personal speech habits of the student. Such an objective is concerned primarily with teaching voice and articulation. The teacher's responsibilities in this case are several: (1) *He must motivate the student to improve.* This can be done by impressing the student with the importance of effective vocal use and clear-cut articulation for successful everyday communication. (2) *He must help the student to build or set up suitable standards for his own personal speech.* These standards should be those of the accepted speech of educated persons in the social and vocational walks of life into which the student plans to go. (3) *He must help the student to achieve these minimum essentials in his own speech:* (a) a voice that is pleasant in quality; (b) suitable control over the elements of pitch, time, loudness, and variation; (c) intelligible and accurate articulation of speech sounds.

It is recognized that these abilities in themselves are important indices of personality; that *adequacy* in them constitutes the essential difference between the "normal" and the defective in speech; that proficiency *beyond* the point of *acceptability* is an important foundation for success in many business and professional occupations; that *unusual skill* in their use is the keystone upon which rest careers in theater and radio, where superior vocal ability and particular clarity are essential.

LOCAL AND REGIONAL EMPHASES

It should be noted, however, that in some localities, especially in large city high schools and colleges, the objectives of improving voice and articulation dominate the entire scheme of speech instruction; they are the principal ends of speech training. This condition results from the fact that in metropolitan areas there are numerous and varied language backgrounds. Often pupils speak a second language (not English) in their homes or nationality groups. These backgrounds, with the effort of the speech teacher, must be molded into patterns recognized as acceptable English speech. This process of amalgamation is closely correlated with the development of the student's ability to speak the English language. In order to achieve such a purpose, the entire first speech course is often devoted to language development *via speech improvement.* Here the speech teacher is confronted with an array of voice and articulation problems that spring from every language background represented in his class. They are many and varied. It is therefore understandable that in these situations the only common denominator is a phonetic one. The instructor's approach is to start from scratch in teaching the correct formation or production of every sound with phonetics as the vehicle. In large eastern city schools it is no accident that speech skills are secondary considerations in the first semester's work, and are usually introduced later with an emphasis on their use as follow-up experiences in which speech-improvement gains may be carried over and applied. Such an emphasis also exists in other schools of similar size and character.

In some schools in our country unusual emphasis is placed upon voice and articulation for other reasons. These originate in a philosophy of speech training that considers the acquisition of a beautiful voice and precise articulation as the principal ends of speech instruction. In such localities usable speech skills are neglected, and too frequently, as a result of the stress that is placed on these factors, the students develop affected, stilted speech habits. In extreme cases where this overemphasis exists, pupils may use stage diction in daily conversation. Such results occur when the teacher fails to recognize that although the development of better habits of voice and articulation may legitimately constitute an *immediate end* during organized class instruction, the *ultimate goal* of acquiring such habits is the contribution they make to greater efficiency in all types of oral communication. In other words, the high school or college student must have speech habits sufficiently well developed to enable him to meet the demands of speech situations in his everyday existence. In the majority of instances he will have little use for stage diction or for such painfully precise articulation that it calls attention to itself.

A REALISTIC APPROACH NEEDED

It should be clear from these examples that the instructor should approach the teaching of voice and articulation with a realistic, common-sense view of the job he has to do in his situation. In most schools he teaches the work as a part of a first course in which he does many other things. He must face a number of practical considerations. The first, his objectives and purposes in such instruction, has been discussed above. In addition are such factors as these: the length of time he can afford to give in class (from the total course time he has for teaching); the number of students in the class; the age of the pupils; the particular kinds of individual problems they present; certain facilities for instruction, e.g., recording equipment, visual aids, and so on; and the skill he possesses. With these is mind the instructor must answer certain pertinent questions regarding the content, organization, and methods he will employ. (1) What information and theory shall be included—nomenclature and terminology, study of the anatomy and the mechanism, phonetics and ear training, description of sounds, essential processes and operations, systems of voice training? (2) When and how shall testing and diagnosis of voice and articulation be done? (3) How much stress shall be placed upon breathing? (4) Can voice recordings be made? If so, how shall they be made and how shall they be utilized? (5) Shall formal drill be employed? In class? Outside class? (6) How can such instruction be individualized in classes of twenty-five to thirty students? (7) Will small-group methods be feasible and successful? How much and what kind of improvement can be expected from class instruction in voice and articulation? (8) How can carryover be secured in the everyday speech of the student so that gains may be permanent parts of his speech behavior?

These are some of the specific questions, usually asked by speech teachers, which this chapter will attempt to answer.

SUGGESTIONS FOR TEACHING VOICE AND ARTICULATION

I. Laying a Foundation.

In laying a foundation for instruction the teacher should provide necessary information and background for an understanding of essential terminology, the structures used, and the processes involved in voice production and articulation. This material will be developed most effectively through lecture, demonstration, and readings of relevant sources.

A. Explain and demonstrate the fundamentals of sound, using tuning forks and resonators. Explain the necessary terminology, such as frequency, wave length, amplitude, overtone, and so on.

B. Discuss hearing, showing how sound is received (heard) in the human body. Use a wall chart showing the ear as a means of clarifying and motivating the discussion. Develop the importance of normal hearing and ear training in learning to speak and in the improvement of speech habits.

C. Discuss the anatomy and physiology of the vocal mechanism. Define and locate the *essential and major* parts of the mechanism. Keep this to a minimum for purposes of clarity. Use a wall chart showing the head and a model of the larynx, if these aids are available.

D. Explain the principles of sound as they relate to the vocal mechanism. Explain the four fundamental processes in the production of speech—breathing, phonation, articulation, resonation—relating them to the parts as explained in C.

Set or strengthen these concepts and information by the use of sound films. "Sound Waves and Their Sources," "Fundamentals of Acoustics," and "The Voice" are excellent.

E. Discuss and explain in this step, which is devoted to diction (articulation) and elementary phonetics, the difference between vowels and consonants, the fundamental movements for the vowels and consonants, and the difference between the voiced and voiceless consonants. Explain the classification of sounds based upon this information and relate it to the previous steps.

F. Know that "defective speech" is relative, since there are few instances in which speech is so perfect it cannot be improved. For practical purposes, Van Riper [1] defines speech as being defective when it deviates so far from the speech of other people that it calls attention to itself, interferes with communication, or causes its possessor to be maladjusted.

G. Learn accurately to recognize common speech defects, especially those of voice and articulation, as well as stuttering and those associated with impaired hearing and other physical disabilities. With the help of a speech therapist, school nurse, doctor, dentist, and psychologist try to discover precisely what is wrong so that the specific therapy needed can be given.

H. Discover with the help of associated personnel the probable causes of the problem.

I. Realize that when treatment is begun, satisfactory results are usually the outcome of working with the whole student. Desire to improve is a strong factor in obtaining the needed cooperation during work on the difficulty. To be successful, specific procedures should maintain the mental and physical health of the student.

II. Analyzing the Needs of the Students in the Class.

The purpose of this procedure is to discover the existing group and individual problems so that instruction can be adjusted to the particular conditions found in the group. Several methods of diagnosis and testing are useful with high school students.

A. Use *speech performance before the class* as a testing device. The two best samples are (1) a short speech, (2) a brief oral reading. These will give a broad screening of students. As the instructor listens, he can make notes on obvious problems in voice and articulation. He can note any persons who have minor disorders. He can also observe basic skills in speaking and reading at the same time.

B. For further testing the following types may be used:

[1] Charles Van Riper, *Speech Correction, Principles and Methods* (New York: Prentice-Hall, Inc.), p. 15.

1. *A loaded passage test.* The student reads a prepared passage containing all the speech sounds in the three positions, initial, medial, and final. The instructor notes incorrect sounds as the student reads. This type of test, particularly useful for checking articulation, can be found in standard textbooks on voice and articulation or speech correction.

2. *A sentence test.* This is also used for testing articulation. Instead of a passage, test sentences are used, one for each sound; each contains the sound in three positions. By marking the accompanying key or check list, the teacher can get a quick record of defective sounds as the student reads the sentence.

3. *A word test.* The student pronounces or repeats words, systematically chosen to cover the possible uses of sounds in various positions. Again, the teacher can mark those that are incorrectly articulated.

4. *Informal speech test.* This makes use of a conversational situation for testing. The student is usually unaware of the testing aspect. The instructor governs the course of the conference, noting vocal characteristics and sounds that occur in the conversation of the pupil. This type of test can be used beneficially to supplement the other types mentioned. It disarms the student and a more accurate sample of his speech is often obtained than is possible in a formalized testing situation.

C. Record the voices of the students and play back the recordings in a conference situation. Analyze the recordings in light of the information and principles developed previously in section I. Use a check sheet to list for the student the particular areas where he needs improvement. This evaluation can be combined with those obtained in all the previous data.

In making voice recordings certain suggestions are relevant:

1. Do not make recordings the first activity in a course. Allow the student to get set and have, perhaps, two platform performances first.

2. Record familiar materials. This will help to reduce ten-

sion and errors from unprepared content. It is often advisable to record a sample of speaking, reading, and conversation on the disc or tape. Some teachers prefer to use much more conversation than prepared material. This proportion can be varied to meet the preference of the teacher and the needs of the situation.

3. Schedule regular appointments long enough to permit recording, playback, and discussion. Twenty minutes will usually suffice. Much can be done in analysis, motivation, and initial attack on problems, and the building of rapport in such conferences.

4. In the appointment session explain briefly the needs for successful recording on the equipment used. Prepare the student by telling him where to sit or stand with respect to the microphone, how loud to speak, and what his attitude toward recording should be. Also, in the playback time, explain the reasons for his saying, "That doesn't sound like me."

5. Have a short trial run first, using the actual material and equipment. This will permit a check on all factors and will help the student to relax. Then stop the student and make the actual record. If time permits rechecking after suggestions are made, make short repeat recordings to cover individual items. This is more feasible when tape is used.

6. Encourage the student to listen for his own errors in articulation and voice.

7. Be specific and accurate in diagnosis; make constructive suggestions.

D. Tabulate findings for the whole class; note the group needs; spot individuals who need special help. If they are particularly aggravated cases in voice and articulation and rhythmical disorders, by all means refer them to the clinic.

E. Secure background information, examine structure, note related factors on individuals in the class for their cumulative records.

F. Plan a sequence for class training to meet the needs of the particular group and work out a plan to care for individuals who need to be handled on extra time.

III. Follow a systematic training procedure to improve the speech of the class for the remainder of the time available.

Any method of dealing with voice and articulation problems or other difficulties in a small group or class inevitably employs sound methods of re-educating the individual student so that desirable habits are retained and faulty ones replaced by correct ones.

Suggestions for Treating Articulatory Disorders

These are the most common speech problems encountered among students. The general classroom teacher or speech instructor can do more for this type of speech problem than for any other. Defects of articulation include (1) omission of sounds, (2) distortion of sounds, (3) substitution of one sound for another, and (4) some combination of these errors. Usually, bad habits resulting from faulty training or learning are responsible for most defects of articulation. However, some defects result from organic conditions, such as abnormal structures in the mouth, tongue, lips, teeth, and palates.

All structural or organic difficulties should be referred to a specialist, who will recommend any treatment needed and will probably teach the student compensatory movements for producing sounds.

Classroom procedure for handling other articulatory problems includes the following:

1. Discover the sounds which are defective or with which the student has difficulty.
2. Make the student aware of the difference between his speech and the correct sound (or sounds).
3. Motivate the student to want to improve or correct his error.
4. Show the student how to produce the sound (in isolation).
    a. Have him *see* you produce the sound correctly and observe the difference from the way he makes it.
       (A mirror will help him see his own method.)
    b. Have him *hear* the sound and distinguish between it and other sounds.
       (A recorder helps in this process.)
    c. Have him *feel* the sound; sometimes manipulation of the lips and jaws is needed.

    d. Explain to him *how* to make the sound.

    e. Have him practice the sound until he can produce it correctly, quickly, and easily.

5. Combine the sound with others, using it initially, finally, medially.

    a. A vowel plus the sound to be corrected is the usual plan; syllables are formed for practice.

    b. When he masters the sound in this combination, use simple words containing the sound.

    c. Continue this with a variety of combinations of the sound in words.

6. Use words containing the new sound in sentences.

7. Carry the sound over into conversation and other types of continuous speech.

8. See that the sound is well established and habituate it.

The teacher will find many suitable drills, games, word lists, stories, and poems in the references listed at the end of this chapter. As a rule these are classified by sounds and include instructions for use.

Suggestions for Treating Voice Disorders

These are relatively rare among high school and college students, but they do occur. Most voice defects are associated with the common cold, nasal obstructions, and laryngitis, although injury to the vocal mechanism and severe emotional problems might be contributing factors. Defects of voice involve the primary attributes of voice, which include (1) *quality,* with problems of harshness, nasality, hoarseness, and breathiness; (2) *pitch,* including levels that are too high, too low, or monotonous; (3) *loudness or intensity,* which may indicate a voice that is too loud, too soft, or no voice at all; (4) *time,* which includes problems of rate, duration, and so on.

All defects of voice should be referred to a specialist for diagnosis, and usually the elimination of the physical condition, which could be the underlying cause.

In the classroom, steps dealing with defects of voice include many of those found above in handling defects of articulation. In addition, the following voice improvement procedures should be used:

1. Establish the responsibility for improvement within the student.
2. Introduce ear training through listening projects involving the analysis of good speech models.
3. Instill an awareness of good health habits, stressing correct posture and the development of proper breathing to ensure adequate breath support for voice production.
4. Strive to develop relaxation through more poise and confidence within the student, since the lack of these qualities contributes to voice problems.
5. Provide speaking and reading experiences that require the student to resort to expressiveness in order to communicate his emotional and intellectual content.
6. Use the tape recorder for practice and evaluation.

Suggestions for Dealing with Stutterers

Stuttering is a disturbance in the rhythm of speech. Many theories have been advanced regarding its cause. It is basically agreed that stuttering is a result of tension and apprehension and is characterized by hesitations, prolongations, and repetitions, plus blocks and extraneous sounds made during the speaking process. Many children and adults have nonfluent speech riddled with hesitations and repetitions. However, when fears and apprehensions concerning speech develop and the individual seeks ways to disguise or avoid his hesitancies and repetitions, secondary symptoms of stuttering, such as facial contortions and other actions, begin to establish themselves.

No classroom teacher should take it upon himself to label a student as a stutterer because he has nonfluent speech. Such an action creates an anxiety state in both the student and his parents. The competent advice of a speech therapist should be sought.

Wendell Johnson's [2] ten-point program for helping a stutterer provides an excellent approach to handling the problem:

1. Help him to face the problem frankly.
2. Build his confidence in his basic physical ability to speak normally.
3. Build his confidence in his ability to handle speaking situations acceptably even as a stutterer.

[2] Wendell Johnson and Others, *Speech Handicapped School Children* (New York: Harper & Row, 1954), pp. 211–57. Reprinted by permission of the publisher.

4. Train him to eliminate unnecessary and undesirable speech mannerisms.
5. Train him to delay and slow down his stuttering reaction.
6. Train him to stutter as easily as possible.
7. Encourage him to talk as much as possible.
8. Encourage him to cultivate his abilities and personality assets.
9. Encourage him in good physical hygiene practices.
10. Take proper steps to prevent the development of stuttering in persons who might otherwise acquire it.

Suggestions for Dealing with Students Having Impaired Hearing

Hearing impairment may result in defective speaking since adequate expression is closely related to good reception. Defects of articulation and voice may be symptoms of hearing loss, because the deaf or hard-of-hearing child is unable to imitate accurately the speech sounds that surround him and that he would normally hear.

There are three types of hearing loss: (1) *conductive*, which is an impairment in either the outer ear or the middle ear resulting from the blocking of the eardrum with an excess accumulation of wax, inflammation of the middle ear, or injury to the eardrum; (2) *perceptive*, which is impairment of the inner ear, resulting from damage to the nerve of hearing through disease, injury, or congenital origin; (3) *mixed*, which is a combination of the first two.

Individuals with impaired hearing fall into three groups: (1) *the congenitally deaf*, which includes those who are born without hearing or lose their hearing before the normal developmental period for speech occurs; (2) *the adventitiously deaf*, which includes those who are born with hearing, who develop speech in the normal manner, but who then are afflicted with a severe hearing loss due to injury or illness; (3) *the hard-of-hearing*, which includes those whose hearing is defective and yet have managed to acquire speech with or without the use of a hearing aid. Congenitally and adventitiously deaf children or students are usually cared for by special teachers, either in a special school or in the regular school. It is very possible, however, for a classroom teacher to have a hard-of-hearing student in his class.

Hard-of-hearing students can be discovered by one or both of two methods. The first method is the screening test, which can be given on a group or individual basis with either a pure tone audiometer or recording devices. The second method is the alert observation of the classroom teacher of the student's physical behavior and speech patterns. Thus he can detect evidences of hearing loss when screening tests are not possible.

Of course, hearing loss needs proper medical attention, but the classroom teacher can do much to conserve whatever hearing the student has. The use of hearing aids and speech reading are great assets to the person who desires to continue his education in the normal classroom situation. Speech improvement procedures, which have been discussed earlier under articulation and voice, must be made a part of a student's classroom program. In addition, the teacher can do much by:

1. Helping the student to understand the nature of his problem and teaching him how to live normally in his environment.
2. Explaining to other students the nature and problems of a hearing loss.
3. Assigning the student activities in which he can participate with some degree of success.
4. Seating the student in a location that will help him see and hear classroom conversation.
5. Giving the student freedom to move about the room whenever necessary for more advantageous hearing.
6. Speaking naturally with normal gesturing to enhance understanding.
7. Utilizing the blackboard for important information, to develop visual supplements to hearing in the student.
8. Being certain that the student comprehends the material and the assignments.

A PLAN FOR A LESSON IN SPEECH IMPROVEMENT [3]

In working with individuals and small groups a practical organization of the lesson is important. Below is a scheme that may be adapted to the situation in which the teacher works. All parts of it need not be included; however, it serves as a starting point for a lesson and gives a workable sequence.

[3] Stanley Ainsworth, *Speech Correction Methods* (New York: Prentice-Hall, Inc., 1948), p. 51.

1. Relaxation
2. Breathing exercises
3. Oral gymnastics
4. Vowel drill—for vowel quality, loudness variations, and so on
5. Consonant practice
   a. Choose one sound for concentrated work, or a voiced and voiceless pair.
   b. Present materials to aid in auditory discrimination.
   c. Drill these sounds by means of isolated production, syllables, words, sentences, jingles, stories, games, dramatics, and so on.
6. Review former sounds, jingles, stories, games, plays, and others.

THE CLASSROOM SPEECH TEACHER AND THE SPEECH CORRECTION PROGRAM

In a total program of speech correction there is no substitute for the trained therapist. His preparation and experience with all kinds of defects are the foundation of the program. He finds, diagnoses, and treats the serious problems in a school. His knowledge of co-operating agencies—doctors, hospitals and clinics, dentists, welfare services, psychologists, and so on—is very valuable. He also guides the classroom speech teacher in his work with speech improvement.

The classroom teacher also performs very important functions in the speech rehabilitation program. The correctionist usually sees the student needing help on a very limited basis, and not in a typical speaking situation, but the classroom teacher has a longer and more normal relationship with him. The cooperation of teacher and specialist is necessary if the student is to benefit from the therapy. The classroom teacher is responsible for follow-up of the clinician's recommendations when the student comes back to his regular classes. Through his participation in the regular speech experiences and extraclass activities, the student gains application for his therapy and is motivated by his success. In addition, the classroom teacher is often an important link between the school, the student, and the home. By maintaining good rapport with the parents, the classroom teacher can ensure out-of-school cooperation in following out the therapy outlined by the speech correctionist. Thus the classroom teacher of speech becomes a very valuable member of the team in speech and hearing rehabilitation.

EXERCISES

1. Visit a speech and hearing clinic, observe a speech or hearing therapy session, and write a report concerning your observation of techniques, approaches, and results.
2. Using your own method, test the speech and hearing of an individual and note any speech and hearing problem that might exist. Outline your approach to the treatment of the existing problems.
3. Using a satisfactory method, test the speech of each person in a class. Write a short paragraph, giving details of your findings for each student.

REFERENCES

AINSWORTH, STANLEY. "Suggestions for a Successful Speech Correction Program in the Public Schools," *Quarterly Journal of Speech,* XXXI (December, 1945), 471–77.

AKIN, JOHNNYE. *And So We Speak: Voice and Articulation.* Englewood Cliffs, N. J.: Prentice-Hall, Inc., 1958.

ANDERSON, VIRGIL. *Improving the Child's Speech.* New York: Oxford University Press, 1953.

BRYNGELSON, BRYNG. "The Classroom Teacher Testing for Speech Defects," *Southern Speech Journal* (March, 1951).

———; MIFANWY CHAPMAN; and ORVETTA HANSEN. *Know Yourself: A Workbook for Those Who Stutter.* Minneapolis: Burgess Publishing Co., 1958.

ECROYD, DONALD H. "A Rationale for the Teaching of Voice and Diction," *Speech Teacher,* XIII (September, 1959), 256–59.

EISENSON, JON. *The Improvement of Voice and Diction.* New York: The Macmillan Co., 1958.

———, and MARDEL OGILVIE. *Speech Correction in the Schools.* New York: The Macmillan Co., 1957.

FAIRBANKS, GRANT. *Practical Voice Practice.* New York: Harper & Bros., 1960.

GRAY, G. W., and C. M. WISE. *Bases of Speech.* New York: Harper & Bros., 1959.

HAHN, ELISE; CHARLES LOMAS; DONALD HARGIS; and DANIEL VANDRAEGEN. *Basic Voice Training for Speech.* New York: McGraw-Hill Book Co., 1957.

JOHNSON, WENDELL, and OTHERS. *Speech-Handicapped School Children.* New York: Harper & Bros., 1956.

———; FREDERICK DARLEY; and D. C. SPRIESTERSBACH. *Diagnostic Manual in Speech Correction.* New York: Harper & Bros., 1952.

KONIGSBERG, EVELYN. "Making Drill Functional," *Speech Teacher,* I (March, 1952), 128–30.

———, and MILDRED WINDECKER. *"Speech Correction in the High School," Speech Teacher,* IV (November, 1955), 247–52.

MULGRAVE, DOROTHY. *Speech: A Handbook of Voice Training, Diction and Public Speaking.* New York: Barnes and Noble, 1954. Chaps. XI–XVIII.

VAN RIPER, CHARLES. *Speech Correction: Principles and Methods.* New York: Prentice-Hall, Inc., 1954.

———. *Speech Therapy: A Book of Readings.* New York: Prentice-Hall, Inc., 1953.

WEST, ROBERT; MERLE ANSBERRY; and ANNA CARR. *The Rehabilitation of Speech.* New York: Harper & Bros., 1957.

WESTLAKE, HAROLD. "The Classroom Teacher and the Speech Correctionist," *Bulletin of the National Association of Secondary School Principals,* XXIX, No. 133 (November, 1945), 61–66.

CHAPTER SEVENTEEN

The Use of Language

The teaching of language is very important in the introductory course in speech. In spite of their many years of instruction in English courses stressing the use of written language, the speech teacher finds among his students a great need for an emphasis upon the use of *oral* language. The language of conversation and of the speaker's platform is not the same as that of the written essay or classroom theme.

Words are indicators and symbols representing things, relationships, and happenings. Most writers and speakers agree that they are essential tools for the development of ideas. Thonssen and Scanlan state that "The extent to which his [the speaker's] control of meanings through words was successful will be revealed when he takes the platform to deliver his talk." [1]

Dewey's viewpoint on this matter is expressed as follows:

Three typical views have been maintained regarding the relation of thought and language; first, that they are identical; second, that words are the garb or clothing of thought but only for carrying it; and third (the view we shall maintain), that while language is not thought, it is necessary for thinking as well as for communication.[2]

In this chapter we shall not use the word *language* as synonymous with *speech,* since the latter term refers to the entire scope of oral communication, but rather we shall use "language" to mean *the choice and use of words and their arrangement in combination so as to carry the thought intelligibly, convincingly, and accurately.*

[1] Lester Thonssen and Ross Scanlan, *Speech Preparation and Delivery* (Philadelphia: J. B. Lippincott Co., 1941), p. 62.
[2] John Dewey, *How We Think* (Boston: D. C. Heath and Co., 1910), p. 230.

The important questions in relation to the teaching of language in the first course are: What shall be the goals of such instruction? What shall we teach? How shall we teach it?

Other relevant questions that develop are:

Can the teacher assume that unity, coherence, and emphasis, as well as grammatical structure and correct usage, have been taught previously in English courses in written composition?

Is it therefore necessary for the student only to adapt this knowledge to the speaking situation?

Shall instruction in language be concentrated in a short unit in the course, or shall the treatment be scattered throughout the entire course?

How much time shall be devoted to such study?

How can language instruction meet individual student problems?

The answers to these questions will in large measure determine content, method, and emphasis.

GOALS IN INSTRUCTION

With reference to goals in teaching language, Irving J. Lee [3] points out that the speaker must meet these if he is to be effective:

1. *He must know how to use correctly the conventional language forms which are recognized and accepted.* This necessitates his having a working knowledge of grammatical principles and correct usage and adequate skill in the mechanics of sentence structure, agreement, case, etc.
2. *He must know how to use language to arrest and hold attention to make his ideas persuasively effective with his listeners.* This necessitates his having a working knowledge of the principles of oral style so that he can create the desired audience response. Therefore, he must know the characteristics of oral style; develop disarming word selection; understand the kinds and uses of various types of sentences; be skillful in the use of definition, examples, illustrations; develop an orderly sequence

---

[3] Irving J. Lee was professor and chairman of the Department of Public Address, School of Speech, Northwestern University. He is the author of *Language Habits in Human Affairs, The Language of Wisdom and Folly,* and *How to Talk to People,* all published by Harper & Bros.

of ideas; employ proper transitions; and know how to employ repetition, climax, rhythm, and figures of speech.

3. *He must meet certain standards of adequacy so that language will fit the "territory" to which he applies it; in short, his use of language must be accurate semantically.* This means that he should avoid ambiguities and oversimplifications; he must realize the need to qualify or restrict statements in order to avoid hasty generalizations; he must be aware of the constant *change* in the things to which language refers; and therefore he should indicate "time limitations" in the use of language.

4. *He must be sure that his language is clear, so that his audience does not mistake his meaning.* This check is in addition to his effectiveness in the first three needs. Sentence length, length and difficulty of words, kinds of sentence, and suitable transitions, all play a part in clarity.

A given speaker can conceivably be effective in every one of these areas; most speakers, however, have some weaknesses and yet enjoy a certain amount of success. A truck driver, for instance, might lack *grammatical skill* (see number 1 above), have only a modest grasp of *accuracy* (number 3), but still might be very successful in *persuasion* (number 2). An atomic scientist conceivably might be meticulously accurate, rather inept in the persuasive use of language, but again, absolutely correct grammatically and mechanically. A Hitler might disregard the third area, be a master of the second, and be adequate in the first. All three of these persons would need *clarity* in language. Most speech instruction has placed a greater stress upon the first area; without punning, it can be said that such teaching merely gives lip service to the teaching of oral style and to developing the persuasive use of language; the third area has been almost completely overlooked in first courses in speech. It is very important that proficiency be developed in *all areas*.

APPROACHES TO TEACHING

A difference of opinion exists regarding how the speech teacher should proceed in teaching the use of language. Some persons contend that he can merely build upon the foundations established in numerous English courses. Therefore, they favor an *indirect* or *in-*

cidental approach to the problem. Others believe the need so important that they advocate *planned* or *direct* instruction, perhaps organized in the form of a short basic unit in language from which further learning may be evolved.

Indirect or Incidental Approach

In this plan, language problems are handled either individually as they arise or, if several students demonstrate the need for assistance, in group instruction. The most appropriate time for such help is in the criticism sessions following platform performances. Some instructors try to integrate such assistance with their teaching of speech preparation, using evaluation sessions to check language use. The following methods may be employed to meet individual needs:

1. Examine preparation outlines, comparing them with the language employed in performance.
2. Assign language critics in each round of speeches.
3. Record careful notes upon language usage and effectiveness in each of the four needs above. Write these upon evaluation sheets with specific errors and recommendations for improvement; hand them to each student as part of regular critiques.
4. List common class errors and needs on the chalk board at the conclusion of each round of performances. Hold class discussions on ways to improve.
5. Tape selected rounds of speeches. Hold playback sessions before the class with both students and teacher, pointing out needs and means of improving language use.
6. Hold individual conferences using teacher observation, evaluation sheets, and replay of tapes to bring matters to the attention of students who need aid.
7. Assign special projects or make "contracts" with individual pupils stressing (a) improved vocabulary or usage, (b) class reports, (c) panel discussions on particular problems, (d) notebook or research assignments.

Direct or Planned Approach

Often the teacher feels that he cannot do this job incidentally. He needs class time and organized instruction to lay foundations and start the development of the student in the direction indicated. After or during such a planned or organized foundation, this training can be supplemented with many of the methods suggested under the indirect approach, particularly following each speaking experience. A minimum of two weeks (ten hours) for such a unit is recommended. However, a third week can be added with considerable gain if time permits. Course schedules will influence this. The speech teacher should expect little background to be adaptable from the previous instruction by English teachers in written composition. If they have succeeded at all in going beyond minimum essentials, their stress probably has been upon grammatical correctness, punctuation, and style. Oral language has certain demands placed upon it, which differ from those of written language. The speech teacher will be wise to review these differences and develop the foundation and characteristics of oral language as used by the speaker.

What should be taught and *how* it should be taught are closely related to the needs of the speaker, as previously expressed. The following section presents a projected unit directed to the achievement of the goals in the field.

A UNIT ON LANGUAGE FOR USE IN
A FIRST COURSE IN SPEECH

Subject: Words and their use; the nature of language.

First Lesson

I. Objectives
  A. To give the student a clear concept of the nature and use of words.
  B. To acquaint the student with the nature of the territory to which words apply.
    1. Observation
    2. Part or all of anything
    3. Change and the temporal character of things
II. Readings
  A. Lee, *Language Habits in Human Affairs,* Chapters 2, 3, 4.
  B. Hayakawa, *Language in Thought and Action,* Chapters 1, 2.

    C. Chase, *The Tyranny of Words,* Chapters 1, 2, 6, 7.

    D. Goldberg, *The Wonder of Words,* Chapter 15.

III. Student Assignment

    A. Have students read from A, B, and one other; they should report their readings in note form.

    B. Give to the class the following list of words, or one similar. Have each person write the first meaning that comes to his mind; also have him mark a + sign before words he likes and a — sign before those he dislikes. Go around the class having each student read his response.

ball	car	Negro
gin	taxes	tough
G.I.	buck	work
music	communist	sweet
television	fun	rich
speech	home	rest
fine	God	labor

      1. Have the student prepare similar lists, indicating his own personal meaning of each word without referring to a dictionary.

      2. Have each student report an experience in which definition, description, or directions have been misunderstood or have been misleading. What attitude should the person have toward such future information?

    C. Give class lecture to cover the following material:

      1. Words are pointers or indicators, not things.

      2. Words have many meanings.

        a. The dictionary gives customary meanings of words; it does not contain all meanings; it needs constant revision.

        b. Every word has an infinite number of meanings.

        c. Avoid confusion by checking what the *other person* means by his language.

        d. Explain the nature of the territory to which words refer; stress observations, the partial (not total) character of experience; the changing order of things and symbols.

        e. Adapt this to the needs of the speaker.

Second Lesson

I. Objectives
   A. To continue the study of language relationships, as they affect the speaker.
   B. To distinguish between connotation, denotation, and between facts and assumptions.
   C. To orientate the student to selected relationship between language and thinking and acquaint him with the possible pitfalls that exist in word usage, as found in the following words and phrases:
      1. "All and some"
      2. "Either, or"
      3. "One word, one meaning"
      4. "Meaning out of context"
      5. Facts and assumptions
      6. "Magic of words"
      7. Inferences and judgments
   D. To stimulate students to see the necessity of using words accurately.
   E. To study concrete and specific words.

II. Readings
   A. Lee, *Language Habits in Human Affairs,* Chapters 7, 8, 9.
   B. Hayakawa, "Story with a Moral" and *Language in Thought and Action,* Chapters 3, 4, 5, 6, 7.

III. Student Assignment
   A. Students should read the references above and take adequate notes.
   B. Each student selects from a newspaper, magazine, or book, an article of about three hundred words. Underline all connotative terms used. Rewrite the article using "unslanted" language. Describe the difference in the reader's conclusion and attitude as he reads the two versions.
   C. Assign an editorial from the local paper for reading. Have students select facts, assumptions, and generalizations that need checking, "either-or" conclusions, one-word meanings, and any other implications contained therein.
   D. Have each student prepare, for the general word on the list below, three concrete words; then have him add to the list

ten more general words that he uses and find three concrete words for each of these: man, fight, walk, answer, store, vehicle, girl, eat, worker, building, athlete, animal, sit, trader.

IV. Method and Procedure

A. Lecture by the instructor and discussion with students on the following topics:
   1. Informative *vs.* directive speaking
   2. Denotation: connotation
   3. Loaded words
   4. Inferences and judgments
   5. Other common faults in word usage
   6. Need for examining word in context
   7. Need for accuracy and concreteness in language

B. Apply reading and lecture material to the assignments.

In III D note particularly the effect of specific words.

Third Lesson

I. Objective

To give the student an opportunity to put into practice in a speech situation the results of the first two lessons. Stress to be upon language that is clear, accurate, concrete; check upon "all and same," facts and assumptions, "either-or," and so on.

II. Student Assignment

A. Each student will prepare a 3–5 minute extemporaneous speech in which he defines a popular concept. He must be sure to clarify the word or phrase, using concrete, accurate, objective language.

Possible suggested subjects: Reactionary, Communism, Success, Nationalism, New Frontier, Loyalty, Treason, Democracy, Courtesy, Liberalism, Freedom of the Press, General Education, Conscience.

B. Each student will prepare a 3–5 minute extemporaneous speech on an occupation or vocation that is of interest to him. Stress theme of specific, accurate language, or specialized language where it is needed.

III. Method and Procedure

A. Each student to deliver his talk after a good outline plan has been made.

B. Criticism of language aspects, especially by the instructor and students.

Fourth Lesson

I. Objectives
   A. To give the students concrete suggestions for building wider, more flexible vocabularies.
   B. To acquaint the student with types of word usage generally to be avoided in effective speaking.
   C. To check upon the student's knowledge of conventional language forms.

II. Readings
   A. Sarett, Foster, and Sarett, *Basic Principles of Speech,* 3rd Edition, Chapter VIII.
   B. Gilmartin, *Building Your Vocabulary.*
   C. Hart, *Twelve Ways to Build a Vocabulary.*
   D. Goldberg, *The Wonder of Words.*

III. Student Assignment
   A. Read one or more of the above references.
   B. Have each student list from his reading at least five suggestions for vocabulary building that he thinks would be most useful to him.
   C. Have each student list ten words he overuses and suggest a synonym for each.
   D. Have each student make a list of ten words he hears but does not readily speak, read, or spell, and use each of these in a sentence.

IV. Method and Procedure
   A. Read to the class the poem, "Hollyhocks," by Lew Sarett. Have the class copy the adjectives and adverbs he uses. Point out the effects the author achieves with these modifiers. Have the class give a synonym for each one selected.
   B. In the following speech by Mrs. Malaprop from *The Rivals* by Sheridan, substitute for the italicized words the correct word from the list below.

   "I would by no means wish a daughter of mine to be a *progeny* of learning: I don't think so much learning becomes a young woman; for instance, I would never let her meddle with Greek or Hebrew; neither would it be necessary for her to handle any of the mathematical, astronomical, diabolical instruments. But, Sir Anthony, I would send her at nine years old, to a boarding school in order for her to learn a little *ingenuity* and artifice. I would have her instructed in *geometry* that she might know something about the *contagious* countries: but above all, Sir Anthony, she should be a mistress of *orthodoxy* that she might not spell and mispronounce words so shamefully as girls usually do; and likewise that she might *reprehend* the true meaning of what she is saying. This is what I would have a woman know—and I don't think there's a *superstitious* article in it."

prodigy	orthography	ingenuity
ambiguous	orthoëpy	contiguous
superfluous	geography	
superficial	comprehend	

C. Discuss the effects upon the listener or reader of the words used in the two selections.
D. Discuss the part vocabulary plays in speech-making, referring back to the material on language and thought in the previous unit.
E. Discuss means of enlarging a vocabulary.
F. Discuss propriety of language in speaking.
  1. The need for adapting language to the occasion, the speaker, and the topic.
  2. Language that usually should be avoided:

archaic words	hackneyed words and
barbarisms	phrases
provincialisms	colorless words
slang	technical terms
foreign words	vogue words
overworked figures of	formal, pompous language
speech	euphemisms
long words	

  3. The need for synonyms and antonyms.

Fifth Lesson

I. Objective

To continue work begun on the first day toward building a wider, more flexible vocabulary for speaking.

II. Student Assignment

A. Write a 100-word précis of a short magazine article, the emphasis being upon economy of words and accuracy in their use.

B. Bring to class ten sentences from a radio talk, magazine, or book to illustrate picturesque or vivid usage of language.

C. Make a list of synonyms (three for each) for the following common words: good, active, brutal, group, school, game, house, walk, speak, quick, smile, awfully, plan.

D. Bring to class a short poem. Be ready to read it and tell how the wording enhances the meaning.

III. Class Procedure

A. Discuss the examples of word usage that the pupils have brought in.

B. Read and discuss the poems.

C. Discuss the elements of vivid word usage: sound words, color words, technical words, picture words, emotionally charged words.

D. Have each student write a short paragraph describing some place he has seen, a new invention, fad, or unusual dish of food.

Sixth Lesson

I. Objective

To use or apply the enriched vocabulary and language usage in a speaking situation.

II. Student Assignment

Each student will prepare an expository-descriptive speech of three minutes in length utilizing language that is clear, accurate, and vivid.

Suggested subjects:

What's in a Name

Verbal Taboos

Interesting Origins of Words

The Use of Language in Modern Advertising

Television Announcers and Continuity

The Effect of Historical Events upon Language

The Coining of New Words

Slang

The Changing Meaning of Words

Sound Words and the Twentieth Century
Overworked Words
Idioms
The Dictionary
The Power of Words
Famous Slogans

III. Classroom Procedure
Have the speeches given in class, criticized, and discussed on accuracy, variety, clarity, and economy in the use of language.

Seventh Lesson

I. Objective
To acquaint students with some of the effective devices of oral style.

II. Readings
Hayakawa, *Language in Thought and Action*, Chapter 12.
Brigance, *Speech Composition*, Chapter 6.
Goldberg, *The Wonder of Words*, Chapters 5, 6, 17.
*Sarett, Foster, and McBurney, *Speech*, Chapter 8.
*Weaver, Borchers, and Smith, *Speaking and Listening*, pages 120–30.

III. Student Assignment
A. Read either of the starred references in II and one other.
B. How many kinds of figures of speech can you name? Give an example of each.
C. List five definite suggestions for gaining greater effect (clarity or impressiveness) in speaking.

IV. Classroom Procedure
A. Discuss qualities of effective style: accuracy, force, suggestiveness, ease, communicativeness, beauty.
B. Discuss definite suggestions for achieving oral style.
1. Speaking in familiar terms
2. Varying the method of statement
3. Amplification
4. Restatement and repetition
5. Objective elements and vividness
a. Direct discourse
(1) Use of first and second person
(2) Direct quotation

          (3) Apostrophe and personification

          (4) Interrogation: direct question, rhetorical question

    b. Epigram

    c. Analogy and antithesis

    d. Allusions

    e. Illustrations

    f. Definitions

    g. Use of slogans

    h. Figures of speech

C. Pass out a mimeographed section of a speech (Lincoln, F. D. Roosevelt, Burke, etc.). Have the students write criticisms of the sections with respect to the use of oral style, underlining examples of the various devices used.

Eighth Lesson

I. Objective

To continue the study of oral style, emphasizing rhetorical elements dealing with coherence, unity, emphasis.

II. Readings

Read in the class speech text the section dealing with principles of unity, coherence, and emphasis.

Baird, *Representative American Speeches.*

Wrage and Baskerville, *American Forum: Speeches on Historic Issues, 1788–1900.*

III. Student Assignment

    A. After reading the materials on unity, coherence, and emphasis, choose a 100-word excerpt from one of the speeches in the texts above. Criticize it for rhetorical style, noting the principles mentioned in the seventh lesson and those developed in the present lesson.

    B. Bring in five magazine advertisements illustrating the use of figures of speech. Classify these according to kind and comment upon their effectiveness.

IV. Classroom Procedure

    A. Discuss rhetorical elements of speech composition:

Unity: purpose, feeling, thought; Coherence: order, transitions; Emphasis: place, space, contrast, climax, antithesis, effective phrases; Sentence structure: variety in length; periodic vs. balanced.

B. Discuss materials brought to class by the students.

C. Pass out mimeographed material of a selection clearly intended to be read silently. Have students rewrite it in "oral style," giving particular attention to the principles listed above.

Ninth Lesson

I. Objective

To evaluate the student's ability to put into practice principles of language usage in an original speaking situation.

II. Student Assignment

Prepare a talk of three to five minutes in length on a topic about which you have a strong feeling or conviction. Try to get your audience to see your point of view. Make use of the principles of effective language.

III. Classroom Procedure

A. Hear talks; these can be regarded as a practical test or examination.

B. Evaluate talks in terms of language effectiveness.

C. If time permits, give a short written review on the language unit.

EXERCISES

1. Select a speech from a recent publication and carefully analyze its vocabulary and language forms.

2. State what you believe to be the specific responsibility of the speech teacher and the specific responsibility of the English teacher in teaching language and suggest how both teachers might best work together to achieve a common goal.

3. Write a paper in which you answer the question: "Should language be taught directly or indirectly in the basic speech course?" Explain your reasons for the method you select.

REFERENCES

BAIRD, A. CRAIG, and FRANKLIN KNOWER. *Essentials of General Speech.* New York: McGraw-Hill Book Co., 1960.

BORCHERS, GLADYS. "An Approach to the Problem of Oral Style," *Quarterly Journal of Speech,* XXII (February, 1936), 114–17.

CHASE, STUART. *The Tyranny of Words*. New York: Harcourt, Brace and Co., 1938.

COOPER, LANE. *Theories of Style*. New York: The Macmillan Co., 1907.

CROCKER, LIONEL. *Public Speaking for College Students*. New York: American Book Co., 1956.

FLESCH, RUDOLPH. *The Art of Plain Talk*. New York: Harper & Bros., 1949.

————. *The Art of Readable Writing*. New York: Harper & Bros., 1949.

GILMARTIN, JOHN. *Building Your Vocabulary*. New York: Prentice-Hall, Inc., 1941.

GOLDBERG, ISAAC. *The Wonder of Words*. New York: Appleton-Century-Crofts, Inc., 1938. Chaps. V, VI, XV–XVII.

HAYAKAWA, S. I. *Language in Thought and Action*. New York: Harcourt, Brace and Co., 1949.

————. *Language: Meaning and Maturity*. New York: Harper & Bros., 1959.

JOHNSON, WENDELL. *People in Quandaries*. New York: Harper & Bros., 1946.

LABRANT, LOU. *We Teach English*. New York: Harcourt, Brace and Co., 1951. Pp. 3–90.

LEE, IRVING. *Language Habits in Human Affairs*. New York: Harper & Bros., 1941. Chaps. I–VIII.

MENCKEN, H. L. *The American Language*. New York: Alfred A. Knopf., Inc., 1936.

OGDEN, C. K., and I. A. RICHARDS. *The Meaning of Meaning*. New York: Harcourt, Brace and Co., 1936.

PROGRESSIVE EDUCATION ASSOCIATION. *Language in General Education*. New York: Appleton-Century-Crofts, Inc., 1940.

ROSENBERGER, MARJORIE. *Mark My Words*. New York: World Book Co., 1952.

WITTY, PAUL. "Some Suggestions for Vocabulary Development in the Public Schools," *Educational Administration and Supervision* (May, 1945), pp. 271–82.

PART THREE

Teaching and Directing
Speech Activities

CHAPTER EIGHTEEN

Administering Activities and Contests

Contests and activities are a major part of a total speech program. Chapter VI developed the philosophy and scope and gave a detailed description of the events possible in such a contest program. This chapter will deal with general and specific problems and suggestions for administering activities and contests.

Although the speech teacher may do a strong job of classroom teaching, he may find even greater demands upon him as a director of activities and contests. Teaching done outside the controlled conditions of course plans and a classroom schedule is more difficult. The informality of after-school sessions, evening rehearsals, and trips out of town presents various problems. One of these is the question of maintaining, at the same time, the necessary motivation for excellent public performance and the desired organization and discipline for achieving results. In addition are all of the administrative details of schedule, auditorium, extra rooms, publicity, finance, transportation, housing, food, materials, and publicity that are inherent in a program of this sort. They place heavy pressures upon the strength and resourcefulness of the speech teacher.

Before proceeding to a detailed discussion of these, it is relevant to consider the general obligations of the director.

GENERAL RESPONSIBILITIES OF THE DIRECTOR

The director should assume the responsibilities of handling speech contests and activities with a full appreciation that the administrator, students, and often the community will judge him by the quality of work he does in this area just as definitely as they evaluate him on his class instruction in speech.

1. *He can determine, or certainly assist in determining, the scope and character of the program to be presented.*

Local conditions will set certain patterns as a starting point for the teacher. He should view the extraclass work in relation to the patterns, to his teaching load, and to the kind of total speech program he hopes to develop. He should consider his own time and energy, the students' interests and abilities, as well as all of the other factors affecting his program (see Chaps. I, IV, V, VI). He might better restrict the scope of the activity program and do better work than spread himself thin trying to do too many things. Since most activities and contests are open to the entire school or community audience, the teacher should always do his best to represent his school and his department with a satisfactory quality of performance.

2. *He selects the students who are to participate and decides what they are to do.*

In contest work this is a critical and vital point. The speech teacher should never relinquish completely nor fail to have a part in determining the persons he must *train* for platform work. The teacher is responsible for results; he should therefore have the authority and right to select his own personnel. In an activity for assembly purposes, this prerogative enables the teacher to include in his program many students who are eager to take part. Many fine educational benefits are thus achieved.

3. *He can select, edit, or cut any selections, plays, or similar material to be used in a contest or activity.*

The teacher's responsibility here rests on supervising the appropriateness and the quality of poetry, prose, dramatic literature, quotations, argument, evidence, or script material that might be used. Quite logically he should be guided by the best standards of literary material; by the conventions and proprieties of the school and community; by the potentialities of the material for acceptance by the audience, critics, or judge; and by his own good taste as an educator and a cultured person. If he is not clearly informed on local custom and tastes, the administrator will tell him, either with or without any leading questions. It is a sensible precaution to consider these matters before the material, program, or play is prepared for presentation, and thus avoid unfortunate consequences.

4. *He directs the training and the preparation of the persons who are to participate.*

This responsibility is solely that of the teacher concerned. The chief requisites are (a) an effective training procedure; (b) sufficient time for preparation; (c) efficient and businesslike rehearsals and staff conferences; (d) a suitable place and facilities for practices and rehearsals; (e) a schedule free from conflicts and outside interruptions; (f) desirable motivation for the activity or contest.

Mastery of these factors will insure as efficient a plan of procedure as the instructor might have in a regular classroom situation. There is no reason for the instructor to be slipshod or careless in speech work that is offered in after-school time. If anything, he should be better organized in order to make the best use of his investment of time and energy.

5. *He secures critics, judges, or audiences for the performance.*

The director of the contest or activity program places the evaluation of his work in the hands of someone else. This may be a paid judge for a debate, extempore speaking, declamation, or oratorical contest. The judge gives his decision and offers suggestions on what is done. It may be a paid or invited critic who discusses the work and gives suggestions, rather than a decision. It may be a school or community audience which likes or dislikes, is stimulated or bored, by what the teacher has done.

If the school is a member of a speech association there are rules of procedure for securing judges. These usually allow some latitude in *who* will be invited to judge. It is of especial importance that the director select persons who are trained in speech, interested in young people, and within the reach of the budget. For all concerned, it is better to pay whatever is necessary to secure a competent judge. All of the time and effort of students and teacher, the anxieties they share with parents and friends, are at stake in such situations. When an evaluation is made, which might in some instances be unfavorable to the teacher's contestant, it should not be the result of ignorance or incompetence, but should be the judgment of a sensitive, discriminating, informed and trained person. Lawyers, ministers, and neighboring school superintendents usually do not make the best judges. They may be cheaper or more accessible, but they do not compare with trained speech teachers in high schools, in colleges, or in universities.

Further details are discussed in Chapter XIX, "Judging Speech Contests."

6. *He is responsible for the financial arrangements involved in the program.*

In planning and conducting extraclass speech work there are many kinds of expenditures, some small and some large. As might be expected, they vary with the kinds of things done and with the extent of the program. Books, pamphlets, plays, script materials, royalty costs, make-up supplies, rental fees for costumes, memberships and registration fees for tournaments, traveling expense, meals and lodging, electrical supplies, lumber, muslin, glue, paints, and hardware are only some of the possibilities. The teacher in charge ultimately becomes an expert on the costs of all items he needs for his work; on the preparation of estimated budgets for plays, operettas, debate trips, and variety shows; on the best methods of presenting anticipated expenditures to the business manager or principal; on the proper ways of requisitioning and payment of all bills for the various projects he directs. He must have the bargaining sense of the businessman, the expediting technique of an executive, and the sytematic accuracy of an auditor. He is responsible for all these details. He must learn to handle them efficiently, and, of course, "always stay within the budget."

The section on financing the program (p. 348) contains further information.

7. *He plans, organizes, and carries out all the details of the program.*

If an outsider were to walk into *some* high schools or colleges on the day of a speech tournament or a school play, it would not take him long to discover the teacher in charge. He would only have to find the member of the faculty with the most harried facial expression, the most disheveled appearance, and a pattern of behavior approaching disintegration. This is indeed a sad commentary upon the planning and organizing ability of the speech teacher. There are no problems in the administration of extraclass speech work that cannot be solved by complete and careful planning of details; systematic organizing of procedure, events, and schedules; and anticipation of any difficulties to be corrected. As one person has said, "A speech teacher must meet the emergency before it emerges." If the director of activities succeeds in doing this, he can appear on the day of the performance with a face that radiates confidence, clothes neatly cleaned and pressed, and a relaxed casual manner that would amaze the most sophisticated adolescent.

Further details of planning and administration are discussed in later sections.

To help the teacher who directs contests, these details of administration will be developed in this chapter: organizing the program; planning the schedule; financing the program; procuring judges; organizing and administering the speech tournament; and handling trips.

Specific methods for selecting students and training will be included in the chapters on individual speaking, discussion and debate, and interpretation.

ORGANIZING A CONTEST PROGRAM

The first steps in organizing a program are publicizing the activity, interesting students, and setting up the first meeting. Publicity should be started as soon as school opens in the fall in order to interest students who might otherwise enter other activities; an early start allows opportunity for participation in debate institutes, practice sessions, and demonstration activities, which are good training opportunities for beginners. It is best to use various methods of publicity for the program. Usable devices include a lead article in the school paper, announcements in the assembly, a series of calls for candidates in the daily bulletin, which is read in home rooms or all classrooms, a news article in the town paper, bulletin-board posters, and personal word-of-mouth advertising.

A particularly successful method of publicizing the program and recruiting students is by personal invitation of the speech teacher. This can be done after he has made a study of the available students, their possible interests, their abilities in speech, and their scholastic achievement. In a college situation, he can invite them individually in conferences held for this purpose. In high school he may use the same method, but may desire to supplement this invitation with a written note to the student and a more lengthy letter to the parents, explaining the program and its benefits. By this means, key students will be included in the program. Because of their intelligence, leadership, and potential speaking ability, they are fine prospects.

Approximately a week of preparation should precede the first meeting. This will give time for publicity to gain attention among the students and will give students a chance to pass the word around among the various groups in the school.

If there has previously been no program in the school, the publicity can point out the possibilities for learning and fun in such a program, describe the activity, stress the achievements of rival schools, and mention awards, trips, and events in the schedule. If there has been a program, news stories can review the past season, mentioning the names of former speakers and those still in school, the results of regional and state tournaments attended, the record of the teams, the trophies and awards earned, and a direct quote from the teacher in charge of the program.

The first meeting should be carefully planned. It should be scheduled at a time when all students can attend, possibly after school or in early evening, depending upon the location of the school (urban or rural), the activity schedule, the availability of facilities, and other local conditions that might affect attendance. The session should combine the purposes of an introduction to debating and other contest events with a mixer and social evening. It is good adolescent psychology to have some cokes and cookies, ice-cream bars, or some easy-to-handle, inexpensive refreshments to "fill out" the evening and "fill in" the student. The coach or director should preside and discuss with the group the purposes of the program, giving a description of each event, explaining what he expects from his students, and outlining the essential information regarding the year's program. If debating is established and members of the previous teams are present, it is good programming to include one or two of them on the schedule for the evening. Students like to hear about things from their fellows, who can tell them straightforwardly many of the things they wish to know from the student's point of view. An opportunity should be given for all present to ask questions so that doubtful points can be cleared up. The students in the group should be introduced by one of the following methods: (1) the teacher can give the name and class of each; (2) name cards can be given out so that students can write their names on them and then pin the cards on; (3) each student can introduce himself in an around-the-circle fashion. The meeting should stress informality, serious purpose in the program, the benefits of the training, the enjoyment that can be had in speech contests, and the personal interest of the director in each of his students.

As a final part of the opening meeting, the director can have the students fill out cards for his file. Helpful items are: name, address, telephone, year in school, subjects in school, previous courses or experience in speech, present major and minor interests in the field of speech and speech contests, other school activities, outside work, and the like.

PLANNING THE SCHEDULE

Each school should frame a contest schedule that fits its own needs. The director knows the goals and scope of the program he wishes to develop. He also is aware of school conditions that will affect his contest activities—students available, budget, facilities, faculty, class load, examinations, other conflicting school events. In planning his year's schedule he considers what affiliations will provide the best training opportunities for his students. For example, in high school, membership in the National Forensic League would provide a pattern of contests that would determine his schedule. In college, belonging to Pi Kappa Delta would do the same thing. Invitational tournaments of all kinds are becoming much more numerous. If he accepts these, they have to fit his plans. State high school speech associations run district, sectional, and state finals. College forensic leagues hold annual events. Regional and national events are sponsored by others.

If the instructor desires, he can schedule himself into a pattern consuming almost every weekend during the school year. This is not desirable. Careful selection of events will help him utilize his energies and those of his students to gain valuable training and yet maintain some balance in his program.

A sensible, productive program is important. It determines the meetings, practice sessions, or rehearsals to be held with students.

To ensure an efficient program throughout, the director should procure the list of available events and dates as early as possible. He can then plan the schedule, make necessary local and travel arrangements, and inform students, parents, and faculty of their obligations.

FINANCING THE PROGRAM

Most colleges and universities have an established budget for forensics, and the director does not have to raise money. Many high schools have a stable forensic budget. Here the usual practice is to allot a certain figure from the general school activities funds. In some schools, however, speech contest programs obtain a certain percentage of the proceeds from the sale of student activity tickets, which admit students to all events in all programs. In less fortunate situations, funds for speech activities are raised by tag sales, special programs, dances, and PTA support.

Both college and high school directors are concerned with the expenditure of their budgets: they check the wisdom of their investment against the benefits from the programs they conduct. Among the various items in the forensic budget, transportation is a large one, depending upon the location of the school and the speech meets it desires to attend. Schools in active speech areas in a metropolitan section can usually run a program on a smaller budget than can schools in remote areas, which have heavy travel expense. Food and housing count up when debaters travel widely. Other items are registration and membership fees, reference materials, duplicating costs, supplies, publicity and promotion, postage, judges' fees, entertainment of visiting speakers, tournament awards and trophies, and annual awards.

College debate budgets have a wide range. A 1950 survey by Carmack[1] showed a range of $25 to $5,000, with most schools grouped between $600 and $1,200. In 1959, Cripe[2] reported a range of $50 to $5,400, with 58 per cent of the 246 schools running over $1,000. Some of these larger budgets supported very large programs, one with 36 debaters in 480 decision debates and 60 programs, another with 36 speakers in 520 decision debates and 60 programs.

[1] Paul Carmack, Ohio State University, 1950.
[2] Nicholas M. Cripe, "A Survey of Debate Programs in 246 American Colleges and Universities," *Speech Teacher,* VIII (March, 1959), 157–60.

High school budgets also vary widely in relation to the strength and scope of the program, as well as the availability of school funds. They usually finance more activities than college programs. Although many high schools expect their speakers to help on their meals and transportation costs, this is not a desirable educational practice. If the school is running the program, it should be willing to provide transportation and food for the students who are giving of their time, energies, and talents to represent the school.

A sample college budget appears below. In this case the school attended events within a radius of not more than three hundred miles.

1.	Reference materials	$ 50.00
2.	Publicity	25.00
3.	Entertainment—visiting schools	50.00
4.	International debate	150.00
5.	Annual home tournament (Awards—$50; meals—$50; judges—$40; postage—$10)	150.00
6.	High school workshop	100.00
7.	Tournaments: (Registration, travel, meals, incidentals)	810.00
	a. 75.00	
	b. 150.00	
	c. 175.00	
	d. 100.00	
	e. 140.00	
	f. 170.00	
8.	Annual awards	60.00
	TOTAL	$1,395.00

TRANSPORTATION AND SAFETY

Safe, comfortable transportation is a must in running a contest program. Many teachers drive their own cars and therefore believe that they can take more students on trips because of allowances for gasoline, tolls, and the like. This may not always be a kindness to the teacher, or to his students, especially if he has not carefully covered each trip with property damage, collision, and liability insurance. He should never move out of his own driveway until he is suitably protected. If the school will not pay the premium, he should do it himself. A better plan is to have school cars, station wagons, or buses, driven by licensed drivers, or to travel by common carriers where liability is not borne by the director-driver.

SUGGESTIONS ON SECURING, PAYMENT, AND TREATMENT OF JUDGES

Securing Judges

The manner of securing judges is usually specified in the rules and regulations of the speech leagues to which schools belong. If no requirement is made, the competing schools should agree in advance upon the method by which judges are to be secured. In some instances this function may be left entirely to the host school. More common practice is for the entertaining school to submit a list of suggestions to the visiting school or schools. Other schools are asked to indicate any objections they may have and suggest additional names. If a number of events are to be judged, a rather extensive and varied list will be necessary. The training, personal qualifications, skill in judging, institutional affiliations, and possible cost are all factors that will influence agreement upon judges. In nominating judges, the list should contain the name, present occupation or position, address or institution where persons are located, and any relevant comments regarding their competence. A sample list, which represents possibilities for a festival or tournament with a variety of events, follows. Duplicate copies could be made and sent to all member schools for comments and additions.

POSSIBLE JUDGES FOR REGIONAL SPEECH CONFERENCE
ELGIN, ILLINOIS, APRIL 15, 1962

John Hawkins, Professor of Speech, University of Wisconsin. Directs debate and oratory, teaches these courses and discussion.

Gladys Fortin, Chairman of Speech Education, School of Speech, South Western University. Knows declamation, interpretative reading, debate, and oratory well.

Henry Mitchell, Director, University Theater, Marquette University, Milwaukee, Wisconsin. Especially well qualified for one-act plays and interpretative reading.

Glen Hills, Coach of Debate, Augustana College, Rock Island, Illinois. Strong in debate, oratory, and declamation.

Mary Black, Department of Speech, Rockford College, Rockford, Illinois. Directs theater production, teaches interpretation, choric speaking, and debate. Versatile and a good critic.

Dorothy Heckelman, Assistant Professor of Speech, Northern Illinois State Teachers College, De Kalb, Illinois. In charge of teacher training in speech. Wide experience in all kinds of speech contests and festivals.

Mason Weekly, Instructor in Public Speaking, School of Speech, Northwestern University. Coaches oratory; a former college debater and coach.

After having distributed such a list to member schools well in advance, the host-school teacher, who is ordinarily the chairman responsible for all arrangements for the tournament, secures replies from all the participating schools. He then compiles a final list and sends invitations to the judges who have been approved. A sample invitation letter follows. The details should be carefully noted.

Elgin High School
Elgin, Illinois
March 15, 1962

Professor John Hawkins
School of Speech
University of Wisconsin

Dear Professor Hawkins:

On April 15, 1962, the Illinois Speech Tournament for District Five will be held at Elgin High School beginning at 9:00 A.M. Events will be Debate, Oratory, Extempore Speaking, Declamation, Interpretative Reading, and One-Act Plays.

We wish to invite you to serve as a critic judge in three rounds of Debate, in Oratory, and in Extempore Speaking, for which we can offer you a fee of $20 plus your traveling expenses. We shall be glad to have you as our guest at a luncheon with the students, teachers, and judges. Your duties will begin at 9:00 A.M. and will be concluded by 3:00 P.M.

We hope that you will be able to accept. May we please have your reply at your earliest convenience?

Sincerely yours,

Roscoe H. Shelwright, Chairman

Payment of Judges

It can hardly be said that payment of judges is universal. It is increasingly true that well-trained and skilled judges cannot be secured

without compensation. Men and women of the caliber which directors of contests will entrust with an evaluation of their work are far
too busy to donate their services. An athletic coach would not dare
to ask an official to referee an interscholastic football game for nothing. The condition is practically the same in speech. The responsibility of judging, the hours of travel, often under dangerous conditions,
the tension of listening and evaluating the performance, and the
critique following it, all demand much in time and effort. It is not
unusual for a judge to spend as much as eight to ten hours in reaching home after an ordinary engagement. Both the schools concerned
and the judges find that a straightforward business arrangement with
an agreement on the fee and expenses in return for services rendered
is best. This removes any feeling of uncertainty on the part of the
schools involved regarding what they may expect from the judge; it
also lets the judge know that they value his time and ability highly
enough to be willing to pay for it. The figure to be paid, with a statement of what it is to cover, as well as the extent of the judge's duties,
should be included in the invitation that is extended him.

Fees will vary in relation to the speech budget of the school or
organization, the custom or regulations in the locality concerned, and
the ability and prestige of the judge involved. Remuneration for a
critic judge is higher than that for a member of a board of judges.
Fees for critic judges in debate in the Middle West run from $10 to
$20 per engagement. Expenses are usually added to this figure.

If possible, it is a courtesy to pay judges as soon as they finish their
work. This can be done by the teacher's arranging with the school
business manager for a cash advance; judges can then sign a receipt
for the amount of fee and expenses. If a requisition is needed before
a check is issued, judges can be asked to submit a statement of expenses, following which the check can be mailed.

Treatment of Judges

A few suggestions are in order regarding the treatment of judges
while they are guests of the school.

1. Always have a student or faculty representative posted to meet
the judges. The person assigned should introduce himself, conduct
the judges to the principal's office, speech room, or lounge designated

as headquarters for the debate. He should also point out cloakrooms, lavatories, and the auditorium in which the contest is to be held.

2. Introduce the judges to the participating coaches and debaters. This is especially important if the event is a single contest. In a tournament situation the host chairman usually presents all the judges to the entire group in a general assembly.

3. Be sure to supply the judges with paper, ballots, and necessary envelopes before the contest.

4. Even though the judges may have voted against your team, be sure to secure and make use of their suggestions for your speakers. These are usually very helpful.

5. Be a good sport; do not argue or protest decisions. Encourage your students by your own example to accept defeat or success gracefully.

6. Allow no conference among the judges before decisions are announced. Each judgment should be arrived at independently.

7. At the conclusion of the contest, extend the same hospitality you would to guests leaving your own home. Be sure to thank the judges for their services.

8. If the judges are late or some emergency prevents their arrival, make the necessary adjustments in cooperation with the representatives of other schools.

ENTERTAINING A DEBATE TOURNAMENT [3]

Nearly every coach at some time or other acts as a host or chairman for a debate tournament. This is a big job; it must be done efficiently and no details should be overlooked. The following plan gives, in some detail, the total planning operation.

I. Early duties and planning.
    A. Decide on alternate dates for tournament.
        1. Consider school activities.
        2. Consider area activities to avoid conflict with state, regional, or district plans.
    B. Get administrative approval for:
        1. A specific date.

[3] Prepared by Glenn W. Timmons, Department of Speech, Allegheny College, Meadville, Pa.

   2. Use of rooms and other facilities.
   3. Cooperation of other staff members.
   4. Financing of tournament, including any deficit that might occur.
   5. Providing awards, if necessary.
  C. Send letter of invitation to schools.
   (Should be sent at least two months in advance, if not earlier.)
   1. Give date of tournament, hours, number of rounds.
   2. Give information regarding style.
    a. Oregon.
    b. Orthodox.
   3. List awards to be given, if any.
   4. State manner in which tournament will be judged.
    a. Expert-judged.
    b. Coach-judged.
     (If coach-judged, every entering team must provide a judge for every two teams.)
   5. List fees, if any.
   6. Give information regarding lodging plans, if it is a two-day affair.
   7. State number of teams that may be entered.
   8. Enclose entry blank.
    (Set deadline for return of this blank, giving yourself ample time for proper planning when you know number of schools entering.)
II. Preliminary arranging and scheduling of events.
  A. Schedule use of rooms through proper authorities.
   1. Rooms in which to hold debates.
    (If six-school tournament, twelve rooms needed.)
   2. Auditorium or large room in which to hold general session.
   3. Hall in which to hold banquet, if one is planned.
  B. Arrange for lodging, if two-day tournament.
   1. On campus.
   2. At hotel.
   3. In private homes.
  C. Arrange for meals.
   1. Through school dietitian or cafeteria manager.

2. Through a church group.
3. Plan for participants to provide own meals.
4. Notify local restaurants of the tournament.
D. Plan schedule of events.
   1. Registration: time and place.
   2. Time and place of general meeting.
      a. Plan welcome by principal, college president, or other official.
      b. Note items to be discussed with group.
      c. Leave ample time for necessary on-the-spot announcements.
   3. Schedule rounds and times of debates (probably four or five rounds).
      a. Schedule debates between teams.
         1. Time.
         2. Room.
      b. Schedule judges.
         1. Be certain no coach judges own team.
         2. Be certain no coach judges a team twice (see No. IV).
      c. Arrange for timekeepers and chairmen.
         1. List time to appear.
         2. List room in which they will preside.
   4. Time and place of closing session.
      a. Presentation of awards.
      b. Suggest places to eat if not provided by school.
E. Plan entertainment.
   1. Banquet.
      a. Time and place.
      b. Arrange for food through dietitian or outside source.
      c. Arrange for decoration of hall.
      d. Arrange for speaker, singers, or whatever other kind of entertainment is desired.
   2. Evening.
      a. Arrange for a dance.
      b. Attendance at a play.
      c. Attendance at basketball game.
      d. Attendance at radio broadcast.
      e. Attendance at swimming meet.

    f. Or it may be possible to divide attendance among two or more events or activities.

III. General planning and gathering of supplies.
    A. Prepare judges' folders or envelopes including:
        1. Instruction sheet.
        2. Decision ballots.
        3. Carbon paper.
        (If ballots provide for written critique, they should be filled in in triplicate. One copy goes to affirmative team, one to negative team, and the original to the tournament chairman.)
        4. Blank paper for note taking.
        5. Envelopes to enclose and seal decisions.
    B. Ask students to act as timekeepers.
        1. Prepare timekeepers' envelopes.
          a. Enclose list of duties.
          b. Enclose time cards.
    C. Ask students to act as chairmen.
        1. Prepare envelopes for chairmen, enclosing list of instructions.
    D. Have plenty of pencils on hand.
    E. Arrange for someone to be at information desk at all times.
    F. Arrange for at least one alternate judge to be available throughout the tournament.
    G. Secure a blackboard, eraser, and chalk to use for announcements and to tabulate results.

IV. Distribution of rounds and judges.
    A. Give number to judges and to school.
        1. Judge #1 ⎫
        2. Affirmative #1 ⎬ Albion College
        3. Negative #1 ⎭
    B. Distribution.
        1. Be certain teams do not meet twice.
        2. Be certain coach does not judge his own team.
        3. Be certain coach does not judge team twice.
        4. As nearly as possible, arrange schedule so that coach does not judge school his own team meets next (this may be difficult to avoid completely).

C. Procedure for setting up rounds.
   1. Letter "A" in chart refers to affirmative.
   2. Letter "N" in chart refers to negative.
   3. Letter "J" in chart refers to judge.

Round 1			Round 2			Round 3			Round 4			Round 5		
A.	N.	J.	A.	N.	J.	A.	N.	J	A.	N.	J.	A.	N.	J.
1	2	3	1	3	6	1	4	2	1	5	4	1	6	5
2	3	4	2	4	1	2	5	3	2	6	5	2	1	6
3	4	5	3	5	2	3	6	4	3	1	6	3	2	1
4	5	6	4	6	3	4	1	5	4	2	1	4	3	2
5	6	1	5	1	4	5	2	6	5	3	2	5	4	3
6	1	2	6	2	5	6	3	1	6	4	3	6	5	4

(This chart may be expanded into the number of rounds desired. Up to a certain point all objectives regarding judge and teams are taken care of.)

D. Mimeographed schedule of debates and program of events for the tournament.

V. Midway planning.
   A. Send program of events to schools entered; include rules for tournament.
   B. Recheck to see that arrangements have been made to cope with all possible or probable situations.
   C. Be certain that you can quickly adapt your schedule of rounds to any last-minute cancellations.

VI. Last-minute planning.
   A. Place envelopes for chairmen in alphabetical order, names on outside of envelope, according to round number.
   B. Place judges' folders in order. If envelopes are used instead of folders they should be placed in chronological order according to the number of the judge and the round and given out at the beginning of each round.
   C. Place timekeepers' envelopes in alphabetical order according to each round.
   D. Check orally or in writing with timekeepers and chairmen.
      1. Remind them of duties.
      2. Tell them time and place of their appearance.
   E. Remind outside speaker of his appearance at opening, general session, or closing general session.

F. Distribute schedules and programs to debaters and coaches at registration desk.

G. Arrange to have results of tournament posted on blackboard or, if facilities make it possible, ditto results so that each person may have a copy.

H. Arrange to have judges' critiques given to proper teams.

I. See that awards to be given are available and in your possession.

J. *Recheck to see that all is taken care of and in order.*

A SAMPLE PROGRAM OF EVENTS AND INSTRUCTION SHEET

WISCONSIN DISTRICT DEBATE TOURNAMENT
West Allis Central High School

Welcome to West Allis Central! Win or lose, we hope your day here will be pleasant and profitable.

TOURNAMENT HEADQUARTERS are in Room 245. Leave your wraps there. Registration is in Room 245 at 9:00 A.M. Buy your meal tickets at the desk (75¢ per plate).

GENERAL MEETING will be in Room 245 at 9:15 A.M.

LOCATION OF ROOMS, REST ROOMS, etc. There are three floors: Basement (Rooms 10-45), First Floor (Rooms 110-148), and Second Floor (Rooms 206-246). The building is U-shaped. Numbers start in the upper left prong of the U and come around to the right. Room 245 is in the upper right prong of the U.

GIRLS' REST ROOMS are on second floor opposite Room 236 and on basement floor near Room 38.

BOYS' REST ROOMS are on second floor opposite Room 216 and on basement floor near Room 12.

FACULTY WOMEN'S LOUNGE is opposite Room 144.

FACULTY MEN'S LOUNGE is off stairway landing opposite Room 144.

THE CAFETERIA is in basement Room 30.

THE CROSS EXAMINATION TECHNIQUE will be used in BOTH DIVISIONS of the tournament, the first rebuttal speech of each side being devoted to the questioning. The rules are as follows:

(1) The question may be directed to either opponent, but either may answer.

(2) Questions must pertain to the evidence or the reasoning offered by the opposing team in the debate.

(3) The questioner controls the time and may properly interrupt a lengthy reply. Any form of time-wasting by the respondent is unethical.

(4) The respondent may decline to answer a question and tersely state the reason for such refusal.

(5) Comment on the answer given may be made by the questioner during the question period, but lengthy comments are to be discouraged.

THE SEMI-FINAL DEBATES will be held in Rooms 144 and 148.
THE CHAMPIONSHIP DEBATE will be held in Room 245.

TOURNAMENT SCHEDULE

9:00 A.M.	Registration, Room 245	11:45–12:45	Lunch in Cafeteria
9:15 A.M.	General Meeting, Room 245	12:50–1:50 P.M.	Round 3
		2:10–3:10 P.M.	Semi-finals
9:30–10:30 A.M.	Round 1	3:20–4:20 P.M.	Finals
10:40–11:40 A.M.	Round 2		

ORGANIZATION OF PLANS FOR AN INTERPRETATIVE READING FESTIVAL [4]

[Situation: State High School, Kalamazoo, Michigan, the Campus Laboratory School of Western Michigan University, is a member of the Big Seven Conference, a group of seven class-B high schools within a radius of fifty miles from Kalamazoo. The event is a one-day Prose and Poetry reading contest to be held on the campus, with State High acting as host school.]

Obviously, the advance preparation for such a festival or contest is of such importance that the success or failure of the entire event may rest on the foresight of the teacher in charge. Following are the steps that should be included in setting up such a contest.

I. *Preparatory Steps*
    A. First: prepare a letter of announcement of the contest, its date, nature, and general regulations. This should be sent to

[4] Prepared by John Pruis, Western Michigan University.

all schools concerned at least three months before the contest is to be held. By general regulations is meant the type of material that may be used, length of readings desired, and so on.

B. Second: follow this with another letter about a month or six weeks before the contest, enclosing a blank form for entrants' names and other information, such as:

1. Prose contest information: each contestant will prepare a seven-minute reading; also, each contestant will be given a copy of prose at the close of the prepared reading. It will consist of approximately five minutes of reading, and the contestant will have about forty-five minutes to prepare for his reading of it. All prepared readings will be heard first, followed by the ones passed out at the contest.

2. Poetry contest information: each contestant will prepare a ten-minute reading. This may be composed of more than one selection, but one selection must be at least five minutes in length.

3. Contest information: (a) Registration: all contestants will register in the lobby of the Little Theatre between 9:30 and 9:50 A.M.; (b) Speaking order: to be determined by lot, the drawing taking place at 9:50 in the lobby of the Little Theatre.

4. Entry blank: name of each contestant (one from each school for each contest) and whether the entry is for Poetry or Prose contest.

5. Luncheon arrangements: a luncheon will be held at 12:00 in the Van Gogh Room of Walwood Hall and Union Building, directly across the street from the Little Theatre. Cost of tickets to be indicated.

6. Exact times of contests: Poetry section at 10:00 A.M. and Prose section at 2:00 P.M.

7. Prizes: prizes will consist of small cash prizes, or books. [This is popular in this area.]

8. Final date for sending in the entry blank.

C. Arrange for rooms: the auditorium of the Little Theatre, the Van Gogh Room for the luncheon, and also, tables in the lobby of the Theatre.

D. Arrange for judges; members of the speech department faculties of Western Michigan University and Kalamazoo College will probably be used. Advise them, by letter, of the date of the contest, type, and time. Indicate which contest you would like to have them judge and ask for a reply (perhaps include a postal card). Acknowledge judge's reply with definite assignment, showing location and time for the contest.

E. Arrange an honorary job for Contest Sponsor; the head of the speech department at Western Michigan will be asked to open the contest with a few words, and also to supervise tabulation of the ballots.

F. Select the prose pieces that will be used as "spot reading" material.

G. Arrange for chairmen for each contest. Students from speech classes can act here. Also, select three or four people to act as ushers, guides, and helpers.

H. Prepare ballots and instructions. Judges will be asked to rank speakers and also indicate percentage scores. Prepare tally sheet for tabulating results. Obtain envelopes to be used when judges turn in ballots.

I. Prepare box and slips numbered 1 through 7 to be used in drawing speaking orders. Better have two sets of numbered slips, one for each contest.

J. Prepare programs showing contestants in each contest. Also include directions for securing luncheon tickets.

K. Secure change and tickets for the luncheon. These should be sold in the lobby of the Little Theatre at time of registration. One of the guides might be assigned to this task.

L. Prepare some sort of entertainment to follow the luncheon; group singing and a short, humorous skit by members of the local speech club are recommended.

M. Arrange for publicity in the local newspaper as well as the high-school weekly.

II. *Duties on Festival Day*

A. Check to see that the Theatre is unlocked, check lights in the auditorium, tables in lobby, ballots, and so on. Check on everything that will be used during the day.

B. Be available at all times for help to visiting coaches and contestants.

This scheme contains all essential details in planning for the entertainment of a festival or contest in individual speech activities. The outline can be adapted to fit extempore speaking, oratory, or declamation, as well as interpretative reading.

HANDLING TRIPS

Trips to speech meets or debate tournaments are strong motivation in a contest program. They can be very enjoyable and educational; however, they can be an instructor's nightmare if they are not well planned.

First, learn all the details of the event to be attended, noting especially: place and time of registration, deadline for entries, contests to be held, fees, housing accommodations, meal service, schedule of events, time for starting and conclusion of the various contests.

Next, be sure to file the entry blank with the necessary fee and the names of participants well in advance of the deadline for entries. Notify students of their assignments.

Then, plan the preparation schedule and meetings to fit the events and the free time of the participating students. Try to avoid last-minute work. Move students ahead as rapidly and soundly as time permits without placing undue pressure upon them. Point up and sharpen preparation as the time draws near, but with specific helps to ensure necessary polish.

Notify students (and parents in a high school situation) through a memorandum in which all arrangements for departure, return, travel, housing, food, necessary clothing, materials and the like are noted. Give specific responsibilities to individuals selected from the traveling squad. Obtain permission and clearance for the trip from parents, dormitory counselors, as needed; if the school asks for written releases, be sure to obtain them.

In planning the trip, be sure to allow ample time for driving, or for air or train schedules, so that arrivals and departures are "easy," if possible.

Build a code of behavior for the students as representatives of their school. Do this by suggestion and example, rather than by rule, wherever they are. This works in the majority of cases. If it does not, "Dutch uncle" talks are in order to set thoughtless students right. Remind them that in contests, in travel, or as visitors at another school, they should follow high standards of social etiquette and sportsmanship. Under no circumstances should a trip be a "letdown" and an escape from approved behavior simply because students are away from home.

See that contestants eat sensibly, get sufficient sleep, and are given a chance to enjoy the mature counsel and help of a director of speech activities while they are "on the spot." Add words of praise and little token rewards such as a special dinner, a show, minor gifts to recognize a job well done.

Finally, trips can be fun. Help make them enjoyable within the limits of a very productive educational framework—the speech contest.

EXERCISES

1. Indicate what you consider to be the major problems encountered in administering speech contests and activities and possible solutions to each.
2. Write an analysis of speech activities and contests as they exist in a speech program with which you are familiar, taking particular note of their administration and their degree of acceptance or rejection by the pupils, the school, and the community.
3. Prepare a plan, with full details and forms, for any type of speech contest or festival you might have to administer.

REFERENCES

BLANDING, DONALD C. "The Speech Contest," Speech Teacher, VI (September, 1957), 193–95.

BRADEN, WALDO (ed.). Speech Methods and Resources. New York: Harper & Bros., 1961. Chap. 10.

BYERS, BURTON H. "Speech Sportsmanship," Speech Teacher, III (March, 1954), 133–35.

DEE, JAMES P. "Bringing the Forensics Program to the Taxpayers," Speech Teacher, IV (September, 1955), 200–3.

FRIEDERICH, WILLARD J., and RUTH WILCOX. Teaching Speech in High Schools. New York: The Macmillan Co., 1953. Chaps. 7 and 8.

GILBERT, EDNA. "Oral Interpretation at Speech Festivals," Speech Teacher, V (March, 1956), 117–20.

NORVELLE, LEE. "Responsibilities of the Theater Director to His University," Quarterly Journal of Speech, XLI (October, 1955), 250–52.

PHILLIPS, GERALD M. "Imagination—The Answer to Tournament Debate," *Speech Teacher*, IX (September, 1960), 207–10.

SCHMIDT, RALPH N. "Some Current Problems in Contest Speech," *Quarterly of Speech*, XXIX (February, 1943), 93–99.

SIEVERS, DAVID W. "The Play Rehearsal Schedule and Its Psychology," *Quarterly Journal of Speech*, XXX (February, 1944), 80–84.

SMITH, CARNEY C. "Practical Procedures in Coaching High-School Debate," *Quarterly Journal of Speech*, XXIX (April, 1943), 222–34.

SORBER, EDNA. "Tournaments: For Better and Better," *Speech Teacher*, VIII (January, 1959), 49–52.

TACEY, WILLIAM S. "Community Speech Programs," *Speech Teacher*, VIII (November, 1959), 310–15.

VON TORNOW, GEORGIANA. "The Drama Festival as a Community Service," *Speech Teacher*, I (January, 1952), 46–51.

WATKINS, LLOYD I. (ed.). "Ethical Problems in Debating—A Symposium," *Speech Teacher*, VIII (March, 1959), 150–56.

CHAPTER NINETEEN

Judging Speech Contests

Every teacher of speech is concerned with two aspects of judging, namely, the various types and methods of judging activities and contests and also his own ability as a judge and critic. In the first aspect, he must know how other judges evaluate this type of performance; in the second, he must be able to explain and justify his own rating of students' performance in contests and activities.

Judging extraclass speech work is not unrelated to evaluating speech performance in the classroom, a problem discussed at some length in Chapter XII. The teacher who does a successful job of class evaluation and criticism will be able to handle judging responsibilities effectively. He will also be aware of the demands he places upon those who evaluate the results of his teaching. Just what is expected of the judge? What should be his attitude and approach? What kind of a person should he be?

NATURE OF THE JUDGE'S FUNCTION

In judging individual speech events, such as extempore speaking or declamation, and such group activities as debating or one-act plays, the judge should serve as an expert critic. He must ask himself, "Which speaker did the highest quality of work? Which debate team did the better debating? Which play had the best production?" All these questions depend on his judgment of the quality of the performance, in relation to the criteria and standards established for performance in the contest; they should not depend on the judge's personal prejudice, political belief, or sympathy for any of the participants.

The problems, methods, and purposes of evaluation in extraclass work are essentially the same as those in the classroom. Added to these are the responsibility of the judge in selecting the highest-ranking speakers, in giving a decision in a debate, or in announcing a quality rating for a one-act play contest. Further, he must explain his judgments and, in some cases, justify them publicly.

QUALIFICATIONS OF A JUDGE

The judge of any contest or activity should be (1) informed and alert; (2) objective, fair, and open-minded; (3) thoroughly familiar with the field of work he is evaluating; (4) well acquainted with the procedures, rules, and problems of the contests he judges; (5) interested in the educational values of speech training; and (6) aware of his function in aiding the students and teachers whose work he appraises.

Outstanding citizens, lawyers, politicians, ministers, or county school superintendents ordinarily fall short of the mark, especially on items 3, 4, and 5. The best judges are persons trained in the speech fields they are to judge—other teachers, directors of forensics, debate coaches, former debaters, educational directors of theater who train actors and put shows on the boards, and the like. Especially in debating is it advisable to check upon alumni connections, possible relatives, friendships, the frequency with which the recommended judge has heard the teams in question, and the geographical location of the prospective critic in relation to the opponent. Having made such preliminary investigations, the teacher can decide upon the type of judging to be used.

TYPES OF JUDGES

Four types of judges are used in this work: (1) the critic or single expert judge; (2) a board of judges; (3) the coach judge; (4) the audience. Depending upon the situation and the kinds of activities conducted, all these types might be used in handling an extraclass program. The two major considerations affecting the type of judging used are (1) the results obtained and (2) the cost.

A Board of Judges

This kind of judging has been used longer than any of the others. A board of three judges is a common arrangement for individual and group speech events. In some instances this number has been expanded to five or seven members; this is often the practice in final state or national contests. The original reason for the board or panel was the greater reliability of judging that numbers provided. Also, it was thought that any special pet ideas, prejudices, or possibilities of undue influence would be removed by increasing the number of judges. Repeated experience and research have shown that the competence and training of judges are much more important than mere numbers. As a result, the tendency has been to seek competence and expertness in judging, even for a board of judges; trained speech teachers and critics are preferred to laymen. Also, the item of expense has had some effect upon the practice of employing three or five judges for contest purposes. Usually, it is possible to find a single expertly trained judge who does as good a job or better for less money than a school would have to pay three judges. Surveys show boards of judges are used by about one-third of the schools participating in contests.

The Critic or Single Expert Judge [1]

The critic or "single expert judge" is just what the title indicates. He is a highly trained individual in the fields of public speaking, interpretation, or drama, one who is recognized as a capable evaluator of performance. He is thoroughly familiar with contest and festival practices. He is not only accepted as an expert by the directors of the schools, but usually has some distinction because of his interest in speech education and in young people. He is usually expected to give oral comments and suggestions to the participants in an effort to assist them in their development. Although some teachers do not wish to trust the selection of winners to a single individual, the trend to utilize critic judges is found in most high schools. The principal reasons for this are (1) confidence in the accuracy of the judgment of the expert; (2) the cost, which is less or certainly no more than for a board of judges; (3) the benefits of suggestion and discussion by the critic judge.

Coach Judges

This type of judging evolved from some of the factors and problems that have been mentioned above. Directors of contests and

---

[1] See Martin Holcomb, "The Critic Judge System," *Quarterly Journal of Speech*, XIX (February, 1933), 23 ff.

activities desired to employ expertly trained personnel; they also desired to reduce contest expenditures. They therefore used the coaches to judge and criticize student performers. The operation of this system is quite simple. In judging individual events, each coach ranks each participant except his own; the ranks are then totaled in the same manner as they are when outside judges are utilized, and the winners are selected by low-rank total (see next section, Methods of Judging). In debating, the coach-judge system necessitates that each coach judge debates between teams other than his own and give his decision. Every effort is made to avoid scheduling a coach so that he will hear in an immediately preceding round the teams that his own debaters will meet next. The success of this system rests upon the ability and the integrity of the coaches themselves. As a rule, the competence of the coach is accepted; it is only in rare instances that a coach will vote against an opponent in order to foster his own ends. If such individuals exist in contest work, it is much wiser and safer to have the judging done by outside experts who have no selfish interests. A large percentage of high schools use coach judges for certain kinds of activities; recent surveys show that about 50 per cent of the schools employ them at some time in evaluating contests and activities.

Audience Decisions

The audience as a method of judging was introduced by Howard Woodward of Western Reserve University. The thinking behind this kind of evaluation was this: A platform performer does his job for the purpose of influencing the members of the audience; why not let the audience judge the effectiveness of his work? The result was the Woodward Shift of Opinion Ballot, which is still used in all audience situations to evaluate the work of speakers of Western Reserve. The method demands that the listener, before he hears anyone speak, mark on a scale on the ballot his opinion on the question to be discussed.

After he has heard the speech, discussion, or debate, he again marks the ballot.[2] The difference between the "before" and "after" position is tabulated numerically and the decision is based on the shifts of audience opinion that the speaker produces. A revised form of the ballot follows.

[2] Howard S. Woodward, "The Measurement and Analysis of Audience Opinions," *Quarterly Journal of Speech*, XIV, (February, 1928), 97 ff.

Date _____

Place _____

This form is filled by a

_____ man _____ woman, whose age

is _____

Occupation _____

THE REASONS FOR MY OPINION ARE:
(before the discussion)

BEFORE THE DISCUSSION
_____ YES (This expresses my belief
on the question.)
_____ NO (This expresses my belief
on the question.)
_____ I am UNDECIDED.

AFTER THE DISCUSSION
Mark only one place.
I have heard the entire dis-
cussion, and now
_____ The only change in my orig-
inal opinion is that I am LESS
SURE it is right.
_____ The only change in my orig-
inal opinion is that I am MORE
SURE it is right.

(after hearing the discussion)

_____ My original opinion has been
changed to YES.
_____ My original opinion has been
changed to NO.
_____ My original opinion has been
changed to UNDECIDED.
_____ NO CHANGE. I vote the same
as before the discussion.

If the speakers and audience both
desire it, a question period will follow the discussion.

Please use the back of this ballot
for your comments on the speaking.
What is good or bad in the ideas
expressed and the manner of speaking?

369

This type of judging does not have high reliability, but it does permit audience participation, arouses interest, and motivates the speakers to meet a real audience situation. Details of scoring can be found in the literature on this type of ballot. Lahman [3] makes some useful additions to this discussion in his book.

METHODS OF JUDGING: INDIVIDUAL PERFORMANCE

Three principal methods of judging are in use today. These are the *rank-order* method, the *percentage total* method, and the *point or quality rating*. The first is employed most widely. As a rule, a percentage ranking is combined with it in order to facilitate tabulations if ties exist between contestants.

Rank-Order

In rank-order evaluation a single judge, or a group of several judges, listens to the participants, and ranks them in order, giving a rank of "1" to the best speaker, "2" to the second best, and so on, until all have been given a numerical rating. If several judges are used, the ranks are computed to determine a final total rank, which indicates the judgment of the committee upon the achievement in the particular speech work being performed. Standard practice is to award first place to the contestant having a majority of first places. If no speaker has a majority, the one with the lowest total rank is declared the winner, and the others are placed in the order of their total ranks. Below is an example of a speaking contest judged by this method.

Distinctive, No. 6, has a majority of first places; he is the winner. Smooth, No. 1 in the speaking order, has a rank total of 10; he wins second place. Third place is in doubt when the judges tabulate the rank totals. Exhibitory, No. 2, and Liberal, No. 5, each has a rank total of 20 for third and fourth. The tie is decided in favor of Exhibitory by pairing these two speakers and noting the number of judges who preferred each. Judges 1, 2, and 4 ranked Exhibitory higher than Liberal. Since he is preferred by three of the five judges, he secures third place. Liberal wins fourth honors.

[3] Carroll Lahman, *Debate Coaching* (New York: H. W. Wilson Co., 1936), pp. 26–28; 244–51.

Speaker	Judge #1	Judge #2	Judge #3	Judge #4	Judge #5	Total Rank	Place in Contest
1. Smooth	2	1	3	1	3	10	II
2. Exhibitory	5	3	5	2	5	20	III
3. Conservative	3	6	6	5	4	24	VI
4. Loud	4	5	4	4	6	23	V
5. Liberal	6	4	2	6	2	20	IV
6. Distinctive	1	2	1	3	1	8	I

Knower [4] has made an interesting study of rank-order methods of evaluating speech contests. He made a survey of judges' rankings in 578 contests, involving 3,962 contestants judged by 1,970 judges who made a total of 13,265 comparative rank-order decisions. The organizations studied were the Northern Oratorical League, the Intercollegiate Oratorical Association, Pi Kappa Delta and Phi Rho Pi national honorary speech organizations, and the National Forensic League. Speech events studied were oratory; extempore speaking; oratorical, dramatic, and humorous declamation; and impromptu speaking. A number of interesting findings were revealed by this study:

1. The usual practice is to use three judges in preliminary rounds, and five to seven judges in final rounds.

2. The average number of contestants per contest is about seven.

3. The mean average deviation in judging speech performance in these contests is slightly over one rank position. In other words, the average judge varies from his colleagues slightly over one rank position in his evaluation of speakers.

[4] Franklin H. Knower, "A Study of Rank-Order Methods of Evaluating Performances in Speech Contests," *Journal of Applied Psychology*, XXIV, No. 5 (October, 1940), 633–44.

4. The amount of variation is influenced by the number of judges, the type of speaking, and the size of the contest.

5. Original speaking, including extempore speaking and oratory, is ranked with greater reliability than is declamation. Extempore speaking is ranked with the greatest reliability. On the basis of correlations run, it would take a panel of sixteen judges to provide a reliability of $+.90$ in judging declamation, and a board of eight judges to provide a reliability of $+.87$ in judging extempore speaking.

6. Judges agree more definitely on the characteristics of speaking they disapprove than they do on the characteristics of speaking they like.

7. Speakers ranked at both ends of the distribution (best and poorest speakers) are ranked with greater reliability than speakers ranked in intermediate positions.

8. Speakers speaking in first or last position are more commonly ranked in an intermediate than in a high or low position; and speakers who are assigned the highest final average rank by judges most frequently speak in next to the last or in some other intermediate position.

Percentage Total

The percentage-total method requires the judge to give a percentage ranking to each speaker. The highest speaker usually receives a rank of 95 and the lowest 75; the range varies with localities. The other speakers are distributed between these two extremes according to their relative excellence. The speaker having the highest total of percentage points is declared the winner. Below is the same contest judged by the percentage-total method. In this case the rankings for the final places are the same as before.

Point or Quality Rating

The point or quality rating is an application of a classroom evaluation technique to contest or activity performance. A controlled judgment method is used with a rating scale indicating the elements of the type of performance to be judged. In the example of this method shown, the activity is interpretative reading and the scale is one used in the State University of Iowa Festival. Readers are

Speaker	Judge #1	Judge #2	Judge #3	Judge #4	Judge #5	Percentage Total	Rank
1. Smooth	90	95	85	95	85	450	II
2. Exhibitory	80	85	80	90	80	415	III
3. Conservative	88	75	75	80	83	401	VI
4. Loud	85	78	83	85	75	406	V
5. Liberal	75	73	90	75	91	414	IV
6. Distinctive	95	93	95	88	95	466	I

evaluated on a seven-point scale, in which the designations are as follows: 7, Superior; 6, Very Good; 5, Good; 4, Adequate; 3, Poor; 2, Very Poor; 1, Inferior. In this case each reader was judged by critics sitting in the rather informal groups of eight or ten students, each of whom shared his choice of literature with the others. The totals of the ratings were then checked against norms that had been built up over a period of years for this scale and the festival. The norms were as follows: above 49, Excellent; 41–49, Good; 32–40, Average; below 32, Below Average. There was no attempt to select a winner, but merely a desire to judge the quality of the work in relation to acceptable standards for interpretative reading. According to the norms, Lewis and Smith are placed in the Excellent category; Haskell is classified as Good; Thomas and Marion are ranked Average; Weiss and Dirks are judged as Below Average. The ratings and the comments are handed to the participants following the festival. To give a simple index on the 1–7 scale, point totals can also be *averaged* by dividing total points by the number of items. Thus Thomas would be 34/9 or 3.77; Lewis 46/9 or 5.1, and so on. Norms can also be computed in decimal form. Such methods can be used in any speech event.

INTERPRETATIVE READING SCALE

Rater: Jones

Date: May 15, 1962

Project: State Festival Prose Reading

Group No. 6 Room 353 U.H.S.

Readers:	Choice of Material	Arrangement of Material	Projection of Thought	Projection of Emotion	Control of Bodily Activity	Rhythm	Pronunciation	Voice Control	Audience Response	Total Score	Comments
1. Thomas	4	5	4	3	2	4	5	3	4	34	Presentation well organized; needs work on voice.
2. Lewis	6	5	5	5	4	5	6	5	5	46	Excellent content effectively presented.
3. Dirks	3	4	3	2	3	3	4	2	3	27	Poor material ineffectively handled.
4. Haskell	5	5	4	4	3	5	5	5	5	41	Well selected and organized; expression inhibited.
5. Smith	6	6	5	5	4	6	6	6	6	50	Unusually well done; physical response a bit weak.
6. Marion	4	4	3	4	4	5	5	4	4	37	Needs a better selection for her use.
7. Weiss	4	4	2	3	3	4	4	3	3	30	Presentation inadequate for the content selected.
8.											
9.											
10.											
11.											
12.											
13.											
14.											
15.											

374

A WORD TO JUDGES

Be sure to carry out your part of the agreement. These suggestions may help to avoid complications.

1. Keep clearly in mind the arrangements for the event for which you are engaged. Check your correspondence with respect to time, place, duties, and so on. It is advisable to carry the confirming letter with you, just in case.

2. Be punctual. Allow enough time to permit your arrival well in advance of the contest. If road conditions are bad, leave earlier. By all means, do not get the reputation of always being late. Your tardiness may ruin the entire schedule of events.

3. Observe the practice and rules of the school into which you go. It is customary for people to remove their hats in high school buildings and not to smoke on the premises. If there are exceptions to such rules, ask the host teacher for his advice and for any information you lack.

4. Treat your assignment as an educational service to the students and teachers. A conscientious judge can be an effective teacher.

5. Be efficient in your work. Come prepared with forms, paper, clipboard, pencil or pen. Do your job effectively. Don't mince words and "crawl" into your decision. State it, explain your reasons tactfully, and invite questions if the time and situation permit.

6. Build good public relations for yourself and for the institutions you represent by the way you handle yourself in your situation. In your critique, be aware of the audience situation and adjust to it. If you find objections from laymen in the audience, handle them with tact and dispatch.

A SIMPLE METHOD OF JUDGING
INDIVIDUAL CONTESTS

Although each person develops his own technique of judging, some suggestions are helpful. This simplified method may offer some aid.

Before the contest the judge is given a program of speakers, a ballot of instructions upon which speakers are to be judged, and several sheets of paper. If he has made no previous preparation for judging, he can quickly use these materials for his evaluation.

The following illustration indicates how six speakers would be evaluated in an oratorical contest. The judge first copies on a blank piece of paper the names of the speakers in the order of their appearance. He quickly rules six vertical columns to the left of the names as indicated in the figure below. To the right he rules three columns, marking one "Composition," the second, "Delivery," and the third, "Total." This layout provides him with a mechanical means of recording a running or continuous ranking of the contest; he records his judgment after each speaker completes his talk. Of course, he can make other written comments on this sheet or upon separate ones, if he desires.

Jones begins the contest. He automatically is marked (1) in column one because he is the only person who has spoken. The judge listens carefully and evaluates the talk according to the established criteria. He gives Jones a percentage ranking of 65 based on a total possible 100. Hoover now speaks. The judge must choose between Jones and Hoover on the total-rank basis. He does this and ranks her (1) ahead of Jones in column two. He also lists a percentage rating for her of 85 points.

I	II	III	IV	V	VI		Comp.	Del.	Total
1	2	.3	4	5	6	Allen Jones	40	25	65
	1	1	2	2	3	Mary Hoover	45	40	85
		2	3	3	4	Harold Brown	40	30	70
			1	1	1	Sam Harris	50	45	95
				4	5	George Borman	46	22	68
					2	Susan Weber	50	40	90

The next speaker, Brown, concludes. The judge now has to choose among three (Jones, Hoover, and Brown) for best speaker. He observes carefully, and decides that Hoover is still (1), but he ranks Brown as superior to Jones, recording them (2) and (3) respectively in column three. He also rates Brown as 70 in percentage.

A fourth speaker is Harris. The judge must now compare him with Jones, Hoover, and Brown. He decides that Harris is outstanding, and the best speaker thus far. He gives him (1) in column four, and ranks the others in the same relative order. Harris has a percentage of 95.

Next is Borman. He must be judged in relation to the first four performers. The judge recognizes Borman as a weak participant but he thinks him superior to Jones. The ranking with five speeches completed (in column five) is now Harris (1), Hoover (2), Brown (3), Borman (4), and Jones (5). Borman's percentage is 68.

The next speaker completes the contest. Where will Weber's work place her? After careful attention to this talk, the judge ranks her as (2) in the contest, and assigns her the percentage of 90. The other speakers are now reranked and the final result has Harris in first place, Weber in second, Hoover in third, Brown in fourth, Borman in fifth, and Jones still in last place.

The judge transfers his ratings to the ballot, signs it, and hands it to the usher. He can then turn his attention to any relevant notes he has taken which may serve him well in a discussion following the contest.

JUDGING INDIVIDUAL SPEECH ACTIVITIES

To help the prospective judge in individual events, a sample ballot (for oratory) is included. Ballots for other activities are similar in form.

BALLOT FOR ORIGINAL ORATORY
NATIONAL FORENSIC LEAGUE

[*Recto*]

Instructions to Judges   Oratory

Since these orations have been written by the contestants delivering them, the judges should consider Thought, Composition, and Delivery. However, as this is a contest in speech rather than in essay writing, the emphasis should be placed on the speech phase. Thought and composition should be considered primarily in the way they are employed to make effective speaking possible.

The orator should not be expected to solve any of the great problems of the day. Rather he should be expected to discuss intelligently, with a degree of originality, in an interesting manner, and with some profit to his audience, the topic he has chosen. He should be given wide latitude in the ideas he expresses, but held closely accountable for the manner in which he expresses them.

The composition should be considered carefully for its rhetoric and diction. The use of appropriate figures of speech, similes and metaphors, balanced sentences, allusions, and other rhetorical devices to make the oration more effective should be noted especially. Use of English should be more than correct; it should reveal a discriminating choice of words and altogether fine literary qualities. It should be especially adapted to oral presentation.

Delivery should be judged for mastery of the usual mechanics of speech—poise, quality and use of voice, and bodily expressiveness; and for the qualities of directness and sincerity which impress the oration upon the minds of the audience.

No particular style of delivery is to be set up as the one correct style to which all contestants must conform. Rather each contestant is to be judged upon the effectiveness of his delivery, free to choose or develop whatever style will best give him that effectiveness with his particular oration.

[*Verso*]

ORATORY

NFL

Round............................ Section............................

ORDER	CONTESTANT	TITLE	RANK
1.			
2.			
3.			
4.			
5.			
6.			
7.			
8.			
9.			

On the basis of the instructions contained on the reverse side of this card, rank the speakers in the order of excellence, 1, 2, 3, 4 (no two alike), and all others 5.

....

JUDGE

EVALUATING OR JUDGING DISCUSSION

Discussion is basically a process of *cooperative* deliberation concerned in most school activities with solving problems. Therefore, in evaluating or judging a discussion in a conference situation (see p. 410), a critic is usually assigned to each discussion group, not for the purpose of picking winners, but to evaluate the skill of the leader and participants in learning and practicing discussion techniques. As a rule, the judge (or critic) uses a check list similar to that on the opposite page to keep a record of activities during the discussion and, if indicated, to rate the members of the group upon the quality of the work done. At the conclusion of the session he usually presents suggestions for improvement of leadership and participation. He may turn in his check list with comments and ratings to the conference headquarters if final standings are to be determined. Because discussion is *relatively* new in the speech field in classroom speech programs and as extraclass activity, much effort has been made to develop such skills among the students participating.

In both classroom and conference situations, evaluation techniques incorporate the use of criteria such as those on the check list; quality ratings of excellent, good, adequate, are given to designate the effectiveness of the performance. In classwork, especially, such methods of judging may be employed to follow daily improvement throughout an entire unit or course in discussion.

In many cases evaluation also includes the use of standard methods of measuring attitudes and information before and after discussion. Practice sometimes indicates the use of a secretary or recorder to report the findings and conclusions of the group, particularly in a conference situation. Thus a total picture of accomplishments may be compiled, mimeographed, or reported at a final legislative session.

JUDGING DEBATING

To the novice debate judge, the whole process may appear quite complicated because of the many details that must be observed; e.g., the notes that must be taken, the criteria that must be followed carefully, and the standards of performance that must be considered in awarding a decision. The judge in a debate, as in other forms of forensic competition, must also be a critic; he must verbally evaluate

CHECK LIST FOR DISCUSSION *

Participants

Names of Participants															
Knowledge of the problem (Information)															
Logic in reasoning															
Skill in following the "pattern"															
Willingness to promote discussion															
Cooperation in thinking and contributing															
Skill in speaking— voice, etc.															
Totals															

The Leader

Skill in stating the problem		Skill in clarifying and summarizing and "pointing up"		
Skill in stimulating participation without intruding		Skill in handling the various kinds of conflict		
Skill in guiding the pattern of reflective thinking		Skill in stimulating cooperative spirit		
Skill in encouraging statement of all points of view		Skill in controlling pace suitable to members and time		

RATING: (1) Poor; (2) Fair; (3) Adequate; (4) Good; (5) Excellent

* Courtesy of Kenneth G. Hance, professor of Speech, Michigan State University.

the performance skills. He must explain why team "A" has done the better debating. His personal views, biases, or sympathy cannot be the basis for his decision. He must fulfill certain personal qualifications already mentioned in this chapter. Since the debate performance involves, as a rule, four speakers and is complex, certain materials and suggestions are presented in the interests of improving judging.

INSTRUCTIONS TO JUDGES IN DEBATE

In discussing instructions to judges, two forms of such directions will be included. One is used in the Michigan High School Forensic Association, the other is a ballot developed by the American Forensic Association. The items on which judging is based are explained briefly in each case but represent certain differences in methods of evaluation. The AFA form includes ratings of teams and speakers in addition to the decision, which is a part of all such forms. It is filled out in duplicate (carbon copy) by the judge. Thus each team can have a copy of the ratings and decision.

American Forensic League Instructions

This ballot uses a point system for individual debaters, a quality rating for teams, as well as a decision. The instructions are very brief and assume that the judge knows the meaning of the criteria for judging debate, the standards he will use for quality ratings, and the bases for a decision.

By tabulating individual debater ratings, team evaluations, and won–lost records, the chairman of the tournament can do an efficient job in recording the results.

Michigan Instructions and Ballots

The judge shall give but one vote, affirmative or negative, basing his decision upon debating standards as set forth below. The judge shall lay aside any prejudice he may have on the question, and shall decide strictly on the merits of the debate as presented, not on what he may think are the merits of the question. He shall not under any circumstances give a "consolation" vote. There shall be no conference of judges after the debate until the decisions have been handed in at the close of the debate. The judge shall write "affirmative" or "negative" on his ballot, sign it and seal it, and hand it to an usher

AMERICAN FORENSIC ASSOCIATION DEBATE BALLOT

Round_____ Room_____ Date_____ Judge_____

Affirmative_____ Negative_____

INDIVIDUAL RATINGS

Check the column on each item which, according to the following scale, best describes your evaluation of the speaker's effectiveness:

1____poor 2____below average 3____average 4____good 5____superior

1st Affirmative_____ 1st Negative_____
(NAME)   (NAME)

	1	2	3	4	5
Analysis					
Evidence					
Argument					
Refutation					
Delivery					

Total _____

	1	2	3	4	5
Analysis					
Evidence					
Argument					
Refutation					
Delivery					

Total _____

2nd Affirmative_____ 2nd Negative_____
(NAME)   (NAME)

	1	2	3	4	5
Analysis					
Evidence					
Argument					
Refutation					
Delivery					

Total _____

	1	2	3	4	5
Analysis					
Evidence					
Argument					
Refutation					
Delivery					

Total _____

TEAM RATINGS

Assign to each team the rating which best describes your judgment of its performance:

1____poor 2____below average 3____average 4____good 5____superior

Affirmative_____ Negative_____

DECISION

In my judgment, the better debating was done by the

_____

(AFFIRMATIVE OR NEGATIVE)

_____

(JUDGE'S SIGNATURE AND SCHOOL)

REASON FOR DECISION:

383

who shall convey it to the presiding officer. The presiding officer shall open the ballots in the presence of the teams and audience and announce the results. He shall not announce the names of the judges on the ballots. The critic judge may give his decision orally, but in all cases this ballot should be filled out, signed, and handed to the person in charge of the debate.

Basis of Decision

The following points should be given primary consideration in arriving at a decision:

1. Case Analysis: Consider the logic and clarity of the case presented. Is the case, as outlined, logically sufficient? Is it clearly organized and easy to follow?

2. Evidence: Evidence consists of facts and authoritative opinions. Consider the pertinency, dependability, and sufficiency of the evidence submitted.

3. Argument: Argument is the reasoning process by which conclusions are drawn from the evidence. Consider the soundness and comprehensiveness of the argument.

4. Refutation: Refutation need not be confined to the rebuttal speeches; in a good debate it will be interspersed throughout. Consider the selectivity, thoroughness, and organization of the refutation. Are the important points chosen for refutation? Are they answered satisfactorily? Is the rebuttal work organized?

5. Delivery: A debater should speak extemporaneously. By extemporaneous speaking we do not mean unprepared speaking. We mean speaking from a previously prepared plan or outline. The debater should be able to compose language on his feet and adjust to situations as they arise. Since a debate is a contest in public speaking, the excessive use of notes or manuscript should count against a speaker. Consider courtesy, audibility, fluency, poise, and the use of good English.

In my opinion the _____ representing _____
                        Aff. or Neg.   School
did the better debating.

. . . .
    Date   Place   Judge
                                    Official Position . . . .

Some Suggestions to Debate Judges

In the forms above, both instructions and the means of recording the decision are made clear. Some brief but specific helps for judges are very much needed to supplement these.

1. Take simple, accurate, meaningful notes, not *voluminous* ones. To facilitate comparisons of arguments, evidence, and refutation, notes may be organized without too much effort. Use two sheets of 8½ × 11 paper. Draw two vertical lines about an inch and a half apart from top to bottom down the center of each sheet, the long way of the paper. Then draw a horizontal line across each at the half-way point of the other dimension as shown on the following page.

The judge uses one sheet for constructive speeches and one for rebuttals. The arguments of each speaker are outlined in the large spaces. The center division is used to note, in abbreviated form, sources of evidence, names of authorities, individual speaker ratings, short comments on delivery, attitude, and teamwork. If notes are written in ink or black pencil, the judge can use a colored-pencil arrow to advantage in denoting clashes or direct refutation. He may care to designate the speaker who answered the point with, "A_1" or "N_2," or some similar notation.

Constructive Speeches		
Aff. #1		Neg. #1
Rebuttal Speeches		
Aff. #2		Neg. #2

By giving a percentage, point, or letter grade for each speaker's total performance, a quick approximation can be obtained of the relative strength of the two teams. In some tournaments a short check list is furnished the judge to facilitate evaluation of each speaker on each of the points on which the debate is to be judged. These are similar to the rating scales used for speaking performance which are explained in Chapter XII.

2. Give careful attention to the debaters. Do not avoid looking at them or assume a bored, indifferent attitude in an effort to appear objective. Even a judge can react like a human being.

3. Remember the affirmative case determines the basic analysis, definitions, and argument in the debate. The negative is obliged to recognize these points and adapt its own to meet the affirmative case. Failure to do so without presenting a different analysis justifying it and without setting forth a negative case based on the new analysis counts against the negative. Even then the affirmative case cannot be ignored.

4. The affirmative has the burden of proving the proposition. Watch for sketchy work, all jammed into the first constructive speech of the affirmative, which sells the affirmative obligation short. The judge must decide whether the affirmative meets the burden of proof in a reasonable manner under the time and conditions of the debate.

5. If a counterproposal is advanced by the negative, the debate hinges upon which team best meets the burden of proof it has assumed regarding the effectiveness of the two solutions or plans presented.

6. Falsification of evidence is not to be tolerated. The judge should vote against a team if he is sure it has indulged in such a practice.

7. Unfair interpretation of the question should count against a team.

8. Deliberate delays in answering arguments and cases that withhold counterplans until very late in the debate should be penalized. Timeliness and "following the ball" are the essence of good debate. The judge should do all he can to encourage this practice.

9. Courtesy and good sportsmanship by speakers should be noted and credited by the judge. Departures from such conduct should be criticized and penalized.

10. Comments and criticism by the judge should be constructive and specific. They can aid the students and their coaches.

JUDGING ONE-ACT PLAY FESTIVALS

Another group activity that must often be served by the judge is the one-act play festival. The majority of such events have been organized to achieve a "Superior," "Excellent," "Good," or "Satisfactory" rating, depending upon the designations agreed upon in a given festival situation. The rules for such festivals are given in the bulletins of the state associations sponsoring them. The criteria for judging and the weight of each are usually specified. A typical pattern is as follows: Acting, 40 per cent; Make-up, 10 per cent; Setting, 20 per cent; Choice of Material, 20 per cent; and Costume, 10 per cent. These elements are quite standard, but the weight assigned to each may vary.

Here again, as was true in debating, the judge must watch a very complex performance and in some way develop his own techniques and methods of evaluation. A list of bases for the judge's evaluation in such festivals follows.

Bases for Judging One Act Plays [5]

1. Choice of Play—Consider not only literary and artistic quality, but also suitability for the occasion, and for the limitations of age, ability, and equipment which the particular group had to meet.

2. Direction—Consider the evidence of a skillful guiding hand in the design of movements and business, the grouping of characters, the regulation of tempo and emphasis, the building of climax, and the development of teamwork in general.

3. Interpretation—Consider whether a sympathetic and intelligent understanding of the author's purpose is conveyed to the audience. Include plot, theme, and characterization. Include both individual and group understanding.

4. Technique—Consider mechanical precision and smoothness, freedom from awkwardness, articulation of lines and business, technical skill in general. Note that (2), above, is concerned rather with design, and (4) with its execution.

5. Voice and Diction—Consider the group as a whole in respect to

[5] *Drama Festivals*, prepared by the Committee on Contests and Festivals, Committee of the American Educational Theatre Association (1945), p. 18, William P. Halstead, Executive Secretary, University of Michigan, Ann Arbor, Mich.

volume, tone quality, and expressiveness of voice, clarity of enunciation, and acceptability of pronunciation. Do not be too much influenced by a single very bad or very good voice, and make due allowance for appropriateness of voice and diction to character.

6. Staging—Consider the taste and appropriateness with which the play is mounted and the skill shown in the handling of equipment, but discount any elaboration that cannot be transferred to the simple conditions available for the finals.

7. Total Effect—Disregard for the moment all analysis; record your spontaneous reaction to the production as a whole. How well did you like it?

The information, methods, and forms that appear in this chapter will be of assistance to the teacher who is judging or who deals with judges evaluating his work. It is impossible, however, to include the one element that is indispensable to judges and judging—experience. Knowledge *plus* experience can contribute much in the training process to developing better judges and improving their methods.

EXERCISES

1. Secure copies of judges' ballots for individual and group speech activities, which are used by various states and schools, then write an evaluation of this material in terms of the criteria included and the method of rating in each ballot.
2. Prepare a plan that you might use in judging individual speech activities and employ this plan in an actual situation.
3. Using the "simple method of judging," prepare your ranking for a class or school contest and write an individual critique for each contestant.

REFERENCES

BECKER, SAM L. "The Ordinal Position Effect," *Quarterly Journal of Speech*, XXIX (April, 1953), 217–19.

———. "Rating Discussants," *Speech Teacher*, V (January, 1956), 60–66.

BRADEN, WALDO W. (ed.). *Speech Methods and Resources*. New York: Harper & Bros., 1961. Chap. X.

CROWELL, LAURA. "Rating Scales as Diagnostic Instruments in Discussion," *Speech Teacher*, II (January, 1953), 26–32.

HALSTEAD, WILLIAM P. *"Who Wins Debates?* A Statistical Study of 1320 Debates," *Quarterly Journal of Speech,* XXVI (April, 1940), 213–21.

HOLCOMB, MARTIN. "The Critic Judge System," *Quarterly Journal of Speech,* XIX (February, 1933), 28–38.

HUNSINGER, PAUL. "Festivals and Changing Patterns," *Speech Teacher,* VII (March, 1958), 93–99.

JOHNSON, EARLE. "How Should Debates Be Judged?" *Quarterly Journal of Speech,* XXI (June, 1935), 396–99.

MATTINGLY, A. S. "The Teacher as a Critic in Interpretation Performances," *Speech Teacher,* VIII (November, 1959), 321–24.

THOMPSON, RICHARD. "Measurements in Contest Speaking," *Quarterly Journal of Speech,* XXI (February, 1935), 81–84.

WINSHIP, F. L. "Judging One Act Play Contests," *Quarterly Journal of Speech,* XXVI (October, 1940), 385–90.

CHAPTER TWENTY

Individual Speaking Activities

Although numerous group activities are conducted in every speech program, major stress is placed upon the *individual* participation and development of the student. Individual activities in original speaking include class instruction emphasizing extemporaneous preparation and delivery in speeches to inform, to explain, to entertain, and the like. The same skill is stressed in contests in extempore speaking. Speaking to convince or to persuade in the classroom prepares the individual for contest experience in original oratory and in the group activities of public discussion and debate. In interpretative speech, classwork is usually in individual interpretation of prose, poetry, and drama. Contest or festival activities include individual training in events using the same types of literature and group activities in choric interpretation, reader's theater, and chamber theater.

This chapter will develop the teaching of *individual* speaking activities—extemporaneous speaking in class or contest, persuasive speaking including oratory, and oratorical declamation. Interpretative activities are treated in Chapter XXII.

These basic forms are practically the same, whether taught in class as parts of courses, or as parts of a program in cocurricular activities. Contest speaking imposes certain restrictions upon them in length, content, preparation, and form. However, the basic teaching methods are much the same. Specific adaptation may be made for contests.

Classwork in individual speech forms builds a body of trained persons who may also apply their talents to contest programs. Similarly, contests provide motivation and training that will fortify students entering courses in speech, or even build a demand for curricular work.

EXTEMPORANEOUS SPEAKING

Extemporaneous preparation and delivery, the basic goal of sound classroom instruction in individual speaking, has been treated earlier in this text. All the materials in the chapters on speech preparation, bodily action, voice and articulation, evaluation, and so on, are directed toward perfecting this skill.

To recall the characteristics of this form, it has as its principal purpose the development of ability in a method necessitating careful preparation and organization, yet it demands that the speaker master a style of presentation that is spontaneous, unmemorized, vital, communicative, and adaptable to the audience he will face. In contest speech, the activity was developed in an effort to find a medium which broke away from the existing trend toward memorization and exhibition that characterized so many traditional oratorical contests. The rules for the extempore contest today are an outgrowth of the desire to create conditions either making memorization virtually impossible, or penalizing it so heavily that it is definitely discouraged. Such rules make more exacting the conditions under which an extempore speech is prepared and delivered. The preparation time is shorter, notes are limited, and judges, rather than classroom teachers, evaluate or rank the speakers. In each situation the speech must meet the same criteria. However, in contests, the standards will probably be higher and may be more rigorously applied.

The following rules are those generally used by most associations in this contest. They govern the activities of the National Forensic League in this event. Variations existing in this pattern will be discussed briefly.

1. *Subjects:* The District Chairman shall obtain from the director of a college or university department of speech a list of thirty topics phrased for contest purposes and based on subjects discussed in standard periodicals during the current school year. The contents of this list shall not be disclosed except as contestants draw their topics therefrom.

This practice is modified somewhat in state associations in which (1) the director of the league prepares the topics and (2) coaches of contestants are present at a session in which the topics are opened and examined. If any topic appears to be poorly stated or unfair in

scope or character, it may be protested by the coach. Should his contestant then draw such a protested topic, he can return it and draw
again.

2. *Drawing:* One hour before the contest is to begin, the first
speaker shall draw three subjects, choose one and return the other
two. The remaining contestants shall draw in like manner, in the
order of speaking at intervals of seven minutes. The entire list of
subjects shall be used for the drawing in each group. A contestant
drawing a subject on which he has previously spoken in the tournament shall return it and draw again.

This practice varies but little in other associations. The chief modifications that have been observed are (1) each contestant is permitted to draw four rather than three subjects; (2) all speakers draw
at the same time instead of at intervals of seven minutes (the length
of time each person is allowed to speak). It should be noted that
the original rule as stated controls the preparation time so that all
speakers have the same length of time in which to organize their
speeches. If all draw together, the first speakers are at a disadvan-
tage; they have less time. The last speaker in a contest of six would
have thirty-five minutes more time in which to get ready.

3. *Preparation:* As soon as he has chosen a topic, the contestant
shall withdraw and prepare his speech without consultation and
without reference to prepared notes. Reference to books and magazines shall be permitted.

This is standard practice in all contests. Ordinarily, the speakers
are given individual rooms in which to work or are allowed to go
to the library of the school in which the contest is held.

4. *Notes:* No speaker shall take to the platform more than fifty
words of notes and the chairman shall be responsible for the enforce-
ment of this rule.

This regulation is quite widespread. There are some states in which
no rule appears governing the amount of note material that may be
used. The excessive use of notes, however, is counted against the
contestant by the judges in all contests of this type.

5. *Time:* Contestants shall speak not less than five minutes nor
more than seven minutes. Timekeepers shall stand and remain standing to denote the expiration of time and at the close of the contest
shall inform the judges of the names of contestants failing to speak
the minimum five minutes. Failure to observe the time limits shall

incur no penalty except that expressed in the rankings of the judges.

The principal deviation from this rule is in the length of the speech required. The five- to seven-minute length is very popular, although some associations extend this time. In Iowa, a question-and-rejoinder period is added. After all contestants have given their speeches, each is asked a question by one of the other speakers, the questioners having been assigned. The contestant must reply to the question in an "on-the-spot" speech of two minutes. This is done to check further upon the possibility of memorization in the first speech and demonstrate to the judges and audience the extemporaneous character of the performance.

6. *Other rules:* Speaking order is determined by lot. Contestants are ranked in the order of their excellence by the judges: 1, 2, 3, and so on. Competing groups are restricted to not less than four nor more than eight in one group.

All these conditions are quite universally established in other societies and associations. In some, an individual point or classification rating is given each speaker in addition to the ranking described above. Average size of contest groups is six speakers.

Choosing Speakers

Choosing speakers for extemporaneous speaking or for any of the other individual contests is done in much the same manner. The first step in the procedure is the announcement of the contest. Such publicity may be secured through a notice in the school's daily bulletin or memorandum issued from the departmental office, through the school and local paper, through posters or bulletin-board displays, through the speech classes as a "special" event, or by the teacher in charge inviting interested or capable students to try out. As a rule, all these methods are employed. In one high school the local motivation was the announcement of the annual school contest sponsored by the Kiwanis Club in the city. This organization was very much interested in encouraging speech training of this kind and offered generous cash prizes to the three best speakers in the school. Another method of initiating such a project is to use an "extemp" contest within the speech classes as a regular assignment in each section. The results obtained in this way furnish the teacher with an excellent picture of prospects in the classes who do well under the conditions explained earlier.

The selection of a school representative is usually accomplished through a local contest, the winner of which becomes the person to go into the first interscholastic contest. There are occasions in which no contest is necessary or desirable. These conditions prevail when the teacher directing the work has selected a student to represent the school. Such a choice is based upon his knowledge of the personal qualities, speech ability, and cooperativeness of the pupil in a training situation. In this case, the contestant is actually hand-picked. There are numerous arguments to support such a method of selection, the principal one being the fact that the speech teacher knows his students better than anyone else; furthermore, he has the responsibility for the training and performance of the student he selects. If the local contest determines absolutely who shall be the school representative, the speech teacher should always have a hand in judging this contest and in selecting the person with whom he must work. As a safeguard against erratic judgment of outside judges, some schools allow the coach of the contest speaker to select any of the first three persons in the local contest as eligible for the interscholastic meet. In this way, the teacher can ultimately choose the person who shows the greatest possibilities as a result of the period of training which is conducted.

These methods of selection can be similarly used in the choice of school representatives in oratory, declamation, or interpretative reading.

A Training Procedure for Extempore Speaking

If the student has not had the first course in speaking, the teacher must start with him from the beginning. The student should possess a certain interest and native ability or, at least, good speech equipment. This means good appearance, satisfactory voice, a good mind, and willingness to learn. Although some teachers have selected persons with speech deviations as contest speakers, this practice is not recommended. The place for therapeutic work in speech is not in a speech contest or festival. Not only will training be made more difficult if this fallacy is accepted, but the emphasis in training will be upon correction rather than upon technique. Also, it is quite possible that the old habits will return in the emotional stress of a public performance. This is especially true if the training period is short.

1. *The student must read widely.*

The first essential is that the student shall have information and ideas. Since the subjects are chosen from the current periodicals, the participant must have complete familiarity with their content. Through the speech department, the school and town libraries, or his home, he must have access to the necessary materials.

2. *The student must have a good memory and should take notes on his reading.*

In covering contemporary issues, the student can facilitate his grasp of facts, opinions, and the course of affairs by listing references under broad classifications, such as Labor Problems, Presidential Possibilities, Nuclear Testing, and similar topics. He can also make outline notes of particular articles that have excellent content and copy quotations or statistics that he wishes to remember. A systematic card filing system will help.

3. *The student must know the principles of speech composition.*

The teacher will have to do a thorough job of instruction on this point. The untrained student will need complete knowledge of the principles. The one who has had course work in speaking may also need a thorough review of fundamental principles.

4. *The student should work out a formula for a convincing talk.*

In getting ready for the contest, the student and teacher must confer and then decide upon a formula that is "sure-fire" with an audience and with critic judges. The experience of the teacher and the originality, interest, and abilities of the student are factors in this step. Good, standard texts in public speaking are the best sources for such a formula, covering introduction, body, and conclusion of the talk.

5. *The student should participate many times in doing the same job he will have to do later, and he should do so under conditions that are as nearly like those of the contest as possible.*

In practice sessions the speaker should "go through all the motions." This means he should draw three topics and choose one. He must learn which topics offer the best possibilities. Usually, those that are very broad, purely factual, or have little audience appeal are poor choices. He should be allowed one hour and no more to organize his material. He should divide his hour about equally for organization and a run-through on delivery. He should present his speech to a real audience. He should be held to the exact time limits of the contest situation. He should be evaluated and criticized on the same bases as those that will be used in the contest. If possible, he should have a number of practices under auditorium conditions if it is known that the contest is to be held in such a place. He should be encouraged to adapt his speech to the conditions and audiences he will meet.

6. *The student should have sufficient time for a thorough period of training.*

While the length of the training period will be determined by the caliber of the student, and there are wide variations in the amount of time different individuals need, a minimum time of one month is recommended for such a contest. Sessions each day or, as a minimum, several times each week are desirable. If the contestant is chosen early in the year and a number of tournaments are in prospect, it is conceivable that the training period will be distributed over several months.

The Speaker in the Contest

If an adequate training period has been possible, the contest itself will present fewer problems. A few suggestions should be noted:

1. Arrive at the contest in plenty of time to look over the ground.
   a. Have a light meal well ahead of contest time.
   b. Get into the auditorium and have a voice check, noting especially the acoustics of the room and the problems it may create, especially in regard to clarity, timing, and loudness.
   c. Find the library and locate the reference works, periodicals, and other necessary materials.
   d. Learn the geography of the building on other details: lavatories, drinking fountains, distance from the preparation rooms to the auditorium, backstage entrance, and so on.

    e. Rest or relax before the contest.

    f. Be on time for drawings of subjects.

    g. Be punctual in arrival for the actual giving of the speech.

2. After drawing the topic, use the time efficiently as has been planned in practice sessions.

    a. Organize carefully according to the formula and any specific adaptations that are indicated.

    b. Use a minimum of notes; in most cases contest speakers will use no notes, having memorized the outline of the talk to be given.

    c. Save an ample portion of the time to have a delivery practice. This should not be overdone; the speech should be *well in hand,* but fresh and vital. It should, however, be fluent and free of hesitations. Be sure to time the speech.

3. On the platform, go to work.

    a. Speak to the audience.

    b. Be sure also to catch the judge directly with the message you have to deliver on the subject drawn.

    c. Be alive; communicate ideas; concentrate on the purpose of the talk.

    d. Watch the time limits so that no penalties are imposed.

ORATORY

Oratory, or "original" oratory as it is sometimes called, is one of the oldest individual speech activities. The term "original" is used to distinguish between a speech written by the student and one written and originally presented by some other speaker. Certain states class both as "oratory." In this chapter we shall designate the latter as *oratorical declamation* and discuss it under that heading.

Oratory, as we shall use the term, is a persuasive speech, written by the student on some problem upon which he has a deep and sincere conviction. After he has completed the manuscript for the speech, the student memorizes it, and delivers the oration in an audience situation (in the presence of judges), if the typical contest conditions are followed.

It is quite possible, however, to teach oratory very effectively as part of a unit or course in persuasive speaking without imposing any

particular contest conditions. Preceding the preparation of an oration would come a study of persuasion. In this, challenging problems of the day could be explored. The theory and technique of
persuasion would be studied. Other speeches would be analyzed for
content, support, style. Individual subjects, selected from the broad
problems, would be investigated, and a careful preparation outline
for a persuasive speech developed. These talks, of a practical, everyday type, would be delivered from notes in extemporaneous delivery
and would be evaluated by the class and the teacher.

Such instruction could lead nicely to the preparation of the contest oration with its limitations of subject, time, form, and style. In
manuscript it could be edited and criticized, memorized, and then
delivered. Thus an instructor could gain double dividends for his
investment in training class speakers and a nucleus of candidates for
his contest program.

There are many concepts of oratory. Over the years they have
changed somewhat. The following statement presents a clear picture
of a modern concept.

What Is an Oration? [1]

An oration is a public speech. Its purpose is to communicate in order
to win a response. It is a refined speech without the refinement distracting. It is a work of art, as much so as a sonnet or an epic. It must have
an object as well as a subject, else it misses its mark—a truth to teach, a
problem of life to solve, an appeal to accept or serve. It must convince
the mind, warm the heart, and move the will.

In an oration the mind is convinced by emotion as well as by argument,
by discernment as much as by debate. An orator is a persuader, and to
persuade he must be utterly persuaded in his own heart.

An oration is carefully styled. Perfection in word choice and sentence
structure needs to be achieved—without the perfection distracting. This
will not deny the speech honesty and simplicity. A good oration will not
say of one who has slipped on the ice, that his perpendicularity suddenly
became a horizontality. It will simply say he fell. Shakespeare was too
wise to make Mark Antony say, "I have neither intellectual acumen, nor
extensive vocabulary, nor ethical significance." He made him say, "I have
neither wit, nor words, nor worth." And he made him say, "poor dumb
mouths" instead of "pitiable, inarticulate orifices."

[1] From an Instruction Sheet for Student Orators prepared by Mason Daly,
formerly instructor in Speech, School of Speech, Northwestern University.

A good oration will have no sanctimonious whining, bombastic bull-roaring, or declamatory tricks.

A good oration will grip an audience's attention at the start and hold it high throughout—with peaks of climax, emotionally gripping—sustained both in delivery and composition.

An oration must be delivered with an intensely communicative attitude, mentally and physically (as in any speech); extremely direct, aware of the audience, out to win a response; physically capable and alive; a finished performance without being studied or mechanical or "canned" in gesture, movement, or vocal variety.

Nearly all forensic leagues sponsor this activity. In addition there are numerous outside contests in which high school students compete. The Hearst newspapers conduct an annual competition in which orations are written on a famous American; subjects have been Hamilton, Lincoln, and others. The American Legion also sponsors one in which speeches are written on the United States Constitution. Numerous other local contests exist.

All of these contests have similar rules. They all specify that the work is to be original with the student; they all restrict the length of the manuscript in words, or in time of delivery. A standard length for high school speeches is ten minutes. The contests usually limit the amount of quoted material that can be included; many set this amount at 150 words. The size of groups in competition is generally set at from four to eight students. Speaking order is determined by lot in the majority of instances; the rank-order method of judging prevails; judges are ordinarily asked to submit some critical comments for each speaker.

Selection and Training of Orators

The suggestions given with respect to choosing speakers in the previous section apply very well here. In preparation, the following list of suggestions to students by Crawford [2] presents a very practical scheme, usable for class or contest.

SUGGESTED STEPS IN THE PREPARATION OF THE ORIGINAL ORATION AND
THE TRAINING OF THE ORATOR

I. Read extensively on current problems. (This is the preliminary exploration, and at least three weeks should be allowed for it.)

[2] Paul Crawford is professor of Speech, Northern Illinois University, De Kalb, Ill. For many years he was director of Forensics at Freeport (Ill.) High School.

A. Read the daily newspapers, especially the front page, the editorial page, and feature articles on political, social, economic, and educational problems.

B. Read magazines such as *Current History, Reader's Digest, The Survey Graphic, The Congressional Digest, School and Society, Time, The Nation, The New Republic, The Commentator, Newsweek, The Nation's Business, Business Week, The Atlantic Monthly, Harper's, U.S. News and World Report.*

C. Read the special school publications on current problems (for example, history classes may take *The American Observer* or one of the many other special publications for high school social science classes).

D. Make brief notations on the problems that seem to you to "cry out" for consideration, for remedial action.

E. List two or three current problems you would like to investigate further.

II. Make a bibliography on each of the problems chosen for further investigation.

A. Use *The Reader's Guide* to find reference material in magazine articles.

B. Use the library's card catalogue to find reference material in books and pamphlets.

C. Use any special index to the particular field of subject matter under investigation, if such an index is available.

D. List the names and addresses of persons in the community who have a special knowledge of the subject and arrange to interview these persons.

III. Select the problem to be dealt with in the oration.

A. Using your bibliography as a guide, review the most important material previously read and investigate the new sources of material.

1. Write a brief summary of each important article, pamphlet, or book. (Take all notes on cards of uniform size.)

2. Record the most significant and striking statistics, examples, illustrations, and opinions of authorities. (Write at the top of each card a heading indicating the point involved in the material on that card.)

B. Consider the possible theses for persuasive speeches involved in each problem. The result of the analysis may be conveniently represented, thus:

General Problem	Title of Oration	Specific Purpose of Oration
Crime	Children Cheated	To persuade the audience that slum clearance is essential to the success of a crime-prevention program.
Crime	The Big House	To persuade the audience that overcrowded and antiquated prisons intensify antisocial tendencies of prisoners.
Crime	"Pardon Me!"	To persuade the audience that the power to pardon and parole convicts should be taken from the governors of the respective states and given to nonpartisan boards of expert criminologists.
Crime	America's Biggest Business	To persuade the audience that the magnitude and interstate character of crime necessitate an expansion of the Federal Bureau of Investigation.
Mental Health	Are We Our Brothers' Keepers?	To persuade the audience that better care is needed for the mentally ill.
Government by the Stampede of Organized Minorities: Pressure Groups versus Majority Rule	The Citizen Abdicates	To persuade the audience that the individual citizen must not be lured by the Utopian promises of pressure groups to surrender his sovereign power to think and act for himself.

C. In light of the analysis of the subjects, the specific purposes, the probable audiences, and the self-examination of the speaker, choose the problem, title, and specific purpose of the oration.

IV. Collect material on the specific thesis chosen.

A. Revise your bibliography, eliminating references to phases of general problems not to be developed in the oration and adding new references to material on the specific thesis chosen.

B. Take notes on cards of uniform size.

1. At the top of each card, write a caption that reveals the main point of the material on the card.

2. Below the caption, give the source of the material.

C. Clip newspaper articles on the subject, especially those containing vivid, concrete illustrative material. Important excerpts may be pasted on cards and captions written at the top.

D. File systematically all notes and clippings.

    V. Organize the material.
- A. Place the cards in three stacks, one for the *Introduction,* the second for the *Body* or *Discussion,* and the third for the *Conclusion.*
- B. Outline the speech, selecting the best material, endeavoring to make full use of the possible elements of interest and persuasion.
- C. Fix the outline in mind.

   VI. Give the speech extemporaneously without notes. (Speak to a class or some other group, if this can possibly be arranged.)

 VII. Profiting by your experience in extemporaneous presentation, write the speech in full.
- A. Carry over into your style the best attributes of your extemporaneous speaking plus those refinements of language that increase the vividness, euphony, personal force, and moving power of the whole speech.
- B. Visualize the audience as you write.
- C. The style should be simple and clear-cut, rather than ornate and highly involved.
- D. Concrete examples and illustrations pump lifeblood into the orator's thesis.
- E. It will be helpful to make a definite list of possible characteristics of effective oral style and to use it as a check list in determining whether you are making the most of the possibilities presented by your material.

VIII. Read the speech aloud.

  IX. Revise the speech.

   X. Practice the delivery of the speech regularly (over a period of several weeks, if possible).
- A. The presentation should be characterized by sincerity, animation, directness of communication.
- B. Artificiality in voice and mere posing are to be avoided.
  - 1. Those audible and visible attributes of delivery that call attention to themselves contribute to the defeat of the speaker's purpose.
  - 2. Those attributes of delivery that make impressive the speaker's thought and feeling and motivate the audience to endorse the speaker's thesis contribute to the achievement of the speaker's goal.
- C. Speak to real audiences (classes, home rooms, clubs, or other groups) whenever possible.

Such a scheme for preparation should be supplemented by a list of suggested subjects for orations; the opportunity should also be given the student to examine models of other contest orations. Numerous other general helps in composition of a speech are suggested in Chapter XIV.

The Orator at the Contest

Most of the suggestions given for extempore speakers in the contest situation apply to the orator. Certain additional points are added here because of the orator's job. In contrast to the extempore speaker, the orator must *memorize* language; he must also make ideas so vivid and convincing to the audience that it will respond to his speech as he wishes it to do. He faces the problem, also, of going stale if he has given his speech many times previously. Under contest conditions, he may lapse into mechanical rather than motivated patterns of delivery.

These suggestions are relevant:

1. Secure time for a good rehearsal session in the auditorium to be used. Size of stage, furniture, distance from the audience, and acoustics are important points to check. Since most orations make greater vocal demands in terms of range, variety, and projection than extempore speeches, this kind of session is of much value.

2. Avoid incessant repetition of the speech before the contest. Most of the patterns have been set during training and they will dominate during a public performance. The frequent delivery of the talk before real audiences is the best insurance of this.

3. Allow time, however, for a period of concentration by the speaker upon his purpose, ideas, and the response he wishes to achieve. This should help him to be more vital and communicative when he speaks.

4. During the contest the speaker should keep his mind on the purpose and ideas he wishes to share with his listeners. He should remember that he is trying to persuade them to believe as he believes. He should note their reactions as he proceeds, and concentrate upon his function as a communicator, not on "giving an exhibition."

ORATORICAL DECLAMATION

This individual speaking event, sometimes called nonoriginal oratory, is an experience in the delivery of a portion or the whole of an original speech of some other person. If the event is conducted with some care and good planning, interesting values may come from the first job to be done, that of selecting a suitable speech. Instead of using the "old standards" or "winners," the teacher can direct his students to read widely from collections of speeches, such as *Vital Speeches, The New York Times,* or other publications that print recent talks. A list of those generally desirable can be prepared. These present interesting opportunities for a study of purpose, ideas, structure, and style with the intent of building interest in criticism of public address. In the Oklahoma State Forensic Association, there is a contest in criticism of a selected public speech.

This preliminary study is usually followed by cutting or editing the speech chosen, to make it conform to the time limits of the contest. The teacher will direct this.

Next is the standard procedure of memorizing the selected text, further analysis, and developing the essentials of effective delivery for the content and audience situation. Since declamation is largely contest activity, careful attention is given in preparation and practice to the criteria and standards for delivery set forth by the state or region in which the declaimer competes.

For years, oratorical declamation has been used as a means of giving practice and experience in platform delivery to younger or less experienced speech students. Properly conducted, it can motivate students and introduce them to outstanding speeches and their organization, besides being a useful exercise in delivery.

EXERCISES

1. Write what you consider to be the pros and cons of each of the individual speech activities, having in mind the teacher in charge, the school, and the student participating.
2. Prepare a training plan and schedule for any individual speaking event you select and justify your procedure.

REFERENCES

BAIRD, A. CRAIG. "The Original Oration as a Speech Activity in the Secondary School," *Bulletin of the National Association of Secondary School Principals,* XXXVI, No. 187 (May, 1952), 117–31.

BRADEN, WALDO W. *Speech Methods and Resources*. New York: Harper & Bros., 1961. Chap. 5.

BRINK, LAUREN. "Extemporaneous Speaking in the English Class," *English Journal*, XXXVI (November, 1947), 474–77.

CRANDELL, S. JUDSON. "The Teaching of Public Speaking in High School," *Quarterly Journal of Speech*, XXVIII (December, 1942), 477–83.

DOWLING, FRED. "Teaching Impromptu Speaking," *Speech Teacher*, VI (September, 1957), 205–8.

FRIEDERICH, W. J., and RUTH A. WILCOX. *Teaching Speech in High Schools*. New York: The Macmillan Co., 1953. Pp. 207–13.

GEHRING, MARY LOUISE. "The High School Oration: Fundamentals," *Speech Teacher*, II (March, 1953), 101–4.

HENDERLINDER, CLAIR R., and EUGENE E. WHITE. "A New Emphasis in Teaching Public Speaking," *Speech Teacher*, I (November, 1952), 265–70.

HOWELL, WILLIAM S. "Training the Speaker: Deductive Logic," *Speech Teacher*, VI (March, 1957), 106–8.

KRUGER, ARTHUR N. "The Extempore Speaking Contest," *Speech Teacher*, V (September, 1956), 214–22.

MELZER, ARNOLD E. *High School Forensics*. New York: H. W. Wilson Co., 1940.

SCHMIDT, RALPH N. "The Teaching of Outlining," *Speech Teacher*, III (January, 1954), 33–35.

WEAVER, ANDREW T., GLADYS BORCHERS, and DONALD K. SMITH. *The Teaching of Speech*. Englewood Cliffs, N. J.: Prentice-Hall, Inc., 1952. Pp. 310–17.

YOUNGERMAN, HENRY C. "Audience Analysis in a Course in Advanced Public Speaking," *Speech Teacher*, II (January, 1953), 58–60.

CHAPTER TWENTY-ONE

Discussion and Debate

Both discussion and debate can be taught in regular courses in the secondary school, either as units in a first course, or in an advanced course in public speaking. However, debate is developed more frequently as a contest activity in high schools. Colleges sometimes teach units on debate and discussion in courses, but their pattern more often allows curricular work in argumentation, discussion, and debate, or separate courses in each. This instruction is generally in addition to a program in intercollegiate forensics.

Recent surveys indicate a growing interest and desire among administrators and speech teachers for inclusion of training in discussion in the extraclass program. This trend arises from the fact that most of the forensic activities—debate, oratory, and extempore speaking—provide training for students in the methods of advocacy. These activities teach persons to gain acceptance for their ideas and propositions by persuasive methods. While these methods are essential in a democracy, it is equally important for students to learn ways of attacking problems, inquiring into them, and seeking solutions for them. Discussion contributes to the education of young people in these techniques of inquiry. The two methods, discussion and debate, complement each other; they may be taught successfully in this relationship and can profitably be included in class and contest programs. Greater emphasis is also being placed on these fields as challenging experiences for superior students. The theory, skills, and training in conference methods and public performance makes them extremely valuable as training for leadership. Therefore, they are both treated in this chapter. The content will follow this order: definitions of the concepts, purposes, and goals; the organization of programs; training of students. Specific plans for tournaments and conferences are found in Chapter XVIII, "Administering Activities and Contests." Judging and evaluation are considered in Chapter XIX, "Judging Speech Contests."

DEFINITIONS

Discussion may be defined as "the co-operative deliberation of problems by persons thinking and conversing together in face-to-face or co-acting groups under the direction of a leader for purposes of understanding and action." [1] This definition means that discussion starts with a problem. The problem may concern the truth or falsity of the question. This is a problem of *fact*. It may raise a question about the goodness or badness of something. This is a problem of *value*. It may deal with whether a given action should or should not be taken. This is a question of *policy*. In attacking the problem, discussion also implies a *cooperative*, not a *competitive* deliberation, which is characterized by reflective thinking. Reflective thinking in a group involves the characteristic pattern of the individual act of reflective thinking as stated by Dewey:

> Upon examination, each instance of reflective thought reveals more or less clearly five distinct steps: (1) a felt difficulty; (2) its location and definition; (3) suggestion of possible solution; (4) development by reasoning of the bearings of the suggestion; (5) further observation and experiment leading to its acceptance or rejection; that is, the conclusion of belief or disbelief.[2]

Inquiry is the core of discussion. Therefore, successful participation in discussion necessitates attitudes of objectivity and cooperation in persons attempting to analyze the problem and find satisfactory solutions for it. The definition also implies the presence of a leader whose principal function is to aid the group in its task of securing understanding or taking action. Finally, it indicates that discussion may be of the face-to-face type, where each participant is a potential contributor, or of the coacting type, in which there is an audience and a single source of stimulation to which the listeners respond. The small committee group is an example of the face-to-

[1] James H. McBurney and Kenneth G. Hance, *Discussion in Human Affairs* (New York: Harper & Row, 1950), p. 10.
[2] John Dewey, *How We Think* (Boston: D. C. Heath and Co., 1910), p. 72.

face discussion; the panel discussion, lecture-forum, or symposium are examples of coacting groups. In discussion there is no attempt to win a decision or capture the vote of an audience. Its purpose is to evolve a solution to a problem which is acceptable to all, if possible.

Newer forms of discussion, non-directive in leadership, have become prominent through group dynamics. These methods get at the same general ends as single-leader discussion, but employ different techniques. This treatment considers *directed* discussion.

Debate usually starts where discussion leaves off. It deals with the *advocacy of a conclusion or a proposition,* often one reached through previous discussion or inquiry. It is this important relationship that should be noted in the study and practice of debate and discussion. In practical situations, when discussion fails to reach a consensus, debate is the next logical step. Debate is a competitive activity in which the participants are committed to arguing opposite sides of a proposition either because of their own convictions or because of the circumstances. Debating in real life most often includes courtroom, or judicial, debating, and parliamentary, or legislative, debating. The debate that is most familiar to high school pupils is an educational method of training students in the techniques of argumentation and debate. It has no exact counterpart in a life situation; however, the techniques may be applied outside the contest performance in situations requiring advocacy. In all these types of debate the speaker tries to argue his position so skillfully that he will win the support of the majority of his audience, the jury, and the judge.

The standard school debate is a contest in which two teams, generally consisting of two members each, argue opposite sides of a given proposition, usually in the presence of judges. Formal rules govern the conduct of such debates. The debate is composed of (1) the constructive speeches and (2) the rebuttal speeches. The affirmative opens the debate and then the sides alternate until each speaker has appeared in the constructive section. The negative then opens the rebuttal and again the sides alternate until each speaker has made his appearance in rebuttal. The usual time allowed is ten minutes for constructive arguments and five minutes for rebuttals. At the end of the debate a decision is given by a board of judges, a critic judge, or the audience.

The principal goals of discussion and debate have already been developed in Chapter V, "Planning Speech Courses and Curricular Programs," and in Chapter VI, "Developing Cocurricular Activity and Contest Programs."

TYPES OF DISCUSSION AND DEBATE

1. *Round-Table Discussion*

This is the most common type of face-to-face discussion; in it the leader and the participants work together in an effort to analyze the problem before them and arrive at a satisfactory solution. Most useful in learning groups, it may also be effective in small groups to determine policy.

2. *Panel Discussion*

The panel discussion is a method by which a few persons carry on a discussion before an audience. It attempts to place the small discussion group before an audience so that the listener can profit from the process of discussion as the leader and the members proceed. Discussion in the panel is spontaneous under the direction of the leader. *There are no set or prepared individual speeches.* The question period that follows is also conducted by the leader.

3. *The Symposium*

This is a method of discussion in which a series of prepared speeches, usually on various phases of a problem, is presented to an audience. Actually, a minimum of two speakers can present a symposium, although three and four members often speak. The chairman introduces each speaker, announces his particular subject, and later conducts a question-answer period.

4. *Lecture-Forum*

The lecture-forum is a method of discussion in which one person presents a public speech, after which the chairman conducts a question-answer period for the audience. This method is very common in public forums, in which a distinguished speaker presents the lecture and the chairman then invites members of the audience to ask questions, which the speaker answers.

5. *The Discussion Progression and Student Congress*

These two activities represent definite departures from traditional debate. In them, each participant engages in several stages, which are essentially discussion methods. The steps in sequence usually follow this plan: (1) a round-table or informal discussion group; (2) a panel discussion; (3) perhaps a symposium; and finally, (4) a legislative or contest debate. The discussion progression devised by Elwood Murray [3] follows five stages:

First Stage. Problem phase. Informal discussion on the subtopic, "What is the problem and to what extent is it significant?"

Second Stage. Problem phase continued. Informal discussion on the subtopic, "What are the most important causes of the problem?"

Third Stage. Solution phase. Informal presentation of various possible solutions.

Fourth Stage. Solution phase continued. Informal debates on the subtopic, "What is the best solution to the problem?"

Fifth Stage. Action phase. Formal public (extemporaneous) speaking on the subtopic, "What, as citizens, will be our program to put into effect the necessary remedies?"

The Student Congress of Delta Sigma Rho, the House of Representatives of the National Forensic League, the Student Senate of the Iowa High School Forensic League, the Purdue University Student Legislature, the Legislative Conference on Public Affairs, and the Public Affairs Discussion Conference of the Ohio Speech League are all projects designed to promote a greater interest and give training in discussion, parliamentary law, and debate in various patterns of organization.

6. *The Symposium-Forum Discussion Contest*

In order to meet some of the criticisms of interscholastic discussion, particularly those of inadequate preparation, unsatisfactory interpersonal methods, and unsuitable evaluative procedures, the Western Conference Debate League used an application of the symposium-forum with favorable results. [4] The procedure was as

[3] Elwood Murray, "The Discussion Progression," *The Speaker*, XXIV, No. 1 (November, 1939), 18–21. Copies of the revised plan are available through the Department of Speech, University of Denver.

[4] Kenneth Anderson and Jerome Polisky, "The Application of the Symposium-Forum to Contest Discussion," *Speech Teacher*, IX (March, 1960), 131–35.

follows, with groups of six to eight students from different schools:

Round I (one hour and thirty minutes)

Symposium: Five-minute individually prepared expository speeches of location, definition, and/or analysis of the problem, followed by four-minute forum periods with questions by a critic judge.

Round II (one hour and thirty minutes)

Cooperative group discussion: Problem defined, limited, and analyzed.

Preparation Time (forty-five minutes)

Students prepare for next round—speeches of advocacy.

Round III (one hour and thirty minutes)

Symposium: Five-minute speeches of advocacy, each followed by four-minute forum periods with questions from other group members.

Round IV (one hour)

Evaluation of Solutions: Speeches presented in Round III are evaluated with selection of *group* solution(s). Resolutions for use in parliamentary debate are also prepared if the conference runs a second day.

7. *The Group Action Tournament* [5]

The University of Kansas initiated a new type of forensic activity in 1958. It attempted to improve the usual discussion by (1) constituting genuine groups with four to six speakers from the *same* school; (2) providing competition among *school* groups, instead of primarily among individuals; (3) stressing preparation more heavily as a basis for evaluation; (4) granting sufficient time for the discussion activity; and (5) judging by what is produced rather than how it proceeds.

The tournament included two phases. The first was the *preparation of a written committee report* on a selected subtopic of the assigned general subject. In one tournament the subtopic was "What can Universities and Colleges Do to Surmount the Problem of Increasing Enrollments?" This "problem" was announced to the students the morning of the first day of the meet. Each team had twenty-four hours to prepare the report. Coaches could be consulted

---

[5] Kim Giffin and Brad Lashbrook, "Group Action in Perspective," *The Speech Teacher,* IX (March, 1960), 127–31.

during this period. At the end of the twenty-four-hour period, four typewritten copies of each team report were handed to the officials. These were judged by three faculty members on analysis, logic, evidence, organization, objectivity, and language.

The second phase *required each discussion team to defend orally,* before three judges, its written report. Ratings were given on approximately the same criteria as those in phase one. Ratings in both phases were totaled, and the team receiving the highest total rating was declared the winner of the Group Action Tournament.

Reactions to this new form were so favorable among students and faculty that this event has been continued at the University of Kansas.

8. *The Problem-Solving Debate*

This is another type of activity that moves in the direction of cooperative deliberation on problems through a discussion medium. It is typical of extraclass speech work in the State of Washington, where it was originated.[6] It provides for three sets of speeches (analysis, solution, and evaluation) by two teams of two or three speakers each. The first speaker presents an unbiased analysis of the problem. He must give all the facts needed for an understanding of the situation that has produced the problem, to discover the factors involved in the solution of the problem, and, if possible, to set up certain criteria by which the solutions may be judged. The duty of the second speaker is to introduce the solution that he and his colleagues believe to be the best one, to show why this solution is the best, and why it would solve the problem. The third speaker on each team is to weigh the solutions presented by both sides; he may disagree or agree, as the case may be. He may question any of the previous speakers, and they must answer briefly and to the point. His conclusion should be to discover the best solution regardless of past beliefs. He may even offer a new solution if it seems warranted.

The three sets of speeches are evaluated in terms of suitable criteria and standards. This debate provides opportunity for (1) an

[6] See Frederick Orr and Albert Franzke, "The University of Washington Problem Solving Debate," *Bulletin of the University of Washington,* Extension Series, No. 8, (January, 1938).

orderly definition and analysis of the problem, including the criteria for the judging of solutions; (2) the introduction of several proposals; (3) the informal give and take of discussion through questions and answers; and (4) a modification of one's original position, even to the point of disagreeing with one's teammates.

9. *The Cross-Question or "Oregon Plan" Debate*

The cross-question debate differs in a number of respects from the standard debate explained earlier. The first affirmative speaker presents the entire affirmative argument. This presentation is longer than the standard time of ten minutes, often running as long as twenty minutes. The first negative speaker presents the entire negative case, using the same total time given the first affirmative. The next part of the debate is the cross-examination stage. The first affirmative speaker is first cross-examined by the second negative speaker; the first negative speaker is cross-examined by the second affirmative speaker. This time also may vary, but it customarily occupies ten minutes for each speaker, if the first speeches have been twenty minutes. The second speaker on each team gives a rebuttal or summarizing speech, often ten minutes in length.

A variation on this plan is used in the National Forensic League state tournaments. The four constructive speeches are given in order as in the standard debate. Instead of the first rebuttal speech, a five-minute cross-examination period is held in which one affirmative speaker questions either or both of his opponents. Each team then has a final rebuttal.

10. *The Direct-Clash Plan*

In this debate, the number of speakers of a team may vary from two to five. The duties of each speaker are different from those of the speakers in a standard debate. The first affirmative defines the terms, explains the affirmative proposal, and explains the issues in the debate. The first negative then replies, pointing out the issues accepted for a clash and those he admits. The debate must then be restricted to those upon which there is disagreement. The preliminary speeches outline the issues, present the affirmative plan and the negative counterproposal, if there is one, and prepare the ground for the introduction of proofs in the speeches that follow. There are slight shifts in this debate from traditional debate procedure in (1) the preliminary period of definition, and (2) the exposition of issues before any argument is presented.[7]

11. *The Jury-Trial Debate*

The essence of this style is that the debaters assume the roles of judge, witnesses, and lawyers, while the audience becomes a jury. The debate proceeds in accordance with some modification of court rules. Witnesses may take the roles of well-known authorities, being restricted to the published opinions of such authorities. This has some interesting possibilities for a change from the standard pattern and appeals to students who wish to use some originality in debate.[8]

ORGANIZING A PROGRAM IN DISCUSSION

Discussion and debate are complementary. Most teachers who offer training in debate should not overlook the opportunity they also have to include work in discussion. First, the various kinds of discussion are excellent vehicles for learning situations in class or squad meetings. Some teachers use these methods in debate sessions without realizing it. Next, the logical pattern of discussion is such that it fits in ideally with the analysis and investigation of the problem from which the debate proposition is developed. The "Units for Discussion and Debate" mentioned later in this chapter show how the debate and discussion processes can be combined in analysis and investigation in a classroom. The same plan will apply in extra-class discussion and debate.

Using Dewey's popular five-step plan for discussion, which is included in most books in the field,[9] the teacher can profitably follow such a pattern and move his whole group of students ahead in the study of the problem. He might even adapt the steps in the forensic progression, which have been mentioned earlier, as the

[7] Edwin H. Paget, "Rules for the Direct Clash Plan," *Quarterly Journal of Speech,* XXIII (October, 1937), 431–33.

[8] Warren A. Guthrie, "The Reserve Plan for Intercollegiate Discussion," *Quarterly Journal of Speech,* XXV (October, 1939), 392–96.

[9] McBurney and Hance, *op. cit.,* Chap. VI. See also A. Craig Baird, *Principles and Types of Discussion* (New York: McGraw-Hill Book Co., Inc., 1943), Chap. V.

basis for a series of debate meetings. If he does not choose to do the latter, he may utilize various types of discussion at successive meetings of his students.

It would be very practical to use a squad meeting of the round-table type for a start. Next, several panel discussions could be used. To present types of solutions and possible plans, the symposium could then be employed. The lecture-forum would be feasible for the introduction of a faculty member or outside expert who could present certain information, to be followed by a question-answer period.

The advantage of the discussion approach is that it requires all the members of the group to make a careful analysis and investigation of the *whole* problem; examine the criteria for any solution that might be proposed; look at all possible solutions and evaluate them; and select the one solution or plan that best meets the problem that has been analyzed. It also makes possible a careful evaluation of the proposed system suggested by the proposition for debate. Further discussion demands thorough and careful investigation with an evaluation of reasoning and argument. This is valuable to both affirmative and negative points of view and prevents streamlined, inadequate preparation, the "whipping together" of a case without complete, basic information. Through this approach the methods, attitudes, and techniques of discussion can be taught in their proper relation to the techniques of advocacy that debating necessitates.

TRAINING STUDENTS IN DISCUSSION

Instruction in discussion, either in class or as part of the speech activities program, offers many interesting possibilities. First, it teaches students problem-solving skills useful throughout life, whether they serve as ordinary citizens or as leaders. The techniques of effective preparation, sound participation, and efficient leadership are extremely valuable tools. Besides being a fundamental need in debate preparation and analysis, discussion makes numerous specific contributions to the school: (1) it is a means of developing competent school leaders; (2) it helps students recognize, formulate, and try to solve school problems; and (3) it helps the community in serving school-organized or outside group discussion programs.

1. *Developing Competent Participants and Leaders*

Every student who engages in discussion activity has to learn how to perform two important functions: (a) he must be competent in the role of a participant, and (b) he must learn the techniques of leading discussion.

The *participant*, of necessity, must be well prepared on the problem. Beyond this he must understand discussion as a method, be familiar with the procedures that are used, be able to present his ideas effectively as a speaker, learn to employ the proper attitude and manner in participation, be able to discern the course of the discussion so that his contribution will be relevant, and, finally, develop an awareness of the progress or result of the discussion. These elements in participation can be studied and applied in the discussion experiences provided at debate meetings, as well as in the other situations that school and community life afford. They will not be developed in this chapter; excellent books on discussion, which present this information in detail, are available.

The *leader* likewise must know the problem and should have made a careful investigation and analysis of it. Leadership in discussion demands certain personal qualities, skill in handling people, and the knowledge of the techniques of discussion leadership. In most school situations, the leader has the responsibility of checking on the arrangements for the discussion, opening the discussion with appropriate remarks regarding the problem and the speakers, guiding the course of the discussion and giving it a satisfactory pattern, making an efficient as well as a democratic process of the discussion he leads, resolving conflicts that arise in ideas and information, tactfully dealing with the persons in the discussion, and properly summarizing and concluding the discussion. A combination of study, repeated experience, and careful evaluation of technique under proper teacher suggestion helps to improve ability in discussion leadership.

2. *Discussion in School Affairs*

There are many interesting opportunities for the use of discussion and the resultant training of students through such experiences in the school. The student council offers such opportunities. Class meetings, usually policy-determining in character, afford further situations. Club meetings are still other potential training grounds. The school assembly can be planned to demonstrate discussion methods and train the speakers and the audience. The many classes in the whole curriculum of academic subjects afford means of employing discussion as a way of exploring subject matter and problems in a given field; at the same time they offer training in methods for those who take part. The speech teacher can develop an effective cooperation among all these agencies for training in discussion.

3. Discussion in the Community

The town meeting may be a working example of discussion in a community. More often, however, discussion finds its place as a tool for inquiry in planned programs, often originated or presented in the high school or college. Students take part in such activities as the Junior Town Meeting of the Air, forums in which youth problems are discussed, and community forums and lecture series. The student is already a junior citizen in the community; through discussion he can learn and put into action the methodologies that make democracy work.

PREPARATION FOR DISCUSSION

Preparation for discussion [10] is not unlike that for debate in many respects. It necessitates the following steps:

1. Choice of a problem.

2. A preliminary analysis of the problem.

3. Investigation and study, with accurate recording of sources and information.

4. Complete analysis and thinking, based upon this investigation, which supplies evidence, arguments, and values on the problems, solutions, and ways of carrying out the solution selected.

5. Writing of a careful, complete discussion outline following the steps in discussion. This is an inventory of one's thinking and information on the problem. Everyone, including the leader, should make such an outline. The leader should supplement this plan with a question-type participation outline which will furnish him with

[10] See McBurney and Hance, *op. cit.*, Chaps. XI–XVI.

the needed scheme for stimulating the responses of the group and the pattern he hopes to achieve.

UNITS FOR A COURSE IN DISCUSSION AND DEBATE

A very excellent course in discussion and debate can be organized for high school or college. In some instances where greater specialization is possible, a full year of work can be taught, with one semester of discussion and one of debate. The following unit headings cover the combination course:

I. Preparation for Argumentation
   A. The place of discussion and debate in a democracy
   B. First steps in discussion: problems; investigation; outlining
   C. Analysis of the basic problem (discussion methods)
   D. Statement and analysis of the debate proposition
II. Construction of the Debate Case
   A. Methods of outlining (the brief)
   B. Development of the case from the issues
   C. Methods of support: evidence; reasoning
   D. Affirmative case; negative case
   E. Development of cases using methods of support
III. Refutation
   A. Openings for refutation
   B. Fallacies
   C. Methods and techniques in refutation
   D. Demonstration and practice in refutation
IV. Oral Language and Delivery
   A. Methods of delivery
   B. Effective oral style
V. Evaluation and Judging in Discussion and Debate

In using discussion as a method of studying school problems or those on an interscholastic level, the discussion conference has been successful. The Ohio Speech League, under the sponsorship of Dr. William Utterback, has held such meetings during recent years as a culmination for a program of discussion held in high schools throughout the state. The program for such a conference appears below.

PUBLIC AFFAIRS DISCUSSION CONFERENCE
NOVEMBER 19–20
FOR
HIGH SCHOOL STUDENTS OF CENTRAL AND SOUTHWESTERN OHIO
AT
OHIO STATE UNIVERSITY—UNIVERSITY HIGH SCHOOL
(O.S.U. CAMPUS AT HIGH STREET AND WOODRUFF AVENUE)

DISCUSSION CONFERENCE PROGRAM
TOPIC: SHALL WE PRESS NOW FOR WORLD FEDERAL GOVERNMENT?

FRIDAY MORNING: November 19

8:30–9:00 Registration and opinion check for discussers. Assemble in Room 100.
"Call to Order," Paul Carmack, Director, Ohio High School Speech League.
"Welcome to the Discussion Conference," Dr. John Ramseyer.
"Welcome to University School," Tom Patton, President of the School Council, University School.

9:15 O.S.U. discussionists will present a sample discussion on the Conference topic.

9:45 An explanation of the methods and procedures to be used in the student discussion sessions. Dr. Wm. E. Utterback, Director, Ohio Discussion Service, WOSU Forum Moderator.

10:00 *SESSION I,* Student Discussion
(The assignment to groups and their respective rooms will be placed on the blackboards in Room 100. The discussers will use the same room in all sessions. Each Session Room will choose a student spokesman and secretary for each session.)
ISSUE I: Would a World Federal Government including all of the present members of the United Nations be preferable to the United Nations?
A. Would it promote the peace more effectively?
B. Would it promote international cooperation more effectively?
C. Would its advantages be worth the sacrifice of national sovereignty involved?

11:10   GENERAL ASSEMBLY, Room 100
          Dr. Utterback presiding:
          Synthesis of reports of the student spokesmen for the vari-
          ous sections with the assistance of the student secretaries.
          Student discussers may offer additions or corrections from
          the floor.
11:50   LUNCH
          The O.S.U. College Road Cafeteria near the University
          High School and other University and High Street eating
          places are suggested because of their proximity.

FRIDAY AFTERNOON:

1:30   *SESSION II*, Student Discussion
          ISSUE II: Would a World Federal Government without
          Russia and her satellites be preferable to the United Na-
          tions?
              A. Would it promote international cooperation more ef-
                 fectively?
              B. Would it preserve the peace more effectively?
2:30   GENERAL ASSEMBLY, Room 100
          Dr. Utterback presiding:
          Synthesis of reports of session spokesmen as in Session I.
3:15   Meeting of Discussion Directors, Room 115.
          Hugh Laughlin, Chairman
          "What should be done with the Conference next year?"
3:15   *SESSION III*, Student Discussion
          ISSUE III: Could World Federal Government be instituted
          now through the process of amending the Charter of the
          United Nations?
              A. Could amendments to the Charter transform the
                 United Nations into a World Federal Government?
              B. Would Russia or any other of the Big Five oppose
                 the necessary amendments?
              C. Could Russian opposition block the amending process?
4:15   GENERAL ASSEMBLY, Room 100
          Synthesis of Session III.
5:00   Adjournment until 8:30 A.M., Saturday Morning.

FRIDAY EVENING:

8:00   Two one-act plays by University School Players
              1. "Happy Journey"
              2. "Flower Shop"
          Admission: Adults—75¢; Students—50¢

8:00   Last performance of "Everyman" at the Ohio State University Theatre, Derby Hall. Admission—$1.20.

8:15   South High School Players at South High School present "Stage Door." Admission—50¢.

SATURDAY MORNING: November 20

8:30   *SESSION IV*, Student Discussion
        ISSUE IV: Could World Federal Government be instituted now by developing "regional arrangements" within the present charter of the United Nations?
        A. Would regional arrangements accomplish the purposes of World Government?
        B. Could such arrangements be achieved?

9:30   GENERAL ASSEMBLY, Room 100
        Synthesis of Session IV.

10:00   *SESSION V*, Student Discussion
        ISSUE V: How would an attempt for agitation to institute World Federal Government now affect international relations?
        A. Would it weaken or strengthen the United Nations?
        B. Would it make World War III more or less probable?

11:00   GENERAL ASSEMBLY, Room 100
        Synthesis of Session V.

11:30   REPORTS, Margaret Willis, Chairman
        Report of Discussion Directors' Meeting
        Announcements
        Report of Impressions of the Experts

11:45   *SUMMATION* of conclusions, agreements, disagreements, and results of the Conference Discussions. Dr. Utterback.

12:00 M.   ADJOURNMENT

CONFERENCE CONSULTANTS

John Bowers   David Stafford

(Members of the Political Science Department of Ohio State University will assist the Conference as resource experts on World Federal Government. If any session runs into difficulties, these experts are "on call" to go to any session where they are needed.)

RULES FOR A STUDENT CONGRESS

The student congress, which appears under different titles as it is sponsored by various associations of high schools, combines experiences in discussion through committee work, parliamentary practice, and legislative debate. The first such venture, and oldest now from standpoint of origin, is the House of Representatives of the National Forensic League. Others now in operation are the Student Senate of the Iowa High School Forensic League, the Purdue University Student Legislature, and the Legislative Conference on Public Affairs of the Ohio Speech League. The rules for these conferences can be procured from the headquarters of these organizations.

DIRECTING THE DEBATE PROGRAM

Choosing the Squad

After the first meeting (Chapter XVI) the teacher will know how many students he will have for his debate squad. Often the group will be small if the program is just starting; if a large turnout greets the teacher in the opening session, he can either carry the whole group through a preliminary training period or eliminate some by a speaking tryout. He will find that debate work in itself is a selective process; he may never have to cut anyone from his squad. Debating demands persons of superior intelligence and good personality who have the potentialities for becoming good speakers. It requires that all who participate have the capacity for hard work and the physical stamina for rigorous extracurricular training. Practical experience shows that all these qualities are needed for success. The debater has to match wits with the keenest minds from other schools; he devotes much time to study and practice in debate, which means that he has to keep up his other work in addition to his forensic activity; he must have the physical energy to engage in long practice sessions, trips, and tournaments. The director of debate can watch his candidates during the training period, observe their abilities in practice debates, and then select hs first-string debaters, and those whom he will carry on the squad as reserves. This plan has the advantage of letting him see what students can do in an actual debate situation.

Some coaches, however, utilize a tryout speech of argumentative type as a method of screening and making initial observations regarding the quality of students. This has value in "taking inventory." Speakers can be evaluated upon all the elements of good composition and delivery; their strengths and weaknesses can be noted, conferences held, and a selection of a squad personnel made at an early time. The coach can then devote his time to the persons he has chosen.

A good working squad may include from eight to twelve debaters; however, squads may vary from a minimum of four to thirty or more.

The Director (Coach) and the Debate Program

Besides the debaters, the director or coach is a key figure in debate training. Not only must he assume all the general responsibilities mentioned earlier for an activity administrator, but he must carry out those particular functions concerned with his debaters.

1. He should have desirable personal qualities.

A successful program rests heavily upon the personality of the director. He must have the capacity for hard work, enjoying long hours spent with young people. He needs patience, tact, and skill to insure the development of his students. He should not expect immediate spectacular results, but should understand that time, experience, and careful instruction yield a superior product. A good sense of humor, a practical knowledge of psychology, the ability to understand students and gain their respect and confidence, all are important. To these he should add a high code of ethics and substantial educational values.

2. He should be well trained.

The best combination of training and experience is found in a person who has a speech major with a concentration in argumentation, discussion, debate, and persuasion, and debate experience that allows him to view debate as part of the total field of speech education. Strong supporting course work in history, economics, political science, and English are valuable. Some persons are successful in this work without training of such depth and breadth, but they would be stronger teachers with greater professional status if they had it.

3. He should understand and know how to work in debate competition.

Debate is by philosophy and practice a competitive activity. A practical director believes in the desirable aspects of such competition and knows how to work in the established pattern. A winning debate squad helps build the entire speech program. It also encourages parental, administrative, and public support. However, winning should not be the *sole* end in debate. It should result from a sound, efficiently conducted educational experience that develops the finest personal intellectual qualities, plus skill in communication, among young people. The director should concentrate upon evolving an outstanding product. In this way he will gain his share of victories among the rewards of effective teaching.

Another part of knowing and working in the competitive pattern is familiarity with tournament debating. Ideally, a solid debate program should give speakers ample opportunity for speaking before audiences. It should also include adequate experiences for competitive participation in tournaments. The coach should know the pros and cons of tournaments.[11]

Certain lacks or weaknesses exist: (1) the absence of post-debate oral critiques; (2) the lack of audiences and the opportunity to convince them, rather than a critic judge, on the strength of one's position; (3) a strong emphasis upon winning, at times, so strong that the won–lost record is a greater motivation than seeking the truth about the issues involved; (4) fewer students, with more "stars" in such competition, because of the highly specialized training demanded; (5) the use of a single proposition; and (6) the competence of judges.

Matching these are the advantages of tournaments: (1) the opportunity for intensive practice in a short time period (one day, for instance); (2) the small per debate cost of tournament debates; (3) the reduction of effort in holding many debates in a tournament at the same time and place; (4) the fact that tournaments are a testing ground for knowledge and ability; (5) the development of good sportsmanship in such competition.

After weighing these items, the coach should similarly consider dual debates with audiences present as part of his program.

---

[11] See David Potter (ed.), *Argumentation and Debate* (New York: Dryden Press, 1954), Chap. 15, and "A Symposium on Debate and Discussion," *Speech Teacher,* IX (March, 1960), 95–131.

4. *He must make materials and library facilities available to the students.*

Certain standard debate references assist squad work. In some localities these are included in the materials sent out by the state association. They include the special issue of the *Congressional Digest, The Reference Shelf,*[12] the *Debater's Handbook,* and the official debate handbook published by the National University Extension Association. The coach is responsible for procuring individual copies of any of these that his budget permits, as well as other special debate handbooks published on a particular question. He should consult with the school and public libraries to put on a reserve shelf other relevant materials with which he may be acquainted. He should leave the actual study and assembly of arguments and evidence to his debaters. He should do such research as is needed for a thorough knowledge of the question or may be helpful in opening up new materials for use by the debaters. The debaters must dig out their information on the proposition. This process is a continuing one, but a good start means that the coach must order the necessary publications and make them accessible.

Often a division of labor in reading, recording, and making out cards is in order. If information can be pooled, a ditto machine becomes a handy instrument for producing duplicate copies of statistical information, quotations, and outlines of plans that are discovered, all of which can be distributed to the whole squad.

5. *He should stress preparation and learning, making decisions regarding selection of evidence, argument, reasoning, and debate cases developed.*

Probably the greatest educational rewards from debate come from the search for knowledge, including evidence, arguments, reasoning, the organization of briefs, and case outlines. These open an expansive area of education in contemporary problems unequalled in any other activity. Greatest stress should be placed here. Within this framework the director must aid in determining value and policy in the use of the materials found. Although student thinking and

[12] These compilations of articles, bibliographies, and sample briefs for debaters are published by H. W. Wilson Co., New York.

suggestion is valuable in this case, the coach has the final authority, based upon his greater maturity and experience.

6. *He should* GUIDE *the thinking of the debaters,* NOT DO IT FOR THEM.

One of the major objectives of debating is the training of students in critical and reflective thinking. Squad meetings and conferences with individual debaters should be guided by the teacher so that together the group will evolve the affirmative and negative cases, plan rebuttals and refutation, test arguments, and weigh evidence.

7. *He should prepare the entire debate schedule, including squad meetings, practice debates, and judged interscholastic debates.*

As director of the program the instructor has the job of organizing all details of scheduling. He may be assisted in this by a faculty manager of debate or activities; in some schools a student manager helps in these matters.

8. *He should keep good records of his program.*

As the season progresses, the director needs to have written information about his squad members: their assignments; dual and tournament participation; wins and losses, critiques and evaluations by coaches, other debaters, and judges; correspondence; invitations; pictures; newspaper clippings, and so on. These records are valuable parts of the training program and prove extremely helpful in all the details of the coach's job. They are also interesting as one compares the achievements of individuals and squads from year to year. Some schools have a debate scrapbook as part of their record-keeping project.

9. *He should develop strong channels for publicity.*

Closely related to the records of the program is the development of reliable, effective means of publicity for the program. The director can use the school paper, daily newspaper, radio and television stations, posters, pictures, and exhibits to implement the publicity for the debate program.

10. *He should provide for awards of various kinds.*

It is customary for certain tangible awards to be provided as recognition for achievement in debate. These vary widely from school to school. In many colleges recognition comes through election to membership in honorary forensic societies, such as Delta Sigma Rho, Phi Kappa Delta, Tau Kappa Alpha, and others. High schools have their counterpart in the National Forensic League. Other means of rewarding achievement are certificates, plaques, trophies, honor rolls, and so on. The director, with his administration and debaters, is responsible for establishing the methods that are appropriate and for providing the awards themselves.

11. *He should secure judges and make all financial arrangements.*

These items, likewise, are part of the coach's job. They are discussed in Chapters XVIII and XIX.

12. *He should teach his students the principles of good sportsmanship in debate.*

Any team reflects the ethics and sportsmanship of its coach. In debate the example of the director is of primary importance. Smith mentions these as essentials which the coach should seek in debate:

If coaches can develop debaters: (1) who will play fair at all times; (2) who will give a square deal to their opponents, to the spectators, and to the judges in their interpretation of their material; (3) who will respect the official or officials of the debate and abide by the decision; (4) who will debate for the joy of debating and for the success of the team; (5) who will cooperate with their teammates and not "try to grandstand"; (6) who will conduct themselves while out of school and out of town in a manner that will be a credit to the institution they represent—we can remove many of the criticisms now leveled at debate activities.[13]

13. *He should plan and carry out a training program that will develop competent debaters.*

Any educationally sound training program should cover these broad areas in debate: (1) the knowledge of the principles of argumentation; (2) the specific rules, practices, and techniques of contest debate; (3) sufficient practice and performance in actual debates to develop skill in those who participate.

Knowledge of the principles of argumentation underlies success-

[13] Carney Smith, "Practical Procedures in Coaching High-School Debate," *Quarterly Journal of Speech,* XXIX (April, 1943), 223.

ful work in debate. These divisions are somewhat standard in the field: (1) the nature and scope of argumentation; (2) propositions; (3) investigation; (4) analysis of the proposition; (5) building a case; (6) evidence; (7) reasoning; (8) outlining or preparing a brief; (9) preparing the argumentative speech; (10) refutation; and (11) delivering the argumentative speech.

Beyond this the coach will have to teach the specific rules, practices, and techniques of contest debate. Principal *additions* to the above may include: organization and procedure in the standard debate and other types to be used; order and duties of speakers; debate cases; obligations of the affirmative and negative; strategy, organization, technique, refutation and rebuttal; methods of note-taking and checking; speech composition; delivery and presentation in debate; platform conduct; and courtesy.

Sufficient practice and performance in actual debates necessitate carefully planned squad meetings, intrasquad competition, the scheduling of an ample number of practice debates before regular competition is scheduled in the association, and the entire schedule of individually-judged debates and tournaments.

The training program is developed in some detail in the next section.

A TRAINING PROGRAM IN DEBATE

There is probably no one procedure or method of training debaters that can be said to be ideal or unqualifiedly better than any other. Every teacher in this field is an individual in his own right and uses the plan that consistently gives him satisfactory results. Two sequences for training are included here as guides for those who have no plan, or for those who wish to check their methods with the intention of making certain changes.

Carney Smith [14] gives a seven-week plan for training a debate squad. This appears in the following outline form:

First Week
 1. Introduce the squad to the objectives and values in debate.
 2. Give preliminary training of students to develop a "questioning mind."

[14] Smith, *op. cit.*, pp. 224–33.

3. Develop an interest in problems of everyday life.
4. Start the investigation of the question for debate.
5. Make tentative definitions of terms.
6. Introduce students to debate materials in the library.
7. Orientate them to the nature of evidence: facts and opinions of authorities.

Second Week
1. Begin the specific search for evidence on the question.
2. Study kinds of evidence, tests for evidence.
3. Conduct round-table discussions with affirmative and negative groups; draw up outlines of possible cases.
4. Present a demonstration debate using veterans.
5. Make recordings of these speeches, if possible.
6. Criticize and show applications of principles, use of argument and evidence.

Third Week
1. Give instructions on the duties of affirmative and negative speakers in a debate.
2. Discuss techniques of affirmative and negative debating.
3. Conduct rounds of practice debates for the entire squad; use tentative pairings and cases.
4. Give thorough criticism of all debates.

Fourth Week
1. Formulate definite cases for affirmative and negative teams.
2. Prepare speech outlines carefully to correspond to cases.
3. Run off practice debates with one veteran–one novice teams.
4. Conduct refutation drills stressing:
   a. Ways of handling arguments.
   b. Methods of refutation.
   c. Preparation of refutation outlines for meeting particular arguments.

Fifth and Sixth Weeks
1. Conduct intrasquad practice debates.
2. Do intensive work on speeches, polishing composition and delivery.
3. Enter practice tournament and individual interscholastic practice debates to give all debaters experience.
4. Pair speakers and rotate sides to give them experience with both sides and different personalities.
5. Note best team combinations.

Seventh Week

1. Select the team or teams who are to debate in judged interscholastic debates.
2. Polish case and delivery, giving detailed criticism in group situations; conduct individual conference.
3. Point up the use of statistics; relationships of individual speeches to the whole case; check selection of material for running refutation and rebuttal points; work on techniques for summary.
4. Give final instructions for first official-judged debates.

A slightly different plan for training is given by Hance.[15] Using the five steps of the teaching cycle given by Morrison—Exploration, Presentation, Assimilation, Organization, and Recitation—he presents five steps in debate preparation which are adaptations from the above scheme. His titles for the steps are: Self-Questioning, which is based upon a carefully prepared self-questioning sheet presented to each student; Getting a Perspective, which involves reading general articles, hearing lectures by experts from the community or school, presentation of material by the coach, the use of short debates, and group discussion; Assimilating, which includes investigation, analysis, discussion, and intrasquad debates; Organizing, which is a stage stressing case organization; and Practicing for Delivery, which is devoted to polishing delivery. A sample of the self-questioning sheet follows.

SELF-QUESTIONING SHEET [16]

Resolved: That the Federal Government should enact legislation requiring the settlement of all labor disputes by compulsory arbitration when voluntary means of settlement have failed. (Constitutionality conceded.)

Background Survey

A. Origin and History
1. When and under what circumstances was the first legislation governing labor relations passed? Its provisions? Why?
2. What were the results of this legislation?

[15] Kenneth Hance, "Adapting the 'Teaching Cycle' to Debate," *Quarterly Journal of Speech*, XXX (December, 1944), 444–50.

[16] Prepared by Kenneth G. Hance, professor of Speech, Michigan State University.

3. What subsequent legislation in this field has been enacted? Its provisions? Why?
4. When did labor unions assume a position of strength?
5. What were the consequences of this situation?
6. When were the various mediation, conciliation, and arbitration boards created? Their nature? Their achievements?

B. Immediate Cause for Debate
    1. Is the war a reason for debating this proposition?
    2. Is the present number of strikes a reason?
    3. Is the present strength of labor unions a reason?
    4. Is existing legislation in this field a reason?
    5. Are specific groups or organizations advocating this plan?

Definition of Terms

A. Terms in the Proposition
    1. What is the meaning of "Federal Government"?
    2. What is the meaning of "settlement"?
    3. What is the meaning of "labor disputes"?
    4. What is the meaning of "compulsory"?
    5. What is the meaning of "arbitration"?
    6. What is the meaning of "voluntary means of settlement"?
    7. What is the meaning of "constitutionality conceded"?

B. Terms Associated with the Proposition
    1. Is any specific agency or arbiter implied?
    2. Is compulsory acceptance of awards implied?
    3. Is conciliation or mediation included in the area of this proposal?
    4. Is the Federal Mediation and Conciliation Service included?

Criteria or Objectives

A. General
    1. What do you wish accomplished by labor legislation?
    2. What should be accomplished by this proposal?
    3. What should be the accomplishments for labor? Capital? The "public"?

B. Specific
    1. Do you wish to preserve labor's right to strike?
    2. Do you wish to prevent strikes?
    3. Do you wish to improve labor-capital relations?
    4. Do you wish to improve labor's opportunity of bettering its position?
    5. Do you wish to protect capital's rights?
    6. Do you wish to protect the "public" from the effects of labor-capital disputes?

7. Do you wish to implement the Bill of Rights as it applies to labor-capital relations?
8. Do you wish to encourage the development and wider use of peaceful means of settling disputes?

The Present Situation

A. Its Nature
   1. What means are available at present for the settlement of labor disputes?
   2. Which of these means are provided for by law?
   3. Which of these means prevent any stoppage of work?
   4. Which of these means provide for conciliation and mediation?
   5. Which provide for arbitration?
   6. What are the effects of these means upon labor? Capital? The "public"?
   7. What is the present situation in labor-capital relations? Number of strikes? Number of persons affected?
   8. What controls are exerted on one or both sides?
   9. What is the Federal Mediation and Conciliation Service? The Railway Labor Board?
   10. What have been their achievements? Limitations?
   11. What is the basic philosophy (underlying assumptions and objectives) of the present situation?
B. Its Adequacy
   1. What are the principal arguments advanced in behalf of it?
   2. Are the points of strength inherent?
   3. What are the principal arguments advanced against it?
   4. Are the weaknesses inherent? Are they results of human frailties in its operation?
   5. Do the weaknesses outweigh the points of strength? Why?
   6. Do these weaknesses justify *some* change?

The Affirmative Proposal

A. Its Nature
   1. What is the precise nature of this proposal?
   2. Does it provide for compulsory acceptance of awards?
   3. Does it outlaw strikes?
   4. Who would administer this plan?
   5. What is the basic philosophy of this proposal?
B. Its Adequacy
   1. What arguments are advanced in behalf of this proposal?
   2. Do they deal with inherent features?

3. Would the plan clearly meet the "need"?
4. What arguments are advanced against this proposal?
5. Where has arbitration worked satisfactorily in the United States? Abroad?
6. Where has it failed?
7. Are these instances of compulsory or voluntary arbitration?
8. Is this proposal analogous to our court system?
9. Is the history of the Federal Mediation and Conciliation Service an argument for or against this proposal? The Railway Labor Board?
10. Would labor be harmed by this proposal?
11. Would management be harmed?
12. Would the "public" be harmed?
13. Would this proposal give too much power to arbiters?
14. Would encouragement be given to "back-stage" or "informal" dealings between the arbiters and the parties to the dispute?
15. Would this proposal remove the inherent points of strength enjoyed by labor? By capital?
16. Would this proposal meet the objectives previously selected?

Alternative Proposals

A. Modifications of the Present System
    1. Would a revision of present legislation be a better plan?
    2. Would the imposition of a "cooling-off" period be better?
    3. Would extension of the services of agencies of conciliation and mediation be better?
    4. Would a program of "education" be better?
B. Proposals in a Different Category
    1. Would legislation outlawing striking and picketing be a better plan?
    2. Would federal regulation of labor unions (incorporation, publication of financial statement, imposition of responsibility for acts of members, etc.) be better?
    3. Would some means of "getting at the cause of disputes" be better?
    4. What is the basic philosophy of each of these proposals?
    5. To what extent would each proposal "meet the need" and also meet the objectives previously selected?

Hance also organizes a time schedule for a squad of from four to twenty-four debaters. It covers a period of nine weeks, with two regular squad meetings planned and one conference or practice session each week. The schedule below indicates (a) the first squad meeting; (b) the second squad meeting; (c) additional conference and practice sessions:

EXPLORATION

First Week
  (a) Orientation, prospectus, introduction to Self-Questioning Sheet
  (b) Review of Self-Questioning Sheet (answers to be written by the debaters)
  (c) Conference with each debater

GETTING A PERSPECTIVE

Second Week
  (a) Lecture by an authority, *or* some other procedure previously announced
  (b) Same as (a)
  (c) Conferences with groups to review the lectures
Third Week
  (a) Short debates (as previously described)
  (b) Partition of the bibliography for individual investigation

ASSIMILATION

Third Week
  (b) Reports on bibliography *or* round tables
Fourth Week
  (a) Reports on bibliography *or* round tables
  (b) Reports on bibliography *or* round tables
  (c) Intrasquad debates (one experienced and one inexperienced member, if possible)

Fifth Week
  (a) Reports on bibliography *or* round tables
  (b) Reports on bibliography *or* round tables
  (c) Intrasquad debates with sides reversed

ORGANIZATION

Sixth Week
  (a) Work on affirmative case (preceded by meeting of experienced debaters)
  (b) Work on negative case (preceded by meeting of experienced debaters)
  (c) Intrasquad debates (teams graded, if possible)

Seventh Week
  (a) Amending and polishing of affirmative case
  (b) Amending and polishing of negative case
  (c) Intrasquad debates

DELIVERY-ORGANIZATION

Eighth Week
  (a) Work with attack and defense, rebuttal speeches, etc.
  (b) Work with attack and defense, rebuttal speeches, etc.
  (c) Intrasquad debates *or* specific work on delivery

Ninth Week
  (a) Demonstration debate by best team to demonstrate cases, attack and defense, delivery, etc.
  (b) Review of bibliography; work on attack and defense
  (c) Intrasquad debates *or* individual practice

PROCEDURE IN THE DEBATE

The day of the debate or tournament is important. The debaters should be given consideration so that unnecessary emotional tensions are not created. If they are to travel, arrangements should be made for a leisurely trip. The coach should ask the cooperation of the administrator so that students may be excused early enough to permit safe driving, a period of rest and relaxation, and a light meal before the debate. Often a movie is a good device to reduce worry or tension. The debaters should arrive at the scene of the contest in ample time to allow them to look over the situation and to enter the debate without the undue pressure of last-minute adjustments.

Even if the debate is at home, a similar schedule should be planned to insure the best possible performance.

During debates the coach should be ready for anything and express no great surprise at what happens. He should keep cool and demonstrate all the attitudes of sportsmanship and poise that he expects of his students. Whether he wins or loses, he should follow those principles. Under no conditions should he "blow his top," "bawl out," or harshly criticize his debaters. He should do all he can to get at the cause of any difficulties calmly and objectively; he should use positive methods and encouragement with his students.

EXERCISES

1. Prepare a list of suitable topics for discussion.
2. Make a list of properly phrased topics for debate.
3. Using either the current high school debate question or a question of national concern, compile a suitable list of references, study the question, and organize a debate brief.
4. Write a paper in which you discuss what you consider to be the principal values of discussion and debate.
5. Prepare a paper in which you develop the pros and cons of tournament debating, followed by your position on the matter. Be sure to support your point of view strongly.

REFERENCES

Andersen, Kenneth, and Jerome B. Polisky. "The Application of the Symposium-Forum to Contest Discussion," *Speech Teacher,* IX (March, 1960), 131–34.

Auer, J. Jeffrey, and Henry L. Eubank. *Handbook for Discussion Leaders.* New York: Harper & Bros., 1954.

Baird, A. Craig. *Argumentation, Discussion, and Debate.* New York: McGraw-Hill Book Co., 1950.

Barnlund, Dean C. "Our Concept of Discussion: Static or Dynamic?" *Speech Teacher,* III (January, 1954), 8–14.

————, and Franklyn S. Haiman. *The Dynamics of Discussion.* Boston: Houghton Mifflin Co., 1960.

Bradley, Bert. "Debate: Practical Training for Gifted Students," *Speech Teacher,* VIII (March, 1959), 134–38.

Buehler, E. C. "Debate and Parliamentary Practice Contribute to Democratic Processes," *Bulletin of the National Association of Secondary School Principals,* XXXVIII (January, 1954), 86–90.

Capp, Glenn R.; Robert Huber; and Wayne C. Eubank. "Debates of Affirmative Speakers," *Speech Teacher,* VIII (March, 1959), 139–49.

Cathcart, Robert S. "Adapting Debate to an Audience," *Speech Teacher,* V (March, 1956), 113–16.

Cripe, Nicholas M. "A Survey of Debate Programs in Two Hundred and Forty-Six American Colleges and Universities," *Speech Teacher,* VIII (March, 1959), 157–60.

Freeley, Austin. "An Anthology of Commentary on Debate," *Speech Teacher,* IX (March, 1960), 121–26.

Giffin, Kim, and Brad Lashbrook. " 'Group Action' in Perspective," *Speech Teacher,* IX (March, 1960), 127–30.

GULLEY, HALBERT E. *Essentials of Discussion and Debate.* New York: Henry Holt and Co., Inc., 1955.

HAIMAN, FRANKLYN S. *Group Leadership and Democratic Action.* Boston: Houghton Mifflin Co., 1951.

KELTNER, JOHN. "The Laboratory Method of Discussion Training at Kansas State College," *Speech Teacher,* VII (September, 1958), 199–208.

McBURNEY, JAMES H., and KENNETH HANCE. *Discussion in Human Affairs.* New York: Harper & Bros., 1950.

———; JAMES M. O'NEILL; and GLEN E. MILLS. *Argumentation and Debate.* New York: The Macmillan Co., 1951.

MILLER, N. EDD. "Some Modifications of Contest Debating," *Speech Teacher,* II (March, 1953), 139–40.

MILLS, GLEN E. "Audiences and Tournaments: Two Forms of Over-Emphasis," *Speech Teacher,* IX (March, 1960), 95–98.

MURPHY, RICHARD. "The Ethics of Debating Both Sides," *Speech Teacher,* VI (January, 1957), 1–9.

MUSGRAVE, GEORGE. *Competitive Debate: Rules and Techniques.* New York: H. W. Wilson Co., 1957.

POTTER, DAVID. *Argumentation and Debate.* New York: Dryden Press, Inc., 1954.

ROBINSON, JAMES L. "Are We 'Overlegalizing' School Debate?" *Speech Teacher,* IX (March, 1960), 109–15.

ROBINSON, KARL F. "Suggested Units on Discussion and Debate for Secondary Schools," *Quarterly Journal of Speech,* XXXII (October, 1946), 385–90.

SATTLER, WILLIAM M., and N. EDD MILLER. *Discussion and Conference.* Englewood Cliffs, N. J.: Prentice-Hall, Inc., 1954.

STURGIS, ALICE F. *Learning Parliamentary Procedure.* New York: McGraw-Hill Book Co., 1953.

WINDES, RUSSEL R., JR. "Competitive Debating: The Speech Program, the Individual and Society," *Speech Teacher,* IX (March, 1960), 99–108.

CHAPTER TWENTY-TWO

Oral Interpretation

Interpretation or oral reading is one of the most important and most popular of speech activities. Charles Laughton and other similar radio, television, and platform readers have done much to promote present interest in the best aspects of this work. Interpretation is the re-creation of literature for an audience through the fundamental processes of oral communication. Such a basic skill should be a part of course work in every speech program; it should also be included in some form in activities outside the classroom.

In relation to the rest of the speech field, skill in interpretation can be, and is, an end in itself. Ability in interpretation also underlies success in acting on the stage, in announcing and acting in radio and television. It is invaluable to the public speaker who wishes to use quoted material in his talk, or who desires to read from manuscript, when necessary, with interest and conviction.

Reading prose, poetry, or drama from the printed page; choric interpretation; reader's theater; chamber theater; declamation—humorous, serious, dramatic; memorized play recitals; original monologues; and the presentation of cuttings from novels or short stories—all these are types of speech activities done under the banner of interpretation in the past and in the present. However, the trend among outstanding, modern teachers in the field is toward reading from the book. This definition from Charlotte Lee confirms this point:

> Interpretation is the art of communicating to an audience, from the printed page, a work of literary art in its intellectual, emotional, and aesthetic entirety.[1]

[1] Charlotte Lee, *Oral Interpretation* (Boston: Houghton Mifflin Co., 1959), p. 7.

She further describes the role of the interpreter in these words:

It is the task of the interpreter to perceive and to communicate to his audience the intellectual, emotional, and artistic or stylistic qualities of his material, not as separate entities, but as a unified and coordinated whole. His responsibility is to communicate the work of another, not to exhibit his own talents or erudition. He achieves communication by means of a trained voice and body, his twofold instrument, controlled by a responsive, informed, and disciplined mind. His aim is to present the material so that it conveys the effect which the author intended. The writer is the creative artist; the interpreter, the re-creative artist.[2]

Thus, in contemporary interpretation emphasis is not being placed upon memorized, often exhibitory, or elocutionary types of performance. In fact, it can be said such traditional types are being excluded by such definitions of oral interpretation as that given above.

Values in good oral communication are placed above those of showmanship. Without completely memorizing his material, the interpreter uses the printed page or his script to establish himself as the middleman between the author and the audience. Emphasis is placed upon suitable selections, careful analysis, and a genuine appreciation for literature as the basis for interpretation. Its artistic purpose is preserved, but presentations become more intelligent, technique less obtrusive and more natural through suitable training.

In secondary school interpretation this trend has led to the inclusion of impromptu reading, verse speaking, poetry and prose reading from selected anthologies, original monologues, and so on, as supplements or replacements for older types of activities. These activities, taught in the speech classroom, in cocurricular festivals, or in English classes, represent a definite trend to use oral methods in teaching literature.

College instruction in interpretation is moving toward organized instruction in units of interpretation in the basic course and toward foundation courses in interpretation that parallel basic courses in speaking. Advanced courses are also offered in many schools. A variety of cocurricular activities usually supplements classroom work, with the presentation of programs by individual interpreters, as well as group projects in choric interpretation, reader's theater, and chamber theater for campus audiences.

2 *Ibid.*, p. 11.

In the treatment of the teaching of interpretation in this chapter, contemporary approaches and forms will be stressed. However, other forms, such as declamation, will be considered because some teachers face the need for dealing with them in their teaching situations.

VALUES AND PURPOSES IN INTERPRETATION

There are many values in studying interpretation. (1) It furnishes a vital approach to the study of all types of literature in both speech and English classes. Thorough analysis of selections is necessary before they are read. Poetry and other types of literature come alive when interpreted orally. Understanding, enjoyment, and appreciation are achieved. (2) It allows students to build values acquired through discovering the finest ideas and emotional sensitivity in literature. (3) It is an expressional experience that gives deep, personal satisfaction to those who participate. Sharing one's ideas and feelings with others through literature not only is good therapy, but when done effectively gives one a real sense of achievement. (4) It develops a basic artistic skill that is desirable for itself as a part of speech education. (5) It provides a foundation and a supplement for other kinds of speech training, such as public speaking, acting in the theater, radio, and television, announcing on radio, and the like. (6) It motivates and provides the vehicle for improvement in the use of voice and in control of bodily expression. (7) It furnishes excellent opportunities in choric interpretation, reader's theater, chamber theater, festivals, or class situations for developing attitudes of confidence, cooperation, responsibility, and sharing with others. These group experiences are invaluable.

METHODS OF TEACHING INTERPRETATION

In this section we shall first discuss general suggestions useful in classroom instruction or activities, and then develop methods applicable to contest and festival work. Consideration will also be given to declamation, as well as to group forms of interpretation—choric interpretation, reader's theater, and chamber theater.

General Suggestions

Successful teaching of interpretation begins with the students' interest in and enjoyment of good literature. Classroom teachers of interpretation in a speech program or teachers of literature in English courses have numerous ways of developing such motivation.

1. *Acquaint students with good literature; make it available to them.*

Today fine literature is available to students at small cost, in convenient form, and is easily procurable. Many anthologies provide collections of literature. Poetry, prose (all types—essays, short stories, biographies, humor, satire, adventure, fiction, and so on), and drama can be found in single, comprehensive volumes. Each of these forms is also collected in specialized works. For example, poetry is usually classified according to author, period, and type. Drama collections include full-length or one-act plays, as well as scenes from longer shows. Classical novels, current fiction, and good periodicals are also important sources.

With paperbacks of reputable works published at low cost, with an extensive offering of titles, the student and teacher of interpretation have a rich reservoir of materials available. This widens the student's possibility for choice of selections. It may also make the cutting of selections for individual use somewhat easier.

The teacher's foresight in providing an "interpretation" shelf of literature in the classroom, school, or public library also aids the process.

2. *Arouse further interest by reading to students and letting them hear good interpretation.*

Students still like to be read to. A good way to arouse interest is by the teacher's reading aloud from works of literature that appeal to a particular group. There are many opportunities today for students to hear others read. Guest readers from outside the school, alumni, older students, and professional readers may be heard in person or over radio and television. Reading hours, recitals, and other special programs on campus afford similar listening experiences.

Commercial records and tapes with excellent materials are another avenue for use by the teacher. These can be auditioned, carefully selected, and played in the classroom as a general motivation for interpretation, or perhaps as special examples for study or evaluation as work progresses. Recording companies such as Caedmon, Columbia, RCA-Victor, Decca, Capitol and others have extensive lists of titles.

3. *Allow students to bring to class selections they enjoy reading to others.*

High school and college students like to share their favorite selections with others. As an added interest-getter, occasional free-choice reading sessions will open the gateway to a knowledge of their tastes, interests, and abilities in reading orally. A sizable list of books and selections they like best may also be obtained with little effort by the teacher.

4. *Teach students a sound, basic method for preparing to interpret.*

The heart of learning how to interpret literature comes from a method of preparation that demands that the student develop a thorough knowledge of the literature he plans to use. This rich experience in study, analysis, and appreciation culminates in the student's sharing his experience through the oral presentation of the selections he chooses.

Charlotte Lee [3] presents a complete scheme for preparation organized around the following outline:

A. Choose an appropriate selection of good literature.
B. Analyze the selection.
    1. Extrinsic factors—universality, individuality, suggestion.
    2. Logical and emotional content: organization.
    3. Author's attitude.
    4. Intrinsic factors—content in relation to unity, harmony, variety, contrast, rhythm, proportion, form, etc.
C. Prepare orally.
    1. Read whole selection aloud; adjust practice periods to needs of reader and difficulty of the selection.
    2. Keep in mind what selection is saying; make your attitude correspond as much as possible with that of author.
    3. Break material into separate parts; note focal points and function of each.
    4. Synthesize the material to check relationships.

[3] *Ibid.,* Chap. III.

5. Adjust practice periods to needs of reader and the difficulty of the selection.
D. Present the selection to the audience.
   1. Rely on previous preparation.
   2. Use appropriate platform methods.
E. Evaluate the performance.
   1. Could the listeners see and hear?
   2. Did they know what you were talking about?
   3. What response did the material call forth from them?
   4. Was it the response your author obviously intended?
   5. Where, if anywhere, did they lose the thread of the thought or mood?
   6. Were there spots where they were aware of you rather than of your material?

Suggestions for Contests and Festivals

Interpretative reading in festivals or contests has made rapid progress. In some states it has largely replaced declamation. The usual pattern, however, consists of a variety of forms including primarily "reading from the book," but with some events retained that permit memorization. Many states also keep declamation in some form. The National Forensic League, for example, includes dramatic interpretation, formerly called dramatic declamation, in its national tournament. Colleges have moved quite definitely toward contemporary definition and practice in interpretation festivals and programs.

Typical State Programs

A representative state program is that under the direction of the Illinois High School Association. It conducts contests in verse reading, prose reading, serious and comedy reading, and original monologue. The first two are reading directly from the book. The last two are memorized. In verse reading, a *required* poem of sonnet length is read by every contestant. Each student also reads a *selected* poem drawn by him from titles prepared by the state office. Both required and selected poems are taken from an anthology announced in the fall by the state headquarters.

Prose reading, eight minutes in length, may be taken from any source. One hour in advance of the contest each student submits five slips, each bearing the title of the source book with the name and page of the selection he has chosen. Immediately preceding the contestant's appearance, the chairman draws one slip. The student reads the selection indicated.

An original monologue, written by the student, portrays a single character in a given situation or miniature drama. A typed copy, suitable for an eight-minute reading, is submitted in advance of the contest.

Serious or comedy reading is done in a memorized presentation of eight minutes, and must contain at least 75 per cent of dialogue between two or more characters. Cuttings from plays or other works are used.

Wisconsin offers another typical state program for high schools. Interpretative reading contests are held annually in prose and poetry, read "from the book." Memorization and properties are not permitted. There is no list of prohibited selections. Play reading has rules specifying that cuttings of fifteen minutes must be read interpretatively, *not acted.* The performance resembles that of reader's theater, employing two to five persons, each reading one individual role. Properties may not be used.

Memorized declamation of a short story, cutting from a play or novel, narrative poem, or an informal essay is retained in Wisconsin. The purpose of this event is to entertain.

At the college and university level, a variety of interpretation events is conducted by state leagues and in invitational meets sponsored by individual institutions. These are usually festivals or special programs using various forms of interpretation.

PREPARING FOR INTERPRETATION AND DECLAMATION CONTESTS AND FESTIVALS

Although the general methods of preparing for interpretation are all applicable to getting students ready for festivals or contests, some additional procedures apply. Each situation has its own rules. Also students are either striving to win or hoping to receive a high evaluation of their performance if winners are not declared.

1. *Select qualified students.*

Qualified students are those who have real interest and possess demonstrated talent to do interpretation. They should be intelligent.

They should have excellent voice and articulation, as well as good physical control and appearance. They should be emotionally poised and secure before audiences. They should have the time and capacity for the hard work of preparation and competition. They should take suggestions readily.

2. *Choose selections of good literature suitable for contests and festivals.*

In contests and festivals selections should have literary merit, appeal, and potential impact upon an audience, a critic, or a judge. Selections should not be chosen *primarily* because of their value for academic study. They should contain wholesome thoughts, emotions, and situations. They should be "timeless," capable of maintaining enduring interest, even after much work has been done on them. They should appeal particularly to the student involved. They should be within his span of re-creative ability. To ensure such qualifications, they should be selected by the student with the advice of his teacher. They should be chosen with an awareness of the type of interpretation to be done. "Cute child" selections should be avoided. Commercial "contest winners" also should be excluded. Sound pieces of literature, properly cut or arranged for presentation, are highly desirable.

3. *Cut the selection (if necessary).*

Most selections of prose and drama require cutting for contest use. A short series of rules of thumb [4] for dramatic materials includes:

a. Choose a focal point for your selection: a central character, one thread of plot, central plot and chief character.
b. Do not try to represent too many characters; it is difficult to handle dialogue with more than two people.
c. Use the characters' names more frequently than the playwright does.
d. "Place" characters in a play-reading by direction of eyes and head, but keep the range of reading within the "angle of the audience."
e. Make your stage directions few and simple.

[4] Patricia Lewis, "May I Cut?" *Masque and Gavel*, III, No. 2 (October, 1942), 8–10.

f. Have an excellent introduction which will set the scene and establish the mood for the reader and the audience.

Many other detailed rules for cutting may be found.[5] It takes skill and some experience to cut effectively.

4. *Analyze the selection carefully.*

For sound analysis of the selection refer to the scheme by Lee, cited earlier. In addition, be sure that the analysis includes a thorough study of the author, his reasons for writing, the conditions that produced the selection that has been chosen, and other related matters. Further analysis must be made of the intellectual or thought content of the piece, as well as the mood and emotional content it contains. The purpose, theme, mood, ideas, and development should belong to the student after such an analysis, and he should be able to tell the story of the selection or relate its principal events readily in his own words.

5. *Read the selection aloud several times, checking the pronunciation of words, articulation, use of voice to convey ideas, emotion, and so on.*

These readings help to call attention to the total effect desired and enable the interpreter to work also on parts of the selection needing particular pointing and attention.

6. *Synthesize (or memorize) the selection.*

In the case of an interpretative reading from the book, this step stresses the development of unity in performance in terms of the emotional and intellectual content. It enables the reader to note his use of techniques in achieving the effects the author intended, which the reader is seeking to develop.

If the selection is to be memorized for declamation or an interpretation requiring memorization, he should be sure to gain complete mastery of his content by his method of committing it to memory. The *whole* method is superior to the *part* method. A combination of reading aloud, recall, and rereading produce good

---

[5] Anne Louise Hirt, *A Handbook of Declamation* (Minneapolis: The Northwestern Press, 1938).

results. Memorizing aloud helps build the desired associations and habits for performance. Frequent, shorter practice periods are better than long periods.

7. *Develop appropriate action, integrating it with voice, through practice.*

The visible aspects of interpretation must be combined with the audible or vocal presentation. So smoothly and appropriately should these be integrated that a single, total effect is achieved.

8. *Use the tape recorder or other recording devices to polish delivery.*

To give the reader a full appreciation of the effects of his performance and possible needed changes, the tape recorder is helpful for playback and listening in preparation. With this device both teacher and student can observe details that can be improved to get the exact vocal effects desired.

9. *Practice before real audiences and under contest conditions.*

In preparing for festival or contest, it is usually helpful to have numerous experiences similar to those that will be met later. Classroom or public audiences with conditions as nearly like those of the contest will provide "seasoning" for declaimers or interpretative readers.

TEACHING GROUP FORMS OF INTERPRETATION

Choric Interpretation

In choric interpretation more than one person interprets the same piece of literature at the same time. This group form dates from the time of its use in the drama of ancient Greece. In recent years it has been very popular in Great Britain and has become an interesting activity in the interpretation field in the United States. Its chief use is for the oral interpretation of poetry. The basic values in this type are the same as those mentioned above for individual work in interpretation. In addition, it is particularly valuable as a method of helping students to gain emotional adjustment.

Two plans are in use for directing choric interpretation: (1) the teacher directing as he would a choir; (2) the teacher out of the picture, giving only starting and incidental direction from a place in the front row of the audience. The latter seems preferable for the average high school or college group.

A group of thirty is a good working size. In organizing a group, voices are either auditioned individually and classified as *light, dark,* and *middle,* with resonance being a more important criterion than pitch or quality alone, or they may be observed in the group by the instructor and then classified. Such classification is important to grouping voices for reading according to the parts indicated in the literature chosen to be read. Semicircular and wedge-shaped formations of the group may be used to facilitate directing and to obtain effects.

In selecting poems for choric interpretation these criteria are important: strong, compelling rhythm; vivid, striking rhythm; variation and contrast in mood or thought or both.

Two principal methods of preparation are used. In the first, the teacher explains the poem, reads it aloud, has the students respond rhythmically, reads it line by line or section by section with students repeating, and continues until the desired interpretation is secured. In the second, a developmental method is employed with steps very similar to those above for individual interpretation: analysis, understanding, and oral practice in which the final product is evolved through a synthesis of pupil and teacher effort and discussion. In each case the teacher prepares a desired arrangement and assigns voices to specific parts of the selection.

Choric interpretation programs afford good possibilities for convocations and assemblies presenting the poetry of selected authors; for Thanksgiving, Christmas, Easter, Armed Forces Day, and other special occasions; and for cooperative programs with English, modern language, and social studies departments. As an interscholastic activity, choric interpretation festivals are held in connection with annual speech meets, or are sometimes developed as invitational events. In the second case, the project in choric interpretation serves as a culminating number after various individual activities have been held. Eastern Illinois University at Charleston, Illinois, has conducted such a program since 1949, utilizing between three and four hundred students.

Reader's Theater

In reader's theater individual techniques of interpretation are adapted to present a work of literature so that each performer in the group interprets only one role. Types of literature used are drama, narrative fiction with considerable dialogue, and dramatic poetry. Reader's theater differs from acting and from chamber theater in that the characters and situations are merely *suggested* by the readers. It does not depend upon a narrator nor upon specific action.

The language of the play, the voices of the interpreters, and the action they suggest carry the reading. Thus, literature chosen should have exceptional dialogue. Readers should be selected for their interpretative skill if public performance is a goal. In a learning situation in class, however, reader's theater can serve as a training vehicle for a group, thus using a number of students at the same time.

Scripts are prepared and usually placed in dark notebook covers in order not to distract the audience as pages are turned. Properties are not ordinarily used extensively. However, reading stands for scripts and high stools for placing characters have become somewhat standard equipment. Costumes, as such, are not needed, but the dress should suggest the character. The color of the dress is also important as an aid to mood or feeling. Straight make-up is sufficient.

The placement of characters on the stage is important. The central character is placed in a position where he will have the center of attention. He may be seated on a stool denoting that he is above two characters on either side of him. He may be placed between two characters less important than he is. In reading, the characters may "play" to one another as they are located on the stage. However, another somewhat more effective method is to have each character, as he speaks, direct his attention to the others as though they were in the audience. Their apparent location will be in a place projected along a line directly in front of their position on the platform. Thus each reader speaks to the audience, yet locates the other character addressed by the direction and place he indicates by his voice and action.

The other characters respond in the same way. Thus, in the diagram, I speaks to II, placing him in a particular location. Then II responds to I, placing him suitably in his location.

Reader's theater has many advantages to offer high schools and colleges. It is a simple, quick method of doing a play. It can employ a number of readers at a single time. It can be run on low budget; no sets or costumes are needed. It can be done in class, for public performance, or as a part of a state program in interpretation, such as the play-reading event in Wisconsin. The time needed for re-

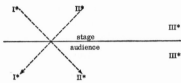

hearsal need not be as long as that for a full-length play. However, for good work, rehearsal time should approximate that of a regular production.

Chamber Theater

This experimental form of group interpretation has been developed and presented in class, for public performance, and over television by Robert Breen of Northwestern University. It involves the presentation of nondramatic prose literature (novel or short story) in dramatic form. The narrative elements are not sacrificed, and full advantage is taken of the use of theatrical devices, such as costumes, properties, scenery, and make-up.

Chamber theater uses two methods of telling a story, those of prose narrative fiction and dramatic fiction. Although these two forms have the same general elements of a character, in action, in a setting, each has distinct advantages. Drama has an advantage over the novel in the immediacy or simultaneity of the action. On the stage the action can be complex, yet it can happen in a moment. In a novel, things happen serially, or one after another, as the author relates them. However, its advantage lies in its ability to explore the inner motivation of an actor at the moment of action. Chamber theater uses both these advantages: (1) immediacy or simultaneity of action, and (2) the exploration of the inner motivation of a character at the moment of action.

In this medium the inner motivation is usually explored by a narrator. At the same time that he reveals the motives, the actor speaks and moves with the illusion of immediacy. The narrator can be used much as a conductor of an orchestra might be employed—to guide or control the situation. He may thus be both actor and commentator, as conditions require. The audience benefits from his commentary, but also sees him *and* the image he brings to its attention.

In the experimental work of chamber theater one must be willing to give up conventions and be content with verbal presentations.

The life of this form is in words, or language.

In producing chamber theater these suggestions are made:

1. Select a short story or novel that can be produced effectively in this form.
2. Read it carefully and decide the role of the narrator.
   a. Is he omniscient, knowing and seeing *all?*
   b. Is he a subjective observer?
   c. Is he an objective observer?
   d. What is his relationship to the other characters?
3. Allocate lines and organize the text.
   a. In general, cut or shorten descriptive passages. However, avoid drastic cuts unless the action can be performed by the actors.
   b. Do not cut the key moments.
   c. Do not cut the climax.
   d. Remember that the organization of events highlights the story and rearrangement should be kept at a minimum.
   e. Cut "He saids," and the like, when necessary.
   f. An actor may take his own narration; he may speak of himself; he may address the audience; he may speak directly to the narrator.
   g. In allocating lines, the balanced sentence may be used effectively, e.g., "It seemed that" (narrator says) "nothing mattered" (actor says).
4. Type the final product as you would a play.
5. Decide upon costumes, properties, scenery, make-up, and other needed items.
6. Cast the show and block the action. Give particular attention to the narrator.
7. Rehearse the show and produce it.

Since there are no set rules for chamber theater, and it is an experimental form of interpretation, the success of the production will depend largely upon the skill, taste, and ingenuity of the director.

EXERCISES

1. Compile a list of suitable selections for an interpretation festival, placing each selection under its proper form or type of interpretation.
2. Indicate the standards you would use for selecting material for interpretation in a high school or college class.
3. Discuss the practicality of incorporating choric interpretation, reader's theater, and chamber theater in the high school speech program and justify your statements.

REFERENCES

AGGERTT, OLIS J., and ELBERT R. BOWEN. *Communicative Reading*. New York: The Macmillan Co., 1956.

COBIN, MARTIN. "Utilizing Television in the Interpretation Program," *Speech Teacher*, VIII (January, 1959), 31–37.

———. *Theory and Technique of Interpretation*. Englewood Cliffs, N. J.: Prentice-Hall, Inc., 1960.

CROCKER, LIONEL, and LOUIS M. EICH. *Oral Reading*. Englewood Cliffs, N. J.: Prentice-Hall, Inc., 1955.

CUNNINGHAM, CORNELIUS C. *Making Words Come Alive*. Dubuque, Iowa: William C. Brown Co., 1951.

GILBERT, EDNA. "Oral Interpretation at Speech Festivals," *Speech Teacher*, V (March, 1956), 117–21.

GRIMES, WILMA. "Paperbacks: The Teacher's Friend: III. Oral Interpretation of Literature," *Speech Teacher* V (January, 1956), 34–36.

———. "Oral Reading Activities in Colleges and Universities," *Speech Teacher* VII (November, 1958), 332–36.

———, and ALETHEA MATTINGLY. *Interpretation: Writer-Reader-Audience*. Belmont, Calif.: Wadsworth Publishing Co., Inc., 1961.

GULLAN, MARJORIE. *The Speech Choir: With American Poetry and English Ballads for Choral Reading*. New York: Harper & Bros., 1937.

HAMM, AGNES. *Choral Speaking Technique*. Milwaukee, Wis.: Tower Press, 1951.

HEDDE, WILHELMINA G., and W. NORWOOD BRIGANCE. *The New American Speech*. Philadelphia; J. B. Lippincott Co., 1957. Chaps. XV–XVII.

HENNEKE, BENJAMIN. *Reading Aloud Effectively*. New York: Rinehart & Co., 1954.

HUNSINGER, PAUL. "Festivals and Changing Patterns," *Speech Teacher,* VII (March, 1958), 93–99.

IRWIN, JOHN V., and MARJORIE ROSENBERGER. *Modern Speech.* New York: Holt, Rinehart, and Winston, Inc., 1961. Chaps. XIX, XX.

LAUGHTON, CHARLES. *Tell Me a Story.* New York: McGraw-Hill Book Co., Inc. 1957.

LEE, CHARLOTTE. *Oral Interpretation.* Boston: Houghton Mifflin Co., 1959.

LOWREY, SARA, and GERTRUDE JOHNSON. *Interpretative Reading.* New York: Appleton-Century-Crofts, Inc., 1953.

PARRISH, WAYLAND MAXFIELD. *Reading Aloud.* New York: Ronald Press, 1953.

WOOLBERT, CHARLES H., and SEVERINA E. NELSON. *The Art of Interpretative Speech.* New York: Appleton-Century-Crofts, Inc., 1956.

CHAPTER TWENTY-THREE

Theater

Theater is probably the oldest and most universally practiced form of speech training. Its origins date to the earliest dramatic forms, not only in the United States, but all the way back to the most ancient civilizations. Today nearly every high school and college has some activity in this field.

In the secondary school, Wallace Smith, Evanston (Illinois) Township High School, a leader in the Secondary School Theatre Conference observes:

I would estimate that of the 30,000 high schools in the nation, 25,000 have some sort of drama program. They are the largest producing group in the world, doing close to 75,000 plays a year.

The nationwide problem at this time, however, lies not in the number of schools doing theatre, but in the attitude of some educators. They believe that theatre is not worthwhile study and that "any English teacher can do it." They believe they have a drama program when somebody coaches a couple of plays a year. The problem is one of *upgrading the work and setting worthy goals to be accomplished by secondary school theatre,* not in getting schools to do plays.

Under pressure from "hard-core" subjects, it is up to well-trained, professionally skilled teachers to do something about this. It cannot be done until there are enough such competent teachers available. There will not be enough of those persons until there are jobs for them. At present about 1200 high school teachers belong to the Secondary School Theatre Conference.

It is the purpose of this organization to establish goals and standards for drama programs and teachers, to integrate them with forward-looking educational ideals, and to encourage the growth of good programs in theatre.

The important role of theater in modern education is clearly supported by the recommendations of the 1960 White House Conference on Children and Youth. Here eight thousand participants gathered to discuss every facet of life affecting young people. These leaders, representing six hundred national organizations, deliberated upon the means by which youth might best be helped "to realize their full potential for a creative life in freedom and dignity." Twenty-one of the final Conference recommendations apply directly or indirectly to education through theater.

Richard Johnson, representative of the American Educational Theatre Association, reports solid endorsement for those specific recommendations:

1. Every child should be given an opportunity to participate in creative dramatics under the guidance of qualified leadership for a basic understanding and critical appreciation of the theatre arts, and as an adjunct to constructive learning.
2. Young people should be given an opportunity to participate in dramatic production under direction of qualified leaders to acquire the emotional and intellectual disciplines inherent in the theatre arts.
3. Colleges and universities should give special attention to:
   a. Creative writing in the dramatic form, stressing the production of quality scripts for new plays and films.
   b. The training of qualified leaders in creative dramatics, theatre arts, and film production.
   c. Touring dramatic productions of high quality to school and community theatre.

Other recommendations called for building more theatres, improving the literary value of material used in dramatic activities of children and youth, launching programs of drama appreciation in schools and religious institutions, placing a greater emphasis on truth and artistry in productions, upgrading the content and performance of radio and television programs for children and youth, making greater use of mass media to disseminate critiques on films and plays, seeking greater public support for good quality high school and college theatre, expanding community theatre efforts to permit children and youth to share and develop their talents, and engaging in more research to determine the impact of theatre on children and youth and how it can be used to develop talents, character and responsibility.[1]

[1] See Richard Johnson, "The White House Conference on Children and Youth," *Educational Theatre Journal* (October, 1960), p. 12.

At present a working committee of the AETA [2] is completing a revised curriculum guide on theater for secondary schools, based upon these recommendations.

Wide scope and continued growth in theater at the college level are indicated by over two thousand theater programs in colleges and universities in the United States, with an estimated ten thousand students enrolled as majors in drama programs. In addition, the Children's Theatre Conference reports nearly two hundred and fifty institutions offering training in creative drama and children's theater to aid a rapidly expanding program in children's theater and community theater.

The tremendous scope of the educational theater work in this country indicates that this agency stands as the foremost means to bring live plays from the world of good dramatic literature to audiences of children and adults. Teachers of theater therefore have a serious and immense responsibility to compete with commercial theater, radio, television, and the films for the minds and energies of their students. Productive experiences as participants in the presenting of plays and rewarding opportunities as audiences should carry over throughout life for students of the drama.

There are stimulating goals for such programs.

GOALS AND VALUES

These objectives can be established from three points of view: the school, the community, and the student.

School Goals

A drama program concerns and affects the entire school. Every student and teacher is a potential participant, either as a part of the production or as a member of the audience. These goals are therefore very relevant:

[2] Committee members include Robert Teeter (Chairman), J. Sterling Morton High School, Cicero, Ill.; Wallace Smith, Evanston Township High School, Evanston, Ill.; Winifred Gahagan, New Trier Township High School, Winnetka, Ill.; Richard C. Johnson, Barrington High School, Barrington, Ill.; Nicholas Wandmacher, Roslyn Heights High School, Roslyn Heights, Long Island, N. Y.; Laurence Olvin, High School of Performing Arts, New York, N. Y.; and Margaret A. Nielsen, North High School, Omaha, Neb.

1. To develop an appreciation and understanding of the theater.
2. To teach standards and skills in evaluating the areas of modern entertainment.
3. To develop a broader aesthetic and cultural background.
4. To integrate and increase the effectiveness of other courses, such as English and history.
5. To provide a means of public relations with parents and others in the community.
6. To give the school publicity and prestige.
7. To raise money for school purposes.

Community Goals

In many communities, the school is the center of numerous activities, educational, social, recreational, and others. The drama program fits solidly into this pattern, especially when three of its goals are:

1. To provide entertainment and recreation.
2. To provide cultural experiences for the community.
3. To share educational achievement with the community.

Student Goals

The goals influencing the experiences of the students are those most commonly considered. They can be classified as those contributing to the general education of the student and those specifically related to theater participation:

1. *General*
   a. To develop an appreciation of the drama as literature, and the elements of acting and production as fine arts.
   b. To contribute to developing basic skills in oral communication.
   c. To help integrate the student's personality so that he can more successfully adjust to his environment through increased cooperation, maturity, judgment, poise, understanding, initiative, and leadership.
   d. To develop creativity.
   e. To enrich the cultural background.
   f. To develop a better understanding of people.
   g. To develop standards and skill in evaluating drama and other forms of cultural entertainment.

2. *Specific*
   a. To know the history of the theater.
   b. To learn standards, criteria, and methods of dramatic criticism.
   c. To understand the work of the playwright and the structure of plays.
   d. To gain skill in developing and projecting a character.
   e. To gain understanding and skill in directing.
   f. To learn the technical skills of backstage production: scenery, lighting, properties, costume, and make-up.
   g. To become aware of good financial and business practice in running a production: publicity, ticket sale, box office, budget, and the like.

FACILITIES AND EQUIPMENT

In an earlier chapter the question of facilities for a speech program has been discussed. Facilities for a drama program vary widely, from a serviceable space for acting to a full-scale little theater with every modern piece of equipment known to the professional theater. Almost every school has its own pattern, determined by needs, budget, educational philosophy, size of the school and community, and the type of program in theater that is conducted.

For specialized equipment, design, and detailed treatment of the question, the teacher should consult authoritative references or experts on the subject.

Some general suggestions follow:

1. *Stage:* Width about 32 feet by 16 feet in height with space above to fly scenery; depth sufficient to allow adequate playing space and room behind a unit set; a fire curtain, just behind the proscenium; a drop or draw act curtain; a painted back wall, sky drop, or curtain across the back of the stage; tormentors to change width of proscenium; teasers to change height of arch; a grid rail to hold pulleys to which drops are attached, and pin rails; a counterweight system, if possible; a sound block or turntable setup for sound effects; sufficient seating space arranged to give desirable sight lines to stage; proper acoustics in the auditorium.
2. *Lighting Equipment.* A modern control board with plenty of

flexibility; six to twelve spotlights, about half mounted in the auditorium with others in the teaser position; three to six others with either floor or hanging mountings or both; two floodlights, olivette type; two floodlights suspended from battens; two six-foot border light sections, hanging mountings; gelatins and similar transparencies for color effects; lamps as needed.

3. *Scene Shop:* Space in same building and close to stage if possible; racks for storing flats and lumber; tool storage with locking facilities; place for mixing and storing paints; hot and cold running water and a large sink; gas plate for heating glue; windows and good lighting equipment; good supply of hand tools; as many power tools as possible: saws, drills, sander, etc.; paints as needed; brushes, rollers, pails, etc.; hardware, nails, screws, racks; unbleached muslin.

4. *Costume Shop:* (A sewing room can sometimes be used.) Storage space for costumes: wardrobes, shelves, boxes; location close to dressing rooms; basic sewing equipment: electric sewing machine, needles, thread, scissors, pins, materials; cutting table with patterns, etc.

5. *Dressing Rooms:* Location close to stage and near costume room; facilities for men and women; mirrors, chairs; racks and hangers for clothes; if possible, a sink with running water.

6. *Make-up Room:* Separate facilities for boys and girls if possible; proper lighting, light over each mirror; adequate mirror and chair space; cabinets for make-up supplies; complete make-up kits with various shades of bases, powders, lipsticks, rouges, eye make-up; cleansing creams and tissues.

7. *Properties' Shop or Room:* Basic pieces of furniture for stage, preferably owned by school: two or three easy chairs, a davenport, a number of tables, a rug that fits the stage, lamps, etc.; other pieces or special furnishings for period plays obtainable on loan; storage space with shelves, cupboards, containers, etc.

ORGANIZING THE PROGRAM

School programs in theater may be organized around a course or department pattern that allows a great proportion of the work to be done in a classroom situation and on school time, or under a cocurricular arrangement, in which the bulk of teaching and production is done through a workshop or club organization on after-school time. In many situations a combination of these two plans is in operation, with theory and laboratories done in a curricular scheme, but the principal rehearsals and crew activity taking place in the after-school period.

Organized Courses and Departments

The most direct and specific way of carrying out the goals of a theater program lies in the organization of courses under the instructional staff to teach the exact theory and skills desired. Such an organization exists in schools where the leadership, budget, and facilities allow this pattern. Such a program may be associated erroneously with large schools exclusively. However, many smaller institutions have excellent and quite extensive curricular offerings because of their local conditions.

A great number of courses is not essential if the planning and treatment of the materials is thorough and comprehensive. The series of unit headings below, suggested by the American Educational Theatre Association, can be taught as individual courses or as parts of longer courses.

Units in Theater

  I. Exploring the Field; investigating the Broad Field of the Theater
 II. History of the Theater
    A. The Greek Period
    B. The Roman Period
    C. Middle Ages
    D. Elizabethan Period
    E. Restoration and Eighteenth-Century Period
    F. Nineteenth-Century Theater
    G. Twentieth-Century Theater
 III. The Play
    A. Dramatic Forms
    B. Structure of the Play
    C. Evaluation of a Play in Production
 IV. The Actor
    A. Fundamentals of Acting

B. Characterization
C. Bodily Action
D. Voice
V. The Director
  A. Play Analysis
  B. Cutting and Adapting a Play
  C. Blocking a Play
  D. Tryouts
  E. Conferences on Production Details and Business
  F. Rehearsals
VI. The Technician
  A. Backstage and Front-Office Organization
  B. Scene Design
  C. Lighting
  D. Stagecraft
  E. Costumes
  F. Make-up
  G. Properties
VII. The Critic and the Audience's Reaction
  A. Criteria for Evaluating Drama
  B. Standards for Criticism
  C. Methods of the Critic

Drama Club or Workshop

Concept and Purpose

The drama club should be the vehicle for organizing dramatic activities in the school, not merely a means of promoting the abilities of the selected few. It should combine two broad functions: (1) the provision of a stimulating drama program for the school, and (2) the development and recognition of achievement by the students who participate. Detailed purposes are discussed in the next section.

The club should allow membership on a wide basis. Chief criteria for membership might include interest; satisfactory personal qualities of cooperativeness, compatibility, integrity, reliability, initiative, and hard work; and demonstrated ability in some phase of the work of the theater. The use of the tryout as the *sole* method of admitting members should be discouraged. Instead or in addition, a system of *active* members and *apprentice* members can be established. The first group might include those persons who have demonstrated a sincere interest, those who have made a service contribution to the club, or those who have given a performance of acceptable quality. The second group might include those persons selected for their interest and personal qualities, but who have yet to demonstrate that they are suitable for active membership.

A point system based on activity could determine this promotion to full status. In this way the organization could admit a larger number of students, those with a wide variety of interests in the field of the drama. With a large membership, the club would be in a position to offer an extensive school service program in theater, at the same time providing training for its members. Recognition of achievement in the field could be accomplished in high school by means of a point-credit system such as the National Thespian Society employs. Certificates, pins, copies of books on acting and play production, and collections of dramatic literature could be used as awards.

The Training Program

One of the major functions of such a club is to train students not just in acting but in all the various areas of the dramatic arts. Such a training program could include all the units under the headings for the courses listed earlier. The club or workshop organization permits students to gain information and practical experience in all areas during their years in school. The major ways of providing such experience include (1) club meetings; (2) performance; (3) observation.

Club Meetings

Club meetings offer many opportunities for study. Sample types of meetings are:

1. Talks or lectures by the sponsor or members on the history of the theater. Slides, film strips, and flat pictures can be used.
2. A panel discussion criticizing a contemporary play or motion picture.
3. A play-reading by a member or a teacher.
4. A guest speaker reviewing plays seen in New York, Chicago, San Francisco, and elsewhere.
5. A film version of a stage success, e.g., *The Glass Menagerie, Hamlet,* or some other.

6. A movie meeting in which the whole club attends a current film of high quality.
7. A similar meeting in which a good film is shown in the school.
8. Transcriptions or recordings of scenes from plays.
9. A talk on costumes with colored slides of a particular period (related to a play to be done by the club).
10. A small group play-reading session in which all participate, each group handling and studying a different play.
11. A demonstration of make-up.
12. A talk by a former or contemporary actor on the profession, its possibilities and difficulties.
13. A lecture-demonstration of the principles of acting.
14. Individual characterizations by members, the sponsor, or guests.
15. Performance of short plays or scenes.
16. A demonstration of the principles of stage lighting.
17. Explanation of blocking and preparation of a prompt book.
18. Demonstration of scene design, painting, properties, arrangement of stage furniture, and so on.
19. A lecture or discussion on directing: its importance, methods, and other aspects.
20. Costume or dress-up session in which each person comes, dressed, made up, and in the character of a role from some play that has been studied.
21. Quiz program on stage terminology, plays, actors, and other pertinent topics.
22. Lecture by a script writer, playwright, scenario writer.
23. Planning session for special dramatic program; creative assembly work, original play writing.
24. Sound effects in the theater: a demonstration and lecture on the use of transcribed and manual effects.

It will be noted that these program suggestions sample every one of the areas in theater that were listed above. It is quite possible to use this kind of program for teaching information, principles, and techniques, as well as for the enjoyment of the club members. It represents a considerable contrast to the club meeting that uses only the performance of some scene from a long play or a one-act as the program to be given. With planning, a series of very rich and broadening experiences in dramatic arts can be presented in the regular club meetings.

Every club will have its own special goals and emphases. Perhaps it may be more beneficial and educational for the club to use its regular meeting time for rehearsal, building and painting, solving of lighting problems, or the planning of publicity for a show to be presented for the school or for a community audience. The sponsor and the students must decide how they wish to spend the time when the group assembles.

Performance

Acting performance is the goal of a great many of the members of every drama club. There are always some, however, who would rather putter with lights until they secure the most serviceable and beautiful stage illumination their equipment will permit. Such an accomplishment is a performance of a very high order for them. Others may love the smell of grease paint and enjoy doing a fine make-up job. Still others may gain great personal satisfaction from designing a set, furnishing the stage, and making a beautiful, highly accurate stage picture. This achievement is the thing they seek most.

The drama club offers a splendid opportunity to combine all the elements of theatrical performance in a direct educational experience for everyone in the organization. The study of plays of high literary quality; the selection of one as a suitable vehicle for the group; the analysis of the plot; the conflicts, the motives underlying the action of the characters; the planning and building of a setting; securing properties, costumes, and lighting the stage; the training of the actors; and the eager expectation of the response of the audience— all these things constitute an example of "learning by doing" which is unique in modern secondary education. Any single show can provide a rich educational experience for everyone who is part of it. Thus, a drama club can give *many* pupils the opportunity to do a great variety of things in theater. Through this training can be developed nuclei of students who can act, run lights, build scenery, get properties, handle the make-up, organize the publicity and ticket sales so that any production attempted can, in time, be staffed with competent personnel. Some students may be more skilled or talented in one area than in another. This does not mean that such individuals should play all of the leads, or always get properties. Club membership necessitates that they learn the whole field, as well as one specialization.

One-Act Plays or Cuttings from Longer Plays

One of the most popular vehicles for drama-club productions is the one-act play or the cutting. Because of short playing time, the need for fewer rehearsals, and the wide variety of plays that can be staged with relative simplicity, they are widely used. It is also possible to have several plays of this type in preparation at one time; the director can do much to block out the action for each cast and begin rehearsals; then the actors go to work under the student director. Periodic checks and rehearsals with the club sponsor can point up the plays before performance. This method enables more students to act; it may not produce the highest quality of performance. Plays prepared in this way can be given for club meetings. The one-acts given for the club can also be presented for assemblies, for noon-hour shows, for parent-teacher meetings, and for other kinds of community service programs.

For public performance it is important for the group to give a piece of superior workmanship. Neither the director nor the students can afford to present a shabby performance in public.

The One-Act Play and the Drama Festival

Clubs in many schools prepare plays for drama festivals. The festivals have grown in popularity because of the general educational values they are able to contribute to the motivation and training of students in drama. Through the careful evaluation by experts in drama of the plays entered by various schools, students receive many valuable suggestions. The festival also gives club members a chance to see many plays given by other schools, to observe the way they do the job, and thus gain by the experience. The motivation of a trip to a festival is also an excellent means of consolidating interest among the members of a drama organization.

Three-Act Plays

Drama clubs often present full-length plays, depending upon the situation. Such ventures are a real challenge and an opportunity for many performance activities by club members. Essential steps in production are the same as those for a one-act show. The details of the scheme vary considerably, however, and can be found in books on play production, as well as in a number of the texts on dramatics for the secondary school.

PRODUCING A PLAY

Choosing the Play

Whether one selects a short play for a festival or a three-act play for public performance, the choice of a play is very important to the director and the actors. In preparation, all persons should read widely among available plays. Certain standards recommended by the AETA may be helpful, particularly for secondary school plays:

1. It should be worth doing, have a suitable theme, and be sincere in its interpretation of life and accurate in its reflection of customs and manners.
2. It should have real literary value. That is, it should be written in acceptable language and in accordance with accepted standards of playwriting. As such it should be emotionally and intellectually stimulating.
3. It should be within the capacities of the student to understand and appreciate.
4. It should challenge the highest creative and artistic abilities of all who are associated with it in production and afford rich opportunities for study.
5. It should be good theater, affording opportunities for sincere acting, and be satisfying as entertainment.
6. It should be free from highly sophisticated or advanced roles, vulgarity or profanity, objectionable subject matter, and sordid and unwholesome presentations of characters and scenes.

There are certain other factors to consider in selecting a play:

1. Is the play adaptable to the physical equipment of the school in which it will be produced?
2. Does it meet the possibilities of the students available for casting? (Number of men, women? Abilities? Experience, etc.?
3. Does it make unreasonable demands upon the budget? Royalty costs, costumes, scenery, lighting, special effects? On the other

hand, does it take its proportionate share of the budget, thereby helping to give good theater to the school?

4. Does it fit in with the other plays that have preceded it or will follow it, giving balance and variety to the program?
5. As a drama project, does the play afford opportunities for participation to a considerable number of students?
6. Does the play come within the interests and qualifications of the faculty members upon whom the responsibility for producing it is placed?

Standards and influencing factors for college plays will vary somewhat from those for secondary school. They may permit more sophisticated or difficult material, greater complexity in staging, costuming, and other technical aspects, depending upon the school involved.

Casting the Play

Each director has or develops his own system of casting. He may use materials from the play he plans to do, similar lines from other dramatic literature, or a combination of both. He may require prepared reading or on-the-spot reading; he may introduce pantomime —prepared or impromptu; he may utilize interviews, data sheets, or other record forms. Here are some suggestions useful in the job of casting:

1. Make copies of the play available for prospective actors. Scripts can be read at school or checked out overnight.
2. Prepare tryout materials from the scripts to be used in the play. These will not be distributed until actual tryout time.
3. Post well in advance the dates, hours, and location of tryouts.
4. Publicize them well, especially if they are *open* tryouts for a whole school or large group. If they are *closed,* be sure that the eligible persons are notified or invited well in advance. The first method is used most frequently in high schools.
5. At the meetings: (a) have all persons reporting fill in information cards; (b) make perfectly clear the nature of the tryouts and the procedure to be followed.
6. Conduct readings by having students first volunteer to read parts they desire from the scenes prepared.

7. Request them to read other parts if it will help the director in casting.
8. After the first round, recall those desired for checking or confirmation of their voices, appearance, and talent or to help decide "close" cases.
9. In selecting characters, cast them for the best part each can do and also make the strongest contribution to the production.
10. Announce the entire cast at once by posting the list and set the first meeting for the group.
11. Hold the first meeting, explain the play, discuss the rehearsal schedule, and work out problems or conflicts.
12. Set the full rehearsal schedule with dates, hours, location, scenes, and characters. Leave space for extra calls.
13. In secondary schools, especially, it may be wise to use a rehearsal contract, signed by the teacher and the student to insure mutual agreement.
14. Also, it is an effective practice to write letters to the parents, clarifying the nature of the project, the schedule, and amount of time involved for both the director and the students.

Organizing Crews and Committees

Every play needs complete and careful organization. There is no place for careless, slipshod operation, taking useless time and energy and disrupting school, class, or student schedules. Such an organization consists of all the personnel needed to aid the faculty director in doing an efficient job. Some schools make extensive use of faculty committees or faculty committee heads; others place all responsibilities upon the students. Following are listed the key points in such an organization. All are responsible to the director:

1. The assistant director
2. The stage manager
3. The technical head
4. Stage crews: scenery, properties, costumes, lights, make-up, sound
5. Finance: (a) expenditures for royalty, scenery, costumes
            (b) income from tickets, advertising, school funds
6. Ticket sale, publicity
7. Program: cast list; credits; advertising
8. House: manager and ushers

The specific duties of each of these groups can be developed in detail by the director and will be found in specialized texts on the theater.

Preparing Scripts

In all probability the director will have marked his script before tryouts. He should next prepare the actors' scripts. This is done with the cast in a rehearsal session in which the characters and director run through the entire script, making changes as indicated with appropriate notations for business, etc. The prompter's script can also be done at this time. Unless the lighting problems are difficult, the technicians for the show can also be present to prepare their lighting and sound scripts.

Rehearsing the Play

The first meeting (already mentioned) has been described as a "mark-up" session. At this rehearsal the director also prepares the cast for the work they are to do. He should explain the essential requirements of promptness, regular attendance, and a businesslike attitude in rehearsal. He should stress the need for an early and complete knowledge of lines. He should point out the need for careful study of the character and the development of all the little things so necessary for a polished performance. He should emphasize the importance of timing in giving lines, in picking up cues, and in action. He should explain the importance of good thinking, flexibility, and resourcefulness on the part of the actor when he is on the stage.

After giving such fundamental directions as these, the director usually reads through the play with the cast so that they will get the total picture. Having done this, he can announce his next rehearsal, the schedule he has prepared, and the deadline on line memorization (usually no scripts after the third rehearsal on average one-acts).

In setting up any rehearsal schedule, the director should plan more than enough meetings for developing the kind of performance he wishes to achieve. It is always easier to eliminate rehearsals than to add them. Such a practice also enables the cast to plan their time so that they can be present at all rehearsals. The schedule may include a number of scene rehearsals for certain characters who will need special work on those sections of the play.

If there are certain important sound effects, music, or special lighting effects, it will be advisable to hold special rehearsals in which these details are carefully planned, cued in, and practiced so that they are absolutely smooth. Ordinarily, two such rehearsals are sufficient, plus one with costumes for achieving the desired results.

Dress rehearsals of complete casts and crews with all details complete should become an established routine in preparing for festival plays. These should be run through without interruption; criticism and suggestions should be given at the conclusion of the performance. If the play is to be given away from home, some minor adaptations may have to be made.

If possible, the director should hold a rehearsal on the stage of the festival theater. This may be dress or not, but it is a valuable insurance against any surprises brought about by the new situation, especially in voice, movement or business, and position of the characters on the stage.

REHEARSAL SCHEDULE FOR THREE-ACT PLAY FOR HIGH SCHOOL

The play: *Our Town* by Thornton Wilder

I. Rehearsals one through six to be spent on character.
    A. First two spent in reading the play and discussion of the play itself and the characters.
    B. Discuss visual appearance of the characters; also walk, setting, and manner. Practice these and begin to incorporate them with lines.
    C. Last three meetings spent on line interpretation. By this time the director should know which scenes are more difficult and which are easier. He should begin work on the more difficult ones first.

II. Rehearsals seven through twelve to be spent on blocking.
    A. The seventh rehearsal to be spent on blocking Act I.
    B. The eighth rehearsal—repeat Act I and begin blocking Act II.
    C. The ninth rehearsal—finish Act II and repeat it.
    D. The tenth rehearsal—finish first two acts; polish rough spots.
    E. The eleventh rehearsal—block Act III.
    F. The twelfth rehearsal—repeat Act III.

III. Rehearsals thirteen through fifteen to be spent on stage business.
   A. Lines should be memorized and props should be available. Such scenery as is necessary to this play should now be on stage.
   Rehearse Act I.
   B. The fourteenth rehearsal—Act II.
   C. The fifteenth rehearsal—Act III.
   Business should include that which is inherent in the play, character business, and anything else that might be used effectively.

IV. Rehearsals sixteen through eighteen to be spent on articulation and projection.
   A. Sixteenth rehearsal—Acts I and II.
   B. Seventeenth rehearsal—Acts II and III.
   C. Eighteenth rehearsal—Act III. Then go back to any weak spots.

V. Rehearsals nineteen through twenty-one to be spent on a complete run-through.
   A. Watch timing.
   B. Watch building and diminishing.
   C. Watch rhythm.
   D. Pull loose ends together.

VI. Twenty-second rehearsal: technical rehearsal.
   A. Final check on costume.
   B. Check props.
   C. Sound effects.
   D. Lights.
   E. Coordinate above with acting.
   F. Smooth over rough spots.

VII. Twenty-third and twenty-fourth rehearsals: Dress.
   A. Let show run through as if in performance—no "cuts."
   B. Criticism at end of each act.
   C. Let crews or a few other people sit out front during twenty-third rehearsal.
   D. Twenty-fourth rehearsal—run through play once. Give a few final instructions and send cast home.

VIII. Performance.

OBSERVATION

No drama-club program is complete without the opportunity for its members to observe dramatic performances in the educational, community, or commercial theater. This statement may be received with some misgivings by teachers in schools that are isolated from those centers in which theatrical possibilities normally exist. Perhaps in such cases, the club program may simply have to suffer from this lack of completeness. However, the experience of seeing professional productions—those done by capable college or community theaters—provides examples of good technique in directing, acting, and staging, which can have a stimulating and direct, practical influence on the work done by high school drama groups. A number of colleges and universities invite high schools in the state to come to their theaters to witness fine productions and to participate in a "drama clinic" which will help them in their programs. If they are approached by letter in advance, box-office managers of shows playing in cities accessible to high school organizations are quick to cooperate in the matter of reserving seats and arranging trips backstage.

Some schools plan weekend or vacation trips to theater centers, such as New York, Chicago, Los Angeles, San Francisco, Miami, New Orleans, or other large cities, depending upon their location. Effective planning combines such visits to the theatre with trips to points of historical interest, museums, and so on. Through travel agencies, railroads or airlines, transportation, meals, lodging, tickets to shows and other scheduled events can be arranged on a tour basis.

Such trips are well supervised by faculty sponsors and are cleared with parents and the administration.

CLUB SPONSORSHIP

After two or three years of successful existence, a drama club should consider applying for membership in the National Thespian Society. Such an affiliation entitles the group to all the services and publications of the Thespian organization and provides a fine working relationship with the other drama clubs and troupes all over the United States.

A Suggested Form of Operation [1]

The plan presented below is one that is in actual operation. The sponsor of the dramatics club, Mr. Blanford Jennings of Clayton (Missouri) High School, states that his organization has been in operation for eighteen years. In a typical year, the club enrolled 235 members from a student body of about seven hundred, and inducted more than fifty members into a troupe of the National Thespian Society in recognition of outstanding service. The bylaws quoted here constitute a plan for the club, which follows the concept and purposes that have been outlined in the previous sections of this chapter.

BY-LAWS

Membership and Advancement

1. Any student, having filled out an application blank and placed it in the hands of the Treasurer together with an enrollment fee of twenty-five cents, is enrolled as an *Apprentice*. To continue membership in the Guild during subsequent school years, the *Apprentice* must either re-enroll, paying the fee, or earn thirty or more points in the Guild. An *Apprentice* has no vote in the Guild and is not eligible to direct one-act plays nor to assist in the direction of three-act plays.

2. Any *Apprentice* earning thirty points or more in the Guild becomes a *Journeyman* and thereby is freed of further fees imposed on *Apprentices* as such.

3. *Any* Journeyman who has earned 120 points or more in the Guild becomes a *Master*.

4. Any *Master* in the Guild may become a *National Thespian* by paying the sum specified for enrollment in that Society and by being regularly initiated.

5. Any *Thespian* who has earned 200 points in the Guild is designated a *Star Thespian*. For each additional hundred points, another star will be awarded up to a maximum of four stars.

[1] Blanford Jennings, "The Dramatics Club," *Bulletin of the National Association of Secondary School Principals*, XXXII, No. 151 (January, 1948), 85–91.

The Point System

6. A. A Point is defined as approximately one hour of work in connection with a school dramatics or stage activity.
    B. Major productions.
        I. Staff:
            1. Chief Usher: 3 points for each performance; Ushers: 2 points for each performance.
            2. Crew Members: 1 to 40 points.
            3. Crew Heads: 10 to 50 points.
            4. Bookholder: 40 to 50 points.
            5. Assistant Director: 40 to 70 points.
        II. Cast:
            Members of the cast may earn from 10 to 70 points in proportion to the length, difficulty, and importance of their parts.
    C. Minor productions: 50 per cent of the points for corresponding work in major productions.
    D. Credits may be increased not to exceed 10 per cent for each performance after the first.

Determination of Points

7. The Director will be advised in assigning the points for any production by the Crew Heads and Assistant Director of the production. The Director's decisions, however, shall be final.

Privileges of Guild Membership

8. A. Any member of the Guild may attend Guild meetings and may take part in productions; may receive instruction in make-up, directing, and other such groups as may be formed; may attend previews of productions when such previews are offered; and may attend free of charge all one-act plays given for the Guild by the Guild.
    B. A *Journeyman* may take part in all elections and may exercise his right to vote in all Guild matters. He is eligible to serve as Director of one-act plays or as Assistant Director of major productions.
    C. A member of National Thespian Troupe 322 will be admitted free, on presentation of his membership card, to any

dramatics production sponsored by the Guild; may work on any crew or committee he wishes provided he places himself under the direction of the Crew Head; may attend any and all rehearsals and other Guild activities. These privileges of *Thespians* do not lapse with the member's graduation.

Finances

9. A. The activities of the Guild shall be financed from enrollment fees, profits from plays, rental or sale of equipment, and any other sources appropriate to its activities.

   B. Should the Guild at any time find itself confronted with such a deficit as might not easily be made up from the above sources, a *pro rata* assessment of the membership may be made after approval by a two-thirds majority of the members voting at any called meeting. (Note: This section has never as yet been invoked. The Guild ordinarily carries a balance of around $300 each year.)

Duties of Officers

10. It shall be the duty of the President to preside over all meetings, appoint committees for the transaction of Guild business, and cooperate with the sponsor in the supervision of Guild activities.

11. It shall be the duty of the Vice-President to assume the duties of the President in the temporary or permanent absence of the latter.

12. It shall be the duty of the Secretary to keep minutes of all meetings, carry on all necessary correspondence, make all required amendments as prescribed by Article VI of the constitution.

13. It shall be the duty of the Recorder to keep the service records of the members up to date and to provide a correct list of the membership on request of the Sponsor or the Principal.

14. It shall be the duty of the Treasurer to receive and care for all revenue of the Guild, to keep a record of receipts and disbursements, and to make a report of the financial condition of the Guild at every called meeting. All vouchers for disbursements must be signed by the Sponsor and the Treasurer.

15. *Apprentices* shall not be eligible to office.

16. Officers for the ensuing year shall be elected at the last called

meeting of the year, and they shall take office at the close of the school year. The term of office shall be one year.

Meetings

17. Meetings shall be called at the President's discretion or on advice of the Sponsor.
18. Members shall be notified of meetings seven days, if possible but in no case less than two days, before the date of a meeting. Two publications in the daily announcements shall be regarded as notification for the purpose of this By-Law, though individual notices shall be sent to members whenever possible.
19. A quorum at any meeting shall consist of a majority of the voting members of the Guild.

Sections 20 and 21 are conventional rules relating to ratifying and amending the bylaws.

EXERCISES

1. Prepare a list of one-act and three-act plays that you consider to be suitable for high school production and set up a chart indicating such important items as plot, setting, type, number of men and women, royalty, publisher, suitability for production, and so on.
2. Select a play for high school presentation and prepare the prompt book for it.
3. Attend a high school play production and write a critical analysis of it, discussing all the elements of production and direction.

REFERENCES

Adix, Vern. *Theatre Stagecraft*. Anchorage, Ky.: Children's Theatre Press, 1956.

Albright, H. D.; W. P. Halstead; and Lee Mitchell. *Principles of Theatre Art*. Boston: Houghton Mifflin Co., 1955.

Barton, Lucy. *Historic Costume for the Stage*. Boston: Walter H. Baker Co., 1938.

Bavely, Ernest. "Dramatic Arts in Secondary Education," *Quarterly Journal of Speech*, XXXII (February, 1946), 40–47.

———. "Play Standards at the High School Level," *Quarterly Journal of Speech*, XXVI (February, 1940), 89–97.

———. "Suggestions for Improving Drama Festivals and Contests, *Quarterly Journal of Speech*, XXVIII (October, 1942), 327–32.

BOLESLAVSKY, RICHARD. *Acting: The First Six Lessons.* New York. Theatre Arts Books, 1949.

BOWMAN, WAYNE. *Modern Theatre Lighting.* New York: Harper & Bros., 1957.

BRADLEY, CAROLYN. *Western World Costume: An Outline History.* New York: Appleton-Century-Crofts, Inc., 1954.

CARTRIGHT, E. S. "Selecting, Casting and Rehearsing the High School Play," *Quarterly Journal of Speech,* XXIX (December, 1943), 443–51.

CHEKHOV, MICHAEL. *To the Actor.* New York: Harper & Bros., 1953.

CORNBERG, SOL, and EMANUEL GEBAUER. *A Stage Crew Handbook.* New York: Harper & Bros., 1957.

CORSON, RICHARD. *Stage Makeup.* New York: Appleton-Century-Crofts, Inc., 1949.

DIETRICH, JOHN E. *Play Direction.* Englewood Cliffs, N. J.: Prentice-Hall, Inc., 1953.

DOLMAN, JOHN, JR. *The Art of Acting.* New York: Harper & Bros., 1949.

———. *The Art of Play Production.* New York: Harper & Bros., 1946.

FRANKLIN, MIRIAM. *Rehearsal.* Englewood Cliffs, N. J.: Prentice-Hall, Inc., 1950.

FRIEDERICH, WILLARD J., and JOHN H. FRASER. *Scenery Design for the Amateur Stage.* New York: The Macmillan Co., 1950.

GASSNER, JOHN (ed.). *A Treasury of the Theatre.* New York: Dryden Press, Inc., Vol. I, 1951; Vol. II, 1950.

———, and PHILIP BARBER. *Producing the Play,* Revised and Enlarged, together with *The New Scene Technician's Handbook.* New York: Dryden Press, Inc., 1953.

HAMMACK, J. ALAN. "Minimum Scenery for High School Productions," *Speech Teacher,* VII (September, 1958), 241–46.

HANSEN, HENNY HARALD. *Costumes and Styles: The Evolution of Fashion from Early Egypt to the Present.* New York: E. P. Dutton & Co., Inc., 1956.

LEES, C. LOWELL. *Play Production and Direction.* Englewood Cliffs, N. J.: Prentice-Hall, Inc., 1948.

LIPSON, LOUIS. *Textbook of Practical Costume Design.* Los Angeles: Cosde Publications, 1941.

McCANDLESS, STANLEY. *A Method of Lighting the Stage.* New York: Theatre Arts, Inc., 1947.

———. *A Syllabus of Stage Lighting.* New Haven, Conn.: By the Author, 1958.

MACGOWAN, KENNETH, and WILLIAM MELNITZ. *The Living Stage: A History of the World Theatre.* Englewood Cliffs, N. J.: Prentice-Hall, Inc., 1955.

Ommanney, Katherine. *The Stage and the School*. New York: McGraw-Hill Book Co., Inc., 1960.

Philippi, Herbert. *Stagecraft and Scene Design*. Boston: Houghton Mifflin Co., 1953.

Plummer, Gail. *The Business of Show Business*. New York: Harper & Bros., 1961.

Portier, Dorothy. "Selecting the High School Play," *Speech Teacher*, II (March, 1953), 109–14.

Seldon, Samuel. *First Steps in Acting*. New York: Appleton-Century-Crofts, Inc., 1947.

———, and Hunton Sellman. *Stage Scenery and Lighting*. New York: Appleton-Century-Crofts, Inc., 1936.

Siks, Geraldine B. *Creative Dramatics: An Art for Children*. New York: Harper & Bros., 1958.

Sliker, Harold. "Theatre Arts in the Secondary School," *Speech Teacher*, IV (January, 1955), 49–53.

Stanislavsky, Constantin. *An Actor Prepares*. New York. Theatre Arts Books, 1949.

Walkup, Fairfax Proudfit. *Dressing the Part*. New York: Appleton-Century-Crofts, Inc., 1950.

Ward, Winifred. *Playmaking with Children*. New York: Appleton-Century-Crofts, Inc., 1957.

CHAPTER TWENTY-FOUR

Radio and Television

Radio and television fit in excellently with other areas in a speech program. These two media are used to transmit many of the products of other parts of the field with little or no modification. Interviews, group discussions, debates, drama, and the various forms of interpretation often need nothing more than the use of broadcasting equipment to convey them to a listening audience seated at a receiving set.

Certain conditions inevitably are different because the usual radio or television audience is not seen by the performers. Thus, the speaker, reader, or discussant must learn how to use the necessary equipment and develop suitable broadcasting techniques to insure satisfactory reception of his content by his audience, wherever it is.

These needs must be served by training in radio and television, whether the person desires to enter the commercial field, to do educational broadcasting, or to make incidental use of the media as an outlet. The basic teaching in radio and television differs but little from teaching in any other skills area in speech. The specialized knowledge and techniques, however, will become part of the student's experience in workshops, after-school activities, or regular classes in radio and television.

There are relatively few such classes in secondary schools. However, the number of schools teaching radio is increasing as FM stations grow in number. Closed- and open-circuit television has aroused greater interest and need for training personnel in technical and performance positions, especially where experimental projects are located. A more common practice is the teaching of a unit in radio or television in a speech course, or on-the-spot training using school or local station equipment when shows are presented. For such schools, or for any others doing even a modest amount of broadcasting, the problem of equipment is a fundamental one. If the administration has the money to spend and desires to install a station, the problem is solved. A radio program compatible with the goals of the station can be developed.

In many other schools, however, the teacher is definitely limited by his equipment. The minimum equipment for radio would include a public-address system, suitable microphones, and a good tape recorder. This meager layout would permit the production of some types of programs, as well as taping them for broadcasting over a commercial station, if telephone lines were not installed to a school studio.

Colleges and universities with a serious interest in training students for radio and television face a more favorable outlook. To offer substantial work they must have good equipment, studios, and trained instructors. In some instances their facilities approach or better those of certain commercial stations. They usually present a series of well-planned courses and laboratory or field training experiences.

The materials in this chapter are not addressed to them. Rather the treatment found here will be directed toward those secondary or college teachers who need some help because of the limitations in their training and equipment. These persons, faced with doing school programs in radio or television, or hopeful of initiating work to motivate students to continue their preparation later, are the objects of the discussion in these pages.

WAYS OF PROVIDING INSTRUCTION

In a limited school situation, three principal possibilities exist for instruction in radio and television broadcasting. These include courses or class units, workshops (which may also include the use of commercial outlets), and school stations. Some schools may use only one of these. However, as programs in teaching broadcasting approach the ideal, all three may be combined to provide depth and variety.

In 1954–55, the United States Office of Education reported in its *Directory of College Courses in Radio and Television* that 300 colleges had at least two courses in broadcasting. Radio workshops on the college level were listed by 269 institutions, while 66 schools reported television workshops. Many of these workshops were very limited in equipment, operating with simple public-address systems, homemade equipment, tape recorders, and the like. Scripts were written by students or obtained from published collections. Ultimately many of these workshops develop into low-power FM stations.

By 1960, courses and programs had expanded rapidly. In the *Fifth Annual Survey of Communications,* completed by Harold Niven at the University of Washington, there were in that year 96 colleges and universities with a major or a strong concentration in broadcasting, leading to a degree. There were 3,009 undergraduates enrolled in such programs. In 49 schools, 422 students were working for the master's degree in the field.

Some broadcasting workshops, usually those at large universities, had excellent professional equipment, including well outfitted television studios and control rooms, cameras, motion picture projectors, kinescope recorders, construction and storage areas, and so on. Since that time newer devices have been added by some schools, such as video tape equipment. Among institutions using workshops to train students for broadcasting are Wayne State University, Northwestern, Wisconsin, State University of Iowa, Iowa State, Michigan, and Syracuse.

In certain situations, these workshops are used with established noncommercial educational AM or FM radio stations. In 1954 there were 23 such AM stations. In the same year 124 FM stations of this type were listed, 40 of which were ten watts, or less. In July, 1955, there were 15 educational television stations on the air, with 8 under construction in major centers, and 6 having been granted permits to construct. Twelve others had applications pending. Commercial FM stations in 1956 totaled 536, with a slow trend increasing this number.

In 1961, the record showed 193 educational FM stations, 38 AM stations, and a category not included in the earlier report, 241 wired-wireless stations. The number of educational television stations had increased to a total of 58, with 16 of these UHF stations, and 42 VHF stations.

These facts show the increasing need and possibilities for training high school and college students in broadcasting. In the next sections, the various ways of providing such instruction will be developed more fully.

Courses and Class Units

Any satisfactory course or class unit includes information and theory plus practical experience to develop skills. Depending upon the situation, the number of units or courses can be extended until considerable specialization is reached. The objectives and headings below indicate possible content for instruction, which would have to be adjusted to conditions.

Objectives

1. To develop the student's appreciation of the significance of radio and television as means of communication and education.
2. To acquaint the student with the history and background of broadcasting.
3. To give the student a sympathetic understanding of public service in broadcasting.
4. To introduce methods of evaluation and audience measurement and present their effect upon programs.
5. To point out new developments in the communications field.
6. To present the structure of broadcasting, the organization and management of stations, independent and affiliated, and of networks.
7. To provide theory and application of the fundamental broadcasting procedures, such as announcing, writing, acting, production, and the like.
8. To develop desirable standards for radio and television performance for the participant and the viewer.

Possible Units or Courses

1. Background and History of Broadcasting
2. Importance of Radio and Television in Modern Affairs
3. The Organization and Structure of Broadcasting: the People, the Government and Regulation, Stations, Networks, etc.
4. The Radio and Television Audience: Broadcasting
5. Providing Programs: Scripts, Program Types, Planning Programs
6. Equipment and Facilities

7. Broadcasting Procedures and Techniques: Writing, Announcing, Acting, Production, etc.
8. Evaluation and the Building of Standards for Broadcasting

Such objectives and areas of instruction must be adapted to school situations. Class units could cover only part of this material. In other situations entire courses might be devoted to a single heading. At Northwestern University, where students may take a major in the field of radio-television-film, the basic introduction consists of a quarter each in the three media. Advanced courses built upon this foundation include Radio and Television Acting, Announcing, Writing for Radio-Television-Film, Radio Production Procedures, Television Procedures, Film Procedures, Continuity Writing for Radio-Television-Film, Program Planning for Radio-Television-Film, Television Station Operation, Television Directing, Television Production, and so on. The school with limited time and teaching personnel must settle for much less than such an array of courses, which are designed for training students for commercial and educational careers.

The Workshop

Objectives

If he has no class time available for radio or television, the speech teacher must turn to cocurricular training. Thomas Rishworth,[1] formerly public-service director for the National Broadcasting Company, points out that radio workshop training is available to almost every school and is adaptable to its needs, equipment, students, and teaching personnel. He also lists these goals for such activities:

1. *The first function of a radio workshop is to develop familiarity with the radio offerings of local and network broadcasts.*

   Through assigned listening after school hours and later reports during class hours on the programs heard, a critical appreciation of radio can be developed which should become an important factor in the listening habits of these young people as they grow older. It is obvious that radio cannot offer everything to the classroom during school hours. Assigned listening may supplement the work of the teacher in many fields.

2. *The second function of the radio workshop is the development of*

[1] See Judith Waller, *Radio, The Fifth Estate* (Boston: Houghton, Mifflin Co., 1946), pp. 438–42.

*further analytical powers through the study of transcriptions or record-
ings of outstanding programs of the past.*

Many of radio's best offerings have been recorded for later reference,
and schools having the necessary playback equipment can tap these
resources as a significant factor in providing the necessary background
for future practical applications of the broadcasting art. The United
States Office of Education, the networks, many college and university
stations, independent educational and professional organizations, and
local broadcasters have recordings available on either a loan or a purchase basis. These recordings can be used as models in the training of
script writers, actors, announcers, producers.

3. *The third function is the production of programs for school consump-
tion alone.*

If the school is properly equipped, the workshop may produce a
daily program of announcements, news, and other features. If the
school lacks a centrally controlled system, perhaps a public-address
system in the assembly hall may provide a substitute. The group may
produce on occasional assembly program. Most certainly a variety of
efforts must first be undertaken within the four walls of the workshop
itself, each student criticizing every other's work, before any display to
a larger public is attempted. No actual broadcast must be permitted
until the group has proved its right to go on the air.

4. *The fourth function of the radio workshop is the actual production of
broadcasts from a local radio station.*

Talent can be discovered in these groups, frequently superior in
quality, and if these exceptional young people can be allowed to
express themselves in terms drawn from their own experience, they
should most certainly be given an opportunity. Youth has something
to say and it should be heard.

Mr. Rishworth adds these further observations:

5. *The radio workshop is not intended to develop professional broadcasters.*

6. *The radio workshop should develop critical standards regarding performance whether the student is in the show or merely a listener.*

These are all significant objectives for the workshop. They present
clearly a point of view and a method of approach to radio through
this type of organized study.

With these goals and those already presented for class units or courses, it should be clear which direction workshop activities should follow; however, it should be noted that throughout all its performance aspects radio has a relation to speech training. Numerous opportunities for continued growth and development exist in the basic skills of speaking and reading, and individual work is possible on the various elements of performance. Radio and television furnish unusual motivation because of their "magic word" influence upon adolescents. The intelligent teacher can make full use of such experiences to continue the training he has begun.

Organizing a Radio Workshop

1. *Membership.* The membership in the radio workshop should be open to all students who are interested in learning about radio broadcasting. The initial call for personnel should not be restricted in any way. The workshop offers countless ways of using the interests and abilities of all students. The sponsor of the workshop should invite everyone and then base restrictions on later schedules. If the group is "convention size," some method of tryout, active and apprentice membership, similar to that described in the drama club, can be devised.

2. *Sponsorship.* Sponsorship should be in the hands of the speech teacher. If he desires, he may invite the representatives of science, music, English, journalism, and social science departments to share permanent responsibilities with him. However, it will be better generally for administration if he invites these people to assist at certain designated times, rather than asking them to act as continuing sponsors.

3. *Meeting Time.* Unless time is provided and facilities are available during the regular school schedule, the meeting should be held after school, and as often as the workshop program and after-school activities permit.

4. *Rules and Internal Organization.* If the students desire to organize as a club, that can be done with some benefit to the operation of the workshop, since it will center certain responsibilities upon particular students. Otherwise, they may wish to organize intraworkshop groups based upon their special interests and abilities. Such subgroups can include: acting, direction, production, sound effects,

technical or engineering, music, etc. These subgroups may be headed by student chairmen, but total administration should be in the hands of the sponsor.

5. *Policy on Programs.* The best training procedures make the shows the complete responsibility of the students with respect to announcing, continuity, script, sound, music, and the principal aspects of production. The direction should be in the hands of the teacher at first, later branching out to those members of the workshop who have ability and who can take responsibility for the job. In some cases, handling of control panels and equipment may be done by a studio or station engineer, who, because of knowledge and training, is best able to operate and repair the expensive equipment.

6. *Areas of Student Activity and Performance.* A good plan is to let students select the areas of their activity and work; some may desire to follow a "round-robin" pattern, learning as many of the aspects of radio as they can. Others may wish to specialize in acting, announcing, writing, sound, confining their study, preparation, and performance to certain parts of the program. The chances are that sufficient variety of interest will be expressed to enable the sponsor to have on hand a casting list for actors, a crew of announcers, a group of writers, and sound technicians, all of whom can be assigned to the shows that are to be done.

7. *Sequence of Study and Work.* Following the objectives and approaches that have already been listed, the first meetings should acquaint the group with the radio medium. It will be possible to combine certain study functions with those of performance and production after the workshop has operated for a time. Early in the semester, auditions should be held for the members of the workshop. Everyone can be heard and a file kept of the persons according to ability to interpret, and according to pitch, quality, loudness, and time in voice, with appropriate description of any special characteristics that would make the voice distinctive or useful in radio. If possible, recordings can be made of these auditions and kept for analysis and study by the members of the workshop. These can later be compared and contrasted with other performances of the same students. A general policy to follow after the workshop is under way is to

integrate all the information, theory, and technique in a given project or in a series of shows, following a certain theme, purpose, educational goal, character, institution, movement, or some other objective.

8. *Suggested Activities for Sponsor and Students*
   a. Talks and lectures by the sponsor and guests.
      1. Orientation. Introducing the student to the workshop and to radio.
      2. History of radio.
      3. Organization of radio.
      4. Control of broadcasting.
      5. Allied service organizations.
      6. Technical aspects of radio.
      7. Sound effects.
      8. Music effects.
      9. Program planning.
      10. Audience measurement.
      11. Types of programs.
      12. The dramatic program.
      13. Talks, interviews, round tables.
      14. Women's, children's, religious, and agricultural programs.
      15. Public service in radio.
      16. New developments in radio.
   b. Reports by the students.
      1. Introducing the student to the significance of radio.
      2. Broadcasting systems.
      3. Networks. Student reports on ABC, NBC, CBS, MBS.
      4. Discuss F.C.C., N.A.B. Display printed advertising not allowed on the air.
      5. Reports on sales organizations, advertising, and promotion.
      6. Reports on technical aspects.
      7. Listen for sound effects in transcription.
      8. Listen for use of music in transcription.
      9. Discuss program planning.
      10. Reports on audience measurement made in school.
      11. Listen to transcription of music program and discuss.

12. Listen to transcription of dramatic program and discuss technique.
13. Reports on talks, interviews, round tables.
14. Reports on women's, children's, religious, and agricultural programs.
15. Discuss educational radio programs, network and local.
16. Vocational opportunities.

c. Laboratory or performance activities.

1. Orientation. Introducing the student to the studio, terms, and signals.
2. Play back three-minute talks (auditions) already recorded. Analyze for rate of speaking, volume, variety and inflection, timing, conversational element. Write suggestions for improvement on script or check sheet.
3. Broadcast three-minute news program or commentary.
4. Broadcast a disc-jockey program.
5. Read three original commercials—one intimate, one punch, and one institutional.
6. Learn to play transcriptions and records.
7. Learn how to produce manual and recorded sound effects.
8. Learn how to handle musical effects.
9. Learn simple microphone techniques—cues, fades, perspective.
10. Learn more simple microphone techniques—action, laugh, cry.
11. Evaluate a music program.
12. Evaluate dramatic program technique.
13. Learn how to use devices in dramatic program (filter, montages, and so on).
14. Interview.
15. Round table.
16. Produce a fifteen-minute dramatic show using all possible techniques mastered. Record it, play it back, and evaluate it.

9. *Types of Programs*

a. Limited equipment.

1. Radio talks and speeches.

    2. Readings and storytelling.

    3. Newcasts and announcements.

    4. Comedy routine (one person).

    5. Comedy program (two persons).

    6. Interview: man-on-the-street.

    7. Commentary.

    8. Book review.

    9. Simple quiz program.

    10. Sportscast.

    11. Special event: on-the-spot commentary.

    12. Disc-jockey program.

    13. Music: solo instrumental—piano, violin, flute, clarinet, trumpet, etc.; solo vocal.

    14. Poetry program: lecture-recital type.

    15. Round table: three people.

    16. Variety—with individual numbers.

  b. More extensive equipment.

    All of the above are possible, plus these as suggestions:

    1. Dramatic shows.

    2. Chorus: vocal music; quartets—instrumental or vocal.

    3. Orchestra or string ensemble.

    4. Dramatizations and adaptations of short stories, novels, Bible stories, fairy tales, sports stories, adventure, travel.

    5. Children's programs.

    6. Women's programs: demonstration or commentator—styles, food, household.

    7. Agricultural programs.

    8. Special-occasion shows.

    9. Public-service shows: community, school.

    10. Town Meeting of the Air; larger round tables.

    11. Audience participation shows.

    12. More elaborate quiz programs.

    13. Assembly programs.

    14. Serials and continued dramatized shows.

The School Station

The growth of noncommercial educational AM and FM stations has been noted earlier in this chapter. These stations cover an estimated 50 per cent of the American people. Most of the FM stations have developed since World War II, when the Federal Communications Commission allocated the 88–92 megacycle band for educational use only.

The FM station offers interesting possibilities for an educational institution. Many colleges, school systems, and high schools have obtained licenses and have built stations. They use the stations to serve a public relations function by informing their listeners in the immediate area of educational events and developments. They also bring school programs of various types to the public. Besides this, their programs provide: (1) direct classroom teaching; (2) supplementary classroom teaching; (3) intraschool broadcasting; (4) informal and out-of-school education; (5) formal adult education; (6) informal adult education; (7) integrated education and entertainment; (8) opportunities for experimentation; (9) outlets for school talent in music, art, speech, and other fields; (10) service and training for students interested in learning broadcasting techniques, and so on.

The last of these functions is necessary in station operation. Announcers, directors, actors, and technicians are essential to successful operation. In some situations the station is the point of origin for classwork in broadcasting, as well as for the expansion of speech programs in the school.

Licenses for stations are granted for a period of three years by the FCC. Applications for licenses must be made in writing to the commission and must specify the following: (1) the need for the station in the school and community; (2) a statement of the financial situation and the names of the responsible parties; (3) a statement of the citizenship, the character, the technical and other qualifications of those who will operate the broadcasting station. Aliens or foreign corporations may not obtain a license.

Further, the applicant must set forth: (1) the location of the proposed station; (2) the frequency and power to be used; (3) the hours of the day and period of the year proposed for operation of the station; and (5) a complete statement of the proposed program service. Additional information must be supplied on the engineering data so that a licensed engineer, legally responsible, will be in charge. A complete drawing of the situation with the height of the proposed tower is also required.

The minimum equipment includes the transmitter, the antenna, a console, at least two good quality microphones, two tape recorders capable of broadcasting quality production, two turntables, a suitable playing arm, soundproofed studios with double glass to separate them from the control room. Other desirable features include subscription to the news services, telephone lines for remote broadcasts, membership in the National Association of Educational Broadcasters, and an ample supply of blank tapes and records. A good file of transcriptions, musical recordings on tape or disc, and sound effects is important.

The cost of installation varies with the type of equipment, studios, antenna, and the the like that are employed. New Trier High School at Winnetka, Illinois, installed an FM station in 1960 with a basic budget of $10,000. Other stations will run somewhat below that figure.

Programming sources are very important to such a station. The most stimulating kinds of programs are those provided live by students, faculty, and community groups. These also provide the greatest means of training students for broadcasting. In planning ahead, some of these may be recorded and played at appropriate times, in order to have enough preplanned programs. There are numerous sources of taped program materials that are available to FM stations for modest cost or without charge.

Membership in the National Association of Educational Broadcasters is a great help. This entitles the member station to receive a weekly newsletter and a valuable journal, attend their conferences, and use their program services. For a fee of $200 per year, the station becomes a member of their network and receives an extensive tape program service.

Free program services providing tapes include the Canadian Broadcasting Company, Montreal, Canada; the British Broadcasting Company, 650 Fifth Avenue, New York, N.Y.; and the United States Armed Forces Programs, Washington 25, D.C.

If a station desires to continue broadcasting, it must renew its license every three years. A statement of the program service for the three-year period must be submitted with the application for renewal. The FCC may compare this statement with the proposed program service, originally submitted, when deciding upon issuing the license for another period of three years.

All these ways of providing training are extremely practical for the school or the teacher with limited facilities or preparation. They offer interesting opportunities for combination and development into more detailed or specialized training as conditions permit.

EXERCISES

1. Visit either a closed-circuit television studio or a commercial television station and prepare a report on your observation, which should include your opinion concerning the use of such media in classroom teaching.
2. Prepare an educational radio script that could be used by students for presentation either over the high school public-address system or the local educational radio station.
3. Prepare a list of radio and television programs that could be used for out-of-school listening assignments, and be prepared to defend your choices, measuring them against suitable standards for radio listening and television viewing.

REFERENCES

ABBOT, WALDO, and RICHARD RIDER. *Handbook of Broadcasting*. New York: McGraw-Hill Book Co., 1957.

BARNHART, LYLE D. *Radio and Television Announcing*. Englewood Cliffs, N. J.: Prentice-Hall, Inc., 1953.

BETTINGER, HOYLAND. *Television Techniques*. Rev. ed. by Sol Cornberg. New York: Harper & Bros., 1955.

BRETZ, RUDY. *Techniques of Television Production*. New York: McGraw-Hill Book Co., 1953.

CARLILE, JOHN S. *Production and Direction of Radio Programs*. Englewood Cliffs, N. J.: Prentice-Hall, Inc., 1946.

CHESTER, GIRAUD, and GARNET GARRISON. *Television and Radio: An Introduction*. New York: Appleton-Century-Crofts, Inc., 1956.

DUERR, EDWIN. *Radio and Television Acting*. New York: Rinehart & Co., 1950.

EMERY, WALTER B. "The Current Status of Educational T.V.," *Quarterly Journal of Speech*, XXXIX (April, 1953), 173–86.

EWBANK, HENRY L., and SHERMAN LAWTON. *Broadcasting: Radio and Television*. New York: Harper & Bros., 1952.

FIELD, STANLEY. *Television and Radio Writing*. Boston: Houghton Mifflin Co., 1958.

HEAD, S. W. *Broadcasting in America: A Survey of Television and Radio.* Boston: Houghton Mifflin Co., 1956.

HENNEKE, BEN GRAF. *The Radio Announcer's Handbook.* New York: Rinehart & Co., 1949.

HUBBELL, RICHARD. *Television Programming and Production.* New York: Rinehart & Co., 1956.

LEVENSON, WILLIAM. *Teaching through Radio and Television.* New York: Rinehart & Co., 1952.

LYON, DONALD. "Is Educational Radio Here to Stay?" *Quarterly Journal of Speech,* XXXVI (October, 1950), 355–59.

MINER, WORTHINGTON. "Training for Television," *Quarterly Journal of Speech,* XXXVI (October, 1950), 351–54.

O'MEARA, CARROLL. *Television Program Production.* New York: Ronald Press, 1955.

ROBERTS, EDWARD BARRY. *Television Writing and Selling.* Boston: The Writer, Inc., 1957.

STASHEFF, EDWARD, and RUDY BRETZ. *The Television Program: Its Writing, Direction, and Production.* New York: A. A. Wyn, Inc., 1951.

TURNBULL, ROBERT B. *Radio and Television Sound Effects.* New York: Rinehart & Co., 1951.

WEISS, HAROLD. "Implementing the Radio Course," *Quarterly Journal of Speech,* XXXII (October, 1946), 335–39.

CHAPTER TWENTY-FIVE

Assemblies and Convocations

School assemblies and convocations serve the broad purpose of convening all or certain parts of the student body for reasons of importance to the administration. In many colleges weekly convocations are held to provide a religious service. Some use such a meeting for other purposes. Universities rarely assemble the student body except for a fall convocation at the beginning of school, baccalaureate, and commencement exercises. The size and purpose of the institution definitely affect this practice. However, the *assembly* has become almost a secondary school tradition. It has important implications for speech teachers; these faculty members may also become closely involved in college convocations.

FUNCTION AND RELATIONSHIP

A recent survey made by high-school principals stated that the school assembly should serve "to integrate the whole school program." Seven important objectives were stressed in the survey: (1) to develop school spirit or unity; (2) to furnish educational-cultural experience; (3) to supply wholesome recreation; (4) to provide guidance; (5) to demonstrate the work of classes; (6) to supplement the work of classes; (7) to motivate the work of classes. Thus it can be seen that the assembly is not just a place where students gather for pure entertainment, even though at times it is presented for that purpose. The major function of the school assembly is an educational one.

The teacher of speech is peculiarly suited because of the nature of his work to make a significant contribution to this program. He should welcome the opportunity of serving on the assembly committee in any school. The chances are that he will be made chairman of this active group, for the principal recognizes that speech activities are superior assembly material and that the speech teacher knows how to organize public performances. With this position virtually assured, the teacher should examine the advantages of such a post. First, it affords him an excellent motivation and outlet for speech and drama activities and classwork. Second, by having charge of the assembly program schedule, he can avoid conflicts of other events with his own use of the stage in construction and rehearsal of plays and for other speech activities.

Similar relationships exist in college situations. Speech professors are by training suited to administer convocations and numerous special events on campus. Deans know this and usually employ such skill wisely.

Some special departmental programs in speech—discussion, debate, oratory, interpretation, honors convocations—have much in common with the assembly.

ADMINISTERING THE PROGRAM

1. *Make a year's schedule.*

As chairman of an assembly committee, the speech teacher will serve with members of other departments who have ideas, ability, and contributions to make from their areas. These persons usually come from the music, art, social studies, physical education, and possibly the science departments, to mention those most frequently included. The first major function of the group is to block out the year's schedule of "must" assemblies. Every school has a number of these, such as the Christmas program, honors programs, athletic rallies, or Homecoming. If there are a certain number of assemblies desired each month, the committee proceeds to develop possibilities for the remaining dates in the schedule. It is here that the speech teacher contributes a considerable list of potential programs from all fields of his work. Dates can be set for dramatic, forensic, interpretation, discussion, or choric-speaking programs as the situation indicates.

In addition to dates, the hour, length, description, facilities, and rehearsals needs should be listed, as well as the faculty member in charge.

2. *Plan outstanding programs.*

The next function is to arrange and plan specific programs. If they are to be truly educational, they should be outstanding. They must be worth every minute spent in selection, preparation, and performance before the student body, teachers, and parents. When the total time of the teacher, participants, and audience is considered, *quality* must be *high* to pay dividends upon the investment.

Kinds of Programs [1]

A. *Programs by Outside Groups*

1. Alumni program. (This is a good one for an opener after the preliminary seating assembly suggested earlier in the article. Alumni are usually available at this time as public schools generally open before colleges. Later in the year, it is difficult to get them.)
2. Outside speakers. (Students will respond well to speakers if they know *how* to talk to high school students and avoid *talking down* to the audience. Careful check should be made on the ability of the speaker. If possible, someone on the assembly committee should hear the speaker before deciding to invite him to speak to the students. The committee should inform the speaker as to the time he is to take, and give him some suggestions for a subject.)
3. Programs by college groups. An occasional program of this nature serves as an excellent example for high school students. Various colleges send groups out to high schools during the year. (A letter to college speech and music departments might open this possibility to you.)
4. A program by a neighboring school, i.e., the exchange assembly.

B. *Programs That Might Be Presented by School Organizations*

1. Hidden talent show. (Another program which is good for early in the year. In some schools this one is sponsored by the staff of the school paper.)
2. Faculty program. (The faculty of one high school presented in assembly a take-off on a popular musical comedy. Students

---

[1] Theodore Skinner, "Suggestions for the High School Assembly," *Quarterly Journal of Speech*, XXXIII (December, 1947), 515–21.

like to see faculty members take their hair down and show that they are human.)

3. Class programs. (Each of the three or four classes of the high school assumes responsibility for working up an assembly. Competition usually leads to good programs.)

4. Programs by school clubs. (The Spanish Club presented an excellent South American program, given in Spanish and costumed in the native dress. It was from this program that the tango number was found for the exchange assembly. Other clubs which might contribute programs are the Hi-Y, Girl Reserve, Girls Athletic Association, Boys Athletic Club, Dramatics, Speech, Student Council, Photography, Art, Future Farmers of America, the school paper staff, yearbook staff, International Relations, French, Science, and Pep Clubs.)

5. A debate. (Certainly there is a place on the schedule for a debate between the school's best team and a strong rival team. Students are usually most attentive if the debaters are experienced.)

C. *Programs That Might Originate in School Classes*

1. Forums or panel discussions on school problems.
2. Gym exhibit.
3. Programs growing out of classwork. (The physics class once gave an assembly in which students explained and demonstrated projects. Various other departments have possible assembly programs growing out of classwork.)
4. A fashion show or parade. (In one assembly the girls from the home economics class modeled dresses they had made. Or again, costumes from different periods could be modeled. Skits might be written on the theme of courtship in grandma's day, mama's day, and daughter's day.)
5. Finals in girls and boys basketball from the intramural program.
6. Parliamentary practice. (We once had a program presented by the speech class in which the members of the class were inmates of an old folks' home holding a meeting. The original script together with the costuming and staging made this an interesting as well as an informative program.)

7. Declamations, orations, and choral speaking. (Another program which could be presented by a speech class or club.)

D. *Music, Dance, and Drama Programs*

1. Group singing. (A very successful program of this type was patterned after one of the radio programs by having an extension cord on the microphone, so that the master of ceremonies could wander up the aisles in order to have various students and faculty members sing solo on parts of the songs. Group singing is best used as a part of a program, not taking more than 10 or 15 minutes at the most.)
2. Band and orchestra concerts. (Again, it is advisable to seek *variety* instead of having a full program of band or orchestra music. Solo numbers might be brought in, or possibly a demonstration by the drum majorettes.)
3. A capella choir, or boys and girls glee club programs. (As with band and orchestra assemblies, it is well to bring in solos, duets, trios, triple trios, etc.)
4. The one-act play. (Always popular.)
5. Hidden talent show.
6. A dance program. (There are many possibilities in this. It might be an interpretative dance program, or could be built around the development of the dance, taking in various periods and ending with a fast jitterbug number. A faculty square dance is also a possibility.)

E. *Miscellaneous Programs*

1. Motion pictures.
2. Quiz programs with audience participation.
3. Programs developed around themes such as fire prevention, safety, citizenship, health, vocations, education, travel, equal rights, United Nations, etc.
4. Programs developed around important seasons or occasions such as the Christmas and Easter program, birthdays of presidents, patriotic holidays, etc. Such programs can be treated in countless ways—student talks, tabloids, dramatizations, panels (all speech activities), and music.
5. Radio programs. (The audience looks at a broadcast. Fun can

be had not only within the program itself, but through the antics of the sound effects man.)

6. A mock political convention. (Can be very successful during a national election year. Also, might be staged around a school election.)

7. Recognition assemblies. (These should be run off quickly, asking the audience to hold applause until all of a given group have been presented. Speeches should be *short*.)

8. Community service program. (Ways in which students can be of help in the community, and opportunities open to student.)

CREATIVE PROGRAMS

Some programs can be developed creatively, using the combined ideas and efforts of the students and the speech teacher. Outstanding examples of such procedures are used by Mary Blackburn at Community High School, Granite City, Illinois; by Doris Niles, at Will Rogers High School, Tulsa, Oklahoma; and by Carolyn Cremeens, formerly at Shorewood High School, Milwaukee, Wisconsin. The procedure used in this type of program is described below: [2]

A. Creating the idea for a definite program:
    1. Analyze the talent within the class. This can be done by giving every member of the class certain skills or activities to perform. Some programs may call for speaking and acting only; others may incorporate song and the dance.
    2. Having a cross section of the talent, the group discusses the program to be presented and its purpose. Each student is asked to bring an original idea and skeleton outline of the program, keeping in mind the talent in the class.
    3. Outlines and ideas are discussed; the best are chosen and the others incorporated when possible. Class members then work individually or in groups, creating specific parts of the show. Group discussions are held and the project is improved and new ideas added.

B. Ideas for various types of programs:
    1. Assemblies for pure entertainment.
    2. Assemblies to advertise school activities.
    3. Commencement programs.

[2] Mary Blackburn, "The Speech Teacher and the High School Assembly Program," *Quarterly Journal of Speech*, XXXIII (February, 1947), 80–83; Doris Niles, "The Beginning Speech Teacher as Director of the High School Assembly," *Speech Teacher*, X (November, 1961), 291–98.

    4. Variety and benefit shows.

    5. Programs for Rotary, Optimists, women's clubs, Lions Club, etc.

    6. Programs for United Fund and Red Cross kick-off dinners, etc.

C. Samples of creative programs developed for these projects:

    1. "All the World's a Stage" (Assembly program)

    2. "The Theater—the Past—the Present—the Future" (Benefit show)

    3. "We Hold These Truths" (Commencement program)

    4. "America Under the Dream Tree" (Children's program)

    5. "United We Stand" (United Fund kick-off dinner)

    6. "Stage Door Canteen" (American Theatre Wing show)

    7. "Sentimental Journey" (Assembly program)

    8. "Rotary on the March" (Rotary program)

    9. "All in a Summer's Day" (Novelty program)

    10. "The Time of Your Life" (Talent show)

3. Develop all details of rehearsal and performance carefully.

After planning the program, the teacher should move toward other details. There is no place for half-done, slipshod work. All mechanical items of rehearsal, facilities, direction, acting, production, publicity, duplicating of programs, timing, auditorium management for performance, must be followed through. The show must go on, efficiently, as planned. Skinner [3] adds further suggestions on these matters.

Some Guiding Ideas for Assemblies

A. *General Policy*

    1. Thirty minutes is probably the best length; few programs can run successfully beyond 40 minutes.

    2. Programs should be decided upon well in advance of the date scheduled, so as to allow for sufficient rehearsal.

    3. If possible, pep rally assemblies should be held in the school gymnasium instead of in the auditorium.

    4. Routine announcements should be held to a minimum, if not eliminated entirely.

    5. Assemblies should not be used as a means of raising money. All programs should be free and open to all students.

    6. Work for wide participation among the student body. See how *many* students can be used throughout the year. Avoid having the same group present all the programs.

[3] Skinner, *op. cit.*, 515–21.

7. Have *students* preside over assemblies, not *faculty members*. (This does not mean that faculty members should not appear before students. Obviously, the school should avail itself, occasionally, of faculty members who are talented.)

8. See that assembly programs are publicized in the local papers and that townspeople are invited to attend.

9. Work for variety among the various programs.

10. The assembly committee should follow up the appearance of guest performances with letters of appreciation.

B. *Preparation of Programs*

1. Programs should be timed to match as closely as possible the established assembly period.

2. Rehearsals should be held in the auditorium. The assembly committee should have representatives to preview each program.

3. Programs should be publicized in the school paper so that students will know what *type* of program to expect. An announcement of the next program might be made at each assembly.

4. Careful attention should be paid to the setting, costuming, properties, lighting, and make-up for assembly programs.

5. Hold dress rehearsals for all programs which would obviously require them.

6. See that assembly programs are publicized in the *local* papers and that townspeople are invited to attend.

7. Have the *conclusion* of the program *planned*, so that the audience knows when the program is over.

8. A member of the assembly committee, preferably a student, should be delegated to meet outside performers and to acquaint them with the facilities of the school. They should be shown the stage, and, time permitting, should have an opportunity for a rehearsal on the stage.

C. *The Performance*

1. All assemblies should begin on time.

2. The curtain should be opened far enough so that all can see.

3. Programs should be run off quickly with no delay between numbers.

4. If a P. A. system is used, check the microphone and the volume in advance.

5. Do not permit students who have appeared in an early number on the program to go out into the audience for the last of the assembly. All performers should have an opportunity to see the

other numbers during rehearsal and should remain backstage for the entire assembly period.

6. Plan for distribution and collection of material used by the audience, such as song sheets.

7. Visiting students who present programs usually are interested in seeing the building; the assembly committee should arrange for a conducted tour.

4. *Evaluate assembles.*

Following an assembly program, the teacher in charge should reflect upon what he has done. First, he can make a personal appraisal. From his own point of view, were his purposes sound and worthy? Did the assembly carry them out clearly, interestingly, effectively? Was the event a challenging educational experience for the participants and the audience? If the program were repeated, would he change the content, method, details, in any way? Was the program technically well done and administered?

From the answers to these questions he should proceed to the students in the show and those in the audience. Next, he can question the faculty, the parents, the principal, and so on. Furnished with honest appraisals, he can look forward to improving his work.

SELECTED ASSEMBLY PROGRAMS

Following are some programs and plan sheets for high school assemblies. They may be of assistance in planning such activities.

UNIVERSITY HIGH SCHOOL

Award and Pep Assembly

Auditorium

1. Opening ceremony: Fred Zeller, President, Student Council, presiding
   a. Call to the Colors: trumpeter and color guard
   b. Pledge of allegiance
   c. Ritual led by Dr. Carpenter
   d. Song
2. Introductory comments: Mr. Lynn
   a. Introduce new faculty members: Miss Weidenback, Mr. Spencer
   b. Remarks
3. Explanation and presentation of Student Council Merit Award: Fred Zeller

4. Response: Mr. Austermiller
5. Athletic recognition: Fred Zeller presiding
   a. Introduce Coach Westwick; football season review
   b. Call for all boys out for football to stand
   c. Captain Halverson presents trophy
   d. Acceptance: Mr. Lynn
   e. Two yells (for football squad and school)
6. Basketball recognition: Fred Zeller presiding
   a. Introduce Jim Rasley; gift presentation
   b. Response: Coach Alley (pep talk)
   c. Yell for coach
   d. Pep talk: Jack Shay
   e. Yell for team
7. Announcements and order of dismissal: Mr. Lynn
8. School song

Here is another plan, for a Christmas program using "Why the Chimes Rang."

UNIVERSITY HIGH SCHOOL

Plan for Christmas Assembly

December 17, 1961

2:30 P.M.

1. Carolers start march through halls; begin on 3rd floor at E. end, proceed to W. down to 2nd, E; on 2nd down to 1st; walk to W. end, down to basement level; proceed to E. end then upstairs and into gymnasium. (Start at 2:15 P.M.)
2. Gymnasium, subdued lighting; decorations on either side of stage to focus attention. Music, either orchestra or piano, playing upon entrance.
3. Chorus proceeds to front of stage; stands on floor level; Mr. Walters leads entire assembly in singing.
4. Lights down as chorus leaves by W. gymnasium door on N. side to reassemble at E. entrance to gymnasium.
5. Narrator begins reading of "Why the Chimes Rang"; string accompaniment. He reads first section of story (up to entrance of procession and characters into cathedral).
6. At this point chorus enters from rear of auditorium, holding flashlight candles so that they shine on their faces; they will sing appropriate Christmas carols as they approach the stage; upon reaching the front of the room before the stage, the group will divide, one file going R.

and the other L. to take their places upon either side of the altar, revealed by the slow opening of the curtain as the procession approaches. The other characters: the priest, the acolyte, the artist, the writer, the rich man and woman, the king, present their gifts in turn to the priest who lays them upon the altar; after each gift all wait to to see whether the chimes will ring. All have given up hope when little brother, unobserved, hands his piece of silver to the priest, who places it upon the altar. The chorus stops its closing song; all watch. Quietly with increasing intensity the chimes are heard to ring (off stage). The chorus takes up its final song with increased vigor, the audience joining in, as all then go into "Holy Night, Silent Night," the audience singing also, and the curtain draws slowly to a close. The lights stay down while the chorus sings one more verse; the lights come up and the program ends.

> Committees:
> General Supervision: Robinson, Austermiller
> Setting: Westwick, Gaiser
> Lighting: Gaiser
> Music: Pierce, Wood (vocal), Walters (instrumental)
> Narration and Pantomime: Robinson
> Decoration (building, stage, auditorium): Patzig
> Programs: Eggert
> Ushers: LeVois
> Costumes: Lloyd, Saggau

It is also desirable to recognize students producing and taking part in an assembly by having their names appear on a mimeographed or dittoed program, which is distributed to the student body. This small recognition is little enough for the many hours of work and effort that the students invest in the production of an assembly.

Another interesting program utilizes various types of literature presented by oral interpreters. The following is a typical assembly.

BROOKSIDE HIGH SCHOOL

Presents a Program
of
INTERPRETATIVE READING

1. An adaptation from *Alice in Wonderland*, by Lewis Carroll.
Donna Harrison.

2. An adaptation from *Antigone,* by Jean Anouilh.
   Joan Peters.
3. An adaptation from *On a Note of Triumph,* by Norman Corwin.
   Earl Grueskin.
4. An adaptation from *The Princess Marries the Page,* by Edna St. Vincent Millay.
   Ellen Mielke.
5. An adaptation from *The Women,* by Clare Booth Luce.
   Henry Lippold.
6. An adaptation from *How Green Is My Valley,* by Llewellyn Jones.
   David Kendall.
7. "Hun-gah" by Ruth McKenna.
   Janet Stewart.
8. An adaptation from *Deep Are the Roots,* by Arnaud d'Asseau and James Gow.
   Larry McKeever.
9. *Cinderella,* by Alice Duer Miller.
   Betty Beyer.

The students appearing on this program have been selected from a group of seventy who elected Interpretative Reading as a course.

EXERCISES

1. Prepare a list of special days and occasions which occur during the school year and give a brief description of a possible assembly program appropriate for each.
2. Plan in detail an assembly for a specific occasion, indicating the necessary procedures, materials, and facilities to ensure its success.
3. State your opinion concerning the use of assemblies and convocations as an educational activity and be prepared to defend your statement.

REFERENCES

ADAMS, AGNES L., and OTHERS. *Sharing Experiences through School Assemblies.* Bulletin of the Association for Childhood Education, 1201 Sixteenth St., N.W., Washington, D.C.

BECKER, ALBERT B. *A School Assemblies Handbook.* A Class Project, Department of Speech, Western Michigan University, Kalamazoo, Mich.

————. *Ideas for Your Next Assembly.* A Class Project, Department of Speech, Western Michigan University, Kalamazoo, Mich.

BLACKBURN, MARY. "The Speech Teacher and the High School Assembly

Program, *Quarterly Journal of Speech*, XXXIII (February, 1947), 80–83.

DICKSON, BELLE L. "Use Your Auditorium," *School Executive*, LXI (January, 1942), 20–21.

EVANS, CLARA. "Elementary School Assemblies," *Social Education*, XII (November, 1949), 39–40.

LOWNDES, POLLY ROBBINS. *Creative Assemblies*. Minneapolis, Minn.: T. S. Denison & Co., Inc., 1961.

SKINNER, THEODORE. "Suggestions for the High School Assembly," *Quarterly Journal of Speech*, XXXIII (December, 1947), 515–21.

THOMPSON, NELLIE ZETTA. *Vitalized Assemblies. 200 Programs for All Occasions*. New York: E. P. Dutton & Co., 1952.

ZACHAR, I. J. "An Assembly Committee at Work," *English Journal*, XXXIV (November, 1945), 476–80.

Appendices

Institutions Granting Graduate Degrees in Speech

This list is taken from "Graduate Theses—An Index of Graduate Work in Speech, XXVIII" by Franklin H. Knower, published in *Speech Monographs,* August, 1961. (Institutions offering the doctorate are noted with an asterisk.)

Adelphi College
Akron, University of
Alabama, University of
Amherst College
Arizona, University of
Arkansas, University of
Art Institute of Chicago

Ball State Teachers College
Baylor University
Bellarmine College
Bob Jones University
Boston University*
Bowling Green State University
Bradley University
Brigham Young University
Brooklyn College

California at Los Angeles, University of
Carnegie Institute of Technology
Catholic University
Colorado, University of
Colorado State College of Education*
Columbia College
Columbia University-Teachers College*
Cornell University*

Denver University*
DePauw University

East Texas State College
Emerson College

Florida, University of*
Florida State University*
Fordham University
Fort Hayes Kansas State College
Fresno State College

George Washington University
Georgia, University of
Grinnell College

Hardin-Simmons College
Hawaii, University of
Houston, University of*

Illinois, University of*
Illinois State Normal University
Indiana State Teachers College
Indiana University*
Iowa, State University of*
Ithaca College

Johns Hopkins University

Kansas, University of
Kansas State Teachers College
Kansas State University
Kent State University
Kentucky, University of

Los Angeles State College
Louisiana State University*

Maine, University of
Marquette University
Maryland, University of
Miami, University of
Miami University
Michigan, University of*
Michigan State University*
Mills College
Minnesota, University of*
Mississippi, University of
Mississippi Southern College
Missouri, University of*
Montana State University
Mt. Holyoke

Nebraska, University of*
New Mexico, University of
New Mexico State College
New York University*
North Carolina, University of*
North Dakota State University
Northern Illinois University
Northwestern University*
Notre Dame University

Occidental College
Ohio State University*
Ohio University*
Ohio Wesleyan University
Oklahoma, University of*
Oklahoma A and M
Oregon, University of

Pacific, College of the
Pacific University
Pennsylvania State University*
Pepperdine College
Pittsburgh, University of*
Potomac University
Purdue University*

Queens College

Redlands, University of
Richmond Professional Institute
Rockford College

Sacramento State College
Saint Louis University
San Diego State College
San Francisco State College
San Jose State College
Smith College
South Dakota, State University of
South Dakota State College
Southern California, University of*
Southern Connecticut State College
Southern Illinois University
Southern Methodist University
Southwestern University
Staley College
Stanford University*
Stephen F. Austin College
Sul Ross State College
Syracuse University*

Temple University
Tennessee, University of
Tennessee Agr. and Ind. State College
Texas, University of*
Texas Christian University
Texas Technological College
Texas Woman's University
Tufts University
Tulane University
Tulsa, University of

Utah, University of*
Utah State University

Vanderbilt University
Virginia, University of

Washington, University of*
Washington State University
Washington University*
Wayne State University*
West Texas State College
West Virginia University
Western Reserve University*
Western State College of Colorado
Whittier College
Wichita, University of
Wisconsin, University of*
Wyoming, University of

Yale University*

Films, Filmstrips, and Recordings

FILMS FOR USE IN THE TEACHING OF SPEECH

Introduction to Speech

Why Study Speech?	11 min. bw		YAF
Controversy, Freedom of Speech, Majority Rule	30 min. bw		NET
Public Opinion	11 min. bw		EBF
Communication: Story of Its Development	11 min.		Coronet
Freedom of Communication	30 min. bw	rental	NET
What Holds People To-gether?	30 min. bw	rental	Indiana U.
Why Do People Misunder-stand Each Other?	30 min. bw		NET
The Man Who Knows It All	30 min. bw		NET

Informal Speaking Situations

CONVERSATION

Ways to Better Conversation	11 min.		Coronet
Conversation	12 min. bw		YAF
Social Courtesy	11 min.		Coronet

INTRODUCTIONS

How Do You Do?	14 min. bw	rental	YAF
Introductions	11 min. bw	rental	Simmel-Meservey
Introductions	11 min. bw		EBF

ON THE TELEPHONE

A Manner of Speaking	25 min. col	loan	Am. Telephone and Telegraph
Your Tell-Tale Voice	20 min. bw	loan	Bell Tel.

Listening

Effective Listening	12 min. bw		McGraw

Group Discussion

Poise and Emotional Adjustment

Language and Linguistics

Say What You Mean	20 min. bw		McGraw
How to choose language that clearly states ideas, etc.			

VOCABULARY

Build Your Vocabulary	11 min.		Coronet
Word Building in Our Language	11 min.		Coronet
The Sounds of Language	30 min. bw	rental	NET
The science of speech sounds. Shows also a demonstration of the speech organs.			

Bodily Action

Public Speaking: Movement and Gesture	11 min.		Coronet
Function of Gestures	10 min. bw		YAF
Using Visuals in Your Speech	14 min.		YAF
Platform Posture and Appearance	9 min. bw		YAF
Marcel Marceau Pantomimes	13 min.	rental	Brandon

Voice and Articulation

SOUND

Fundamentals of Acoustics	11 min.		EBF
Sound Waves and Their Source	11 min. bw		EBF

THE HUMAN VOICE

Your Voice	11 min. bw	rental	EBF
Using Your Voice	10 min. bw		YAF
Pictures of the Human Vocal Cords in Operation	6 min. silent bw	rental	Indiana

Speech Preparation

INTRODUCTION

Speak Up	13 min. bw and col	rental	Alturas Films
Speech Preparation	16 min. bw		C–B Films
Speech: Planning Your Talk	13 min. bw		YAF
How to Prepare a Class Report	11 min.		Coronet

FINDING INFORMATION

Know Your Library	11 min.		Coronet
Keys to the Library	15 min.	rental	Library Films

OUTLINING AND NOTE-TAKING

Importance of Making Notes	11 min.		Coronet
Building an Outline	11 min.		Coronet
Making Sense with Outlines	11 min.		Coronet

COMMUNICATION

Making Yourself Understood	14 min. bw		EBF
How to Say What You Mean	30 min. bw	rental	NET
Getting Yourself Across	21 min. bw		McGraw

Parliamentary Procedure

Parliamentary Procedures	11 min.		Coronet
Parliamentary Procedure in Action	13½ min.		Coronet
Conducting a Meeting	12 min. bw		YAF
Effective Listening	15 min. bw		YAF
The Task of the Listener	30 min. bw	rental	NET
How to Observe	11 min.		Coronet
What Is a Good Observer?	30 min. bw		NET

Interpretation of Poetry and Prose

PROSE

Literature Appreciation: How to Read Novels	13½ min.		Coronet
Literature Appreciation: How to Read Essays	13½ min.		Coronet

POETRY AND DRAMA APPRECI-
ATION

Literature Appreciation: How to Read Plays	11 min.		Coronet
Literature Appreciation: How to Read Poetry	11 min.		Coronet
Telling Stories to Children	27 min.	rental	Michigan U.

POETS SPEAK

Langston Hughes	29 min. bw	rental	NET
Carl Sandburg Discusses His Works	13½ min.		Coronet
Robert Frost: Part I Discusses why and how he writes poetry. Reads some of his own works.	30 min. bw	rental	NET
Robert Frost: Part II Discusses the fundamental meaning of poetry. Talks about the fun of writing, listening to words, and telling stories in poetry.	30 min. bw	rental	NET

Robert Frost: Part III Discusses what the reader gets from poetry, what the components of poetry are.	30 min. bw	rental	NET
Robert Frost: Part IV Discusses what it means to write a poem.	30 min. bw	rental	NET
Robert Frost: Part V Explains why poetry should have meaning and what the meaning should be.	30 min. bw	rental	NET
Robert Frost: Part VI Discusses themes in poetry and his basic philosophy of writing.	30 min. bw	rental	NET
Robert Frost: Part VII Discusses his philosophy of poetry, religion, etc.	30 min. bw	rental	NET

Drama and the Theater

DRAMA—BACKGROUND AND
  HISTORY

The Theater: A Fine Art Compares theater with other forms of art.	29 min. bw	rental	NET
Drama: How It Began Takes up the Greek theater and chorus technique.	30 min. bw	rental	NET
Acting: How It Began Discusses the Greek theater and drama in the Middle Ages.	30 min. bw	rental	NET
Acting Comes of Age A history of acting.	30 min. bw	rental	NET
Drama: The Renaissance Describes different types of stages.	30 min. bw	rental	NET
Acting: The Renaissance Uses Shakespeare's actors as examples.	30 min. bw	rental	NET
Drama Comes of Age Discusses realism.	30 min. bw	rental	NET
Drama: The Twentieth Century Discusses expressionism.	30 min. bw	rental	NET
Acting: The Twentieth Century	30 min. bw	rental	NET

The Actor: Character Creation for Illusion The visualization and expression of character for the actor.	29 min. bw	rental	NET
Movement and Gesture: Action for Illusion Discusses stage acting problems.	20 min. bw	rental	NET
Dialogue: Speaking for Illusion Illustrates the three kinds of dialogue.	30 min. bw	rental	NET

DIRECTING AND MANAGING

Curtain Time A survey of casting, directing, rehearsals, costumes, props, sets, publicity, finances, etc.	30 min. bw		EBF
The Play: Idea for Illusion The directors responsibility—analyzing and interpreting the play.	29 min. bw	rental	NET
Scenic Styles: Design for Illusion	29 min. bw	rental	NET
Stage and Backstage: Space for Illusion Discusses the role of the different crews.	29 min. bw	rental	NET
Auditorium and Stage: The Medium for Illusion The function of the stage and the auditorium.	29 min. bw	rental	NET
ABC of Hand Tools: Part I	19 min.	loan	GM
ABC of Hand Tools: Part II	15 min.	loan	GM

PRODUCTION: LIGHTING AND SOUND

Spots and Floods: Lights for Illusion	29 min. bw	rental	NET
Color and Light: Stage Technician	7 min.	rental	U. of Calif.
Elements of Electrical Circuits	11 min.		EBF
Series and Parallel Circuits	11 min.		EBF
Light Waves and Their Use	10 min.		EBF
Music and Effects: Sound for Illusion	29 min. bw	rental	NET

PRODUCTION: MAKEUP

Makeup for the Theater	13 min. col	rental	UCLA
Basic steps—no character makeup. Stage lighting on the face.			
Character Makeup for Men	17 min.		U. of Minn.
Makeup—Straight and Old Age	16 min. col	rental	Bureau of A–V Instruction
Cloth and Color: Costumes for Illusion	29 min. bw	rental	NET
Making Theatrical Wigs	11 min. bw	rental	UCLA
Mask Making	20 min. silent		Yale

APPRECIATION AND ANALYSIS

Shakespeare and Stratford-on-Avon	14 min. silent	rental	B&H
Julius Caesar	33 min. bw		McGraw
Macbeth	16 min.	rental	BIF
Midsummer Night's Dream	13½ min.		Coronet

Radio and Television

RADIO

Radio Broadcasting Today	19 min.	rental	U. of Mich.
On the Air	28 min.	loan	Westinghouse
Lessons from the Air	14 min. bw	rental	BIF

TELEVISION PRODUCTION

Staging for TV	30 min. bw		NET
Television Directing: Part I	30 min. bw		NET
Television Directing: Part II	30 min. bw		NET
Problems that face the technician.			
Television Lighting	30 min. bw		NET

Puppetry

ABC of Puppet Making	silent	rental	Bailey
ABC of Puppets: Type I	14 min. silent;	rental	Bailey
	10 min. sound	rental	
ABC of Puppets: Type II	14 min. silent;	rental	Bailey
Describes the operation and stage.	10 min. sound	rental	
Puppetry: String Marionettes	10 min.	rental	EBF
Make a Hand Puppet	10 min. silent	rental	Library Films
Puppet Bodies and Costumes; Puppet Stage and Scenery			Bacon and Vincent

FILMSTRIPS FOR THE TEACHING OF SPEECH

Communication

How to Converse	40 bw	rental	SVE
Relation of Personality to Communication	40 bw	rental	SVE

MASS COMMUNICATION

Motion Pictures	47 bw	rental	McGraw
Television	47 bw	rental	McGraw
Newspapers	47 bw	rental	McGraw
Radio	47 bw	rental	McGraw

Language

How Context Changes Meanings	23 col	rental	McGraw
How Words Grow in Meaning	23 col	rental	McGraw
How Words Work Together	23 col	rental	McGraw
Words—Origin, Uses and Spelling	36 bw	rental	SVE

Voice and Articulation

How We Produce Sounds and Speech	49 bw	rental	McGraw
Mechanism of Breathing	65 bw	rental	EBF
The Respiratory System	42 col	rental	McGraw

Speech Preparation

Use Your Library for Better Grades and Fun Too!	81 bw	rental	SVE
The Card Catalog	42 bw	rental	McGraw
The Dewey Decimal System	42 bw	rental	McGraw
Your Dictionary and How to Use it Set of six filmstrips.	25 col	rental	SVE
Dictionary: Part I	42 bw	rental	McGraw
The Encyclopedia	42 bw	rental	McGraw
Exploring TV Illustration for use of the encyclopedia.	45 col	rental	McGraw
One-Volume Encyclopedia	45 col	rental	McGraw
Almanacs and Yearbooks	45 col	rental	McGraw
Gazetteers and Atlases	45 col	rental	McGraw
Reader's Guide	45 col	rental	McGraw
Aids in Writing and Reading	45 col	rental	McGraw
Books for Biography	45 col	rental	McGraw
The Book Library series.	42 bw	rental	McGraw

PUBLIC SPEAKING

How to Prepare a Speech	40 bw	rental	SVE
The Power of Speech Comes with record.	bw	rental	Nat'l Safety Council
The Key to Good Speaking Recording.	bw	rental	Nat'l Safety Council
How to Deliver a Speech	40 bw	rental	SVE
Butterflies in Your Stomach	bw	rental	Nat'l Safety Council
On Your Feet	bw	rental	Nat'l Safety Council
Now You're Talking	bw	rental	Nat'l Safety Council

Listening

Information; Persuasion; Propaganda	40 bw	rental	SVE
Tell the Difference between Essentials and Details	40 bw	rental	SVE
Discover the Purpose of a Speaker	40 bw	rental	SVE
Tell the Difference between Facts and Opinions	40 bw	rental	SVE

Parliamentary Law

Parliamentary Rules of Order	59 bw	rental	U. of Mich.
How to Conduct a Meeting Using Parliamentary Procedure	col	rental	Bailey

Interpretation of Literature

UNDERSTANDING LITERATURE

How to Read a One-Act Play	50 col	rental	McGraw
Interpretation and Evaluation of the Short Story	32 bw	rental	SVE
How to Read a Short Story	50 col	rental	McGraw
How to Read a Narrative Poem	50 col	rental	McGraw
How to Read an Historical Novel	50 col	rental	McGraw

LITERATURE APPRECIATION

American Author Series Louisa May Alcott Samuel Clemens (Mark Twain) Henry Wadsworth Longfellow) Washington Irving Edgar Allan Poe John Greenleaf Whittier	col	rental	Young America

American Poets Series William Cullen Bryant Emily Dickinson James Russell Lowell Edgar Allan Poe Walt Whitman	49 col	rental	EBF

MECHANICS OF POETRY

Getting the Meaning from Poetry	48 col	rental	McGraw
Rhythm in Poetry	48 col	rental	McGraw
Stanza Forms and Forms of Verse	48 col	rental	McGraw
Sound Effects in Poetry	48 col	rental	McGraw
Figures in Speech	48 col	rental	McGraw
How to Write a Poem	48 col	rental	McGraw

Drama and the Theater

HISTORY AND TECHNIQUE

Development of the Physical Theater	55 bw	rental	Comma
Ancient Greek Theater of Epidauros	56 col	rental	Comma
Theater of Dionysus, I	39 col	rental	Comma
Theater of Dionysus, II	41 col	rental	Comma
Hellenistic Theater of Priene	43 col	rental	Comma
Roman Theater of Orange	51 col	rental	Comma
Basic Stage Movement	58 bw		Paramount

STAGECRAFT

Stage Machinery and Equipment	71 col	rental	Comma
Shop Machinery and Tools	40 col	rental	Comma
Stage Hardware	53 col	rental	Comma
Stairs	34 col	rental	Comma
Ramps	29 col	rental	Comma
Platforms	26 col	rental	Comma
Parallels	33 col	rental	Comma
The Simple Flat	67 col	rental	Comma
The Complex Flat	49 col	rental	Comma
Handling Flats	32 col	rental	Comma

LIGHTING

Basic Stage Lighting Three parts.	60 col 40 bw 42 bw		Paramount
Basic Stage Lighting Equipment	40 col	rental	Comma
Back, Side and Fill Lighting	36 col	rental	Comma
Area Lighting	36 col	rental	Comma

MAKEUP AND COSTUMES

Makeup for the Stage With 32-page booklet.	70 col		Paramount
Women's Clothing of the Western World	28 col	rental	Comma
Costumes of the Scottish Highlands	43 col		The Wool Bureau, Inc.
Men's Clothing of the Western World	35 col	rental	Comma

APPRECIATION

Sophocles' Electra	30 col	rental	Comma

Television

How TV Works	49 bw	rental	McGraw

LIST OF FILM PRODUCERS AND DISTRIBUTORS

AF: A. F. Films (now Film Images, Inc.), 18 East 60th St., New York 22, N.Y.

Alturas: Alturas Films, Box 1211, Santa Barbara, Calif.

Am Cent: American Central Manufacturers Corp., St. Charles, Ill.

AFR: American Film Registry, 28 East Jackson, Chicago 4, Ill.

AmMusNH: American Museum of Natural History, Central Park West at 79th St., New York 24, N.Y.

AT&T: American Telephone and Telegraph Co. (Bell Telephone Company, nearest branch).

Art: Art Films, 650 Ocean Ave., Brooklyn, N.Y.

Association: Association Films, 347 Madison Ave., New York 17, N.Y.

Bailey: Bailey Films, Inc., 6509 De Longpre Ave., Hollywood 28, Calif.

BH: Bell and Howell, 1801 Larchmont Ave., Chicago 13, Ill.

Brandon: Brandon Films, 200 West 57th St., New York 19, N.Y.

Bray: Bray Studios, Inc., 729 Seventh Ave., New York 29, N.Y.

BIS: British Information Services, 30 Rockefeller Plaza, New York 20, N.Y.

BurAVInstr: Bureau of A–V Instruction, University of Wisconsin Extension Division, Madison, Wis.

California: California, University of, Dept. of Visual Instruction, Berkeley 4, Calif.

UofCal: California, University of, at Los Angeles, Film Dept., University Extension, Los Angeles 24, Calif.

CB Films: C–B Educational Films, 690 Market St., San Francisco 4, Calif.

CC Indiana: Celluloid College, Indiana University Audio-Visual Center, Bloomington, Ind.

Classic: Classic Films, Bell and Howell, Inc., 1801 Larchmont Ave., Chicago 13, Ill.

CollegeFilm: College Film Center, 84 East Randolph St., Chicago 1, Ill.

Columbia: Columbia University, Teachers College, Bureau of Publications, 525 West 120th St., New York 27, N.Y.

Comma: Comma, 1535 Ivar, Hollywood, Calif.

Coronet: Coronet Films, Coronet Bldg., Chicago 1, Ill.

Edited
Pictures: Edited Pictures Systems, Inc., 165 West 46th St., New York
                     19, N.Y.
EBF: Encyclopaedia Britannica Films, Inc., 1150 Wilmette Ave.,
                     Wilmette, Ill.
FREC: Federal Radio Educational Commission, Office of Educa-
                     tion, Washington 25, D.C.
FilmPub: Film Publishers, Inc., 12 East 44th St., New York 17, N.Y.
Ganz: Ganz, William J., 40 East 49th St., New York, N.Y.
Gateway: Gateway Products, Inc., 1859 Powell St., San Francisco 11,
                     Calif.
GE: General Electric Corp., Visual Education Service, Schenec-
                     tady, N.Y.
GM: General Motors Corp., 3044 West Grand Blvd., Detroit 2,
                     Mich.
Ideal: Ideal Pictures Corp., 65 East South Water St., Chicago 15,
                     Ill.
Indiana U: Indiana University Audio-Visual Center, Bloomington, Ind.
InstF: Instructional Films, 1150 Wilmette Ave., Wilmette, Ill.
International: International Film Bureau, 57 East Jackson Blvd., Chicago
                     4, Ill.
IntTh&TV: International Theatrical and Television Corp., 25 West 45th
                     St., New York 19, N.Y.
UofIowa: Iowa, State University of, Bureau of Visual Instruction Ex-
                     tension Division, Iowa City, Iowa.
IowaState: Iowa State College, Visual Instruction Service, Ames, Iowa.
JamHandy: Jam Handy Organization, 2821 East Grand Blvd., Detroit
                     11, Mich.
Library: Library Films, Inc., 25 West 45th St., New York, 36, N.Y.
McGraw: McGraw-Hill Co., Text-Film Dept., 330 West 42nd St., New
                     York 36, N.Y.
Mahnke: Mahnke, Carl F., Productions, 215 East 3rd St., Des Moines
                     9, Iowa.
MichiganU: Michigan, University of, Audio-Visual Education Center,
                     4028 Administrations Bldg., Ann Arbor, Mich.
UofMinn: Minnesota, University of, Audio-Visual Education Service,
                     Westbrook Hall, Minneapolis 14, Minn.
ModTkgPict: Modern Talking Pictures Service, 45 Rockefeller Plaza, New
                     York 20, N.Y.
MusModArt: Museum of Modern Art, 11 East 53rd St., New York 19,
                     N.Y.
NatFilmBd
Canada: National Film Board of Canada, 1270 Ave. of the Americas,
                     New York 20, N.Y.
NatSafety
Council: National Safety Council, 425 North Michigan Ave., Chicago,
                     Ill.
NET: NET Film Service, Audio-Visual Center, Indiana University,
                     Bloomington, Ind.
Official: Official Films, 776 Grand Ave., Ridgefield, N. J.
Penn State: Pennsylvania State College, Psychological Cinema Register,
                     State College, Pa.

ReligFilm:	Religious Film Association, 220 Fifth Ave., New York, 1, N.Y.
Simmel Meservey:	Simmel-Meservey, Inc., 854 South Robertson Blvd., Los Angeles 35, Calif.
Sterling:	Sterling Films, 316 West 57th St., New York 19, N.Y.
TchgFilmCust:	Teaching Film Custodians, 25 West 43rd St., New York 36, N.Y.
UnitedWorld:	United World Films, 1445 Park Ave., New York 29, N.Y.
VocGuid:	Vocational Guidance Films, Indiana University Audio-Visual Center, Bloomington, Ind.
Wayne:	Wayne University, Audio-Visual Materials Consultation Bureau, Detroit 4, Mich.
Westinghouse:	Westinghouse Electric Corp., 306 Fourth Ave., PO Box 1017, Pittsburgh, Pa.
Wilding:	Wilding Picture Products for Coopers, Indiana University Audio-Visual Center, Bloomington, Ind.
Yale:	Yale University, Dept. of Drama, New Haven, Conn.
YAF:	Young America Films, Inc., 18 East 41st St., New York 17, N.Y.

LIST OF FILMSTRIP PRODUCERS AND DISTRIBUTORS

Bailey:	Bailey Films, Inc., 6509 De Longpre Ave., Hollywood 28, Calif.
Comma:	Comma, 1535 Ivar, Hollywood, Calif.
EBF:	Encyclopaedia Britannica Films, Inc., 1150 Wilmette Ave., Wilmette, Ill.
Life:	Life Filmstrips, 9 Rockefeller Plaza, New York 20, N.Y.
McGraw:	McGraw-Hill Book Co., 330 West 42nd St., New York 18, N.Y.
NatSafety Council:	National Safety Council, 425 North Michigan, Chicago, Ill.
Paramount:	Paramount Theatrical Supplies, 32 West 20th St., New York 11, N.Y.
SVE:	Society for Visual Education, 1345 West Diversey, Chicago, Ill.
Wayne:	Wayne University, Audio-Visual Materials Consultation Bureau, Detroit 4, Mich.
YAF:	Young America Films, Inc., 18 East 41st St., New York 17, N.Y.

RECORDINGS FOR USE IN SPEECH

Following is a list of records arranged according to the supplier:

THE AMERICAN BOOK COMPANY *

Blow the Man Down, Old Sea Chantey, by Woody Guthrie
Moby Dick (Herman Melville), by Charles Laughton
Paul Bunyan and the Howlin' River, by Walter Huston
Rip Van Winkle (Washington Irving), by Walter Huston
Hamlet Soliloquies (Shakespeare), by John Gielgud
Romeo and Juliet (Shakespeare), by Gielgud and Brown

*The first eight selections are Decca recordings.

World Literature, Series 2, by Alexander Scourby, Ames Bros., and Agnes Moorehead

INCLUDES:

The Highwayman
Edward, Edward
Sea Fever
If
Barbara Fritchie
Go Down, Moses

World Literature, Series 5, by Alexander Scourby, Ethel Everett, Walter Huston, Carl Sandburg, and Richard Dyer Bennett

INCLUDES:

The Creation
Abraham Lincoln Walks at Midnight
Annabel Lee
The Rhodora
The Tide Rises, The Tide Falls
Parting
Success
The Blind Men and the Elephant
Prayers of Steel; Grass; Swapping-Song

Hamlet (Shakespeare), by John Gielgud
Romeo and Juliet (Shakespeare), by John Gielgud

CAPITOL RECORDING

Cyrano de Bergerac

CAEDMON RECORDS

This company has the most complete and varied list available of recordings of all types of literature by poets, actors, playwrights, and others. Write Caedmon Records, 277 Fifth Avenue, New York 16, N.Y., for a catalog.

COLUMBIA RECORDS

Paris '90 (solo production), by Cornelia Otis Skinner
Don Juan in Hell (George Bernard Shaw), by Charles Boyer, Charles Laughton, Sir Cedric Hardwicke, and Agnes Moorehead
You Are There: The Signing of the Magna Charta; The Battle of Gettysburg, as reported by CBS correspondents on CBS radio programs
Macbeth (Shakespeare), by Orson Wells and the Mercury Theater Cast

DECCA RECORDINGS

Parnassus: A Treasury of the Spoken Word—Famous Poems That Tell Great Stories, by Agnes Moorehead, Fredric March, Arnold Moss, and others

INCLUDES:

William Shakespeare, immortal scenes and sonnets
The Heroic Soul, poems of patriotism
The Fun Makers, an evening with the humorists
Words to Live By, prayers and inspirations
The Heart Speaks, lyrics of love
Carl Sandburg Reads His Poems

Medea, by Judith Anderson and supporting cast—poetic drama
Readings from the Bible, by Charles Laughton
Abraham Lincoln, Poetry of Carl Sandburg, Edwin Markham, Walt Whitman, Rosemary Benét, Vachel Lindsay, read by Walter Huston, Carl Sandburg, Orson Welles, Agnes Moorehead
Robert Frost Reads the Poems of Robert Frost

The Presidential Years (1932–1945), the voice of F.D.R.
Sorry, Wrong Number, by Agnes Moorehead (dramatic reading)
Tell-Tale Heart, Annabel Lee, Silence, by James Mason
EDUCATIONAL AUDIO-VISUAL, INC.
Forms of Poetry, with student text
INSTITUTE FOR DEMOCRATIC EDUCATION
These Small Things, by Macdonald Carey
The Lesson, by Mary L. Harrison
LINGUAPHONE INSTITUTE
The Sounds of English, by W. D. Greet
Poems, by E. E. Cummings
America Was Promises, by Archibald MacLeish
Hamlet, Act II, Scene 2, by John Gielgud
American Dialect Series
British Dialect Series
Lincoln's Gettysburg Address and Lincoln's Second Inaugural Address, by
Raymond Massey
NATIONAL COUNCIL OF TEACHERS OF ENGLISH
Shakespeare, by John Barrymore
Poems, by Ogden Nash (reading his own)
General American Vowels, by J. A. Kenyon
His Own Poems, by Dylan Thomas
The Appreciation of Poetry, by Norman Corwin
Great Themes in Poetry, by Basil Rathbone
Poetry of Edna St. Vincent Millay, by Judith Anderson
Poetry Recordings of Robert Frost, by Robert Frost
Poetry Recordings of Vachel Lindsay, by Vachel Lindsay
PARAMOUNT
Golden Age of the Theatre, by Edwin Booth, Sarah Bernhardt, Ellen Terry,
John Barrymore, Julia Marlowe, George M. Cohan, Jane Cowl, and Joseph
Jefferson
A Tribute to Eugene O'Neill, by Broadway cast
SAM GOODY
Bible Stories, by Ronald Colman
The Greatest Story Ever Told, by Fulton Oursler
Anthology of English Lyrics, by Cornelia Otis Skinner
Keats: Two Odes, by Vincent Price
Ike from Abiline, by Henry Fonda
Readings from His Works, by Archibald MacLeish
The Power of Positive Thinking, by Dr. Norman Vincent Peale
Sermon on the Mount, by David Ross
Abraham Lincoln, by Carl Sandburg
Private Lives, by Noel Coward and Gertrude Lawrence
RCA VICTOR RECORDS
Anthology of English Verse, by Cornelia Otis Skinner
The White Cliffs of Dover (Alice Duer Miller), by Lynn Fontanne
Hamlet (Shakespeare), by Sir Laurence Olivier
Hamlet (Shakespeare), by John Gielgud
A Christmas Carol (Dickens), by Ernest Chappell
Macbeth, by Old Vic Company
Why the Chimes Rang (Elizabeth McFadden), by Ted Malone
Poet's Gold, by Helen Hayes, Thomas Mitchell, Raymond Massey

THEATER MASTERWORK
Hedda Gabler (Ibsen), by Eva Le Gallienne and Richard Waring
An Evening with Shakespeare, by Wesley Addy, Staats Cotsworth
The Importance of Being Earnest (Oscar Wilde), by Maurice Evans and Lucille Watson
INSTITUTE FOR DEMOCRATIC EDUCATION
The Man in the Plane, by Richard Widmark
An American Comes Home, by Faye Emerson
Jane Addams, by Wendy Barrie
Samuel Gompers, by Jay Jostyn

TAPES, SCRIPTS, AND TRANSCRIPTIONS FOR SPEECH

BRITISH INFORMATION SERVICES: (SCRIPTS) each 14:30 min.
Dylan Thomas in America
Five Poems by Dylan Thomas, read by Mr. Thomas
Why Poets Write, by Dame Edith Sitwell
KENT STATE UNIVERSITY: (TAPES) each 30 min.
Words with Music gives a descriptive biography of the poet and relates his work to the times in which he lived. These programs are recited by Paul Mathews.
The Poetry of William Shakespeare
The Poetry of William Wordsworth and His Friend Samuel Taylor Coleridge
The Poetry of Francis Thompson
Poems by Shelley and Keats
The Works of Oscar Wilde and Charlotte Meaux
The Poetic Prose of Thomas Wolfe, by Otto Carl Storr
SHAKESPEAREAN SERIES
Introduction to Shakespeare. Introduces the material that is to follow in the remaining programs by pointing up some of Shakespeare's outstanding contributions to literature.
The Shakesperean Plot. Discusses the three parts of a play—the beginning, the middle, and the end—and illustrates these parts from *Romeo and Juliet.*
The Shakespearean Character. Illustrates how a writer gets across to his audience the character of actors. *Antony and Cleopatra* provides the illustrations.
Diction and Speech. Discusses those techniques and methods employed by Shakespeare to provide the best kind of speech for every occasion, high and low, plain and elaborate, description, argument, oratory, meditation. Emphasis is on his sheer command of words.
How Shakespeare Uses Words. By drawing illustrations from *Julius Caesar,* this program considers how Shakespeare, by use of words, makes his characters and us do what he wants.
The Shakespearean Atmosphere. Discusses and illustrates from several plays various kinds of atmosphere such as romance, kind of weather, horror, and pathos as portrayed by Shakespeare.
Continuation of the Atmosphere Theme. Illustrations for this program are drawn from *Macbeth* with its horror and terror.
The Shakespearean Comedy. Illustrates the many subtle ways by means of which Shakespeare introduced comedy into his plays.
Should Controls over Radio, TV, and the Movies Be Increased? Illustrates good discussion techniques using 1950–51 Minnesota high school topic and outline. K. W. Ziebarth and his group.

Index